D1540164

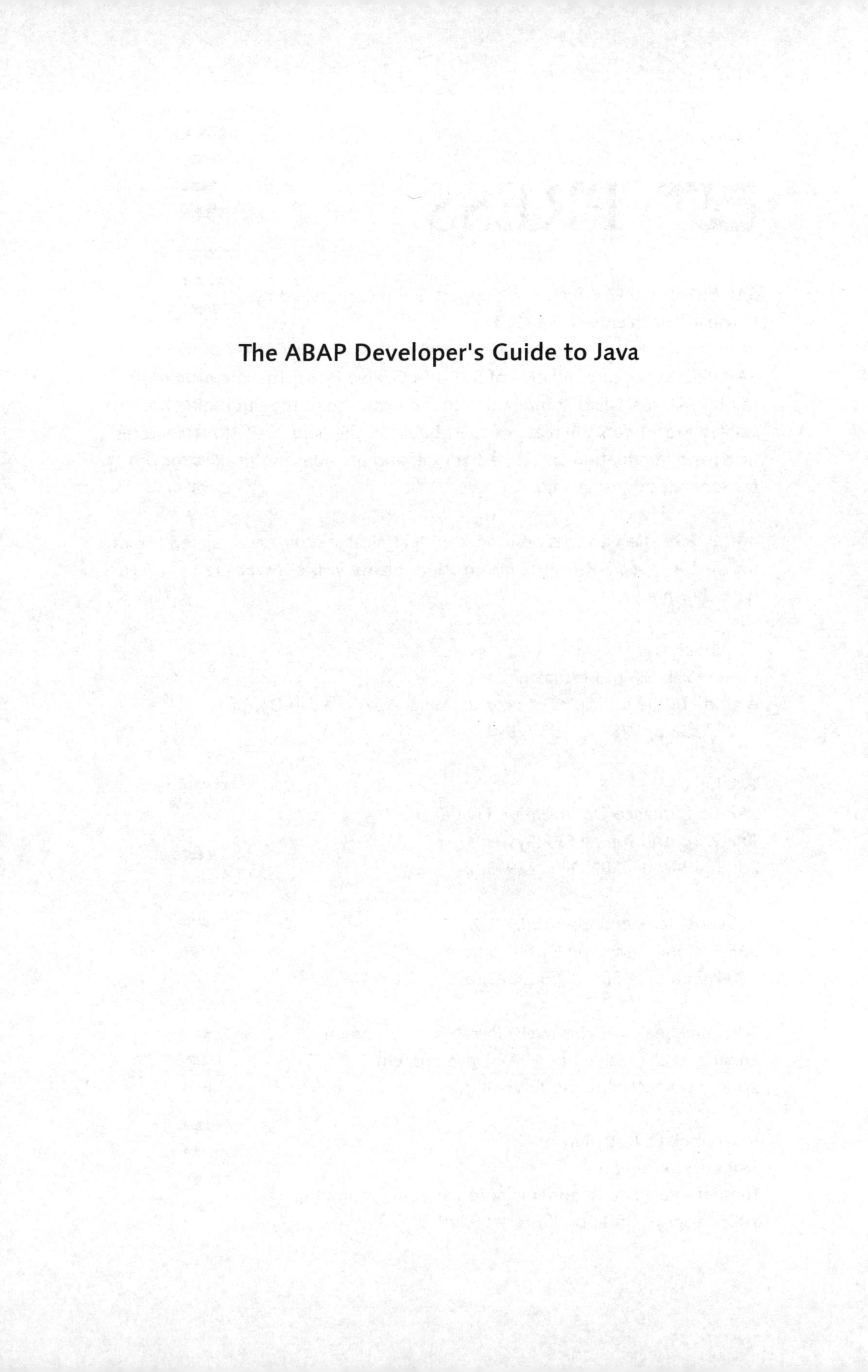

The ABAP Developer's Guide to Java

SAP PRESS and SAP Technical Support Guides are issued by
Bernhard Hochlehnert, SAP AG

SAP PRESS is a joint initiative of SAP and Galileo Press. The know-how offered by SAP specialists combined with the expertise of the publishing house Galileo Press offers the reader expert books in the field. SAP PRESS features first-hand information and expert advice, and provides useful skills for professional decision-making.

SAP PRESS offers a variety of books on technical and business related topics for the SAP user. For further information, please visit our website: *www.sap-press.com*.

C. Whealy
Inside Web Dynpro for Java
A guide to the principles of programming in SAP's Web Dynpro
2005, 356 pp., ISBN 1-59229-038-8

T. Schneider
SAP Performance Optimization Guide
Analyzing and Tuning SAP Systems
2003, 494 pp., ISBN 1-59229-022-1

A. Schneider-Neureither (Ed.)
SAP System Landscape Optimization
2004, 220 pp., ISBN 1-59229-026-4

W. Heuvelmans, A. Krouwels, B. Meijs, R. Sommen
Enhancing the Quality of ABAP Development
2004, 500 pp., ISBN 1-59229-030-2

A. Goebel, D. Ritthaler
SAP Enterprise Portal
The definite guide to administration and programming
2005, approx. 350 pp., ISBN 1-59229-018-3

Andreas Schneider-Neureither, Bernd Noll,
Andreas Schlindwein, André Schüngel,
Dominik Wittenbeck

The ABAP® Developer's Guide to Java

SAP PRESS

SAP PRESS is an imprint of Galileo Press,
Fort Lee (NJ), USA
Bonn, Germany

German Edition first published 2004 by Galileo Press.

Translation Jeffrey S. Zalkind for Lemoine International, Inc., Salt Lake City, UT
Copy Editor Nancy Etscovitz, UCG, Inc., Boston, MA
Cover Design department, Cologne, Germany

ISBN 1-59229-027-2

Contents

Foreword **9**

1 Introduction **11**

2 Technology Overview **17**

2.1 **Enterprise Services Architecture** ... 18
2.2 **SAP NetWeaver** ... 19
2.2.1 People Integration ... 20
2.2.2 Information Integration ... 20
2.2.3 Process Integration ... 20
2.2.4 Application Integration ... 20
2.2.5 Life Cycle Management ... 21
2.2.6 Composite Application Framework ... 21
2.3 **System Architecture of the SAP Web Application Server** ... 21
2.3.1 Presentation Layer ... 23
2.3.2 Application Layer ... 24
2.3.3 Database Layer ... 24
2.4 **Major Components of the SAP Web Application Server** ... 24
2.4.1 The Internet Communication Manager (ICM) ... 24
2.4.2 The ABAP Runtime Environment ... 26
2.4.3 The J2EE Engine ... 26
2.4.4 The Integration Engine ... 28
2.5 **Database Integration** ... 30
2.5.1 Database Independence ... 30
2.5.2 Client Capability ... 31
2.5.3 Caching and Trace Mechanisms ... 31
2.5.4 Transaction Capability ... 31
2.5.5 Object-Relational Mapping ... 32
2.5.6 Native SQL ... 32
2.6 **Web Services** ... 33
2.6.1 What Are Web Services? ... 33
2.6.2 The Web Service Paradigm ... 33
2.6.3 The SAP Web Application Server as Web Service Client ... 35
2.6.4 The SAP Web Application Server as Web Service Provider ... 35
2.6.5 Outlook ... 36
2.7 **Frontends** ... 36
2.7.1 SAP GUI for Windows ... 36
2.7.2 SAP GUI for Java ... 38

2.7.3 SAP GUI for HTML ... 40
2.7.4 Pure Browser Interface (BSP, JSP) ... 42
2.7.5 Web Dynpro ... 44

2.8 Authorization System ... **46**
2.8.1 Authorizations in the ABAP Personality ... 46
2.8.2 Authorizations in the Java Personality ... 48
2.8.3 Security of J2EE Applications ... 51

2.9 Versioning and Transport System ... **54**
2.9.1 Versioning ... 54
2.9.2 Transport System ... 56
2.9.3 Versioning and Transport Process under Java ... 58

2.10 Availability, Performance, Scalability ... **59**

2.11 Integration Options for ABAP and J2EE ... **60**
2.11.1 J2EE Calls ABAP ... 60
2.11.2 ABAP Calls J2EE ... 61

3 The "ResMan" Example Project 63

3.1 Prerequisites ... **63**
3.1.1 Business Benefit ... 63
3.1.2 Functional Prerequisites ... 64
3.1.3 Technical Prerequisites ... 65

3.2 The Data Model ... **65**

3.3 Technical Implementation of the Prerequisites ... **69**

4 The Programming Languages of the SAP Web Application Server 71

4.1 ABAP and ABAP Objects ... **71**
4.1.1 Typical Activities ... 71
4.1.2 Basic Terminology and Concepts ... 72
4.1.3 Variables and Data Types ... 74
4.1.4 The Most Important Commands and Language Constructs ... 78

4.2 Java ... **90**
4.2.1 Basic Terminology and Concepts ... 90
4.2.2 Object-Oriented Programming ... 91
4.2.3 A First Example Program in Java ... 93
4.2.4 Comments ... 94
4.2.5 Identifiers and Keywords ... 95
4.2.6 Data Types, Variables, and Constants ... 96
4.2.7 Operators ... 101
4.2.8 Control Structures ... 107
4.2.9 Exception Handling ... 112
4.2.10 Methods ... 114
4.2.11 Classes and Objects ... 115

4.2.12 Packages 123
4.2.13 Inheritance 124
4.2.14 Preventing Overwriting and Inheritance 127
4.2.15 Encapsulation 128
4.2.16 Abstract Classes and Methods 129
4.2.17 Interfaces 129
4.2.18 Summary of the Most Important Modifiers 131
4.2.19 Programming Conventions 131

5 Development Tools and Objects 137

5.1 ABAP 137
5.1.1 The ABAP Development Environment 138
5.1.2 ABAP Dictionary and Data Modeler 141
5.1.3 Development Objects 143
5.1.4 Transport System and Versioning 157
5.1.5 Testing 165
5.2 J2EE 166
5.2.1 Architecture 167
5.2.2 Development Environment 207
5.2.3 Development Objects 216
5.2.4 Java Dictionary 223
5.2.5 Deploy Process 233
5.2.6 Collaboration Tools 237
5.2.7 Versioning 240
5.2.8 Testing 248

6 Application Layers 255

6.1 Retrieval Logic and Persistence 255
6.1.1 ABAP 255
6.1.2 Java 260
6.2 Middleware: Connectivity Between Applications 297
6.2.1 RFC 298
6.2.2 JCo 298
6.2.3 EJB Proxy Class 312
6.2.4 More Interfaces 314
6.2.5 Web Services 315
6.3 Business Logic 344
6.3.1 ABAP 345
6.3.2 Java 347
6.4 Presentation Logic 361
6.4.1 ABAP 362
6.4.2 Java 369

7 Application Design 421

7.1 A Typical Problem ... 421
7.2 Design Patterns ... 422
7.2.1 MVC ... 422
7.2.2 Façade ... 428
7.2.3 Adapters ... 430
7.2.4 Driver Model ... 431
7.2.5 Lazy Initialization ... 434
7.3 Developing an ABAP Web Application ... 436
7.4 Developing a J2EE Web Application ... 438

8 Performance Aspects 441

8.1 Performance under ABAP ... 441
8.1.1 Rules for Boosting Performance ... 442
8.1.2 Performance Analysis Tools ... 443
8.2 Performance under Java ... 445
8.2.1 Rules for Boosting Performance ... 447
8.2.2 Performance Analysis Tools ... 450

9 Outlook 455

A Glossary 459

B Sources and Further Reading 479

C About the Authors 481

Index 485

Foreword

Several years ago, SAP AG announced that future application development would take place in parallel in both Java and ABAP. This paradigm shift for SAP Development was launched successfully with Version 6.20 of the SAP Web Application Server (SAP Web AS). The current release, SAP Web AS 6.40, now supports both development tracks fully and reliably, giving SAP developers a platform with an incomparable arsenal of modern and proven technologies to develop powerful, professional, and stable applications.

This twin-track development has received little attention in customer products to date, however, due in large part to a lack of information among ABAP developers, who are unfamiliar with Java and J2EE syntax and concepts, as well as their distinct implementation and integration in SAP Web AS.

This book is aimed at correcting this information deficit. Not only will it illustrate the various options that the new technologies in SAP Web AS provide—in detail and with a practical focus—but also provide experienced ABAP developers with a defined, efficient migration path to this new world of SAP development.

This book is intended primarily for accomplished ABAP developers and IT managers who want to learn how to harness the great potential of the new SAP technology and integrate it into their own IT strategies to achieve a successful outcome.

We, the authors, aren't afraid to criticize, either. As experienced developers and consultants who apply these technologies in customer systems on a daily basis, we examine the individual concepts and technologies in detail, and always with a critical eye toward their practical usability.

Writing this book—coupled with our daily consulting work—demanded a tremendous effort of the authors. This effort would not have been possible were it not for the support of both our coworkers and our families. Our special thanks go out to all of them.

We would particularly like to thank Ulrich Klingels from SAP NetWeaver Product Management, whose detailed comments enriched this book. We also want to thank Florian Zimniak at Galileo Press—who provided valuable advice, assistance, and motivation for our last book in the SAP PRESS series—for his professional support and coordination efforts and Nancy

Etscovitz at SAP PRESS for her editorial help with this translation. Our thanks also go to everyone at SNP who supported or otherwise assisted us with this book project, whether directly or indirectly. Last but not least, we thank Bernhard Hochlehnert of *SAPinfo*, who gave us the impetus for our book projects.

We trust that you will find this book to be a useful tool for familiarizing yourself with the new technologies and implementing them successfully in your projects.

We hope that this is a pleasant, stimulating read for you!

Andreas Schneider-Neureither
Heidelberg, November 2004

1 Introduction

Java has occupied a firm position in SAP's platform strategy. SAP's focus on Java and open standards has resulted in a variety of new technologies that have collectively established a foothold in the previously more proprietary SAP world. The importance of these technologies and the Java programming language will continue to increase exponentially—for the practical tasks of SAP programmers as well. This book will help you get started with these new technologies.

SAP and Java

When SAP announced in 2001 that Java and ABAP would receive equal footing as programming languages for SAP systems, it was clear that this proclamation was more than evolutionary—it was, in fact, a minor revolution. It also represented a milestone because it sent a clear signal that SAP, after years of concentrating on proprietary technologies, would begin to build on "external" technologies, open standards, and interoperability with other systems.

In the three years since, in which the initial visions and announcements have turned into tangible products and solutions, everyone—SAP strategists, developers, and users alike—has had his or her own experiences (and not all of them positive).

Vision and Reality

But not all of the expectations and hopes that the Java announcement raised at the time have come to fruition; turning the visions into tangible applications proved to be much more demanding and exhausting than originally planned, as is so often the case. Despite SAP's vast experience in developing complex software systems, implementing the fundamental elements of the "old" SAP world with the new technologies proved to be a much more complex undertaking in many cases. Two prominent examples of these difficulties, the locking concept and the Transport Organizer, are described in detail in later chapters.

Even today, several obstacles that prevent giving Java technologies an equal ranking with the ABAP world remain, although the current release of the SAP Web Application Server (SAP Web AS 6.40) is a much closer approximation of the original vision.

Strategic SAP Issue

Even though some of the original motives and objectives no longer apply (the job market for IT experts has changed radically in the last few years, for example), there are still sound reasons in favor of opening the system and integrating Java and Java-based technology. It is also clear that SAP is not going to change its basic direction—too much money has already been spent on the "pacification" of the new technologies, and too many SAP strategies depend on resolutely pursuing the objectives to their completion. Nor is there any doubt that SAP will do so. A large portion of the software currently being developed at SAP by more than 1000 developers is no longer written in ABAP, but in Java.

The Development of ABAP

In the past, SAP developers could count themselves among the few "fortunate" IT specialists who didn't have to learn a new programming language every few years to augment their skill base and maintain their market value. Although development of the ABAP programming language continued, the changes were evolutionary in nature and tended to be distributed incrementally across the new SAP releases. Most of the major changes to the language scope and development philosophy resulted from the introduction of ABAP Objects and the Internet Transaction Server (ITS), but conventional ABAP developers could avoid these latest developments with a bit of skill, and create perfectly functioning SAP programs without a sound knowledge of ABAP Objects and HTMLB (HyperText Markup Language for Business).

ABAP Objects Optional

Of course, this trend was facilitated by SAP's desire to keep the language as downward compatible as possible, which meant that a combination of old and new syntax was permitted, and various tools were provided to avoid forcing developers to cope with the new language constructs. A primary example of these tools are the function modules that serve as wrappers for the object-oriented (OO) functionality, making the implicit use of ABAP Objects possible in a conventional manner.

ABAP Objects in Practice

Faced with occasional, yet unavoidable encounters with the new OO syntax in the system, however, many "old school" ABAP programmers chose not to simply live with their ignorance and unawareness of the new functions. Instead, they took courses and learned about ABAP Objects. But, despite their new training, very few of the programmers were able to employ object-oriented coding in practice. This was only rarely due to a lack of understanding or acceptance of the object-oriented approaches; however; in most cases, ABAP Objects were not used simply because new applications are seldom developed from scratch. Instead, existing applications are extended and enhanced with new functions. And as most SAP applications originated in the pre-ABAP Objects era, they weren't designed or developed with an object-oriented approach in mind. It doesn't make much sense to use OO for their enhancements, either.

ABAP to Java

The technological transition from ABAP/ABAP Objects to Java and J2EE will be far from seamless. The differences between the underlying concepts and technologies are simply too great. The focus on Java, for example, not only implies a new programming language, but also a completely different Basis technology. And it isn't just the technology that differs; the entire application development philosophy is fundamentally distinct. Consequently, for many commands and concepts, there is not a one-to-one correspondence between the ABAP and Java worlds.

"Sit Out" Java?

The technological transformation of SAP applications from ABAP to Java-based applications can also be ignored for awhile. The existing base of ABAP applications, whose complex business logic adds value for enterprises, is enormous. All of these applications will continue to exist, and it will only rarely be practical or cost-effective to port them to Java (nor is there any technological need to do so).

Therefore, ABAP developers who don't want to deal with the world of Java don't have to worry about their jobs in the interim. Even many years from now, there will still be a wide variety of critical SAP applications that have been developed in ABAP and that will have to be maintained and enhanced in ABAP as well.

Target Readership

This book, however, is intended for all those developers who do *not* want to limit themselves to maintaining these legacy applications in the future. It is targeted at ABAP developers (and other interested parties) who want to broaden their scope and discover exactly what lies behind the overstated buzzwords in those slick marketing brochures.

Given the frequency with which SAP already uses the new technologies to implement its products, it's apparent that the future of SAP development does *not* belong to ABAP. So, if you want to play a role in the world of SAP, we suggest that you begin dabbling with those new technologies now.

If you're receptive to the new SAP technologies and deal with them *actively*, this book will help you get started. In contrast to the "new equals good" approach of most other literature on the subject, this book provides a critical review of the new technology from a practical perspective.

Developers

This volume is therefore intended primarily for ABAP developers who want to (or have to) learn about this new world hands-on. Reinforced by specific examples and comparisons with familiar, proven technologies in the ABAP world, it contains an introduction to all relevant aspects of practical Java development with SAP Web AS. It is not intended to be a comprehensive tutorial of Java and J2EE architecture; the sheer scope and complexity of the subject matter prevent this from occurring. If you're looking for assistance in this area to help you with your daily (project) work, we recommend the numerous, outstanding publications listed in the bibliography of this book. The primary goal of this book is to describe the conceptual and architectural aspects of the new technologies and stress the similarities and differences between them and ABAP.

Decision-Makers

Another target audience for this book includes decision-makers whose daily responsibilities do not include developing software (or not any more), who will find an abundance of relevant information to help them steer design decisions in the right direction. This book will help you understand the functionality and philosophy of the new technologies, and point out its potential uses and limits in clear detail.

Book Structure

The structure of the book is the result of our attempt to illustrate the concepts and technologies based on practical examples and comparisons with the "old world":

Our Workshop

In **Chapter 2**, "Technology Overview," we examine the technology available in SAP Web AS 6.40 and discuss its integration in SAP's overall technology strategy, focusing primarily on the relevant functions and procedures from a developer's perspective.

The Example Project

To demonstrate the practical use of the technologies and techniques introduced in the book, the individual chapters contain numerous examples, which involve a fictitious IT project. This example project is introduced in **Chapter 3**, "The ResMan Example Project," which also specifies the professional and technical requirements.

Old Stuff and New Stuff

Chapter 4, "The Programming Languages of the SAP Web Application Server," first deals with the "old" ABAP world, and briefly discusses the most important features of the ABAP programming language as a refresher. This is followed by a summary of the major aspects of the Java programming language, which provides the fundamentals for the subsequent chapters.

The Tools

Chapter 5, "Development Tools and Objects," deals with the available development tools. We first review the familiar tools and development objects from the world of ABAP, and then move on to examine their relevant equivalents in the Java environment in detail. An introduction to the architecture of J2EE applications provides a foundation for the latter.

Chapter 6, "Application Layers," deals with the individual layers of a modern software application in detail. The performance and functions of the ABAP and Java tools are described for each layer.

Layers

Chapter 7, "Application Design," takes a "best practice" approach to describing the available, practical options for designing applications.

Best Practices

Chapter 8, "Performance Aspects," provides recommendations for optimizing application performance based on current Web AS technologies.

Lastly, **Chapter 9**, "Outlook," hints at the future path of SAP's technology, and describes the consequences this will have for strategy and operational IT.

The Future

But enough introduction—it's time to get started together with the "brave new world" of SAP application development. Have fun!

2 Technology Overview

Developing successful applications with the SAP Web Application Server requires a sound understanding of the underlying technology and architecture. This chapter will help you understand the basics, without boring you with non-development-related details.

Challenges to IT

The challenges to and demands on IT infrastructures are increasing constantly. Mounting costs and strong competition characterize nearly every industry sector. More than ever before, enterprises are being forced to cut costs, optimize processes, and expand (or at least defend) their market position through improved customer relationships and shorter product development cycles, to name just two approaches.

Many of these objectives would be out of reach if it weren't for the intelligent, extensive use of information technology. Therefore, the importance of enterprise IT is increasing apace as the enterprise IT infrastructure plays an increasingly critical role.

Beyond the Dot.com Era

After the end of the dot.com era—that fast-moving, lively world of e-commerce in which speed, looks, and marketing were more important than solid, demand-based projects—both users and IT vendors learned their lessons from their vast experiences, many of them bad.

Now, their attention has returned to essential enterprise requirements and re-learning the fact that IT performs a service, and is not an end in itself. Information technology must support enterprise goals with practical projects, a robust infrastructure, and optimized technology for the task—and all at the lowest possible costs.

Web technologies are still important; however, now, they have to be embedded in sensible, integrated IT strategies.

Transformation of the SAP Technology

SAP AG, the largest vendor of enterprise resource software in the world, has had many of the same experiences as its customers. The SAP technology has also changed dramatically in recent years and in prior releases, and continues to evolve. The conventional three-tier R/3 client/server architecture, which was used for many years, has been enhanced repeatedly, opening SAP systems to the "outside world"—for access to and from non-SAP systems—towards a service-oriented architecture (SOA).

ITS The *SAP Internet Transaction Server* (ITS) was a typical child of the dot.com era—a quick and dirty solution, complex, error-prone, and lacking clean integration with the SAP infrastructure—and therefore proved to be an unhappy chapter in the lives of developers and system administrators, which hopefully will soon be cast onto the heap of IT history.

SAP Web Application Server With the current release of *SAP Web Application Server* (SAP Web AS), however, SAP has developed a powerful, scaleable, robust platform that meets all the technical requirements posed on a modern, professional application server with Web integration.

It forms the technological basis for many modules in the current SAP strategy and represents the foundation of current and future SAP products.

This chapter discusses SAP's overall strategy, as well as how the SAP Web AS fits into it.

2.1 Enterprise Services Architecture

SAP introduced its new overall strategy in early 2003. Since then, the *Enterprise Services Architecture* (ESA), SAP's implementation of the SOA concept, has formed the "ideological" framework for current and future development of the SAP technology. The technological basis of the ESA strategy is *SAP NetWeaver*.

ESA and SAP NetWeaver are not revolutionary concepts; instead, they represent the evolutionary development of existing concepts and technologies, which were previously known as *mySAP technology* and implemented large parts of the current strategies.

Web Services The ESA platform offers Web services as a way to make IT environments more flexible with interoperability and deployment of cross-system functions. Simultaneously, it builds on existing solutions to protect legacy investment while still providing innovative solutions.

In particular, the ESA concept enables developers to integrate heterogeneous applications and allows for their simple, flexible, and location-independent use by end users.

Service-Oriented Architecture In the service-oriented architecture of ESA, all applications are treated as services. SAP's technical implementation is based on a combination of proven, innovative, open, standardized, and Web-based technologies.

These technologies form the backbone of the SAP NetWeaver platform—the foundation for all of SAP's new business solutions.

The most important benefit promised by the ESA strategy is a reduction of the *total cost of ownership* (TCO) by integrating heterogeneous infrastructures and reducing overall complexity.

Benefit: TCO

2.2 SAP NetWeaver

SAP NetWeaver is a product that encompasses many different technical components. It implements SAP's vision of a comprehensive integration and application platform for both intra-enterprise and cross-enterprise solutions.

Its approach to integration is broad-based and aims to provide technology that makes it possible to integrate systems, processes, technologies, and people across enterprise boundaries with relatively little effort (read: low costs).

Unlike earlier strategies, in addition to offering universal Web services, SAP NetWeaver's approach also entails an explicit portal to technologies used by other (competing) Web application servers, specifically IBM WebSphere and Microsoft .NET.

A rough overview of the SAP NetWeaver architecture is shown in Figure 2.1.

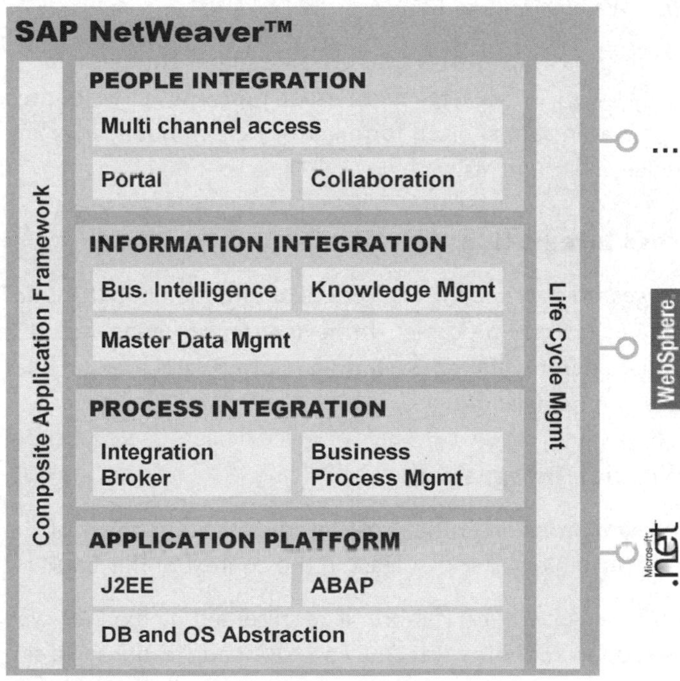

Figure 2.1 SAP NetWeaver Architecture

2.2.1 People Integration

Collaboration

The *SAP Enterprise Portal* already provides technology that makes it possible to give users (both within and outside the enterprise) role-based access to SAP and non-SAP applications under one "roof"—in a largely standardized, customizable user interface.

The SAP Enterprise Portal also provides groupware-like functions, to promote fast, efficient communication and collaboration within teams. These functions are grouped together under the umbrella of *collaboration*.

The *SAP Mobile Infrastructure* enables access to information over a multitude of user devices (such as Internet, WAP, voice control, handhelds, offline access).

2.2.2 Information Integration

Integration

SAP Enterprise Portal also deals with *Knowledge Management* (KM) issues. It features powerful functions for managing, distributing, and retrieving unstructured information and external content.

A proven module for *Business Intelligence*—the collection, preparation, analysis, and distribution of mission-critical information—is the *SAP Business information Warehouse* (SAP BW).

Master Data Management (MDM) is a fairly new component that ensures that master data (such as business partners or products) is distributed enterprise-wide and in standardized form across system boundaries and in heterogeneous environments.

2.2.3 Process Integration

The *SAP Exchange Infrastructure* (XI) is a central information hub that integrates internal and external processes, retrieving, transforming, and distributing information from different systems and processes based on rules and XML/SOAP communication.

2.2.4 Application Integration

Application integration involves the most interesting component of the SAP NetWeaver technology stack, at least in the context of this book.

The SAP NetWeaver *Application Platform* is represented by the SAP Web AS. It features support for both Java/J2EE and ABAP applications in a single environment, has powerful development tools for both platforms, and offers independence from any particular database system or server operating system. Along with its native Web services, the SAP Web AS also features excellent scalability and robustness.

2.2.5 Life Cycle Management

Life Cycle Management

Functions to support the software life cycle—including design, development, distribution, versioning, testing, operating, change management, and monitoring—are available at all levels of the technology stack.

2.2.6 Composite Application Framework

Composite Applications

The complete SAP NetWeaver technology provides all the tools and components required to develop and apply *xApps*.

xApps are finished applications that use the technologies and modules across the entire NetWeaver technology stack, to combine SAP and non-SAP components and integrate them in a powerful, homogenous application. xApps are based on the Enterprise Server Architecture (ESA) and use Web service standards. The *Composite Application Framework* is SAP's development and runtime environment for xApps.

Several xApps are already available. One of the first xApps is SAP xRPM *(SAP xApp Resource and Program Management)*, which helps control and carry out research and development processes of IT projects. It integrates application components of various systems.

Another available program is SAP xMA *(SAP xApp Mergers and Acquisitions)*, which accelerates, controls, and makes known the business processes involved in mergers and acquisitions.

Other xApps include SAP xPD *(SAP xApp Product Definition)* and SAP xEM *(SAP xApp Emission Management)*. SAP xPD simplifies the design and development process for new products; SAP xEM helps enterprises comply with regulations and meet defined standards for greenhouse gas emissions.

2.3 System Architecture of the SAP Web Application Server

The original three-tier architecture that was introduced with SAP R/3 is still generally valid, and forms the foundation for implementing applications based on the SAP Web AS. Its basic principle is a clear separation between the presentation, application, and database layers.

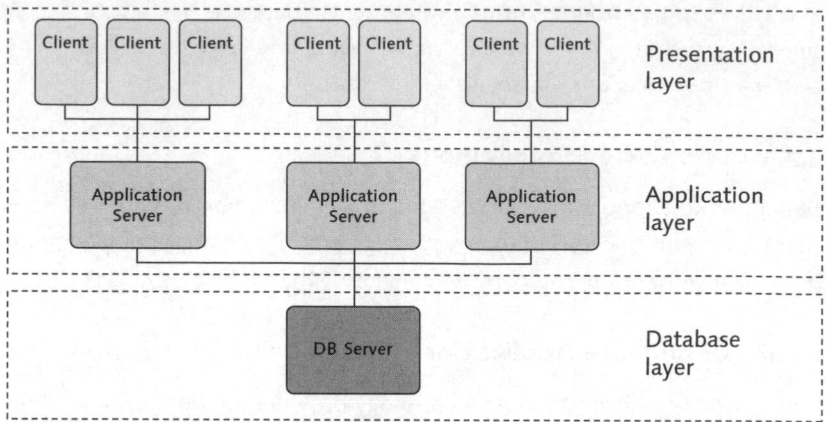

Figure 2.2 Conventional Three-Tier Architecture

Advantages of the Layer Model

One major advantage of this separation of layers is the excellent scalability of the supported application. The individual layers can be distributed to different computers to achieve greater overall performance.

The conventional three-tier architecture, which has proven itself in countless implementations in recent years and was an important reason for the resounding success of SAP R/3, has been given major extensions, to create a true Web application server and enable the integration of open standards.

A visual mapping of how the three-tier architecture is applied to the SAP Web AS is illustrated in Figure 2.3.

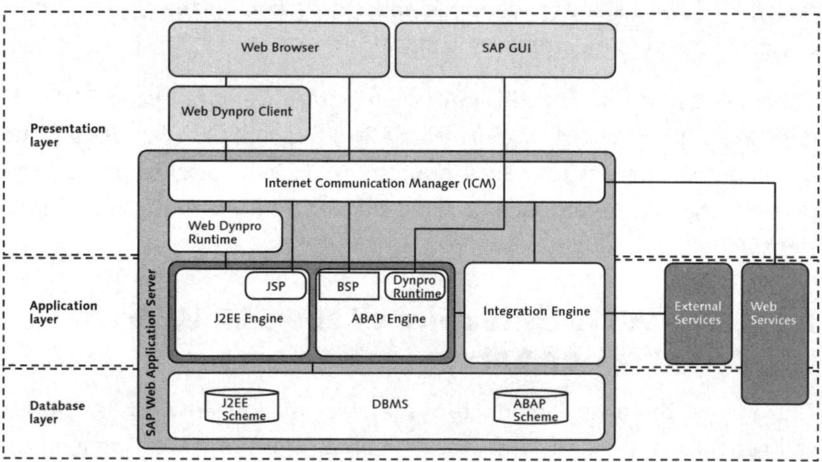

Figure 2.3 Three-Tier Architecture of SAP Web AS 6.30

2.3.1 Presentation Layer

The *presentation layer*, or *client layer*, is the user interface for interaction and navigation. It is usually represented by a graphical user interface (GUI).

Web Browser

Whereas a dedicated SAP GUI was required as a client on PCs and workstations in the early days of R/3, the current version of the SAP Web AS features support for a wide variety of user devices. The most important of these, especially in the Web environment, involves using a Web browser as client.

Web Dynpro

In particular, the Web Dynpro technology makes extensive use of this type of communication with the application server and uses a highly efficient, innovative procedure to turn the browser into an extremely powerful client. In this model, a browser-based client—with which the user interacts—communicates with a server component, which, in turn, "talks" to the application server.

The SAP Web AS also supports conventional techniques for creating Web frontends and provides two powerful technologies in parallel to do so:

- *Business Server Pages* (BSPs) can be used to develop Web frontends that communicate with the ABAP Engine in the application layer. **BSP**
- *Java Server Pages* (JSPs) make it possible to create Web frontends whose "call partner" in the application layer is the J2EE Engine. **JSP**

Benefits

The main advantages of browser-based client technology—aside from flexibility of display—include the fact that only a slight administration effort is required for distribution (no client installations) and its high availability (operating system independence, large number of installed browsers).

For more details regarding the Web Dynpro technology and how it works, see Section 6.4.2.

ICM

The *Internet Communication Manager* (ICM) plays a central role for Web-based client technologies on the SAP Web AS. It not only carries out the tasks of a conventional Web server (processing HTTP requests, for instance) and manages the entire IP communication on the SAP Web AS, but also distributes the client requests to the responsible engines in the application layer.

2.3.2 Application Layer

Business Logic The *application layer* should be considered the most important part of an application because the entire business logic is modeled within it. It is responsible for processing the business data.

Processing The application layer accepts the data from the presentation layer (entered by the user, for example), collects additional data (from a database table via the database layer, for example), and processes it. The result of this processing is then passed on to the other layers—for example, made accessible to the user through the presentation layer and written to database tables through the database layer.

Integration Engine The *Integration Engine* enables external systems to address the application layer and integrate functions from external systems.

A major feature of the application layer in the SAP Web AS is that business logic can be implemented both in the ABAP/ABAP Objects programming language and in Java. A detailed description of these *personalities*, along with the most important components of the SAP Web AS, follows in the sections below.

Other special features in the application layer of the SAP Web AS are its operating system independence and its capabilities for flexible load distribution across multiple servers.

2.3.3 Database Layer

Persistence The *database layer* is responsible for the retrieval and storage of all persistent data. It provides its services to the applications independently of the underlying database system and supports both transaction processing and object-relational mapping.

Other major features of the database layer on the SAP Web AS are its operating system independence and its integrated mechanisms for performance optimization (caching).

2.4 Major Components of the SAP Web Application Server

2.4.1 The Internet Communication Manager (ICM)

The *Internet Communication Manager* (ICM) is a primary component of the SAP Web AS. It represents the link between the components on the server and the outside world that is accessible through Internet protocols.

Plug-Ins

The protocols supported by the ICM are provided by *plug-ins*, which are loaded as necessary. The most important plug-ins are currently those for HTTP(S) and SMTP. An additional (provided) component does the encrypting and decrypting of the data stream under the secure HTTPS.

As an integral component of the SAP Web AS, the ICM provides all the necessary basic technology to act both as an HTTP(S) server, to communicate with clients/Web browsers, and as an HTTP(S) client, to communicate with other Internet servers.

Worker Threads

The ICM is an independent process that is started and monitored by the dispatcher. It distributes incoming requests to *worker threads*, which, in turn, start work processes through the dispatcher. Communication between the work process and worker thread takes place through *memory pipes*.

Sessions

In addition to controlling incoming and outgoing requests, the ICM also manages connection and session information to assign and supply the correct status and user contexts to the respective requests.

Server Cache

Another important component of the ICM is the *server cache*. This is a server-side buffer that caches frequently requested (usually static) HTTP objects, such as image files, and delivers them directly from the ICM when requested, and not from a work process. This approach can boost performance significantly. Transaction SMICM contains various functions for administering the ICM and the server cache, among other things.

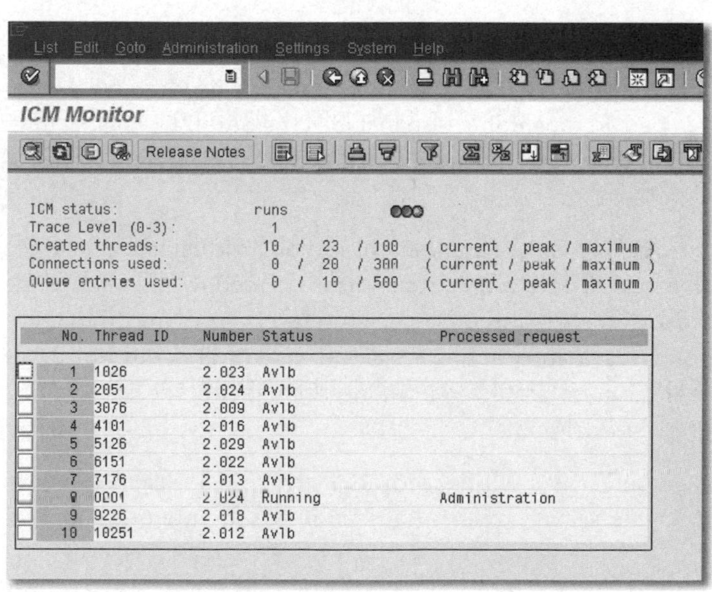

Figure 2.4 Administering the ICM with Transaction SMICM

2.4.2 The ABAP Runtime Environment

The *ABAP runtime environment*—also know as the *ABAP personality*—designates the component of the SAP Web AS that is responsible for running programs that were written in the ABAP programming language.

ABAP is an interpreter language, which means the ABAP source text is not compiled directly to machine language and run by a processor. Instead, it is transformed to a byte code—the *Intermediate Language* (IL).

ABAP VM This byte code is executed at runtime by the *ABAP Virtual Machine* (VM), which forms the core of the ABAP personality. The ABAP VM triggers and monitors the execution of every IL command by the processors.

This "managed code" principle ensures that the multitude of parallel processes does not interfere with one another and that no single process can take control of the entire server—causing a server crash or monopolizing all the CPU time, for example. It provides for controlled, secure, stable system operations—basic prerequisites for running mission-critical applications.

Another advantage of this approach is that it is platform-independent. Specifically, ABAP developers don't have to worry about porting their programs to other platforms—SAP handles this task by porting the ABAP VM to other operating systems.

2.4.3 The J2EE Engine

Starting with Release 6.20, SAP's Web AS not only features the proven ABAP runtime environment, but also includes the SAP J2EE Engine, integrating an additional, non-proprietary platform for application development on a single server.

Java VM Similar to the ABAP VM, Java applications run on a virtual machine in the SAP J2EE Engine. The Java source code is transformed to an intermediate code—*Java byte code*—that the Java VM interprets and runs on the processor. As such, Java applications are never given full control over the main CPUs and can be protected from interfering with one another in a secure processing environment.

The SAP J2EE Server is a full-fledged J2EE engine with all the features required to create secure, robust, transaction-based enterprise applications.

Various standardized functions and components provide nearly everything required to solve complex enterprise tasks with component-based software: transaction control, database integration, component-based development, load distribution, and more.

Release 6.30 and higher of the SAP J2EE Engine are fully compatible with J2EE 1.3 specifications. In addition to the pure Java platform, the J2EE platform also provides native support for a multitude of standards and application programming interfaces (APIs).

Standards

The most important technologies supported by the SAP J2EE Engine are:

- Enterprise JavaBeans 2.0 with
  - Session beans, entity beans
  - Message-driven beans
  - Container-managed persistence
  - Query language
- Web support
  - JSP
  - Java servlets
  - HTTP(S)
- APIs
  - Java Connector Architecture (JCA)
  - Java Message Service (JMS)
  - Java Naming and Directory Interface (JNDI)
  - Java Database Connectivity (JDBC)
  - Remote Method Invocation (RMI)
  - Java Transaction API (JTA), Java Transaction Service (JTS)
  - Java Cryptography Architecture (JCA), Java Cryptography Extension (JCE)
  - Java Mail
  - Java Authentication and Authorization Service (JAAS)
- XML support
  - XML parser with Java API for XML messaging (JAXM)
  - XML schema support and validation
  - Java API for processing XML (JAXP)

- SOAP support (including attachments)
- XSLT 1.1 processor

Detailed explanations of these technologies and their relevance for developing practical applications in the Java environment are available in Section 5.2.1.

2.4.4 The Integration Engine

The integration layer is responsible for enabling communication between the business layer and different systems and applications.

It is not a single process, but rather various technologies that are used to integrate other (SAP and non-SAP) systems or provide functions for other systems.

The most important categories are described below.

Connectors

Connectors, which SAP usually supplies free of charge, are middleware that connect external systems to the SAP ABAP Engine.

Business Connector

The *SAP Business Connector* provides a bidirectional XML interface and even supports asynchronous communication. It uses the existing RFC, BAPI, and IDoc interfaces and translates the calls to and from XML. It is implemented as an independent component outside of the actual SAP R/3 System.

It no longer plays a strategic role in SAP's NetWeaver strategy as its functions are now fully covered by the *SAP Exchange Infrastructure* (SAP XI).

JCo

The *SAP Java Connector* (JCo) is a collection of Java classes that enables bidirectional communication between Java applications and the ABAP Engine.

The underlying RFC protocol enables communication in both directions, that is:

1. All "remote-capable" function modules in the ABAP world can be called from within the Java world.
2. Functions can be deployed in the Java world and called (with `Call Function`) from within the ABAP world.

The JCo is an integrated component of SAP Web AS Release 2.0 and higher and will represent a strategic medium for communicating between the Java/J2EE and ABAP personalities in future versions.

You'll learn more about options for communicating between the ABAP and Java personalities in Section 2.11.

Similar to the JCo, the *SAP .NET Connector* enables two-way communication between the ABAP Engine and Microsoft .NET applications. **.NET**

This forerunner of the .NET Connector also offers options that are comparable with the JCo to access functions of the ABAP Engine (via RFC) from within programming languages supported by *COM/DCOM*. **COM/DCOM**

ALE and EDI

ALE *(Application Link Enabling)* is a technology to support the controlled exchange of business data between distributed SAP applications within an enterprise.

The applications are not integrated through a central database. Instead, the applications access local, redundant databases and use *IDocs* (intermediate documents) to exchange information. **IDocs**

EDI *(Electronic Data Interchange)* uses the same basic technology (IDocs) in the SAP environment after conversion, but, by definition, is also used to exchange data between two business partners.

RFC

RFC *(Remote Function Call)* is SAP's proprietary communication protocol for calling functions in other systems over a network connection.

It supports both passed parameters and results parameters, which can also contain complex structures and data types. RFC is the preferred protocol for synchronous data transfer—especially for communicating with RFC-capable non-R/3 systems.

Web Services and SOAP

In contrast to the proprietary RFC, Web services are an open-standards interface technology for publishing, locating, and using software components in other systems over the Internet/intranet.

Web services are based on XML, SOAP, WSDL, and UDDI (see Section 2.6). The SOAP protocol is the most comparable with RFC. A character- **SOAP** based transport protocol (such as HTTP or SMTP) is used to execute function calls, which can contain transfer or return parameters in external systems.

Web services, the future technology for integrating processes between enterprises, play a central role in SAP's overall strategy and in the SAP Web AS. Web services can be used and rendered in both the ABAP and Java worlds starting from Release 6.20 of the Web AS.

Integration Engine The *Integration Engine* is one of many components of the SAP Web AS that supports communication via Web services through the *SOAP Runtime*. This engine also plays a critical role in the context of the SAP XI.

For more information on Web services, see Section 6.2.5.

2.5 Database Integration

Persistent data storage is one of the most demanding challenges for a business application.

Requirements Important features of a professional solution for meeting these demands include:

- Database independence
- Client capability
- Caching and trace mechanisms
- Transaction capability
- Object-relational mapping

Early versions of the SAP Web AS already provided outstanding support for these features in the ABAP personality. Release 6.30 is the first serious attempt to expand these features to the Java world in the SAP Web AS. The abstraction technology used for the database layer is called *Open SQL*.

2.5.1 Database Independence

The virtual machines of the ABAP and Java personalities make the application layer platform-independent. Open SQL performs the same task for the database layer.

Open SQL encapsulates the database interfaces of many different database vendors. The various database management systems (such as Oracle, IBM DB2, SAP DB/MaxDB, or Informix) each "speak" a different SQL syntax and have completely different interfaces, especially where system services are involved.

Homogenizing Heterogeneous SQL Dialects

Open SQL hides these heterogeneous interfaces behind a syntax that is standardized for all databases and which the Open SQL Engine translates transparently into commands for the specific installed DBMS. Although this entails reducing the SQL syntax to the least common denominator, it provides invaluable advantages when it comes to porting applications to other databases.

2.5.2 Client Capability

Another important feature of Open SQL, and one that helps application developers avoid mistakes, is its ability to *automatically* add a client assignment to all database table accesses (read or write).

Consequently, datasets from different enterprises (subsidiaries) can be saved together in the same DBMS tables, without the developer having to worry about their explicit separation.

2.5.3 Caching and Trace Mechanisms

Open SQL's ability to buffer parts of tables (or even entire tables) in main memory can increase performance dramatically during read operations.

Caching complete SQL statements also boosts performance—independent of the caching mechanisms in the underlying database system.

Powerful trace mechanisms enable detailed logging of database access, giving you several database-independent starting points for troubleshooting, logging, and optimizing database access.

2.5.4 Transaction Capability

Support of the transaction concept is one of Open SQL's most important features. The transaction concept supports developers through effective mechanisms that largely preclude the problems that can otherwise arise in multiuser operations.

ACID

From the application view, the developer has an "all or nothing" view of the database in accordance with the ACID principle, which means transactions have the following characteristics:

- **Atomicity**
  Either all the changes involved in the transaction are successful and valid or none are.
- **Consistency**
  If the transaction is successful, the database remains consistent in accordance with the defined integrity conditions.
- **Isolation**
  All changes and actions performed within one transaction remain invisible to other parallel transactions.
- **Durability**
  After the changes of a transaction are released, the system must ensure the persistence of the changes despite any potential errors.

2.5.5 Object-Relational Mapping

When object-oriented languages (such as ABAP Objects and Java) are used, it is advisable to use techniques to store the objects.

In other words, in contrast to strictly relational persistence—in which object attributes have to be written to tables or read from them explicitly—an application developer does not have to worry about these tasks. Instead, the database abstraction layer takes care of data retrieval and object persistency in the database whenever needed.

In the world of ABAP Objects, Open SQL performs this task. Various J2EE-based techniques and SAP-specific solution approaches exist for the Java world and are described in more detail in Section 6.1.2.

2.5.6 Native SQL

Unlike Open SQL, native SQL supports the complete set of SQL commands for each respective database vendor.

Technique for Exceptional Cases

Although use of native SQL from both personalities is feasible, it is not recommended in most cases, as all the advantages described above—especially guaranteed portability—are lost.

At most, native SQL should be used for one-time data migration or similar exceptional cases, in which specific vendor-supported features are required for a specific task.

2.6 Web Services

2.6.1 What Are Web Services?

Web services represent self-contained, self-descriptive, modular business logic that is published, located, and executed based on Internet standards. Web services represent a form of standardized, XML-based middleware, whose success is due in part to major support from the software industry.

Protocols

The largest software vendors around the world have established standard procedures and protocols for automated, cross-platform integration:

- SOAP (Simple Object Access Protocol)
- WSDL (Web Services Description Language)
- UDDI (Universal Description, Discovery, and Integration)

A decisive advantage of Web services, compared to other middleware technologies like CORBA or DCOM, is their flexibility and independence from platform, programming language, and even transport protocol.

Their platform independence results from the direct use of generally accepted Internet technologies. Their independence of programming language comes from a technology stack based completely on XML, which is supported by every serious programming language. Another decisive bonus of Web services is their nearly free choice of transport protocol: The messages used for Web service communication can be based on HTTP, SMTP, or FTP, and can also be adapted to any future character-based protocol.

Interpretation

To interpret Web services, the service provider merely needs a handler on the server side, to detect when a Web service message is received and has to be converted to a function call. As the different protocols show, contrary to strictly synchronous RFC calls, assorted other communication modes—both synchronous and asynchronous—can exist. Section 6.2 explores this subject in greater detail.

2.6.2 The Web Service Paradigm

The general process flow of a Web service call is as follows (also see Figure 2.5):

1. The Web service requestor (the "calling" program), acting as the client, places a request with the service directory, with search criteria for a

certain type of service. This service directory is called the UDDI (Universal Description, Discovery, and Integration) directory. Its interface, the UDDI Inquiry API, is also available as a Web service-like mechanism.

2. This central service directory contains a list of all known Web services, that is, all Web services that were recorded under certain criteria in this directory. The service provider has published its services previously, either manually or automatically with the UDDI Publish API. The service directory gives the client a reference, in the form of a URL with the interface description of the service—the WSDL *(Web Service Description Language)*.
3. The client requests the WSDL definition of the Web service to use from the service provider. It contains all the necessary information for the service—including the available functions, a description of the necessary parameters, the URL of the service to call, or the transport protocol used.
4. The client sends a SOAP request to call a function of the Web service; in the process, input parameters are passed on and (usually after the service provider runs the function) return values are received.

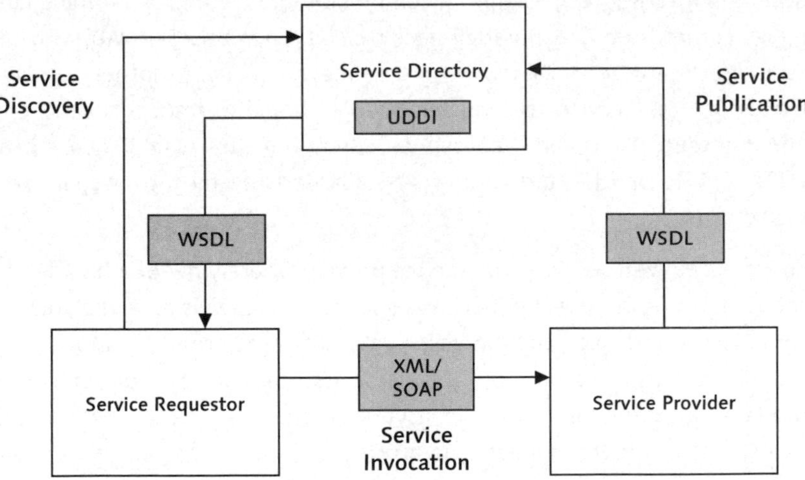

Figure 2.5 The Web Service Paradigm

2.6.3 The SAP Web Application Server as Web Service Client

Web services can be accessed from the SAP Web AS in two ways:

1. **Low-level, based on SOAP Runtime**
   ABAP Objects classes are supplied as a SOAP framework (which is distributed as an include) to call the Web services directly from within the applications. To do so, a SOAP document must be manually parameterized, serialized, and dispatched, and its reply interpreted.
2. **High-level, based on proxy classes of the Integration Builder**
   The Integration Builder—a component of the SAP Exchange Infrastructure (XI)—can be used to generate proxy classes, which can be integrated easily with existing programs. These classes encapsulate the technical parameters and methods of a Web service as a native-speaking proxy, which means they can be included in applications relatively simply.

Because HTTP is normally used to communicate with Web services, the Internet Communication Manager (ICM) is used for low-level communication in both directions between the SAP Web AS and the Web services.

Web Service Clients with Java

Starting with Release 6.40 of SAP Web AS, the *SAP NetWeaver Developer Studio* (NWDS) now also has powerful Java tools for generating Java-based Web service clients automatically, based on the WSDL description of the service in question.

2.6.4 The SAP Web Application Server as Web Service Provider

The role of Web service provider is performed adequately even by Release 6.20 of the SAP Web Application Server, despite several technical restrictions. All remote-capable function modules are deployed as Web services automatically. Although it does not integrate UDDI fully, each SAP Web AS has an easy-to-use WSDL browser to manually locate Web services as Web-based BSP applications. The interface description of any service can be queried and the clients can be implemented in any programming language. In addition, SAP Web AS 6.40 features sophisticated mechanisms for configuring visibility, transaction processing, and security aspects of the deployed Web services.

2.6.5 Outlook

Web services will continue to increase in importance in future SAP releases—not only because they provide the basis for simple, standardized, cost-effective integration scenarios in heterogeneous application landscapes, but also because Web services have assumed a central role in the implementation of the *Enterprise Services Architecture* (ESA).

Encapsulated Database Access

SAP still has the vision of encapsulating data retrieval—which even today employs object-relational database access—to the extent that future applications will no longer access the database directly. Instead, data retrieval and persistence will be provided as Web services.

This would create a service-oriented abstraction of the application and database layers. The application is completely independent in this scenario, regardless of whether the data supplier or recipient is a local application, some other database, some other application server within the company, or a service provider on the other side of the globe.

Of course, the security, stability, performance, and quality of the communications are essential here. It will certainly take time until this concept is ready for the market, but the idea of such a scenario is extremely attractive—especially under integration and technical development aspects—and ultimately realistic in the long term.

2.7 Frontends

Different graphical user interfaces are available for giving users access to SAP systems. The advantages and disadvantages of the most important technologies are discussed briefly below.

2.7.1 SAP GUI for Windows

Classic

SAP GUI for Windows was developed for Windows operating systems. In addition to the standard functions provided by every member of the SAP GUI family, SAP GUI for Windows features deep integration with the Microsoft Office Suite, as well as links to mySAP components such as *mySAP Supply Chain Management* (mySAP SCM). The connection to the SAP system uses the proprietary DIAG protocol, which is based on TCP/IP. Although SAP GUI for Windows cannot be embedded seamlessly in the SAP Enterprise Portal, individual transactions can be accessed through links.

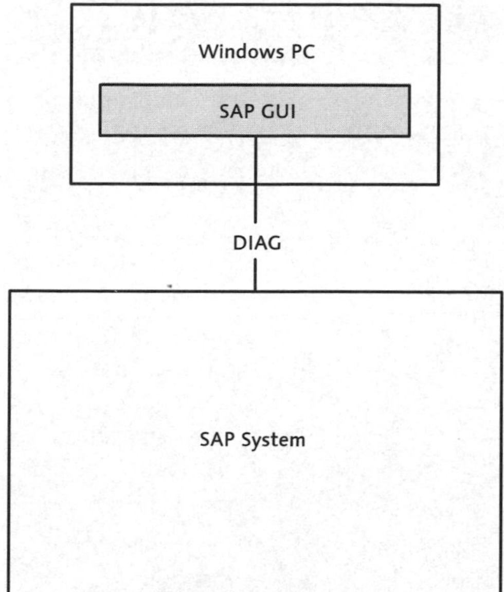

Figure 2.6 SAP GUI for Windows

- Requirements
  - All Windows operating systems from Windows 95 (including Windows CE) or
  - ECitrix Metaframe
- Advantages
  - All transactions and settings are available
  - Support for more than 20 languages
  - Multiple work sessions possible
  - Office integration with a high degree of automation
- Disadvantages
  - Client installation required on every PC

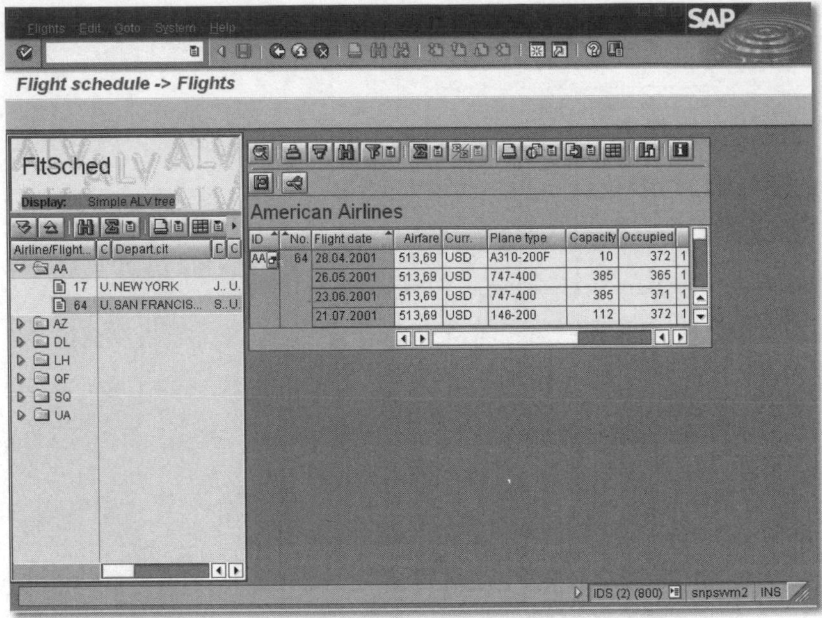

Figure 2.7 SAP User Interface for Windows

2.7.2 SAP GUI for Java

Multifunctional

SAP GUI for Java was developed to achieve platform independence for SAP desktop frontends. This GUI uses JavaBeans (not to be confused with Enterprise Java Beans, EJBs) to provide functions, all based on a combination of Java and C++. The contribution of C/C++ takes the form of libraries that are saved on the desktop and used by SAP GUI for Java to supply functions such as network communication, file transfer, and others. SAP GUI for Java is installed as a desktop application and communicates directly with the SAP Web Application Server.

The full functions of the application are also available when it is started as an applet in a browser, which means it can be seamlessly integrated as a frame in the Enterprise Portal.

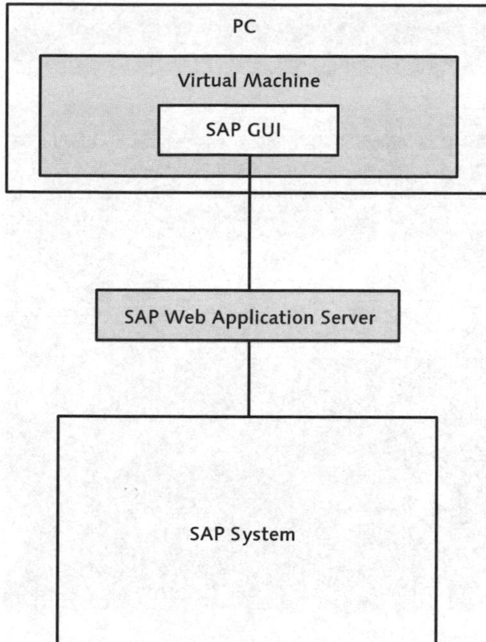

Figure 2.8 SAP GUI for Java

- Requirements
  - Any operating system that supports the Java Virtual Machine or JVM (such as OS/2, Apple Macintosh, Linux, Solaris, AIX, Tru64, HP-UX)
  - Java VM installation (if not already included in the OS) or VM installation as browser plug-in
- Advantages
  - Platform independence
  - Multiple work sessions possible
- Disadvantages
  - Client installation required on every PC
  - Poor performance
  - No office integration
  - Some displays are restricted
  - Limited transaction access
  - Limited Enjoy controls
  - No GuiXT support

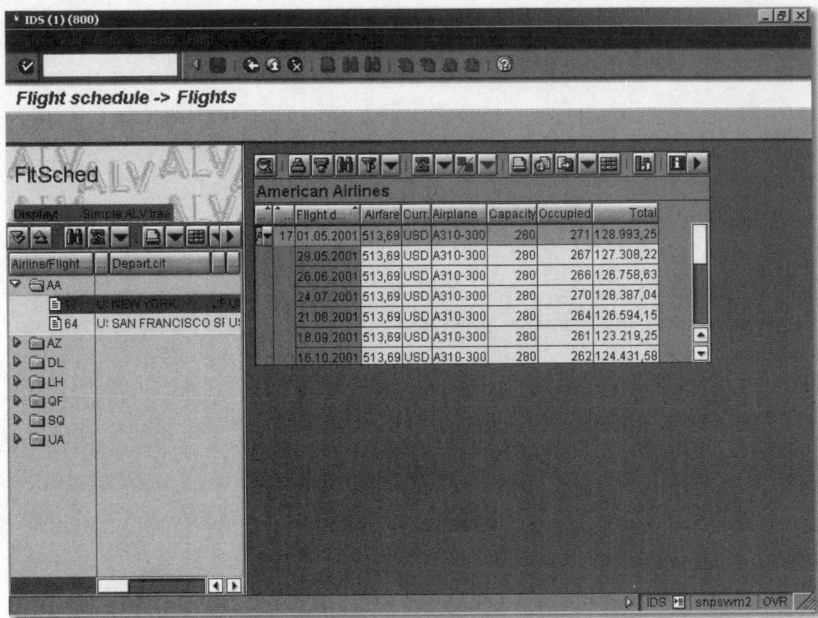

Figure 2.9 SAP User Interface for Java

2.7.3 SAP GUI for HTML

Exotic

SAP GUI for HTML enables you to access certain transactions through a Web browser. An installed SAP Internet Transaction Server (ITS) is also required, which performs the actual conversion to HTML, taking any existing templates into account. SAP ITS services are used to convert screen elements in SAP transactions to HTML. Although not all the elements can be translated to HTML, all the standard elements (such as tables, lists, menu trees, and so on) are supported. Processing business transactions with a Web browser requires transactions that have been developed specifically for execution in the Internet or an Intranet: Internet Application Components (IAC).[1]

Data transfer can be handled by a standard 56K modem. SAP GUI for HTML can be integrated seamlessly in an Enterprise Portal (EP), just like any other browser-based application.

1 SAP Web Application Server 6.40 integrates both SAP GUI for HTML and IAC as services.

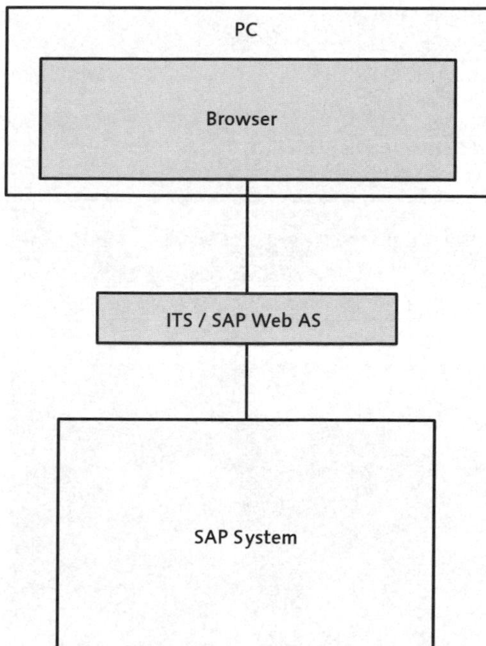

Figure 2.10 SAP GUI for HTML

- Requirements
  - Internet Explorer 5.5 or Netscape Navigator 7 and later
- Advantages
  - No installation
  - Simple handling
  - Web-capable
- Disadvantages
  - Limited display of images and transactions
  - Highly limited Enjoy controls
  - SAP GUI scripting is not possible
  - Only one session (multisession transactions are not supported)
  - Network load is three times higher than with GUI for Windows/Java
  - Slow page display
  - Difficult to debug and trace
  - High administrative effort required
  - Inadequate display (structure, clarity)

- Some specific programming is required
- Does not support flexible design
- No office integration
- No input wizards and no input verification

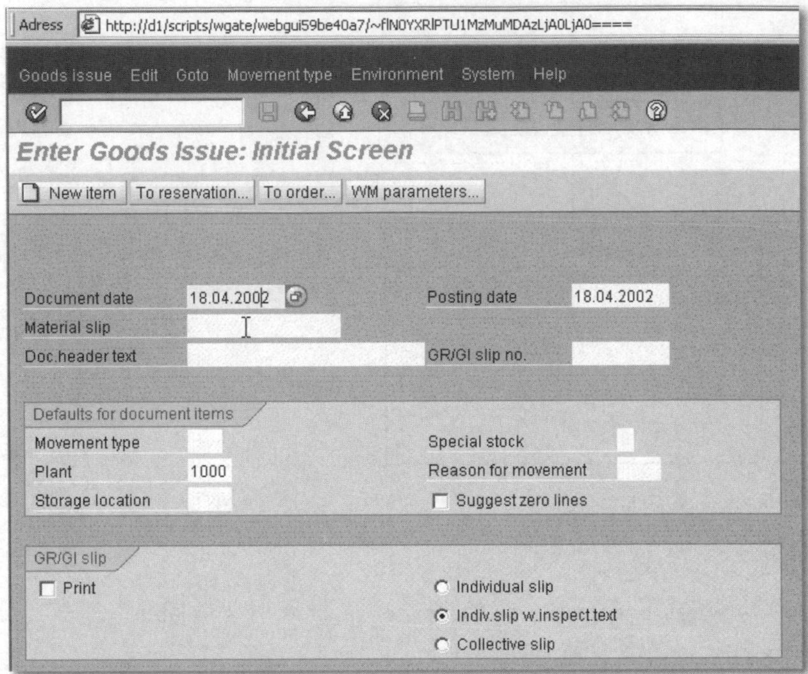

Figure 2.11 SAP User Interface for HTML

2.7.4 Pure Browser Interface (BSP, JSP)

Lean Server-side scripts are used to generate HTML that can be displayed in a Web browser. The ITS or SAP Web AS serves as the runtime environment. Display options are limited due to the HTML specifications.

Tag libraries, which contain predefined visual elements, can be used to develop JSPs and BSP.

In SAP Web AS 6.20 and later, the MVC (model view controller) design concept can be implemented in BSP. In this design pattern, the display pages are separated from the data model and the program flow is optimized.

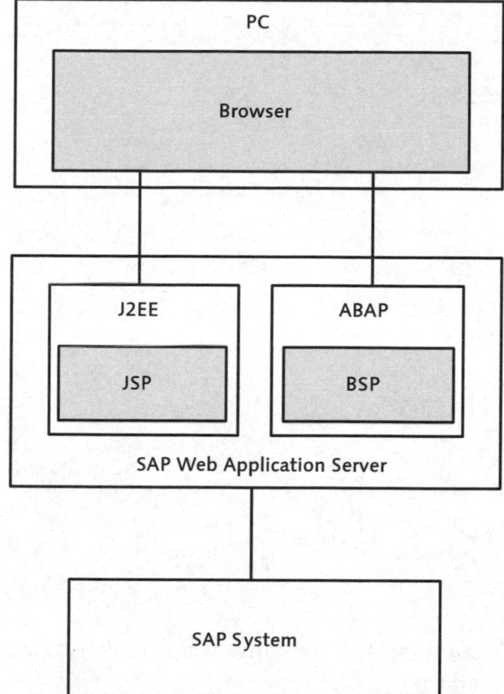

Figure 2.12 Client Using Server-Side Script Languages

- Requirements
  - Internet Explorer 5.5 or Netscape Navigator 7 and later
- Advantages
  - No installation
  - Simple handling
  - Web-capable
- Disadvantages
  - Separate development of user interface and flow logic
  - No Enjoy controls
  - SAP GUI scripting is not possible
  - High network load
  - Slow page display
  - No office integration
  - No input wizards and no input verification

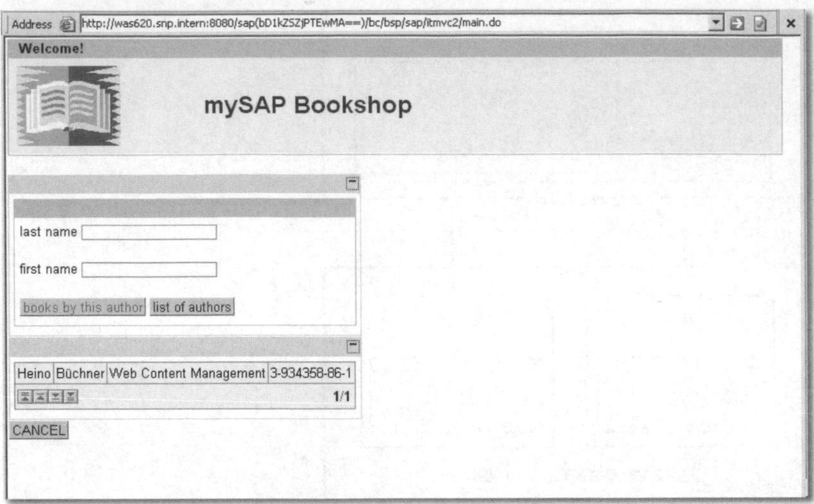

Figure 2.13 Example of BSP Using MVC

2.7.5 Web Dynpro

Future-Proof

Web Dynpro technology will combine the benefits of both Web-based GUIs and Windows/Java-based GUIs.

Web Dynpros can be created using a WYSIWYG developer interface in the SAP NWDS. The process is similar to that of conventional screens (dynpros). What is new is that the results are saved in an abstract descriptive language. This metacode is then used to generate new classes for the most important system environments (Java and ABAP).[2] In turn, these classes serve the applications on the various clients—in the form of dynamic HTML pages, for example.

This program flow support is also implemented in accordance with the MVC concept.

Communication with the SAP system is optimized by a JavaScript-based delta technique that transmits only the changes to a page; the page itself can be refreshed without constantly reloading the entire view. This technology is harmonized with the Enterprise Portal (EP), of course. The applications can be integrated fully into the EP, with support for client-side events and styles.

2 Theoretically possible for .NET as well, but not implemented yet.

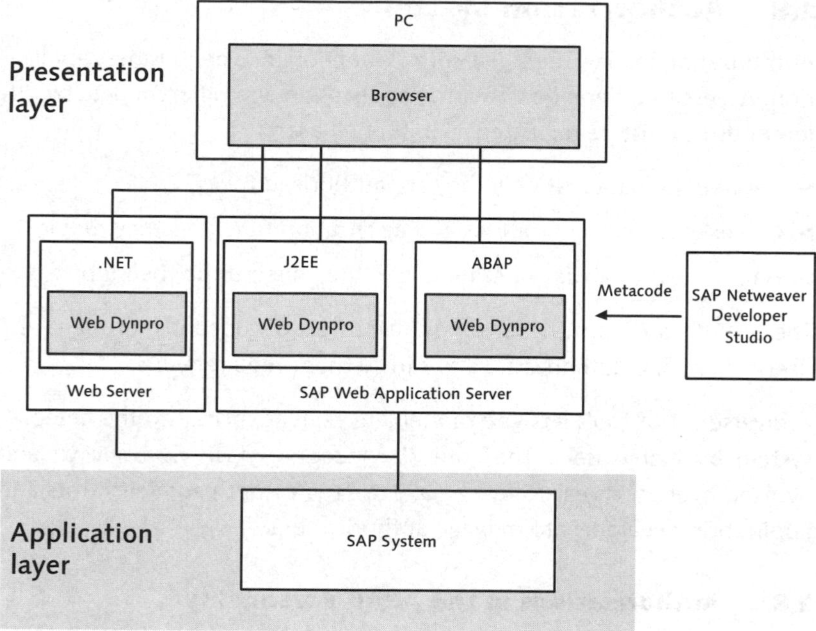

Figure 2.14 Web Dynpro Technology

- Requirements
  - Internet Explorer 5.5 or Netscape Navigator 7 and later
  - Integration with PDAs and smart phones possible
- Advantages
  - Low network load
  - No installation
  - Simple handling
  - Web-capable
  - Supports all future transactions
  - Support for multiple languages, input verification, input wizard
  - Improved error handling
- Disadvantages
  - Not available until SAP Web Application Server 6.40
  - Old transactions have to be transformed (which currently is not guaranteed in all cases)
  - The technology is not that widespread yet

2.8 Authorization System

Authorization management is a critical function in every business application. Access to different parts of the application and different data by different users must be regulated such that all users:

- Can see the data that only they are authorized to see
- Can execute the applications and application functions they require
- Have access to all data and functions they need to do their jobs

The SAP Web AS provides a sophisticated set of functions for managing users, roles, and authorizations to satisfy these requirements.

A diverse set of tools lets you model and regulate access to the complex system by many users. The control concepts, which have grown and evolved over their years of use, make it easy for both administrators and application developers to manage authorizations.

2.8.1 Authorizations in the ABAP Personality

The authorization system protects sensitive data against unauthorized access or modification. At the same time, it ensures that users have access to all relevant functions. It uses a hierarchical control system that can be used to assign authorizations that are extremely granular, yet still efficient.

The smallest element in the hierarchy is the *authorization field*, which defines an elementary data field for use in the authorization check.

Authorization Objects

Several authorization fields can be combined to form an *authorization object*. An authorization object is a table containing up to 10 authorization fields that are linked by "AND" operators. To simplify administration of authorization objects, each object belongs to an *object class.*

An *authorization* is a specific instance of an authorization object, as shown in Figure 2.15.

Figure 2.15 shows one possible aspect of the authorization concept for the ResMan project, the example project introduced in the next chapter. There are three different authorizations within the application: read and write authorizations for all resources with type "A," a read authorization for all resources with type "B," and a write authorization for all resources with type "R." To implement them, the fields from the master data table are linked with the possible activities. The authorizations can be maintained individually or created automatically when a new resource type is created.

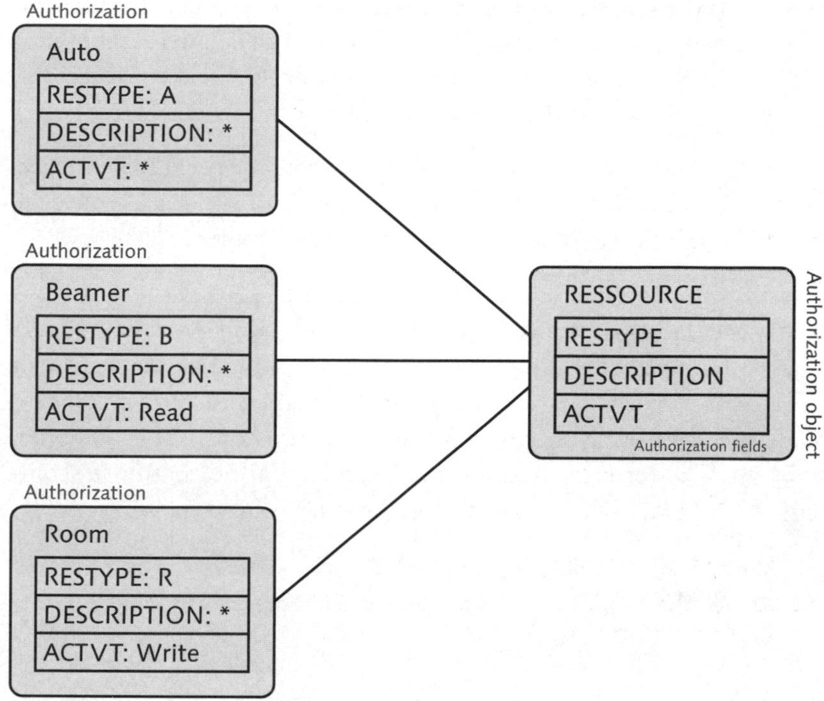

Figure 2.15 Assignment of Authorizations to an Authorization Object

An *authorization profile* groups together multiple, predefined authorizations from the same application. For large applications, these profiles can be aggregated further to form *composite profiles*. Most developers provide profiles along with their applications that correspond to the typical areas of use.

Assigning Authorizations

Every user has a *user master record*, which contains all the authorization profiles and composite profiles. It defines which authorizations apply to the individual user.

Role

Authorization profiles and composite profiles influence authorization assignment within an application. In contrast, the *role* describes the user's total set of activities at the enterprise. It groups the different profiles from the individual application together and defines them for cross-application activities. Accordingly, a role defines which applications, Internet links, reports, files, MiniApps, and so on a user can access. A SAP System already contains numerous standardized roles, such as system administrator, developer, and accountant. Of course, you can also define your own roles or group several roles together to form *composite roles*.

The authorization check takes place at two levels. First, the user/role management functions automatically implement all defined authorization settings. The most obvious effect of this approach is that users see only those applications that they are authorized to use.

Secondly, developers can conduct authorization checks in their application programs. This enables them to define specifically which individuals are authorized to perform which postings, for example.

The ABAP `AUTHORITY-CHECK` statement allows you to check a user's authorization for a specific authorization object against a defined set of values. Authorization checks are supported all the way down to data level, which means you can even restrict access to a certain company code. System field `sy-subrc` contains the return code of the authorization check and can be used for branching within the control structure. Listing 2.1 shows an example of an authorization check.

```
AUTHORITY-CHECK OBJECT 'Z_BO_TYP'
ID 'Z_BF_TYP' FIELD 'A'
ID 'ACTVT' FIELD '01'.

IF sy-subrc <> 0.
...
ENDIF.
...
```

Listing 2.1 The Displayed Coding Checks Whether the Current User Is Authorized to Perform Activity "01" for Resource Type "A"

2.8.2 Authorizations in the Java Personality

The issues of security and authorizations were considered at an early stage of Java development, which resulted in a more demanding security model than is found in most other programming languages. One reason for this approach was the existence of applets, which are downloaded from the Internet and therefore had to be as secure as possible. Not even "malevolent" applets should be capable of committing serious damage to the computer, the operating system, or user resources. The initial emphasis was more on technical security and less on role-based authorizations.

Security in the Language Concept

Security in Java began with the implementation of the very language concept itself. Contrary to programming languages like C++, Java does not permit direct access to the main memory, nor does it support pointer arithmetic. Memory management is fully automated (garbage collection), so buffer overflows are nearly impossible. Type conversions are checked at runtime, which prevents illegal types; the same type of technical security implemented in ABAP for all intents and purposes. When byte code is downloaded from the Internet, as is required for all applets, the byte code verifier ensures that only valid instructions from the Intermediate Language are used, that all methods have valid signatures, that Goto statements point to the start of a statement, and that all expressions are typed correctly.

Sandbox Model

In the Java version of JDK 1.0, a *sandbox security model* defines the access and authorizations of Java applications. In this model, applications that were loaded locally are rated as trusted and given unconditional access to all resources. In contrast, applets are rated as not trustworthy, because they're usually downloaded from a network and therefore pose a security risk. Their capability for action is therefore highly restricted, which means an applet can be executed only from within the virtual sandbox, minimizing all security risks to the Java Virtual Machine (JVM) or the underlying system. It is impossible to gain access to the file system.

Signed Applets

It quickly became apparent, however, that this security model was too restrictive for various application areas. Consequently, *signed applets* were born. Signed applets are Java archives that can be signed with a private digital key. Therefore, applets can be granted the same authorizations as local applications, as long as they come from trusted sources.

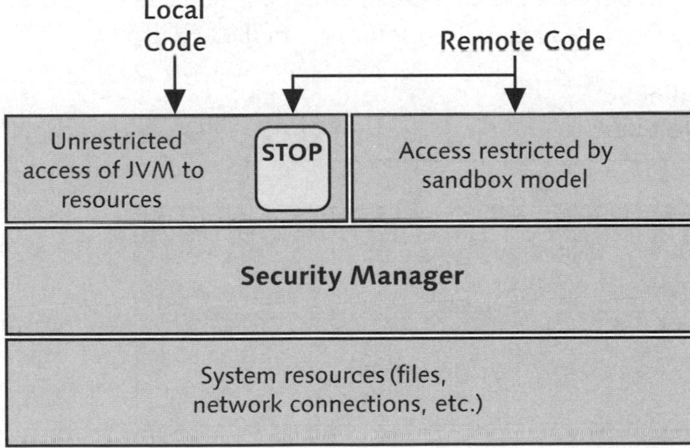

Figure 2.16 Security Concept in Java 1.0

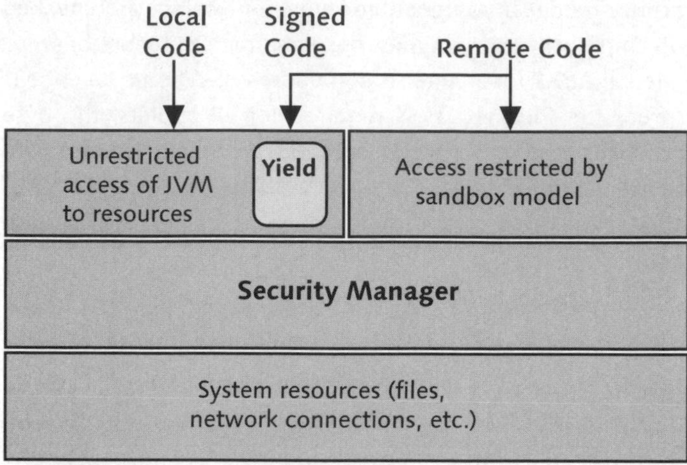

Figure 2.17 Security Concept in Java 1.1

Security Settings and Permissions

This concept was still inadequate, however, as it gave only one applet full access to a resource. There were also desires to run applications in a sandbox even if their origin could not be determined. Consequently, the existing security models were revised once again in Java 2. The major difference between the current security model and its predecessors is that it cannot only differentiate between trusted and restricted applications, but also supports fine-grained security through the granting of restrictions and permissions to these applications. If no restrictions or permissions are set, these applications are still considered to be "unrestricted" by default, giving them unrestricted access to resources as in JDK 1.2.

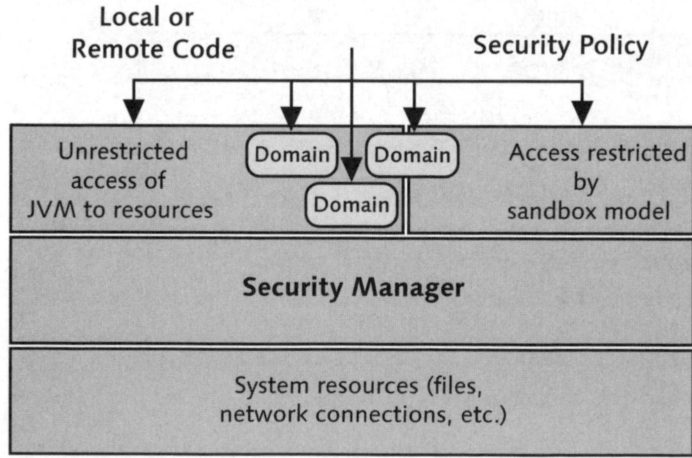

Figure 2.18 Security Concept in Java 1.2

The Java 2 security model is based on coordinated interaction between various components intended to guarantee security. This interaction is illustrated in Figure 2.19.

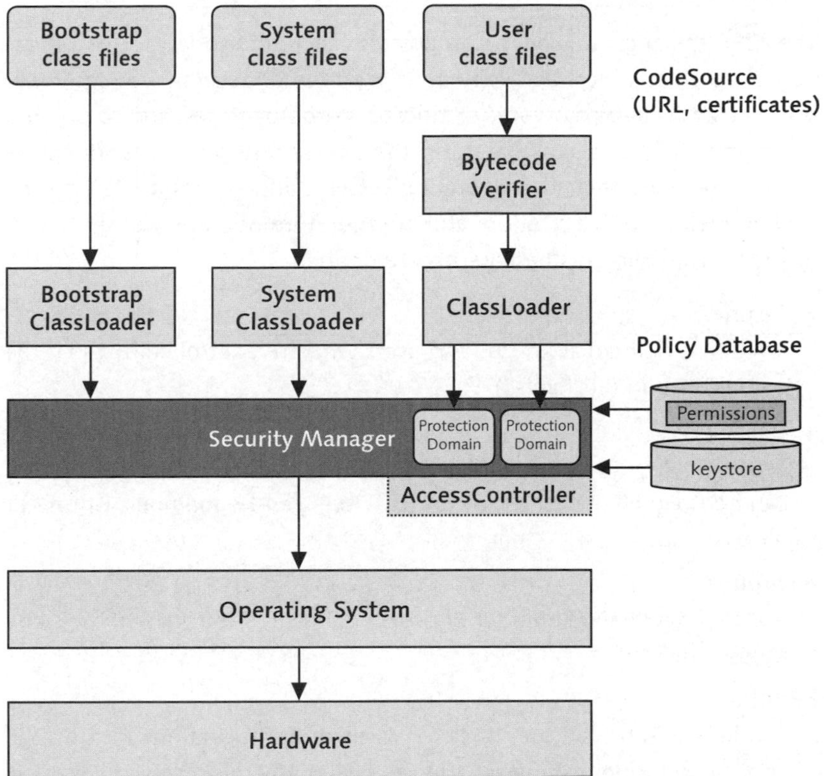

Figure 2.19 Java Security Model

You may ask yourself whether an authorization concept is available for individual users, like the one you know from the ABAP world. Options for user authorizations are certainly available, however, you must implement them yourself. See Section 5.2.1 for more information.

2.8.3 Security of J2EE Applications

The information in the previous section applies equally to J2SE and J2EE applications. The J2EE specifications also define additional security mechanisms for J2EE applications.s

In realistic scenarios, J2EE applications do not have to deal with a single user, but instead with many concurrent users. This fact resulted in increased security requirements of J2EE applications. Consider a Web shop, for example, where customers, staff of the integrated department stores, and the shop operator's service team all have access to a single, shared system. Obviously, business data has to be protected against unauthorized access and manipulation in such scenarios.

Abstract Security Model

The J2EE specifications define an abstract security model. This is necessary because technical details such as the type of access data (combination of user ID and password, certificate, Kerberos ticket, and so on) and the storage of the access data and the access authorizations (directory service, database, text file, operating system, and so on) are left to the J2EE implementer's discretion, and are therefore not a part of the specifications. The following basic terms are defined:

- **Realm**
  A realm is defined as groups and users who are controlled by the same authentication mechanism.
- **User**
  A user is an individual—either a person or a computer program—that can be uniquely identified by an ID. Users can be members of one or more groups.
- **Groups**
  A group is a defined number of users who have been granted the same access privileges.
- **Roles**
  A role is an abstract identifier for a set of authorizations in the J2EE application. Roles can be assigned to both individual users and groups.

Authentication

Authentication describes the procedure in which the user and service verify their identities with one another. We differentiate between two scenarios in J2EE applications:

- **Web tier**
  When applications with a Web interface are involved, the user is authenticated via HTTP against the Web container.
- **Client tier**
  In rich-client applications, which have their own Java-implemented user interfaces instead of the Web browser, authentication is performed in the client container, which functions as a security barrier around the actual rich client.

Both procedures supply the user ID of the authenticating calling program. This means application developers don't have to contend with authentication details, as they're the sole responsibility of the application container.

Web-Tier Authentication

The three most widely used, basic procedures for authentication with the Web container are:

- **Basic authentication**
  This procedure is defined in the HTTP/1.0 specifications. The first time a user calls a Web application, he or she is prompted to enter a user ID and password in a dialog box generated by the browser. The access data for authentication consists of the combination of user ID and password.
- **Form-based authentication**
  The access data (usually also a combination of user ID and password) is transmitted via an HTML form.
- **X.509 authentication**
  In this procedure, the application server and browser exchange certificates.

We should point out that both basic and form-based authorization are the more vulnerable procedures, as the access data in both procedures is transmitted in the clear or merely encoded with base64. HTTPS must be used as a security transport protocol; otherwise, any TCP packet analyzer will be able to obtain the access data by spoofing IP packets.

Authorization

Authorization mechanisms ensure that authenticated users can access the resources and perform only those actions for which they are authorized based on their assigned roles.

In the J2EE architecture, containers serve as barriers between the calling programs and the components contained in the container (such as Enterprise JavaBeans, EJBs). Configuring the EJB container using the deployment descriptor makes it possible to define authorization mechanisms declaratively, as the following fragment from a descriptor shows, in which the authorization to call a special method of an EJB is assigned to a specific role:

```
<method-permission>
       <role-name>customer</role-name>
       <method>
             <ejb-name>BookBean</ejb-name>
             <method-name>getAbstract</method-name>
       </method>
```

```
    ...
</method-permission>
```

In addition to this declarative method, authorization can also be implemented within the program, using methods such as `EJBContext.isCallerInRole()` and `HttpServletRequest.isUserInRole()`.

There are advantages and disadvantages to both the declarative and program-based methods for verifying authorization. The major advantages of the declarative method are its greater transparency and its flexibility in configuring the application. Nonetheless, we can imagine highly complex scenarios in which only the program-based approach can provide the necessary degree of detail.

In closing, we should mention that the security of J2EE applications is ultimately dependent on the interaction between the developer, deployment manager, administrator, and application architect. The J2EE architecture supports this team by defining an abstract security model and by clearly separating the areas of responsibility for their respective tasks.

2.9 Versioning and Transport System

To ensure that different program versions can be clearly distinguished from one another in major development projects, and that the existing data and programs are always consistent, the SAP Web Application Server (SAP Web AS) primarily uses two techniques: versioning and transport management.

2.9.1 Versioning

In today's large software development projects, hundreds of employees often work on a single program. The SAP Web AS uses sophisticated versioning mechanisms to coordinate this work and ensure that everyone is working with uniform versions across all stages of the development cycle. SAP Web AS makes certain that the same, consistent program excerpts are used in the development, quality management, documentation, and translation phases.

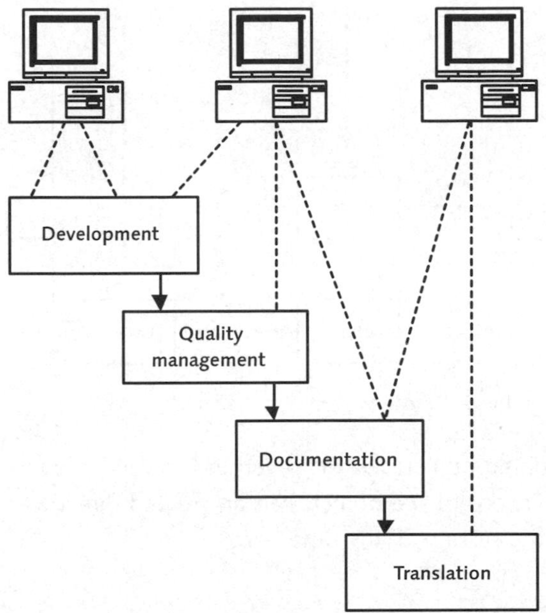

Figure 2.20 Different Users Work on Different Parts of a Development Project Concurrently

Consistency in Development

This approach also enables data exchange between departments. Developers have access to the requirements and specifications in knowledge management and document management, for example. All the text elements used in the program (messages, labels, long texts) can be used in the documentation, while Knowledge Warehouse functions let you supplement them with online help texts. All texts can then be translated in the SAP System or sent to translation programs through defined interfaces.

Each object (source texts, data models, tables, views, and texts) is automatically assigned a current, active version in the system, and is replaced by the new version during activation. The old versions form a history and can be restored if necessary. Developers can activate a tested program as the current version at any time.

During transports, all changed objects are copied from one SAP System to the next (from development system to test system, for example) in a change request. At the same time, the current version is maintained in version management.

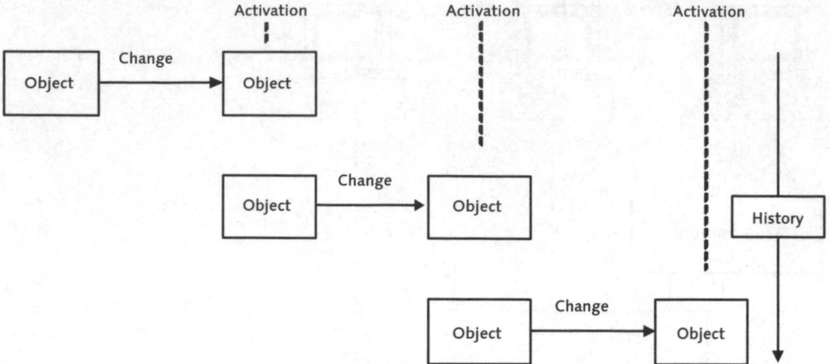

Figure 2.21 Object Versioning in the SAP System

After the import, the updated objects are displayed in the version overview. If necessary, new versions of the objects can be created directly to trace the import state in the system at any time.

2.9.2 Transport System

The SAP Web AS employs a *Transport Management System* (TMS) to ensure that the system remains consistent and available throughout the change process. When the TMS is used, individual components can be enhanced and revised with only a minimum of downtime.

Activities During Development

At the start of a development project, the development manager creates a change request in the Transport Organizer. The employees involved and an ID number are assigned to this request. A change request usually contains only logically related objects that are always executed together. Consequently, they can be transported and managed in a self-contained unit.

Transporting Changes

The Transport Organizer assigns each employee a task; in turn, the employees assign the elements they change to that task. Employees who have completed their work can release their tasks. As soon as all the corresponding tasks have been released, the development manager can release the complete change request, and the transport to another SAP System can begin.

Transport Through the Systems

Typically, an SAP installation consists of at least three independent systems:

1. The *development system* is the runtime environment for new developments and Customizing.
2. All changes to programs and Customizing settings are then tested in detail in the *quality assurance system*.
3. Once all the tests are passed, the changes are ultimately transported to the *production system*.

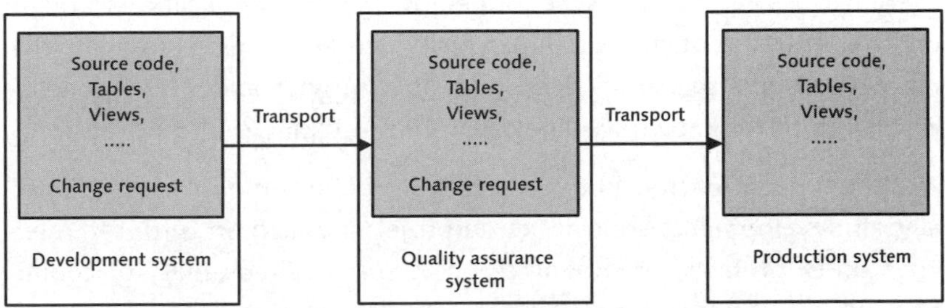

Figure 2.22 Transporting Changes in an SAP Landscape

4. The TMS uses change requests to manage all imports and exports, keeping disturbances of ongoing system operations to a minimum. When objects are updated, the old objects continue to be accessed during the transport process. Once the transport request has been executed completely, all the objects contained therein are considered and called together as the new version.

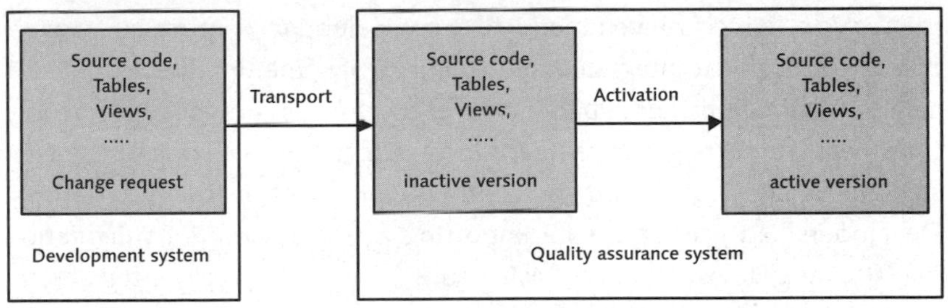

Figure 2.23 Transport and Activation Process

5. The TMS also monitors and manages all changes to the Customizing of an application.

2.9.3 Versioning and Transport Process under Java

Components of Distributed Development

A versioning mechanism is integrated in SAP NetWeaver Developer Studio (NWDS): the Design Time Repository (DTR), which manages all development objects (tables, Java classes, Web Dynpros, project files) centrally. It provides for versioning of all project components and enables their synchronization among all involved developers. The Component Build Service (CBS) saves Java archives and builds packages from the contents of the DTR on request by IDE NWDS. The Software Logistics (SL) component consists primarily of a Change Management Service (CMS), which manages the software versioning, and a Software Delivery Manager (SDM), who is responsible for deploying a Java application throughout the entire production system. Consequently, the development environment covers the entire life cycle of a project and offers effective workarounds for known weaknesses from the J2EE world.

Project-Oriented Approach

The general approach is both project-oriented and modularized. Generally, all developments are considered projects, which, in turn, can reference other projects, promoting the cross-project reusability of coding. Specifically, referencing one or more existing projects in a new project makes all the existing classes and packages in the referenced projects available in the new project. *Assembly projects* involve grouping existing projects together to form distribution packages, as well as configuring them with visual tools for use in the respective target container (deployment). Without the appropriate tools, deployment itself can be a complex, time-consuming process in the J2EE world. SAP NWDS features a full range of efficient tools to save developers from this manual work.

Another drawback of J2EE is inherent in its deployment-driven development cycle, which prevents effective code debugging prior to deployment. Although the integrated debugging environment in the SAP NWDS cannot eliminate this drawback completely, it is a big help. You probably think that connecting a developer's local IDE to the development system requires a major installation and configuration effort. If so, you're wrong: Developers can gain access by importing a single, simple configuration file. The Java Development Infrastructure (JDI) is seamlessly integrated in the Developer Studio. While each developer works locally on his or her system, the overall teamwork is synchronized centrally. These synchronization routines are almost entirely all automatic; developers only have to ensure that they're connected.

2.10 Availability, Performance, Scalability

Is Java Really Slow?

Java is still considered by some to be a language with substandard performance, due to its initial problems in this area. Despite Java's early history, this characterization is unfair, as the days in which the AWT (Advanced Windowing Toolkit—a technology to build frontends for desktop application) and Swing GUI technologies (a successor of AWT) were the sole measure of performance are numbered.

It is generally true that programming languages that use platform-independent byte code tend to be slower, because the respective virtual machine always has to convert the source code into platform-dependent instructions; nonetheless, the ongoing optimization of the JVM has made this aspect nearly irrelevant for overall performance. Because both ABAP and, recently, Microsoft (with its .NET technology) are taking a VM approach to achieve platform independence, the Java-based J2EE Enterprise Platform is evidence of a clear trend within the SAP Web Application Server as well.

Performance Traps in Application Development

Many pitfalls in performance optimization lie outside the platform, in the application-specific coding; the use of inefficient SQL statements or unnecessary redirects through remote calls are just two examples. Therefore, if application programmers complain about poor performance on a particular platform, it might make sense for the IT manager to verify the programmers' qualifications. The strategies described in Chapter 8 deserve particular attention.

Tools for Performance Optimization

In addition to the performance optimization mechanisms already available on the Java/J2EE platform, the current SAP Web AS offers new tools for achieving this objective in SAP NWDS. In this environment, extended monitoring and statistics functions, or *profilers*, help you to check the efficiency and runtime behavior of coding.

They reduce the processing time in case of performance problems and increase platform performance with a *distributed statistics record* (DSR), along with integration in a *Computing Center Management System* (CCMS).

The former involves analyzing statistics records, which provide information about system performance. This information is based on measurements of response times of the J2EE Engine, along with the installed applications and databases, which are subjected to an analytical comparison.

The CCMS configures, monitors, and controls the J2EE personality of the SAP System. In SAP Web Application Server 6.40, the CCMS has been enhanced with services that permanently monitor critical system parameters.

2.11 Integration Options for ABAP and J2EE

Because the two personalities available in the SAP Web Application Server, ABAP and J2EE, can be used together (and not just as alternatives), the first question on your mind is probably "How can I do that?" This section describes the various options for enabling access between the personalities.

The current Release 6.40 of the SAP Web Application Server still divides responsibilities between the two platforms fairly clearly: While ABAP contains the business logic and allows access to the functions and modules, Java is primarily responsible for distributing and presenting applications over the Web.

2.11.1 J2EE Calls ABAP

Two basic options are available to implement the typical application case in which a business component is used from within a J2EE-based Web application.

RFC Call with JCo

The Traditional Method

Function modules and BAPIs can be started through RFC calls in Java and J2EE applications, similar to the inherent procedure within the SAP System. The *Java Connector* (JCo) enables native use of the SAP-specific binary protocol. JCo acts as a client that provides the functions of an ABAP function module, which acts as the server, to the surrounding context. The stub/server architecture described in Section 5.2.1 can be used for this. (In an environment of distributed computing, the stub is an exact representation of the interface of a server or service. The implementation of the stub's method does not contain business logic but remote calls to the server or service where the business logic is centrally held and processed.) The JCo interface makes it possible to transfer most data types in both directions.

Web Service with ABAP Use from J2EE

The New Method

Alternatively, remote-capable function modules can also be addressed through the SOAP interface—a Web service interface that is independent of any given platform and transport protocol. Within a Java program, a client program is generated automatically (based on the interface description of a stub class) and used. The problems with transferring complex parameters that were caused by the canonical representation of data types in Release 6.20 have been corrected in Release 6.40. In the new version, an ABAP Workbench extension for generating and distributing Web services replaces the previous SOAP Runtime, which permits only the publishing of new ABAP types.

2.11.2 ABAP Calls J2EE

In some cases, such as for data encryption, Java's general superiority in the areas of infrastructure and extensibility through third-party products can make it necessary for an ABAP application to use the business logic of a J2EE application. Three different types of connectivity are currently available for dealing with such situations.

RFC Server with JCo

The Complex Method

The first option, which is completely transparent on the ABAP side, is to implement and deploy an RFC server using the Java Connector. This requires a relatively large effort, however, both in terms of the architecture and the implementation. Consequently, two other methods for integrating Java-side business logic have become more popular in the interim.

EJB Proxy Class Access from ABAP

The Interim Solution

Java components can also be accessed from the remote interface (see Section 5.2) of an Enterprise JavaBean—or, more specifically, a session bean that encapsulates the business logic. The EJB proxy can be generated automatically at design time as an ABAP Objects class. At runtime, the ABAP class uses HTTP requests to address a Web application on the J2EE server, which, in turn, converts these requests to native EJB calls. This interface, which has suffered from several technical/infrastructure difficulties in the past, is being replaced by a new, Web service-based variant in future system architectures. Accordingly, it will play only a limited role in a future where integration projects are defined primarily by Web services.

Web Service Using Java from ABAP

The Future Method

In the mid- to long-term, using Java-based Web services from within ABAP (and vice versa) will be how the two personalities are integrated. In a Web AS 6.20-based landscape, SOAP Runtime has various classes for formulating SOAP-based RFC calls, sending them to a Web service, and analyzing the results. In addition to relatively simple services, however, SOAP Runtime is far from a runaway success. The implementation of clients is a relatively complex process, and the underlying XML technology does not meet all the demands of a modern XML parser. The fact that ABAP data types can be rendered in only canonical form often causes difficulties when more complex data has to be transferred.

Fortunately, the relevant SAP tutorials on SOAP Runtime are relatively open regarding the weakness of the implementation, which helps to avoid unpleasant surprises during development.

The stability and capabilities of SOAP Runtime have been greatly enhanced in the SAP Web Application Server 6.40, improving the use of Web services in both design time and runtime.

3 The "ResMan" Example Project

The examples in this book all share a practical background: The "ResMan" project, which is introduced in this chapter, helps to illustrate the tutorials and context-specific information used in later chapters.

Scenario

The fictitious "Resource Manager" project, or "ResMan," is a scenario that is used for practical demonstration of the techniques and technologies that are described in full in the later chapters of this book.

Please note that the resulting applications do not purport to be complete, and do not—by any means—represent a commercially viable solution.

Nor will they win any beauty contests for layout, modern user guidance, or other features. The primary focus is on the functionality and how it can be implemented with the tools currently available on the SAP Web Application Server (SAP Web AS).

3.1 Prerequisites

Our sample scenario involves deploying an application that will enable employees at an enterprise to reserve resources over intranet and Internet.

Resources

Resources are objects such as:

- Rooms and premises (for meetings and business events, for example)
- Vehicles
- Overhead projectors
- Laptops
- Cell phones

Therefore, resources refer to pooled resources that are required for a certain amount of time and then are generally available again.

3.1.1 Business Benefit

The business benefit of the application is derived in large part from the following factors:

- **Reduction of administration and communication effort**
  The existing reservation process—calling or sending email to the person responsible for resource planning—is relatively inefficient and limits staff capacity unnecessarily. As in most self-service scenarios, the ability to retrieve data and make a reservation results in a much faster process that benefits everyone involved:
  - Independence and freedom from time and staff constraints for the requestor
  - Relief from routine activities and excessive phone calls for the resource planner
- **Overlaps and duplicate bookings are no longer possible**
  Minimizes the risk that employees arrive for a training course, for example, only to discover that no room or overhead projector has been booked, which also minimizes the risk of wasting valuable working time.
- **Resource bottlenecks can be detected early on**
  The early procurement of additional resources helps to avoid unnecessary costs (such as surcharges for rush reservations).
- **Resource utilization can be documented**
  The resource planner can see which resources are currently in use at any time, and how often they were used in the past. This information can be analyzed to derive usage statistics for future procurement planning, for example.

3.1.2 Functional Prerequisites

User Department Criteria

From the user department's perspective, the new application should feature the following functions:

- Overview of
- All resources
- Utilized resources
- Available resources
- Options to book a resource—with check of overlaps
- Options to cancel one's own bookings

3.1.3 Technical Prerequisites

IT-Relevant Criteria

To integrate seamlessly in the existing IT landscape, the solution must meet the following technical prerequisites:

- ▶ Web-based user interface that can be used with a current Web browser version (Internet Explorer ≥ 5.5, Netscape ≥ 6)
- ▶ Exclusive use of SAP technology (Web AS 6.20 – Web AS 6.40)
- ▶ Modular structure of the application (extensibility)
- ▶ If necessary, it should be possible to add multilingual capability to the application (user interface and data) at short notice.
- ▶ All functions should be available in a single-screen user interface; that is, the user has access to all necessary information and functions in a single screen and does not have to toggle from one screen to another.

3.2 The Data Model

To implement these requirements, a data model is required to map the application details to reflect the actual application.

The Principle of Simplicity

The data model on which all subsequent implementations are based is intentionally limited to the bare necessities, to keep the application complexity to a minimum.

For the most part, the data model consists of several master data tables for the resources and their attributes, plus one table where the transaction data—the reservations in this case—is saved.

The texts for the master data tables are saved in separate text tables, to enable multilingual support if necessary.

The table names all have the prefix "ZRM_", placing them in the customer namespace.

Tables

Table Name	Description
ZRM_RES_MASTER	Resource master data
ZRM_RES_TYPE	Resource types
ZRM_RES_TYPET	Text table for resource types
ZRM_RES_ATTRS	Attribute master data (assignment of attributes to resources)
ZRM_RES_ATTRST	Text table for attribute master data

Table 3.1 Overview of Database Tables

Table Name	Description
ZRM_RES_ATTR	Attribute values (specific instantiation)
ZRM_RES_RES	Reservations

Table 3.1 Overview of Database Tables (cont.)

The relationships between the tables, along with the primary and foreign keys, are illustrated in Figure 3.1.

Data Model

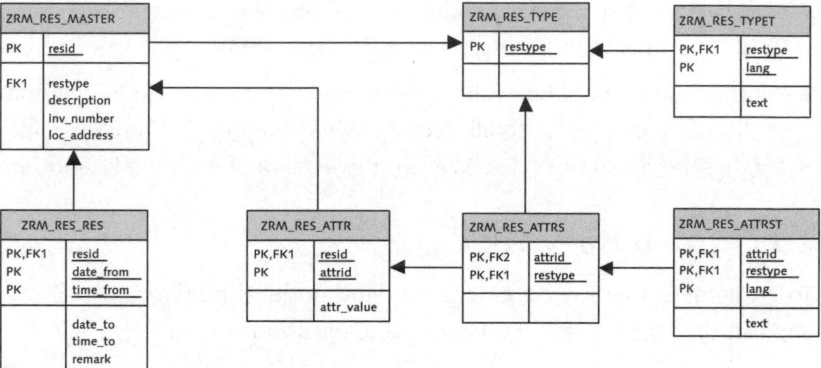

Figure 3.1 Data Model of the ResMan Application

The table structures in detail:

Fields:				
Name	**Description**	**Data Type**	**Length**	**Key**
MANDT	Client	CLNT	3	X
RESID	Resource ID	CHAR	12	X
RESTYPE	Resource type	CHAR	2	
DESCRIPTION	Description	CHAR	255	
INV_NUMBER	Inventory number	CHAR	25	
LOC_ADDRESS	Location address ID	CHAR	10	
Foreign Key:				
Field	**Table**			
RESTYPE	ZRM_RES_TYPE			

Table 3.2 Structure of Table ZRM_RES_MASTER, Resource Master Data

Fields:				
Name	**Description**	**Data Type**	**Length**	**Key**
MANDT	Client	CLNT	3	X
RESTYPE	Resource type	CHAR	2	X
Foreign Key:				
Field	**Table**			

Table 3.3 Structure of Table ZRM_RES_TYPE, Resource Types

Fields:				
Name	**Description**	**Data Type**	**Length**	**Key**
MANDT	Client	CLNT	3	X
RESTYPE	Resource type	CHAR	2	X
LANG	Language	LANG	1	X
TEXT	Description	CHAR	128	
Foreign Key:				
Field	**Table**			
RESTYPE	ZRM_RES_TYPE			

Table 3.4 Structure of Table ZRM_RES_TYPET, Text Table for Resource Types

Fields:				
Name	**Description**	**Data Type**	**Length**	**Key**
MANDT	Client	CLNT	3	X
ATTRID	Attribute ID	CHAR	12	X
RESTYPE	Resource type	CHAR	2	X

Table 3.5 Structure of Table ZRM_RES_ATTRS, Attribute Master Data

Foreign Key:				
Field	**Table**			
RESTYPE	ZRM_RES_TYPE			

Table 3.5 Structure of Table ZRM_RES_ATTRS, Attribute Master Data (cont.)

Fields:				
Name	**Description**	**Data Type**	**Length**	**Key**
MANDT	Client	CLNT	3	X
ATTRID	Attribute ID	CHAR	12	X
RESTYPE	Resource type	CHAR	2	X
LANG	Language	LANG	1	X
TEXT	Description	CHAR	127	
Foreign Key:				
Field	**Table**			
ATTRID	ZRM_RES_ATTRS			
RESTYPE	ZRM_RES_ATTRS			

Table 3.6 Structure of Table ZRM_RES_ATTRST, Text Table for Attribute Master Data

Fields:				
Name	**Description**	**Data Type**	**Length**	**Key**
MANDT	Client	CLNT	3	X
RESID	Resource ID	CHAR	12	X
ATTRID	Attribute ID	CHAR	12	X
ATTR_VALUE	Attribute value	CHAR	127	
Foreign Key:				
Field	**Table**			
RESID	ZRM_RES_MASTER			
ATTRID	ZRM_RES_ATTRS			

Table 3.7 Structure of Table ZRM_RES_ATTR, Attribute Values

Fields:				
Name	**Description**	**Data Type**	**Length**	**Key**
MANDT	Client	CLNT	3	X
RESID	Resource ID	CHAR	12	X
DATE_FROM	Date from	DATS	8	X
TIME_FROM	Time from	TIMS	6	X
DATE_TO	Date to	DATS	8	
TIME_TO	Time to	TIMS	6	
REMARK	Remark	CHAR	255	
Foreign Key:				
Field	**Table**			
RESID	ZRM_RES_MASTER			

Table 3.8 Structure of Table ZRM_RES_RES, Reservations

3.3 Technical Implementation of the Prerequisites

The application functionality now has to be implemented based on the data model. SAP Web Application Server 6.40 provides a multitude of technical options to build these functions—options that are examined in careful detail in the subsequent chapters.

Principle: Reuse

The detailed implementation is highly dependent on which technology is used. Nonetheless, our application development will aim to achieve a high degree of reusability from the start, independently of which technology is used for the actual implementation.

Modularization

Therefore, in both the ABAP and Java worlds, we will split the application into reusable modules that we can use to separate the data processing logic from the processing logic and presentation logic. The application has been split into the following elementary modules:

Module	Function	Remark
ZRM_RES_GETLIST	Create list of resources	Selection option: All, Only Utilized, Only Available
ZRM_RES_BOOK	Book resource	With error handling in case of overlap
ZRM_RES_CANCEL	Cancel booking	

Table 3.9 Elementary Modules of the Application

This separation will make it possible to reuse core functions of the application later, across platform boundaries. The above modules will be implemented as function modules, and then used as components of the business logic within the framework of the presentation layer of screens, Web Dynpro, and BSP applications.

4 The Programming Languages of the SAP Web Application Server

Java has established itself as an all-purpose programming language in recent years, and SAP is now building on its strengths. After a brief summary of the main features of ABAP and ABAP Objects, this chapter will explain the basic and most important terminology in Java, and compare and contrast it with the corresponding ABAP statements and constructs where relevant.

SAP's reasons for establishing Java as a second programming language alongside ABAP are twofold: first, to give the many millions of Java developers a new platform within the SAP System, to ease their entry into the SAP world; and secondly, to keep SAP's options open with regard to future technologies. Therefore, Java programming skills will become increasingly important for future SAP projects, alongside ABAP expertise.

Before Java is examined in any detail, this chapter will first describe several of the basic ABAP features, to give you a direct comparison between the two languages.

4.1 ABAP and ABAP Objects

4.1.1 Typical Activities

ABAP, which stands for *Advanced Business Application Programming*, is a programming language that has undergone a major transformation in recent years. Originally designed as a reporting language, it was enhanced over time to form a fully fledged fourth-generation programming language, and an integrated set of SQL commands was added with the Open SQL statements. Following the introduction of ABAP Objects between Releases 4.0 and 4.6, it is now possible to use modern, object-oriented programming techniques in ABAP, while simultaneously retaining its organic programming concepts.

Even today, reporting is still one of the most important tasks of ABAP programs. Although programs such as SAP Query now provide many preconfigured reporting options, sometimes there is no alternative to developing a program or selection screen yourself.

While programs that run in dialog are frequently limited to outputting and processing small amounts of data, batch processing can deal with extremely large data volumes without user interaction. Examples of batch operations include the automatic import of master data and transport requests.

Read and write operations, or selecting and manipulating data from database tables, lie at the center of most ABAP programs.

4.1.2 Basic Terminology and Concepts

Program Structure

An ABAP program can generally be divided into two sections:

- **Declarative section**
  Definition of global data. The values defined in this section are visible throughout the entire program.
- **Procedural section**
  Processing blocks

Syntax Elements

Every ABAP program consists of a number of statements. These statements always start with a keyword and end with a period.

The different ABAP program types that can be used to create programs are described in brief below.

Executable Programs

The `REPORT` statement starts an executable program. Executable programs can be started using transaction codes and the `SUBMIT` statement; they can also contain all ABAP processing blocks—aside from function modules—and multiple local classes.

Module Pools

The `PROGRAM` statement starts a module pool. Module pools can only be run through transaction codes, and can contain all ABAP processing blocks—aside from function modules and reporting blocks—and multiple local classes.

Subroutine Pools

Like module pools, the `PROGRAM` statement also starts a subroutine pool. Aside from the `LOAD-OF-PROGRAM` event block, however, subroutine pools can contain only subroutines as administration blocks. They are loaded through external subroutines and not executed directly. Module pools and subroutine pools are used within programs, as a modularization technique for comprehensive, largely context-independent functions such as string handling, conversion routines, and the like.

Function Groups

The `FUNCTION-POOL` statement starts a function group (function pool). Function groups are not usually executed directly, but instead loaded when function modules are called. These function modules, the modular units within function groups, encapsulate reusable application and data retrieval logic. Aside from reporting blocks, all ABAP processing blocks can be used within function modules. Function groups can be created in either the Function Builder or the Object Navigator.

Interface Pools

Keyword `INTERFACE-POOL` starts an interface pool, which cannot contain any of its own screens or any ABAP processing blocks. Interface pools define a global interface that can be implemented in any local or global classes. The interface concept involves designing an abstract definition, for example, of methods in a class, including input and output parameters. Every class that implements an abstract interface of this kind has to flesh out all the methods defined in that interface, that is, provide the program code for the method. When different classes implement the same interface, this ensures compatibility among the users of that class.

Class Pools

The `CLASS-POOL` statement starts a class pool. Class pools can contain a global class and multiple local classes, and are loaded either via the use of their global class or via transaction codes that are linked with the global classes. Local classes are used as object instances or static method calls in the global class, which forms the processing framework.

Include Programs

Include programs are strictly ABAP source text libraries, and therefore don't have an introductory statement. They are fundamentally different from the other program types because they don't represent independent compiling units with their own memory areas. Include programs can be integrated with the `INCLUDE` statement—anywhere within another program—to roll out logical program components and to help reduce complexity in large programs. Module pools, function groups, and class pools can be divided into include programs in the ABAP Workbench.

4.1.3 Variables and Data Types

Data Objects

To process data that is located in a persistent storage medium, such as a database or a file, at runtime, it has to be transferred into internal data constructs that can be processed directly by the runtime environment. Then, this data must made available in the main memory of the executed program. The concept of the *data type* involves typing data in accordance with its use. Data types can generally be divided into modifiable and non-modifiable data types.

The non-modifiable data—constants and literals—is used along with variables, work areas, and internal tables, which represent the data types that can be modified at runtime. Data objects are split by visibility into local, global, and external objects. The visibility of a data object indicates the places where that data object can be accessed within the program.

Local data objects, for example, can be accessed only in the subroutines and methods where they are defined. Conversely, global data objects can be accessed from anywhere within the program. External data objects are assigned to the programs by parameter ID in the SPA/GPA buffer.

Non-Modifiable Data Objects

Literals

ABAP differentiates among four types of literals: character string, numeric string, floating-point number, and hexadecimal number. Literals are case-sensitive character strings of any length that are enclosed by single quotes. An exception to this is the numeric literals, which can also be defined without surrounding single quotes.

Constants

The value of a constant cannot be changed. Therefore, its definition is similar to that of the data declaration statement described further below. The constants are assigned values through literals. The syntax for constants is defined as follows:

```
CONSTANTS <c_...> [TYPE ...] [DECIMALS..] VALUE ,....'
```

Modifiable Data Objects

Variables

Two different statements can be used to define variables in an ABAP program:

- `DATA`
- `PARAMETERS`

Variables are assigned to a data type within the `DATA` statement and can have their own default values. The syntax is defined as follows:

```
DATA <var...> [TYPE ..] [DECIMALS ..] [VALUE ...]
```

The data type can be defined locally (using the TYPES statement in the program), defined through elementary types, or defined through references to objects in the ABAP Dictionary.

Parameters

A *parameter* is a specific type of variable. The parameter statement behaves similarly to the DATA statement, except that a program displays the parameters as input fields in a selection screen before the program is executed further. Therefore, this statement permits the user to enter values in the program. The syntax for the parameter statement is:

```
PARAMETERS <p_...> [TYPE ..] DEFAULT ...
```

You can use the following additions in the parameter statement to configure specific uses and screen designs:

- **OBLIGATORY**
  Required entry field. A value must be entered in this field.
- **AS CHECKBOX**
  The input field is displayed as a checkbox.
- **RADIOBUTTON**
  The input field is displayed as a radio button. Radio buttons are arranged in groups.

Data Types

Each data object has a data type, which determines how the data object is saved in memory and which type of data the object in question can be assigned.

In addition to the standard data types defined in ABAP, new data types can be defined independently in the ABAP Dictionary, as cross-program types, or even as local types in the ABAP program itself. The available types can then be used to create instances, which inherit the properties of the data type and use memory.

Anonymous Data Type

In ABAP, data objects can also be created from data types that aren't defined completely with TYPES. These data types are sometimes called *anonymous data types*, while data types defined with TYPES are called *named data types*.

The data types used in ABAP can generally be divided into elementary data types, reference types, and complex data types, all of which comprise a data type hierarchy.

Elementary Data Types *Elementary data types* are data types that aren't composed from other data types. We differentiate between fixed-length and variable-length data types. In this case, a fixed length means that the size of the data object has to be specified in the declaration, and cannot be changed during the program flow. Of the basic data types defined in ABAP, `i`, `p`, `f`, `c`, `n`, `d`, `t`, and `x` are all elementary data types with fixed lengths, while types `string` and `xstring` are elementary data types with a variable length.

Reference Type Reference types are data types that point to a reference of an instantiated object. Data objects that are generated from reference types are called *reference variables* or *pointers*—data references imply data objects, while object references imply objects derived from classes. The following syntax is used for data references:

```
TYPES | DATA ... TYPE REF TO data
```

Accordingly, the syntax for object references is:

```
TYPES | DATA ... TYPE REF TO {class|interface}
```

Complex Data Types Another important kind of data type is the *complex data type*. Data objects that are generated from complex data types are not elementary in memory; instead, they form a logical structure. We differentiate between two kinds of complex data types: structured types, which can be composed of any other data types, and table-like types, which possess a row type that can be repeated in memory as often as necessary.

Structure Type A *structure type* is created somewhat like a regular data type. The statements

```
TYPES BEGIN OF <structype>
...
TYPES END OF   <structype>.
```

enclose the components of the structure type. Other type definitions can be written between these two statements, and deep nesting of types is possible. The structure of the row type of an internal table can even be used as the structure type, for example:

```
TYPE LINE OF <itabtype>.
```

or

```
LIKE LINE OF <itab>.
```

A data object that was created from a structure type is called a *structure* or *field list*.

An *internal table* is a temporary table that is generated and filled at program runtime. It is deleted again at the end of the program. It consists of several identically-structured rows and has a structure similar to that of a database table.

Internal Table

We differentiate between three types of internal table, which differ in the way their internal table is accessed:

- Standard table
- Sorted table
- Hashed table

The first two table types are accessed through indexes, while the last type is accessed by key field. The internal tables have the following syntax:

```
DATA <it_...> TYPE [STANDARD|SORTED|HASHED] TABLE OF...
```

Or simply:

```
DATA <it_...> TYPE ...
```

In the latter variant, the referenced data type has to be defined as a table type either locally, through the `TYPES` statement:

```
TYPES <t_...> TYPE [STANDARD|SORTED|HASHED] TABLE OF...
```

or globally in the ABAP Dictionary. In particular, a unique key must be specified with `UNIQUE` for a hashed table.

Internal tables can be filled and processed. The statements for filling internal tables are `APPEND`, `INSERT`, and so forth, while `READ TABLE`, `LOOP`, `SORT`, and so on also use internal tables.

Field Symbols

Field symbols are placeholders or symbolic names for existing data objects. They don't require any separate memory of their own for a field, but instead point to a data object, which can be assigned to the field symbol dynamically at runtime. The major advantage of this approach is that operations can be developed without having to know which data objects are really available at runtime. Field symbols can also be used to typecast data objects, as they don't have to handle the contents of a data object as its type would otherwise require. The following example program with one field symbol should help to illustrate this typecasting of data objects:

```
REPORT example_field_symbol.
FIELD-SYMBOLS <fs> TYPE ANY.
DATA: charvar(10) TYPE c,
      numvar(5)   TYPE n.
ASSIGN charvar TO <fs>.
<fs> = 'Example Text'.
ASSIGN numvar TO <fs>.
<fs> = '12345'.
WRITE:/ charvar, numvar.
```

Listing 4.1 Example for Using Field Symbols

The above listing declares one data object with type `c`, one data object with type `n`, and one field symbol. The `ASSIGN` statement assigns the data objects to the field symbol and fills them with values through the field symbol. The closing output of data objects `charvar` and `numvar` shows that the assignment via field symbol worked properly.

4.1.4 The Most Important Commands and Language Constructs

In addition to the control structures and loops used in ABAP, this section also explains the simple output of values on the screen, commands for data retrieval and manipulation, and the basics of object-oriented programming with ABAP Objects.

Control Structures

The `IF ... ENDIF` and `CASE ... ENDCASE` statements are the control structures featured in ABAP. They can be used to check conditions during the program flow and branch to different sections of a code block.

IF Statement The `IF` statement formulates a logical condition. If the condition is true, the corresponding statement block is executed, and processing continues with `ENDIF`. If the expression is false, the other conditions are checked; if no other condition is true, the `ELSE` statement block is executed. You can use any number of `ELSEIF` statements and a maximum of one `ELSE` statement. You can also nest the control structures. In the example below, we use an `IF` structure to check the value of a data object and output it with the `WRITE` statement.

```
REPORT s_if.
IF i_demo IS INITIAL.
   WRITE: / 'Value was not set!'.
```

```
ELSE IF i_demo <= 0.
   WRITE: / 'Value is less than or equal to 0!'.
ELSE .
   WRITE: / 'Value is greater than 0!'.
ENDIF.
```

Listing 4.2 Program Branching with the IF Statement

The CASE ... ENDCASE control structure is similar to IF, except it doesn't use logical expressions; instead, it compares a data object directly with other data objects or values.

CASE Statement

```
REPORT s_case.
CASE i_demo.
  WHEN 0 OR -1.
    WRITE: / 'Value is 0 or -1!'.
  WHEN 1.
    WRITE: / 'Value is 1!'.
  WHEN OTHERS.
    WRITE: / 'Value is less than -1 or greater than 1!'.
  ENDCASE.
```

Listing 4.3 Program Branching with the CASE Statement

The above listing checks the value of data object i_demo and branches to the appropriate statement blocks. Like the IF control structure, the CASE control structure can be nested to any depth.

Loops are sequences of program statements that can be executed repeatedly. ABAP features the WHILE ... ENDWHILE loop and the DO ... ENDDO loops for this purpose.

The WHILE statement is used for conditional loops, that is, a sequence of program statements is executed repeatedly, controlled by a condition that changes during execution.

WHILE Loop

```
REPORT s_while.
DATA: i_limit TYPE i VALUE 10.
WHILE i_limit > 0.
   WRITE: / 'Loop number:', sy-index.
   i_limit = i_limit - 1.
ENDWHILE.
```

Listing 4.4 Example of WHILE Loop

DO Loop In contrast to the WHILE ... ENDWHILE loop, the DO ... ENDDO loop does not depend on a logical condition; instead, it can be programmed to repeat the sequence of instructions until left with an EXIT statement or the defined number of passes is reached.

```
REPORT s_do.
DO 5 TIMES.
  WRITE: / 'Loop 1: Pass number', sy-index.
ENDDO.

DO
  WRITE: / 'Loop 2: Pass number', sy-index.
  IF sy-index = 5.
    EXIT.
  ENDIF.
ENDDO.
```

Listing 4.5 Example of DO Loop

In addition to the EXIT statement, which completely exits the loop, other loop controls are CHECK—which checks a logical condition and skips the remaining coding in the current statement block if the condition is false—and CONTINUE, which stops execution of the current loop pass without checking a condition.

Open SQL Statements

The main activities of ABAP are accessing, selecting, and manipulating large datasets that are usually saved in a centralized database. This is done using ABAP Open SQL statements, which map the Data Manipulation Language (DML) functions that are supported by all database systems to ABAP. The Open SQL interface converts these Open SQL statements to database-specific SQL later. This section summarizes the most important Open SQL statements.

SELECT The SELECT statement is used to import data from one or more database tables into a data object. The resulting set can be a single table row or a table-like structure—an internal table. Generally, four pieces of information are required to read data: What is to be read (SELECT from), from where (FROM source), where it will be placed (INTO target), and under which conditions it should be read (WHERE cond). In addition to these four clauses, the SELECT statement has three other clauses that oversee data summarization and sorting. The general syntax of a SELECT statement is:

```
SELECT result
   FROM source
   INTO | APPENDING target
   [[FOR ALL ENTRIES IN itab] WHERE cond]
   [GROUP BY cols] [HAVING group_cond]
   [ORDER BY sort_args].
...
[ENDSELECT.]
```

There are several ways of using a simple SELECT query to fill an internal database table:

- Import rows into the internal directly:

  ```
  SELECT * FROM table INTO TABLE OF it...
  WHERE arg1 = ...
  ```

- Import single rows into a work area and then insert them into an internal table:

  ```
  SELECT * FROM table INTO [CORRESPONDING FIELDS ] s...
           WHERE arg1 = ...
  ENDSELECT.
  ```

The SELECT and ENDSELECT statements set the values of global system fields SY-SUBRC and SY-DBCNT, which can be used to validate the query results.

SY-SUBRC	Meaning
0	At least one result was passed on.
4	The resulting set is blank—no result was passed on.
8	The FOR UPDATE addition was used in the result, but the WHERE clause did not include a complete primary key.

Table 4.1 SY-SUBRC Values for the SELECT Statement

The INSERT statement is used to add new lines to the database. Its syntax is: **INSERT**

```
INSERT [INTO] target VALUES | FROM [TABLE] source.
```

The target value determines the database table into which the values specified in source will be inserted. Several options are available for using an INSERT statement:

```
INSERT INTO demotable VALUES wa_demo.
```

or

```
INSERT demotable FROM wa_demo.
```

Because both statements insert the content of work area wa_demo into database table demotable, they are equivalent to one another. The work area should have the same structure as the database table. Multiple rows can be added at the same time to improve performance:

```
INSERT demotable FROM TABLE demo_tab
```

UPDATE The Open SQL UPDATE statement is used to modify data in a database table. Its syntax is:

```
UPDATE target SET | FROM [TABLE] source.
```

The target value determines which data records will be changed, while source determines which information is written into which columns of the selected data records.

Simple example of an UPDATE statement:

```
UPDATE demotable SET
   value_1 = ... ,
   value_2 = value_2 + ...
WHERE ...
```

The above statement changes value_1 and value_2 in all rows of table demotable that meet the conditions defined in the WHERE clause.

You can also use the following statement to replace an entire row:

```
UPDATE demotable FROM wa_demo.
```

Or, for multiple rows:

```
UPDATE demotable FROM demo_tab.
```

MODIFY If you don't know, prior to a database change, whether the data record to be changed already exists or has to be created first, you can use the Open SQL MODIFY statement. For performance reasons, however, we do not recommend generally replacing INSERT and UPDATE commands with

MODIFY, because MODIFY always performs an internal SELECT first, to determine whether the record has to be inserted or changed.

The following syntax is used to change individual rows:

```
MODIFY demotable FROM wa_demo.
```

The following syntax is used to change multiple rows:

```
MODIFY demotable FROM TABLE demo_tab.
```

DELETE

The Open SQL DELETE statement deletes data records from a database table. The data records to be deleted are selected either by the information in the WHERE clause or using a work area. Its syntax is:

```
DELETE FROM target [WHERE <cond>|FROM [TABLE] source].
```

In order to avoid deleting the wrong rows, you should exercise extreme caution when formulating DELETE statements. If you inadvertently omit WHERE conditions or specify a blank internal table, all the rows in the table will be deleted.

For example:

- Deleting with a WHERE condition:

  ```
  DELETE FROM demotable WHERE value_1 = 10 AND ...
  ```

- Defining deletion conditions with a work area:

  ```
  DELETE demotable FROM wa_demo.
  ```

- Defining deletion conditions with an internal table:

  ```
  DELETE demotable FROM TABLE demo_tab.
  ```

Object-Oriented Programming

ABAP Objects

While a procedure-based language makes it theoretically possible to modularize complex program flows within subtasks, it lacks many of the options and simplifications that object-oriented programming provides for organizing program sections.

Conversely, ABAP Objects deals with entire objects. Logically related data is grouped together as attributes of an object; an attribute can also represent another object. A basic principle of object-oriented systems is that instead of using direct procedures to process the data of an object, the capabilities of an object are deployed as object methods. This way of thinking makes it easier to use the actual data, as only the object itself has to know the actual data structures contained within its methods. External program segments that use these objects merely have to be aware of their capabilities—their methods—to use them, and do not deal directly with structures at deeper levels.

Two major concepts are the basis of all object-oriented programming—reusability and modularity (the latter including the logical encapsulation of functions described above).

When individual program segments can be reused, the corresponding coding has to be written only once, and can then be included in other programs in order to avoid having to repeatedly write the coding over again. This improves the readability and ease of maintenance of the coding, while also saving on valuable programming resources.

Classes This reusability is achieved by using modules of object-oriented systems, which are called *classes*. In ABAP Objects, classes can be either implemented locally in the program or defined globally in the Class Builder.

A local class is defined with the statement `CLASS ... ENDCLASS`. The ABAP source coding that implements the class and its methods is entered between these segments. A full class definition includes a declaration section and an implementation section.

The syntax for the declaration section is:

```
CLASS lc_... DEFINITION.
...
ENDCLASS.
```

All the required components are defined between these two statements. They describe the state and behavior of objects. Specifically, these include:

- `ATTRIBUTES`
- `METHODS`
- `EVENTS`

The class declaration is divided into three different visibility areas:

```
CLASS lc_... DEFINITION.
   PUBLIC SECTION.
   PROTECTED SECTION.
   PRIVATE SECTION.
ENDCLASS.
```

The visibility information for a method, its names, and its parameters constitute its *signature*. The signature usually follows the method body, which contains the actual implementation. Interfaces are an exception to this, as they contain only signatures and have to be implemented by a class.

Signature

Therefore, the visibility areas of methods and classes meet one of the most important requirements of an object-oriented language, namely, encapsulation. Programmers should be careful to define as little as possible in the public section, in order to do the following:

1. Provide a well-designed interface for the users of the objects
2. Avoid bothering the user with irrelevant object details that should really be managed internally

The class definition belongs to the declaration, and should therefore be placed in the global data declaration of a program.

If a method is declared in the class, the class will also need an implementation section. You use the following statement to create it:

```
CLASS cl_.. IMPLEMENTATION.
  ...
ENDCLASS.
```

Use the following statement to create an object:

```
CREATE OBJECT cref_...
```

The reference variables, which contain the object in the coding, are typed with the statement:

```
DATA cref TYPE REF TO cl
```

Methods

As described above, methods describe the behavior or capabilities of an object. Methods generally have interfaces (parameters) that can supply them with data and return it as well. These interfaces and the type of method call used may be reminiscent of function modules, but, in contrast, methods have a call-independent context, because the data can remain in the object, as object attributes, beyond the call itself. You use the following language construct to define methods:

```
METHOD m_... ENDMETHOD.
```

This statement is allowed in both classes and interfaces. As mentioned above, methods are components of a class. They are called with the

CALL METHOD statement. The following interface parameters can be defined as additions:

- **EXPORTING**
  Pass on parameters
- **IMPORTING**
  Pass parameters on to the calling program
- **CHANGING**
  Send and receive parameters
- **RECEIVING**
  Return an actual parameter that was defined in METHODS with RETURNING
- **EXCEPTIONS**
  Exception handling
- **PARAMETER TABLE**
  The method can be supplied with dynamic parameters. The parameter table is a hashed table with table type ABAP_PARMBIND_T.
- **EXCEPTIONS TABLE**
  This parameter can be used to catch exceptions dynamically. The parameter table is a hashed table with table type ABAP_EXCPBIND_T.

The first five additions are used for regular, static calls of methods, while the last two additions apply to method calls in which the transfer parameters are supplied dynamically.

Here is a simple example of the interaction between the individual components:

```
REPORT  z_test_class.
********************Declaration section***************
*-------------------------------------------------------*
*       CLASS resource_management DEFINITION
*-------------------------------------------------------*
CLASS cl_resource_management DEFINITION.
  PUBLIC SECTION.
    METHODS change_date IMPORTING i_date
                                  TYPE sy-date
                        EXPORTING e_date
                                  TYPE sy-date
                        EXCEPTIONS ex_1
ENDCLASS.
```

```
DATA: l_res_man TYPE REF TO cl_resource_management,
      n_date    TYPE        sy-date.
PARAMETERS p_date TYPE sy-date.
START-OF-SELECTION.
  CREATE OBJECT l_res_man.
  CALL METHOD l_res_man->change_date
              EXPORTING  i_date = p_date
              IMPORTING  e_date = n_date
              EXCEPTIONS ex_1    = 1.
  IF sy-subrc <> 0.
    WRITE 'Error!'.
  ELSE.
    WRITE n_date.
  ENDIF.
*---------------------------------------------------------*
*       CLASS resource_management IMPLEMENTATION
*---------------------------------------------------------*
CLASS cl_resource_management IMPLEMENTATION.
  METHOD change_date.
    IF i_date IS INITIAL.
      RAISE ex_1.
    ENDIF.
    COMPUTE e_date = i_date + 7.
  ENDMETHOD.
ENDCLASS.
```

Listing 4.6 Example of a Simple Class in ABAP Objects

Interfaces

The components of interfaces define the external visibility of the interfaces of a class. Classes allow an extension of the public interface. They are implemented in the declaration section of the class.

As you can see, the INTERFACES statement is declared only in the public section of the class definition. The exact same components can be defined in the interface statement as in a class definition:

```
INTERFACE in_date.
  DATA v_date.
  METHODS prevmonth.
ENDINTERFACE.
```

To implement an interface definition, you can insert the INTERFACES statement within a class definition, as this documents the class's intention to deploy the bodies of the method signatures defined in the respective interfaces. This extends a class definition with the components in the INTERFACES statement:

```
CLASS ... DEFINITION.
   PUBLIC SECTION.
      DATA ...
      METHODS...
      INTERFACES in_date
   PROTECTED SECTION.
      .....
ENDCLASS.
```

The components of the INTERFACES statement become a fully-fledged part of the class. You use the identifier IN_..~COMP to address the components within the implementation of the class:

```
CLASS IMPLEMENTATION.
   METHODS A1.
      CALCULATE ..In_date~v_date
   ENDMETHODS.

   METHODS in_date~prevmonth.
      .....
   ENDMETHODS.
ENDCLASS.
```

Inheritance Another important concept in object-oriented programming is inheritance. Under inheritance, existing classes can be passed on to a new class during its definition. To do so, you use the INHERITING FROM addition to the CLASS ... DEFINITION statement. The properties of a previously defined class are appended to the new class. This makes the new class a subclass and the existing class becomes a superclass. In the jargon, the subclass inherits the properties of the superclass.

Please note, however, that only the PUBLIC and PROTECTED components of the superclass are visible and can be used in the subclass. In contrast, PRIVATE classes are only visible within the respective class.

The definition of a class is enclosed by the following coding:

```
CLASS cl_sub DEFINITION INHERITING FROM cl_super.
[class definition]
ENDCLASS.
```

Abstract Class

Classes also have other additions and statements. You can use the addition ABSTRACT, for example, to create an abstract class. Abstract classes have at least one abstract method—that is, at least one method that consists only of a signature. Abstract classes cannot be used to create any specific instances, just as interfaces cannot either. You can only instantiate subclasses of abstract classes that implement the abstract methods of their abstract superclasses. Like interfaces, abstract classes are used to define hard interfaces for a largely anonymous community of developers, and for delegation in later development phases. If abstract classes or interfaces violate the conventions described above, the syntax check will detect this violation and prevent the development object from being activated.

Abstract classes are especially useful to implement processes in which certain parts of the process are known to be required, but whose procedures are unknown or have to be interchangeable.

Final Class

The FINAL addition defines a final class from which no further subclasses can be derived. One logical application of such a construct is as an unchangeable set of values, to model a set of constants, for example. If a class is both ABSTRACT and FINAL at the same time, only its static components can be used.

Events

You use the EVENTS or CLASS-EVENTS statements to define events. EVENTS creates an instance-dependent event; CLASS-EVENTS creates an instance-independent (static) event.

The syntax for declaring an event is:

```
EVENTS evt [EXPORTING { VALUE(ei) typing
                        [OPTIONAL | {DEFAULT defi}] } ].
```

Events are declared within the class definition and can then be triggered with the RAISE EVENT comment. Note that instance methods can trigger both instance-dependent and static events, whereas static methods can trigger only static events. When an event is triggered, execution of the method is interrupted and the methods registered in the event handler are processed; execution of the original method then continues.

Events are used especially for the loose coupling of dependencies between classes. This is the case, for example, when the class or object that triggers an event cannot know anything at design time about the objects that only register as handlers for this event at runtime.

4.2 Java

4.2.1 Basic Terminology and Concepts

Java is much more than just another programming language. The basic approach behind the language is far deeper, and was virtually revolutionary at the time it was invented. Its platform independence and innate object orientation set Java apart from all other prevalent programming languages. As a whole, Java is based on three pillars:

- The Java Virtual Machine (JVM)
- The Java/J2EE platform
- The Java programming language

The Java Virtual Machine (JVM)

The most basic difference between Java and many other programming languages is that the compiled programs are not only executable on the operating system where they were developed; rather, they are executable on all operating systems for which a *Java Virtual Machine* (JVM) is available. The JVM is a separate runtime environment that forms the interface between Java programs and the operating system. Compiled Java source code consists of *Java byte code*, which the JVM interprets and translates into the platform-specific machine language.

The architectural concept of the virtual machine is also implemented in the ABAP runtime, which means a platform-independent byte code is created first and then converted to platform-specific commands by the virtual machine.

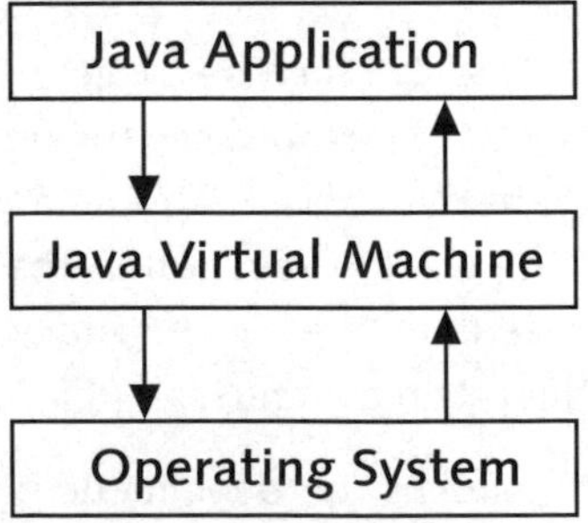

Figure 4.1 Position of the Java Virtual Machine Between the Java Application and the Operating System

The Java Platform

The second pillar, which is just as important as the JVM, is the Java platform, which consists of a large set of predefined classes. The platform already provides functions for nearly every area in the supplied *packages*. The programming interface of these predefined packages is entirely comparable to that of a full operating system.

J2SE and J2EE

Different versions of the Java platform are available. The *J2SE Standard Edition* is the first choice of developers of applets and desktop applications. It contains all the main Java technologies and is the most widespread edition. There is also the *J2EE Enterprise Edition*, which is designed especially for complex, mission-critical applications. It builds on J2SE and also features many enhanced functions, which are described in detail in Section 5.2. This chapter deals exclusively with the basic technologies of the Standard Edition, in particular, to analyze the syntax structure of Java programs and concepts of the language in comparison to ABAP.

J2ME

In addition to the above editions of the Java platform, there is also a *J2ME Micro Edition*, which was developed for small, mobile systems such as PDAs and smart phones.

The Programming Language

The Java programming language was designed to be easy to learn. It uses only a few syntax constructs (in contrast to ABAP, for example)—a fact that has made it extremely popular. Java wins people over with its simple syntax, which circumvents the complexities that afflict many other languages, and its wide range of functions. The syntax of Java is similar to C (or C++); however, it is otherwise fundamentally different from C regarding its object orientation and object independence.

Of course, the SAP NetWeaver Developer Studio represents a development environment for Java in the SAP environment that is on a par with the ABAP Workbench. It is described in detail in Section 5.2.2. To provide you with a better understanding of the material, we will first introduce the basic concepts and paradigms of Java development.

4.2.2 Object-Oriented Programming

Data in the Foreground

Object-Oriented Programming (OOP) began to replace structured programming as the dominant paradigm in the early 1990s. Instead of structured programming, the focus was now on the data, not on the algorithms and functions used to process it. An object defines itself by the data and properties that it reveals to the outside. The functions that manipulate this data are also part of the object, but are not in the foreground and are concealed from other objects. Therefore, the determining factor is not how a function is implemented within an object, but which interfaces can be used to access it. If an object is working correctly, you only have to worry about its interface specifications, not its implementation.

Objects An object-oriented program consists of a set of objects with specific properties and functions. These objects interact by sending messages to one another. In the object-oriented terminology, functions are called *methods*, while the data refers to the *attributes* of an object. When an object wants to send a message to another object, it calls that object's method. The attributes can be reached only through their corresponding methods. Each object covers a specific range of activities within a program. If an object has to solve a task that lies outside its range, it accesses another object whose range includes that task, and assigns it to the object to solve. The result can be sent back as another message. But the range of activities of an object, and therefore its complexity, should not be chosen too broadly. Small objects with strict specifications will make it much easier to design and troubleshoot your program.

Key Characteristics of Objects Each object differs from every other object in at least one of the following key characteristics:

- Object behavior
- Object state
- Object identity

All the objects that were instantiated from the same class have the same behavior. An object's behavior is defined from the methods that can be used to address it. An object's state is also initially derived from the *class definition*. The state can change over time, however, when messages are sent to the object and cause its attributes to change. But its state and behavior alone do not set an object completely apart from all other objects. Each object also has its own identity, which is used to address it.

Client/Server The calling object is the *client*; the called object is the *server*. This relationship between the two objects is not static—it can change as soon as communication flows in the other direction.

Classes But how are objects created? First, you need a kind of template, which is called a *class*. Classes specify the "shapes" of objects. An object is an instance of a class, while a class can have any number of instances. Section 4.2.11 explains how to create classes and objects in Java.

Java already includes thousands of classes, each of which covers a certain range of activities. To write your own program, you have to generate your own classes and instantiate them. In Java, unlike with ABAP, you cannot write a complex program without resorting to object-oriented concepts.

Inheritance Concept

There are different types of relationships between objects. One of them is the inheritance relationship. Java has an absolute base class called `Object`, from which all other classes are derived. An inheritance relationship describes a hierarchy between two classes. The higher-level class acts as a superclass, which "bequeaths" all its properties to the lower-level base class. The base class can use these properties as if they were its own. It can also extend them or overwrite them. In turn, the base class can act as a superclass for other classes. The implementation of the inheritance concept in Java is discussed in Section 4.2.13.

Encapsulation

Encapsulating data and functions to form objects is another key concept of OOP. An object is a specific collection of properties, methods, and attributes. If you want to access an object from outside, you must use the object's public methods and their interfaces to do so. Each object's internal workings are irrelevant to the other objects. Only this approach makes reusable classes possible for use elsewhere in the program or even in other programs. Therefore, think of an object as a type of "black box." Section 4.2.15 describes the implementation of this concept in more detail.

4.2.3 A First Example Program in Java

The following short Java program calculates the square value of an integer.

```
/* Program to calculate the square value
* of an integer
*/
// Class Definition
public class Square {
  // This method starts the program
  public static void main (String args[]) {
    // Read user inputs
    int input = Integer.parseInt(args[0]);
    // Call method to square and save
```

```
    // the result in a variable
    int output = square(input);
    // Output the result
    System.out.println(output);
    // End of main method
  }

  // This method calculates the square of a number
  public static int square(int input) {
    // Return result with type Integer
    return input * input;
  // End of square method
  }
// End of square class
}
```

Listing 4.7 Example Program for Calculating the Square Value of an Integer

Save the program in a file called *Square.java*; the file name is case-sensitive. You can then use *javac*, the Java compiler, to compile it into a file that the Java interpreter can execute:

```
javac Square.java
```

The result is a file called *Square.class*, which *java*, the Java interpreter, can now execute. The program expects the integer to be squared as an argument:

```
java Square 5
25
```

After you have read the complete section 4.2, you will be able to understand programs as well as execute them. The meanings of the individual program elements are described below.

4.2.4 Comments

There are three different types of comments in Java. Single-line comments begin with a double slash: //:

```
String test = "ABAP2Java";  //Initialize variables
```

In contrast to the ABAP environment, you can use the Java notation for single-line comments anywhere in the source text—you don't have to differentiate between comments that start at the beginning of the line and those that start in the middle.

Multiline comments begin with /* and end with */. Setting additional asterisks at the start of each line is not absolutely necessary, but highlights the comments better:

```
/* This is a multiline comment that could
* appear anywhere in the source text.
*/
```

Unfortunately, ABAP does not feature an equivalent to the Java multiline comment function.

Doc Comments

There is also the special doc comment, which can appear at the start of a Java class file, interface, method, or field definition. It is used to embed the documentation of the entire class, with its methods, in the source text. The comments enable the automated, structured publication of the documentation on other media later on. This option is described in detail in Section 4.2.19 (see documentation conventions).

4.2.5 Identifiers and Keywords

The term "identifier" encompasses all generic names for source text elements. You can generally choose your identifiers at your discretion. The Unicode character set gives developers even more options for using identifiers than other programming languages. In Java, an identifier must start with a letter, an underscore, or a currency symbol (such as i or $). However, you should note that Java programming conventions encourage you to avoid using currency symbols whenever possible. There are no restrictions to any characters from the second place onwards, with the exception of punctuation marks.

Identifiers are a standard programming tool for declaring objects—such as classes, variables, and so on—within a validity area and referencing them again elsewhere. The term "validity area" is extremely important in Java development, to ensure the interoperability of software, packages, and even code snippets from different vendors, and avoid unwanted system responses caused by the random selection of identical identifiers.

The keywords listed below are reserved in Java and cannot be used as identifiers.

abstract	do	if	package	synchronized
boolean	double	implements	private	this
break	else	import	protected	throws
case	false	int	return	transient
catch	final	interface	short	true
char	finally	long	static	try
class	float	native	strictfp	void
const	for	new	super	volatile
continue	goto	null	switch	while
default				

Table 4.2 Java Keywords

4.2.6 Data Types, Variables, and Constants

The preceding keywords, which are described in detail later on in this chapter, already represent the full scope of the Java language. Therefore, you only have to deal with far fewer reserved terms that you would in ABAP programming. Java supports higher-level events, remote calls, and other models with concepts that are implemented in the class architecture, instead of using additional language constructs. This usually makes it easier to get started in new areas, as there are no syntax components that have to be observed, only architectural components.

Primitive Data Types

Java supports a total of eight different basic data types as is shown in the following table:

Type	Contents	Size	Value range
`boolean`	true/false	1 bit	–
`byte`	integer	8 bits	–128 to 127
`short`	integer	16 bits	–32768 to 32767

Table 4.3 Basic Data Types in Java

Type	Contents	Size	Value range
int	integer	32 bits	–2,147,483,648 to 2,147,483,647
long	integer	64 bits	–9,223,372,036,854,775,808 to 9,223,372,036,854,775,807
float	floating point number	32 bits	±1.4E-45 to ±3.4028235E+38
double	floating point number	64 bits	±4.9E-324 to ±1.7976931348623157E+308
char	Unicode	16 bits	\u0000 to \uFFFF

Table 4.3 Basic Data Types in Java (cont.)

Data type `char` is not based on the 7-bit ASCII character set, like so many other languages, but instead on the 16-bit Unicode character set. Consequently, Unicode can represent nearly every written language in the world. The Unicode characters are saved in UTF-8 encoding, which makes it possible to reuse existing ASCII/8-bit Latin-1 texts. You won't notice any difference in practice. You can continue coding your source texts in pure ASCII if you want. The following escape sequences are defined for special characters:

Escape Sequence	Character Value
\b	Backspace
\t	Tab
\n	Next line
\f	Page feed
\r	Carriage return
\«	Double quote
\'	Single quote
\\	Backslash
\xxx	Latin-1 character; xxx is an octal number between 0 and 377.
\uxxxx	Unicode character; xxxx are four hexadecimal digits. Unicode can be used anywhere in Java programs.

Table 4.4 Escape Sequences of the char Data Type for Special Characters

These sequences also apply to data type `String`, which is a class, and not a primitive data type. Because it is used very often, however, and much easier to handle as a primitive data type, it behaves like one in Java.

Octal and Hexadecimal

All integer values are generally signed. It is also possible to portray them in octal notation, with a preceding 0, or in hexadecimal notation with a leading 0x.

```
0x7B   //Decimal 123 in hexadecimal notation
0173   //Decimal 123 in octal notation
```

Value ranges cannot overflow in Java. If the value range of an integer value is exceeded, it wraps: A `short` type value with 32767 +1 becomes –32768.

Integer literals are always 32 bits wide at first. If defined with a trailing `l` or `L`, they become a 64-bit wide `long` value.

Floating point literals are also 32 bits wide at first and correspond to the `float` data type. The double precision of the 64-bit-wide `double` type is achieved by entering a trailing `f` or `F`. Floating point literals always have to contain a decimal point or a trailing `f`; otherwise, the compiler will interpret them as integers. Scientific notation for powers of 10 can be designated with the letters `e` or `E`:

```
2.6783e04   //corresponds to 2.6783 x 104, or 26783
3.05e-5     //corresponds to 3.05 x 10-5, or 0.0000305
```

Octal or hexadecimal notation is not possible for floating-point numbers.

In addition, four special values exist for floating point numbers that can arise when the value range is exceeded:

Special Value	Cause	Example
Positive infinity	Value range exceeded	float pos = 1.0 / 0.0;
Negative infinity	Value range exceeded	float neg = –1.0 / 0.0;
NaN (not a number)	Result of an illegal operation	float nan = 0.0 / 0.0;
Null	Value range undershot	float x = –1.0 / pos;

Table 4.5 Special Values for Floating-Point Numbers

Variables

You use the following scheme to declare a variable in Java:

```
Data_type Name;
```

You use the equals operator (=) for initialization:

```
Name = Value;
```

Because each data type is absolutely self-descriptive and all data types are implemented as a class (aside from the primitive data types, such as integers or Boolean values), it is apparent that tables and complex values are encapsulated in tables. Therefore, Java can usually forego complex declaration procedures, which are the norm in the ABAP world, provided that every data type is implemented as a class.

Constants

You use keyword `final` to define constants. As in many other languages, the Java convention is to write constants in all caps in order to distinguish them from variables:

```
final double E = 2.71828;
```

This method of declaring constants is a prime example of the general Java approach, in which logical combinations of existing language constructs are generally preferred over creating new language constructs.

Type Conversions

With the exception of `boolean`, which cannot be converted into any other primitive data type nor be the target of any type conversion itself, the underlying Unicode coding enables you to convert any primitive type into any other existing type. This also applies to converting a `char` value to an integer or floating point number.

Cast

We typically differentiate between widening and narrowing type conversion. In a widening conversion, values with a narrow value range are copied to a type with a wider value range. This is performed implicitly, which means the `?=` construct for the widening cast (or up cast) familiar from ABAP is unknown in Java. Conversely, narrowing conversions—from a wider value range to a narrow one—are not possible without further effort. They require a *cast*, which forces such a conversion, and can result in the loss of data.

In contrast to the implicit casting in ABAP, casting in Java is explicit, with a simple type conversion:

```
int i = (int) 11.123;  //a forced conversion
```

Arrays

Arrays are reference types that are composed from primitive data types, which means they can contain a multitude of simple literals. Arrays can be created from any primitive data type. To do so, you first need an array variable with type "array values." You use the new operator to create an array in memory. The array variable refers to the array through an assignment. The array then addressed through the array variable. You can do all of this within a single statement:

```
char abc[] = new char[25];
```

An index is used to access the individual elements of an array:

```
abc[0] = 'a';
abc[25] = 'z';
```

The first element of the array is accessed through index 0 in Java, in contrast to ABAP, where it is accessed through index 1.

You can also use an *array literal* to create an array:

```
char abc[] = {'a','b','c','d','e','f'};
```

The new operator is implicit in this case. The size of the array is determined from the number of values within the curly brackets.

Multidimensional Arrays

Multidimensional arrays, which are implemented in Java as "arrays in arrays," can be created in a similar manner. You simply add another pair of square brackets to the declaration for each additional dimension:

```
String abcMatrix[][] = new String[25][25];
```

The memory has to be assigned for the first dimension first, however. The other dimensions can be assigned manually:

```
String abcMatrix[][] = new String[25][];
abcMatrix[0] = new String[25];
abcMatrix[25] = new String[24];
```

The advantage of this syntax is that you can select different numbers of elements for the nth dimension.

Multidimensional array literals are also supported, and are implemented using nested curly brackets:

```
String abcMatrix[][] = { {"aa","ab","ac"}
                         {"ba","bb","bc"}
                         {"ca","cb","cc"} };
```

This handling of arrays can be extended to any other dimensions.

You can use keyword `null` to explicitly represent the absence of an array:

null

```
char abc[] = null;
```

The ABAP environment does not use arrays in this form. Internal tables are usually the ABAP counterpart to arrays. However, the objects of java class `Vector` are even more like internal tables than arrays, functionally speaking. These objects can also be processed in loop constructs; furthermore, they can contain any other objects as row elements. This technique—using iteration-capable objects to enable sequential access to subobjects and their attributes—is quite widespread in Java and, as already mentioned, is supported by native loop constructs, as will be demonstrated later.

4.2.7 Operators

Arithmetic Operators

Arithmetic operators can be used with all primitive data types except `boolean`. Either floating point or integer arithmetic is used, depending on the operators. This is particularly important for the division operator:

```
5/2       //Result 2
5/2.0     //Result 2.5
5/0       //Returns an error
5/0.0     //Result positive infinity
```

The modulo operator, %, calculates the remainder of a division, and behaves identically for both integer and floating-point operands:

```
5%2       //Result 1
```

The increment and decrement operators increase or decrease the operand by one, respectively. We differentiate between postfix and prefix notation:

Increment and Decrement Operators

```
int i=1;      //i=1
int j=++i;    //j=2
j=i++;        //j remains 2
```

In the prefix case, the operand is increased before the expression is evaluated; in the postfix case, the expression is evaluated first.

Operator	Meaning
+	Addition
-	Subtraction
*	Multiplication
/	Division
%	Modulo
++	Increment
--	Decrement

Table 4.6 Arithmetic Operators in Java

The flexibility that these operators give developers is not entirely supported in ABAP, especially with regard to incrementing and decrementing values.

We should point out, however, that the excessive use of operators in Java can result in confusing coding, especially when incremental assignments are used in statements.

Bit Operators

Bit operators can be used only with `int` and `char` operands. These operators use and manipulate operands at the bit level.

Operator	Meaning
~	Ones complement
&	bit AND
|	bit OR
^	bit XOR

Table 4.7 Logical Bit Operators

The following truth table illustrates the meanings of the operators:

A	B	A|B	A&B	A^B	~A
0	0	0	0	0	1
1	0	1	0	1	0

<table>
<tr><th>A</th><th>B</th><th>A|B</th><th>A&B</th><th>A^B</th><th>~A</th></tr>
<tr><td>0</td><td>1</td><td>1</td><td>0</td><td>1</td><td>1</td></tr>
<tr><td>1</td><td>1</td><td>1</td><td>1</td><td>0</td><td>0</td></tr>
</table>

Bit Shift Operators

The shift operators—<<, >>>, and >>—shift the bits of the left operand to the left or right by the number of places specified in the right operand. The places that are "squeezed out" to the left or right are lost. When << and >>> are used, the places are filled with zeros; if >> is used, they are filled with the originally highest bit.

```
12 >>> 2      // 00001100 >>> 10 = 00000011 = 3
17 << 5       // 00010001 << 101 = 00100000 = 32
```

Operator	Meaning
>>	Shift to the right
>>>	Shift to the right and fill with zeros
<<	Shift to the left

Table 4.8 Shift Operators

Relational Operators

The results of relational operators always have type `boolean`. The "equal to" operator returns primitive data type `true` when the compared values are really equal in value. When operands with a reference data type (array or object) are used, the references are checked for equivalency. The same applies to the "not equal to" operator. As you will see, relational operators are used primarily in program branching and loop constructs.

Operator	Meaning
==	Equal to
!=	Not equal to
>	Greater than
<	Less than
>=	Greater than or equal to
<=	Less than or equal to

Table 4.9 Relational Operators

Boolean Operators

Boolean operators are used primarily to concatenate the results of logical operators. The results (or operands) must have type `boolean`. The result of a Boolean operation is always another Boolean value.

Short-Circuit Evaluation

The `&&` and `||` operators are generally used more frequently than `&` and `|`, which evaluate the right side of the expression in all cases, even if it isn't necessary. The `&&` and `||` operators don't do this; instead, they end as soon as they calculate the left side of the expression (this method is called *short-circuit evaluation*). The `^` operator is also typically used as a logical bit operator.

Operator	Meaning
&	Logical AND
|	Logical OR
^	Logical XOR
||	OR with short-circuit evaluation
&&	AND with short-circuit evaluation
!	Logical NOT
==	Equal to
!=	Not equal to

Table 4.10 Boolean Operators in Java

Assignment Operators

Assignment operators assign a value to a variable. In addition to the regular assignment operator—the = operator—Java has many short forms that link the assignment with another operator, enabling an abbreviated syntax of the expressions.

```
i = i / 5;      // this syntax can be
i /= 5;         // abbreviated like this
```

Operator	Meaning
+=	Addition assignment
-=	Subtraction assignment
*=	Multiplication assignment
/=	Division assignment

Table 4.11 Assignment Operators in Java

Operator	Meaning
%=	Modulo assignment
&=	AND assignment
|=	OR assignment
^=	XOR assignment
>>=	Assignment by right shift
>>>=	Assignment by right shift, filled with zeros
<<=	Assignment by left shift

Table 4.11 Assignment Operators in Java (cont.)

Other Operators

The point operator, (.), is used to access the members of a class—the attributes and methods. Its exact meaning is described in Section 4.2.11.

instanceof

The `instanceof` operator can be applied only to objects or arrays (reference types). The left side of the expression must contain a reference, while the right side contains a reference type. If the type in the reference is the same as the reference type in the expression, the result is `true`; if not, it is `false`:

```
char abc[] = new char[6];
abc[] instanceof char[];     //returns true
abc[] instanceof int[];      //returns false
```

new

You use the `new` operator to create objects and arrays in memory; it is analogous to the keyword `CREATE OBJECT` in ABAP. It's followed by the reference type (the name of the class to instantiate) and, in parentheses, the arguments that are assigned to the constructor of the object or array to create.

The operator for type conversion `(data type)` expects a primitive data type within the parentheses, into which the operand after the parentheses will be converted:

```
(long) 256    //Cast an int value to long type
```

The + operator, aside from adding numeric values, can be used to concat enate strings.

```
String app = "ResMan";
String statement = "Our" + app + "is a great app!";
```

This also works if only one operand has type `String`. All other data types are converted to strings implicitly.

Operator	Meaning
.	Reference to members of a class
`instanceof`	Compares a reference with a type
`new`	Creates objects and arrays
`(data type)`	Type conversion, cast
+	String concatenation

Table 4.12 Other Operators in Java

Priorities

The priority of the operators can be influenced via the use of parentheses.

High priority			
()	[]	.	
++	--	~	!
*	/	%	
+	-		
>>	>>>	<<	
>	>=	<	<=
==	!=		
&			
^			
|			
&&			
||			
?:			
=	op=		
Low priority			

Table 4.13 Operator Priorities

4.2.8 Control Structures

{...}

Curly brackets allow you to create *composed statements* and *statement blocks*. You can use a statement block anywhere that you can use a single statement. Statement blocks can be used together with all other control constructs.

This encapsulation process is fundamentally different from the syntax in ABAP programs, in which all control structures are concluded with END....

If

The if statement behaves exactly like it does in most other languages:

```
if (i==0) {
  System.out.println("i equals 0");
} else {
  System.out.println("i does not equal 0");
}
```

If only one statement follows the condition else, you can end it with a semicolon. You don't need to encapsulate it in curly brackets. The condition must return a boolean value that the if can evaluate. If the condition returns true, the first statement block is executed; if it returns false, the else block is executed. Of course, the else block is not mandatory.

You can also nest if control structures:

```
if (i==5) {
  if (j==6) {
    System.out.println("i times j is 30");
  }
} else
  System.out.println("i times j is not 30");
}
```

Appending a condition to an else statement helps you structure if ... else branching better:

```
if (i==0) {
  System.out.println("i equals 0");
} else if (i==1) {
```

```
  System.out.println("i equals 1");
} else if (i==2) {
  System.out.println("i equals 2");
} else {
  System.out.println("i does not equal 0, 1 or 2");
}
```

Switch

The switch statement is similar to the if statement. It is the only abbreviated form of if ... else control structures with conditional else branches. The parentheses after switch contain the variable with type int whose value you want to examine. Numeric constants appear as possible values for the respective variables after case. You must enter break to end the subsequent statement block. The statement block after the default statement is carried out if the variable does not correspond to any of the constants.

```
switch (i) {
  case 0:
    System.out.println("i equals 0");
    break;
  case 1:
    System.out.println("i equals 1");
    break;
  case 2:
    System.out.println("i equals 1");
    break;
  default:
    System.out.println("i does not equal 0, 1 or 2");
    break;
}
```

The equivalent to switch in Java is the CASE statement in ABAP. It does not require a statement like break to exit a specific case; if this is necessary, WHEN is used instead of case. The default case is introduced in ABAP with WHEN OTHERS.

While

The while loop is the basic loop statement in Java:

```
int i=0;
while(i<10) {
  System.out.println(i);
  i++;
}
```

Similar to the if control structure, the curly brackets can be omitted if only one statement occurs within the loop. The expression in parentheses after while has to return a value with type boolean. If true is returned, the contents of the loop are executed. If false is returned, the statement is continued after the statement block in the while loop.

The familiar statement used in ABAP for iteration in a results list in an internal table, LOOP AT table_name INTO row_name, is not implemented as a language construct in Java. A while loop is used in combination with an iteration-capable function, as shown below, to provide efficient, elegant access to the resulting set:

```
while(recordSet.next()) {
  System.out.println(recordSet.getField("field_name"));
}
```

Do

The do corresponds to the while loop, in which the loop header appears at the end of the loop, which means the interpreter executes the loop body at least once:

```
int i=0;
do {
  System.out.println(i);
  i++;
} while (i<10);
```

This statement is implemented in ABAP with DO n TIMES, whose function is more equivalent to the for loop in Java.

For

A for loop is basically a special variant of a while loop, and is widely used. This control structure features easy-to-use syntax:

```
for(int i=1;i<10;i++)
  System.out.println(i);
```

In this case, declaration (or only initialization), control printout, and incrementing take place in a single statement. The loop body can be reduced, and in the above example, it is not even necessary to create a statement block with curly brackets. We don't recommend using this syntax, however, as it makes the program unnecessarily difficult to analyze.

While it is also possible to perform multiple initializations and increments in the loop header, this can also impair the readability of the coding. If you choose to do so, you must separate the values with commas:

```
for(int i=0, j=20;i=j;i++,j--) {
  System.out.println("i is "+ j-i +" less than j");
}
```

The variables are visible only in the loop body.

Endless Loops All three expressions in the loop header are optional and any of them can be omitted if desired. Of course, if you don't use any expressions, you'll create an endless loop, which you should avoid at all costs.

```
for(;;) {
  System.out.println("To infinity and beyond...");
}
```

Break

You can use the `break` statement to exit `while`, `do`, and `for` loops:

```
for(int i=0;i<10;i++) {
  System.out.println(i);
  if (i==5)
    break;
}
```

After a break statement, the interpreter continues processing after the end of the loop.

This statement is also used in the `switch` control structure. In this case, the interpreter jumps to the end of the `switch` block.

The equivalent command to `break` in Java, for exiting loops, is `EXIT` in ABAP; the `EXIT` statement can also be used elsewhere, for example, to exit function modules and methods.

Continue

The continue statement behaves similarly to the break statement, with the exception that the loop is not exited completely; instead, the next loop pass starts, and everything between continue and the loop header is ignored:

```
for(int i=1;i<=100;i++) {
  if (i%2 != 0)
    continue;
  System.out.println(i + "is an even number.");
}
```

continue has a similar function as a keyword in both Java and ABAP.

Return

You use the return statement to pass methods from a called method back to the calling method. It is usually followed by an expression as a return value, with the type of the method. The interpreter returns immediately after a return statement, without considering any subsequent statements of the method. Methods are described in detail in Section 4.2.10.

```
public float divide(float divisor, float dividend) {
  float quotient = divisor / dividend;
  return quotient;     //returns quotient
}
```

Methods with type void—that is, methods without a return value—use return without a return value. The keyword EXIT is used to exit the current module within ABAP function modules and methods. Export and return parameters must be set previously through explicit assignment, and are independent of the language construct itself.

Synchronized

You can use the synchronized statement to protect statement blocks such that only one thread can access them.

Threads

Threads are similar to processes, but work within a process and therefore don't have their own memory area. Threads make it possible to process program flows in parallel. Because threads share a common memory area, however, some statement blocks can be critical.

The synchronized statement defines that one thread must finish processing a critical block before the next thread can begin processing that same block. The expression has to contain a reference to an array or an object after synchronized. Before the statement block is interpreted, an exclusive lock is set for the referenced array or object, and persists until the thread finishes processing the statement block.

```
int arr[] = new int[10];
synchronized(arr) {
  for (int i=0;i<10;i++) {
    arr[i] = i*i;
  }
}
```

You can also use synchronized for complete methods, which means only one thread can call the method at the same time:

```
synchronized int square (int i) {
  return i*i;
}
```

You only have to use synchronized if multiple threads access the same data in a program.

4.2.9 Exception Handling

Throw

The throw statement is used to catch *exceptions* or errors. To do so, throw defines the exception object that is created when the exception occurs. If the interpreter runs across a throw statement, it stops the regular program flow and jumps to the exception handler, a try ... catch ... finally block. It searches for this block in the directly adjacent statement block first. If nothing is defined there, it searches the next higher block, and so on. If no exception handler is defined in the entire program, the program is terminated and an error message is output. Here is a simple example for using throw:

```
int arr[] = new int[9];
for(int i=0;i<10;i++) {
  arr[i] = i*i;
  if (i>9)
   throw new ArrayIndexOutOfBoundsException("Error");
}
```

In ABAP, exceptions are triggered by keyword raise, followed by the name of the EXCEPTION class or one of the exceptions defined in the exception list at the current encapsulation level.

The throws statement, which forms part of the method definition, indicates which exceptions the method can generate: throws

```
public int divide(int a, int b) throws ArithmeticException
{
if(b == 0) {
        // An exception occurred
        throw new ArithmeticException("Divisor is zero.");
} else {
        // Calculation possible, no exception
        return a / b;
}
}
```

In the above example, exception ArithmeticException is generated only when argument b of the method is null. The throws statement informs the byte code compiler that the method might trigger this exception.

In ABAP, possible exceptions are not specified in methods or function modules using a special keyword like throws, but instead defined in the list of possible exceptions in the Workbench itself.

Try ... Catch ... Finally

Used together, try ... catch ... finally blocks form an exception handler to deal with exceptions, which are either raised manually with throw or generated automatically by the system.

try begins the statement block, in which one or more exceptions can be defined with catch, followed by the cleanup operations defined under finally. Although the latter two statements are optional, a try statement block without exception handling makes little sense.

catch intercepts a possible exception and handles it within its statement block. The argument is always an object with type Throwable or one of its subclasses. If an exception occurs in the try block, the interpreter locates a catch block that has the suitable type and then executes the corresponding statements.

finally forms the closing statement block of the exception handler. It contains instructions that are always executed, regardless of whether the previous try and catch blocks pass on the control flow with return, continue, or break. It is normally used to clean up the statements in the try block.

```
int arr[] = new int[9];
try {
  for (int i=10;i>0;i--)
    arr[i] = i*3/i;
} catch (ArithmeticException exp1) {
  System.out.println("Calculation error");
} catch (ArrayIndexOutOfBoundsException exp2) {
  System.out.println("Index outside of array");
} finally {
  System.out.println("Exception handling finished.");
}
```

In general, the TRY ... CATCH mechanism under ABAP is equivalent to exception control in Java, except for a few syntax peculiarities. The only difference is that ABAP uses CLEANUP instead of finally.

4.2.10 Methods

Methods are special statement blocks that can be called from within other statement blocks through their method headers, or *method signatures*. A method is divided into header and body. The body is simply any sequence of statements that implement the method specifications in the signature.

Method Signature

The method header specifies the method and contains the following elements:

- Name of the method
- Type of value returned by the method
- Interface specifications, that is, types and names of method parameters (optional)
- Method modifiers (optional)
- Exception types that can be raised by the method (optional)

The signature has a fixed structure:

```
modifier type name (parameters) [throws exceptions]
```

Modifiers affect the response of the method in various ways. They are described in detail in Section 4.2.15.

The type specifies the return value of the method, which can be primitive data types, arrays, or objects. If no value is returned, the keyword `void` must be used.

Overloading

The name of the method is an identifier, and subject to the restrictions of identifiers. Identically named methods can exist in parallel, as long as their interface specifications or parameter passing is different. This approach is used to "overload" methods: The interpreter determines which method to execute, depending on how many parameters (and which ones) are passed on in the call.

ABAP does not support overloading in this form, because method names must be unique within a class. Optional parameters are supported, however, similar to function modules, providing an easy way to simulate the overloading of methods with different signatures.

Parameters

The list of parameters must be enclosed in parentheses. If the method is not to be given any parameters, the parentheses remain blank. Each parameter consists of a type and a parameter identifier. Multiple parameters are separated by commas. If a method call occurs anywhere within a program, it must contain its name and—if present in the method signature—the parameters. The sequence and types of the arguments must agree with the parameters of the method. The types can differ, however, if an implicit (widening) type conversion is possible; if not, the arguments must be transformed to the correct format before the record call.

Exception handling with `throws` was discussed in Section 4.2.9 above.

A complete method specification could look like this:

```
public long takeRoot (long number, short root) throws Ill
egalArgumentException {
  // Method body
}
```

4.2.11 Classes and Objects

The *class* is a central concept of object-oriented software development. Because Java is a self-contained, object-oriented language, classes are its most important modularization unit. You cannot program in Java without using classes. The Java compiler cannot recognize Java coding without the class that surrounds it. A class consists of attributes, that is, variables and methods, also called its *members*. Every statement in Java must be contained within a method and every method must be a member of a class.

Terminology In the terminology of structured programming, a class corresponds to a self-defined type. Methods correspond to functions, while attributes correspond to variables. This separate terminology is not merely semantic, however, but stems from the different approach to program coding used in object-oriented software development.

Objects When classes define a data type, you also need values that are based on that data type and can be used in a program. The value of a class is called an *object*. Just as the data type specifies the value range and possible operations for a value, the class specifies an object's behavior and its properties—the behavior in the methods and the properties in the attributes. The properties of an object collectively form its state.

To create an object, you must instantiate a class. Therefore, the class acts like a template for an object. You can create any amount of objects from a class.

Defining a Class

You create classes in Java with the keyword `class`, the name, and a pair of curly brackets. Therefore, the simplest statement for creating a class looks like this:

```
class ClassName {..}
```

Members You should always start the name of the class with an uppercase letter. The class body then contains the definitions of the class members (its methods and attributes). The convention is to list the attributes in the class first, followed by the methods.

Example of a class:

```
class Resource {
  private int remainingOperatingTime;
  private int costPerHour;
  public boolean Available;
  public Resource(int remainingOperatingTime, int costs)
    {
    this.remainingOperatingTime =
         remainingOperatingTime;
    this.costPerHour = costs;
    this.available = true;
```

```
  }
  public int getRemainingOperatingTime() {
    return this.remainingOperatingTime;
  }
  public void setRemainingOperatingTime(
  int remainingOperatingTime) {
    this.remainingOperatingTime = remainingOperatingTime;
  }
  public int getcostPerHour() {
    return this.costPerHour;
  }
  public void setcostPerHour(int costs) {
    this.costPerHour = costs;
  }
  public void output() {
    System.out.println("This resource has: ");
    System.out.println(this.remainingOperatingTime
                       + " remaining operating time");
    if (this.available==true) {
      System.out.println(" and is available.");
    } else {
      System.out.println(" and is not available.");
    }
  }
}
```

Constructors

`Resource()` is a special method, the class constructor. When an object is created from the class, this method is called implicitly and the statements contained therein are executed. The object attributes are usually initialized here. The constructor must contain the name of the class and does not have a default type. Constructors can be overloaded, just like normal methods. If no explicit constructor is specified in a class, Java supplies an implicit standard constructor, which does not require any parameters and does not initialize any values.

this

The `this` keyword—similar to `ME` in ABAP—is used to emphasize that the member in question is an attribute or method of the same class definition. While you can also address a member without a preceding `this` keyword, using the `this` keyword will help to improve the clarity and readability of the source text. The use of `this` is required only if the method contains a local variable with the same name, in addition to the attribute, which is the case in constructor Resource() in the example.

Creating an Object

To create an object in the class engine, you must generate a reference variable that you can use to address the object, just as you would with an array:

```
Resource myResource;
```

The object itself is generated using keyword new and a call of the class constructor:

```
myResource = new Resource(1000,10);
```

Of course, these two statements could also be contained in a single line.

null Reference variables can also be set to point explicitly at "nothing." The keyword for this is null. However, this keyword does not refer to the numeric null (zero); rather, it is a reference to a blank memory location:

```
Resource myResource = null;
```

Addressing the Methods and Attributes

Now that you've created an object, you'll probably want to work with it. To do so, you have to access the attributes and methods of the object. You do this with the point operator (.). It is preceded by the name of the object (or its reference variable) and followed by the attribute to be changed or the method to call (with parameters):

```
myResource.setusefulLife(900);
myResource.usefulLife = 900;
```

Set and Get Methods These statements both have the same effect, namely, setting attribute usefulLife to a new value. The second variant, in which the attribute is addressed directly and does not use a method. The first variant, in which the attribute is set using a set method, is much more elegant. The concept of encapsulating objects, in which methods must be used to access attributes, is implemented properly in this case. This applies equally to read and write access. Get methods are responsible for read access to attributes:

```
int costPerHour = myResource.getcostPerHour();
```

Class Members and Instance Members

The members of a class can also be differentiated between members that are static and those that can be instantiated, in addition to differentiating between attributes and methods.

static

Class members are designated with the keyword `static`:

```
public static String name = "myResource";
```

They are considered static because they are only one component of a class and cannot be instantiated in objects. This applies to both methods and attributes. Class attributes are comparable to global variables in structured programming. A class attribute can be accessed directly within a class by using its name. From outside the class, the attribute can be accessed through the preceding class name:

```
Resource.costPerHour = 24;
```

The definition of class methods is very similar:

```
public static int costPerHour(int costs,
                                          int hours) {
       return costs / hours;
}
```

Class methods can also be called directly by name within the class, and with the preceding class name outside the class.

```
Resource.costPerHour(24, 6);
```

Note that class methods can use only class variables and other class methods, not instance attributes or instance methods.

Instance members are attributes and methods that aren't really components of the classes, but only instances. If a class is not instantiated, it cannot be accessed. Every member without the keyword `static` in the signature is an instance member.

Addressing Instance Attributes

Instance attributes are addressed by name only within the class definition; otherwise, they're specified with the preceding object name and the name of the instance attribute:

```
Resource myResource = new Resource(1000, 18);
myResource.usefulLife = 2000;
```

Instance methods, like instance attributes, are addressed using only their name within the class definition, and otherwise, using the object name and method name:

```
Resource myResource = new Resource(1000, 18);
int life = myResource.getusefulLife();
```

Instance methods can also access class methods. The reverse case—class methods accessing instance methods—is not possible, as mentioned above.

Automatic Initialization

Also note that Java initializes class attributes and instance attributes automatically, in contrast to local variables. Primitive attributes are initialized with `null` or `false`, while references are initialized with keyword `null`.

The main() Method

The `main()` method is a special class method. It can be used to start a Java program. The `main()` method has the following signature:

```
public static void main (String args[])
```

Parameter `String args[]` is needed as soon as you want to pass arguments on to the program. Each argument (separated by blanks) is saved in an array of strings and is available in the program itself.

The following program queries the arguments it was passed and outputs them:

```
class Echo {
  public static void main (String args[]) {
    for(int i=0;i<10;i++)
      System.out.println("Argument"+ i + ":" +args[i]);
  }
}
```

Because ABAP is not completely object-oriented, in contrast to Java, the mechanism of the static `main()` method is represented by the context surrounding the objects, such as a report program. You will not encounter the `main()` method in a J2EE environment either, because the container architecture already ensures that the objects are initialized.

Copying and Comparing Objects and Arrays

To copy a primitive value, you need only a few statements:

```
char abc1 = 'a';
char abc2 = abc1;
```

Variable abc2 now contains the same value as abc1. This means the value actually exists twice.

Reference variables are somewhat different:

```
int arr1[] = new int[10];
int arr2[] = arr1[];
```

Reference variable arr2[] now contains the same reference to the array as arr1[]. This means the array object in the memory can be accessed through both reference variables. The array does not really exist twice. When you run the following statements

```
arr1[0] = 5;
arr2[0] = 10;
```

in sequence, then arr1[0] has value 10.

You get the same response when you copy objects:

```
Resource myResource = new Resource(1000, 12);
Resource yourResource = myResource;
```

Only one object exists, but there are two references to it.

clone()

To truly copy an object, you must use a special method called clone():

```
Resource myResource   = new Resource(1000, 12);
Resource yourResource = (Resource)
                        myResource.clone();
myResource.setTime(2000);
yourResource.setTime(1000);
System.out.println(myRessource.getTime());
```

The program outputs the value 3000, and not 1000, because two references and two objects exist. The cast is needed to transform the return value from clone() to the correct type. You also use clone() for arrays:

```
int arr1[] = new int[10];
int arr2[] = (int[]) arr1[].clone();
```

While you can always clone arrays, you can only clone objects if the `Cloneable` interface is implemented in the class definition. If someone attempts to clone an object that cannot be cloned, an exception is raised.

Reference Equivalence

Primitive values are handled differently than objects and arrays in comparisons as well, not only during copying. When you compare two primitive values, the interpreter simply checks whether the contents of the values are identical. When you compare two reference types, conversely, you declare the references with one another, not the arrays and objects themselves. Therefore, the equals-operator (==) operator—which compares if two values are equal and is used in if/else and other statements that require a Boolean decision (true/false)—used here checks whether two reference variables point to the same object or array:

```
Resource snpResource = new Resource(2000,18);
Resource sapResource = (Resource) snpResource.clone();
Resource ibmResource = snpResource;
if (snpResource == sapResource)
  System.out.println("Incorrect!!");
else if (snpResource == ibmRessource)
  System.out.println("Correct!!");
```

equals()

To test two objects or arrays for equivalence, you use the `equals()` method, which all objects possess. Please note, however, that `equals()` checks only for equivalence of the reference at first as well. If you really want to check whether the objects are identical, you will have to overwrite and implement `equals()` again in each respective class definition. The String class has an implementation of this type:

```
String myString = "Learning Java is fun.";
String yourString = "Learning ABAP is fun.";
if (myString.equals(yourString))
  System.out.println("Both strings are identical");
```

You can also use `equals()` to test arrays for equivalence.

Garbage Collection and Finalization of Objects

Until now, you have repeatedly generated objects and arrays, while the working memory was allocated implicitly. You have not learned how to release memory or delete objects, because this is seldom an issue in Java. Java is able to detect which objects and arrays are no longer used and automatically releases the memory they occupied for use by other objects. An object is considered to be "garbage" if no references point to it. This integrated Java mechanism is called the "garbage collector."

4.2.12 Packages

Commercial applications generally use software components from different software makers and distributors. An excellent example of this is Microsoft's Internet Explorer, which incorporates software from RSA, the JPEG Group, and others. One major problem that arises during the integration of different software components is the issue of naming conventions. If vendor A defines a class with name X and vendor B coincidentally uses the same name, the vendors' software cannot be integrated in the same final product, because it isn't clear which class is intended when X is addressed.

Packages were developed as a simple solution to this problem in Java. Several classes can be grouped together to form a package, for example, when the classes have a similar range of activities or a similar origin.

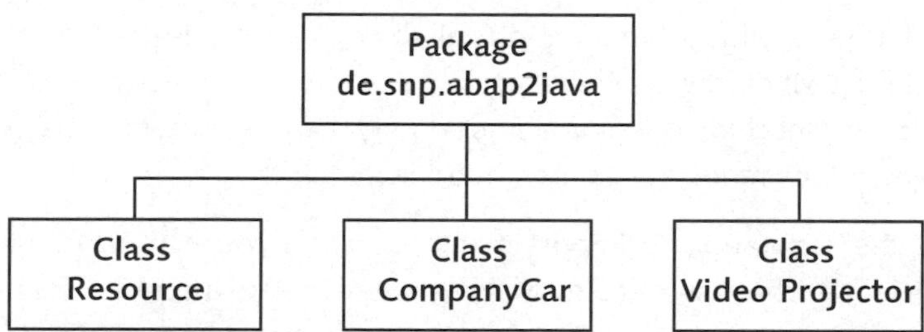

Figure 4.2 Package with Classes

The Java platform itself consists entirely of packages. The `java.io` package, for example, contains all the classes used to import and export data media. The `java.awt` package contains many classes for building user interfaces, and so on. The packages that start with `java`, `javax`, and `sun` are already reserved; you cannot use these names for your own packages.

Notation for Proprietary Packages

The naming conventions for packages defined by Sun, the developer of Java, state that proprietary packages should be named, starting with the Internet domain name in reverse notation, for example:

```
package de.snp.abap2java;
```

All classes that start with this statement belong to `package de.snp.abap2java`, and can access each other easily, simply by invoking the class name. For the Java interpreter to locate these classes, however, they have to be contained in an appropriate subdirectory, /de/snp/abap2java, relative to the current directory. If no package is defined for a class, it belongs to the default package. Other classes that don't have a package statement must invoke the class name to access it. For namespace problems described above, using default packages makes sense for only small, local standalone projects.

Namespaces in ABAP

In the ABAP Workbench, development objects are assigned to *namespaces*, which SAP manages centrally. In general, all development objects within a namespace use that designation as a prefix before their proper names.

import

If you want to use classes other than those defined in your own package, and don't want to have to invoke the complete package name every time, you can set the import statement at the start of a class definition. If you want to compose a class that writes data to the hard drive, for example, you should import package java.io:

```
import java.io.*;
```

The asterisk (*) is a wildcard that imports all the classes of this package at the same time, which means they can all be addressed directly in our class. The important thing is that you import only the classes, and not any subpackages, which require separate import statements.

If you use the * notation to import many packages, you may run into name collisions—when two classes of the same name are imported from different packages. Another version of the import statement can help you deal with such cases: If you want to import only a particular class, you can specify the class after the package:

```
import java.io.FileWriter;
```

The java.lang package plays a special role on the Java platform—it contains the elementary components of the language and is available directly in any class, even without an import statement.

4.2.13 Inheritance

If you want to expand or specialize the functions of an existing class, but also retain it as a more general, higher-level class, we recommend creating a derived class. Java features the inheritance mechanism for this task. A derived class is simply a copy of the higher-level class at first, and can then be extended as needed.

Extending Classes

We now want to extend our Resource class so it can model company cars as well. The existing class should remain, however, and function as a more general superclass.

```
 class CompanyCar extends Resource {
   private String brand;
   CompanyCar(int costs, int remainingOperatingTime,
                             String brand) {
     super(remainingOperatingTime,costs);
     this.brand = brand;
   }
   public String getBrand() {
     return this.brand;
   }
   public void setBrand(String brand) {
     this.brand= brand;
   }
}
```

extends

As you can see, two new keywords now appear: super and extends. You use extends to assign the derived class to the superclass. Consequently, the derived class inherits all the methods and attributes from the superclass, which can be used as if they were in the derived class. All other members of the derived class are extensions. The ABAP Workbench follows this same principle within the Class Builder, using the same keywords.

super

super() in the constructor calls the constructor of the superclass and passes the parameters on to it. Note that super() must always be the first statement in the subclass constructor. You can also use super to address a member of the superclass explicitly from within the subclass, for example:

```
super.setusefulLife(20000);
```

This usage is similar to the keyword this. It is necessary whenever members of the derived class overload identically named members of the superclass, which means they cannot be invoked using only their names.

Inheritance is a central feature of object-oriented programming in Java, and is used extensively. You cannot form multiple superclasses of a derived class in Java, however; only simple hierarchy formation between classes is possible.

Hiding Attributes

You can define an instance or class attribute in a subclass that has the same name of an attribute inherited from a superclass in order to hide the inherited attributes. If you defined an additional attribute called usefulLife in class CompanyCar, for example, this would hide the inherited usefulLife attribute, and you would have to use keyword super to access it. You can also use a cast to convert a subclass to a superclass in order to access hidden attributes:

```
CompanyCar car = new CompanyCar(20000,5,"BMW");
System.out.println(((Resource) car).costPerHour);
```

The attribute of class Resource, not of class CompanyCar, is now accessed.

Class attributes behave similarly to instance attributes in their hide response, with the exception, of course, that class attributes still cannot be accessed uniquely even if the class name is invoked.

Overwriting Methods

In addition to extending classes with new methods, you can overwrite and specialize superclass methods from within the subclass:

```
public void output() {
  System.out.println("This " + this.brand
    +"company car has: ");
  System.out.println(this.remainingOperatingTime
    + " hours of remaining operating time, ");
  System.out.println(this.costsPerHour
    + " i costs per hour ");
  if (this.available==true) {
    System.out.println(" and is available.");
  } else {
    System.out.println(" and is not available.");
  }
}
```

Within the Class Builder in the ABAP Workbench, this process is called *redefining a method*.

Here, the overwritten output() method of class Resource can be accessed only with a preceding super. If the method is called for a class object, the overwriting version is used. Class methods can only be hidden, but not overwritten. In most cases, however, class methods should be called with a preceding class name to avoid potential problems. Class methods cannot overwrite instance methods.

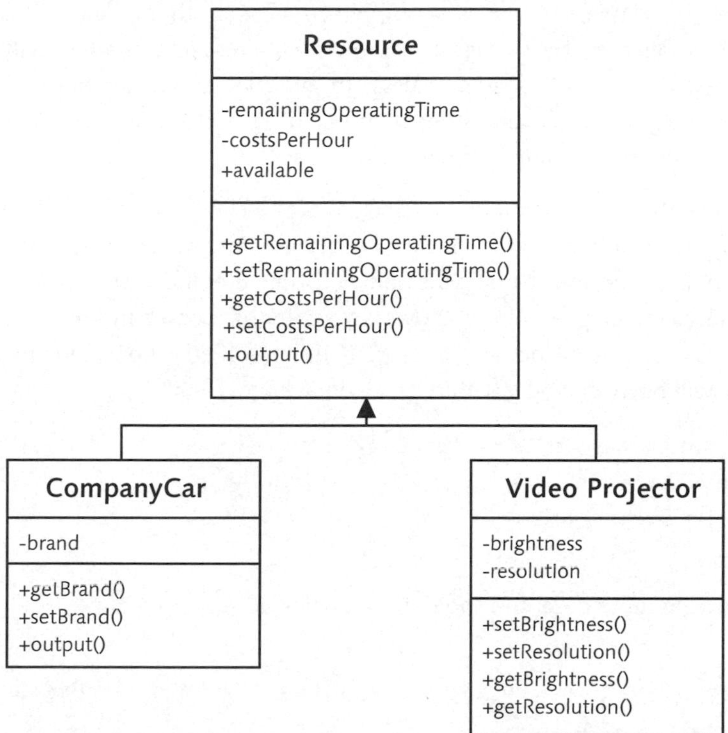

Figure 4.3 Inheritance

4.2.14 Preventing Overwriting and Inheritance

final

You can use keyword `final` for more than just defining constants. If you place `final` before a class signature, it prevents inheritance for that class:

```
final class CompanyCar {..}
```

No other derived classes can be formed from the preceding class.

If you want to prevent a method from being overwritten, you can also add `final` to the signature:

```
public final void output() {..}
```

These two principles are implemented at the visual level in the ABAP Workbench, but the effects are largely the same.

4.2.15 Encapsulation

To keep the programming interface of a class as clean as possible and ensure that objects are consistent, you should limit the visibility of the members of classes, or even completely classes themselves. This approach is called *encapsulating* data. The visibility restrictions affect only other classes that want external access. In general, every member of a class can always access every other member of that class. Java provides several modifiers for limiting visibility and access.

Visibility

You can use the `public` modifier to declare that a class, an interface (see next chapter), or a member is visible to everyone. The modifier `private` permits only a member to be accessed by other members of the same class. The modifier `protected` allows access by all classes in the same package, as well as all derived classes. If no modifier is specified, the member will be visible only within its own package.

```
public int setusefulLife(int life) {..}
private static char abc;
protected String brand;
...
```

The following table describes the dependencies:

Meaning	private	none	protected	public
Visible within its own class	Yes	Yes	Yes	Yes
Visible for derived classes in same package	No	Yes	Yes	Yes
Visible for non-derived classes in same package	No	Yes	Yes	Yes
Visible for derived classes in other packages	No	No	Yes	Yes
Visible for non-derived classes in other packages	No	No	No	Yes

Table 4.14 Visibility in Java

In addition, the access modifier of the class has priority over the access modifier for the class members for the `public` modifier. Therefore, if a method is declared as `public`, but the corresponding class does not have a modifier, the visibility rules when no modifier is specified (which is not possible in ABAP) also apply to the method.

Inheritance behaves similarly to visibility: Members that have been defined private members cannot be inherited.

4.2.16 Abstract Classes and Methods

Abstract classes contain at least one abstract method without an implementation. Abstract classes and methods are used to form higher-level basic classes that cannot (and should not) be instantiated themselves. Therefore, abstract constructors are impossible by definition. At least one method of an abstract method has not been implemented, and consists only of the method signature and closing semicolon. When other classes inherit the abstract methods, they must implement them; otherwise, they'll become abstract classes themselves.

abstract

You use the keyword abstract to make classes and methods abstract. If a class contains an abstract method, the class must also be defined as abstract. Static methods cannot be abstract, converse to ABAP Objects.

Let's assume that we now want to model a projector, in addition to a company car. To do so, we can define our Resource class as an abstract superclass that contains all the similarities between company car and projector.

You already implemented class CompanyCar in Section 4.2.13. Now, you only have to extend its signature:

```
class CompanyCar extends Resource {..}
```

The abstract class Resource could now resemble the following:

```
abstract class Resource {
  int usefulLife;
  abstract int getRemainingOperatingTime();
  abstract void setRemainingOperatingTime(

  int remainingOperatingTime);
  abstract void output();
}
```

You cannot use the keyword final with abstract classes, because an abstract class without derived classes does not make sense.

4.2.17 Interfaces

Interfaces are a special form of abstract classes that contain only interface definitions; that is, they don't contain any method headers as implementations. They cannot be instantiated and, therefore, don't have constructors either. Interfaces are always implicitly public and cannot be affected by modifiers. Moreover, all the attributes of an interface are implicitly assigned the keywords `final` and `static`. Therefore, an interface defines what has to be done, but not how to do it:

```
public interface CostControl {
  public void setcostPerYear(int costs,
                             int years);
  public int getcostPerYear();
}
```

implements

This is left up to the classes, which implement the interface in the class signature with keyword `implements`. All the methods that are defined in the interface must be implemented in the corresponding class. If just one method is not implemented, the class implicitly becomes an abstract class and cannot be instantiated.

```
public class CompanyCar implements CostControl {
  // previous class definition
  int costPerYear;
  public void setcostPerYear(int costs, int years) {
    // Implementation of method from interface
    this.costPerYear = costs / years;
  }
  public int getcostPerYear() {
    // Implementation of method from interface
    return this.costPerYear;
  }
}
```

Implementing Multiple Classes

A class can also implement multiple interfaces. If this occurs, the interfaces are separated by commas in the signature. This is different from the `extends` clause, which can contain only one argument. Multiple inheritance is not supported in Java, therefore, a class can inherit values from only one superclass, not several. Interfaces provide a way to pass interface definitions and constants on to other classes independently of the inheritance mechanism. The methods have to be implemented again in every class, however. Therefore, it may be advisable to define an abstract superclass in which several methods are already implemented, but you will have to observe the restrictions involved with inheritance in this case.

4.2.18 Summary of the Most Important Modifiers

Table 4.13 summarizes the most important Java modifiers.

Modifier	Use	Meaning
`abstract`	Class Interface Method	Defines a class, interface, or method as abstract. The implementation must take place in derived classes. An interface is always implicitly abstract.
`final`	Class Method Attribute Variable	Defines a class that cannot be derived. If final appears in the signature of a method, that method cannot be overwritten. final interacts with fields and local variables to transform them into constants.
`private`	Member	private members can only be accessed from within their own class.
`protected`	Member	protected members can only be accessed from within their own package and in derived classes.
`public`	Class Interface Member	Indicates that a class, interface, or member can be accessed anywhere. If a class is not public, its members cannot be public either.
`static`	Class Method Attribute	When classes are involved, static only makes sense for inner classes (which are not discussed in this book). static turns methods into static class methods and attributes into static class attributes.
`synchronized`	Method	Indicates the method is available to only one thread at a time.
`transient`	Attribute	Important for serializing objects. Attributes with this modifier are not serialized.
none	Class Interface Member	If no modifier is placed before a class, interface, or method, it is visible only within its package.

Table 4.15 The Most Important Modifiers

4.2.19 Programming Conventions

Naming Conventions

The naming conventions for identifiers are generally recognized; you should follow them all the time. Adhering to the conventions will make it easier for everyone else to read and maintain the source text. The names should be as brief and descriptive as possible, except for globally visible class names, where longer, mnemonic identifiers are preferred to identify the purpose of the class instantly. The same applies to class attributes and constants. Method names have restricted visibility and can therefore have shorter names. Avoid using abbreviations whenever possible, unless they're widely used and understood. Identifiers for local variables, such as index variables, do not have to be mnemonic and can therefore be kept short. While the dollar sign ($) is allowed in identifiers, you should avoid it whenever possible. Similarly, although names can use the entire Unicode character set, we recommend restricting yourself to English terms.

Package names must be unique. Therefore, one established convention is to use the inverse name of your Internet domain as a prefix.

Class names always begin with an uppercase letter, followed by a mix of uppercase and lowercase. Each word in the name begins with a capital letter.

Interface names follow the same conventions as class names. If an interface characterizes a class, an adjective is used, such as "executable" or "accessible."

Method names always begin with a lowercase letter, followed by a mix of uppercase and lowercase. Each additional word in the name begins with a capital letter. The first word is usually a verb (such as "set,","get," "output," and so on).

Attribute names follow the same conventions as methods, but constant attributes follow other rules: They are written in all caps. If a constant name consists of several words, they are separated by underscores. Attribute names should always be selected to describe their own function or content.

Parameter names and local variables follow the same naming conventions as attributes. However, you should keep parameters as short as possible—ideally one word that describes its purpose—as they also appear in the interface definition.

Naming Conventions under ABAP

In contrast to Java, in which the naming conventions are highly case-sensitive, the development objects in ABAP are all managed in all caps. Therefore, the typical Java conventions cannot be followed. The underscore (_) is generally used to separate multiword names.

Documentation Conventions

To document APIs of customer classes, Java provides a special comment type, the *doc comment*. You should place doc comments directly before the definition of a class, interface, method, or attribute. You start a doc comment with /** and conclude it with */. In contrast to the conventional multiline comment, doc comments support using some HTML tags, as well as several specific doc comment tags:

```
/**
* This class defines a <i>company car</i>.
* It is a subclass of <i>Resource</i>.
* @author SNP AG
* @version 1.0
*/
class CompanyCar extends Resource {
  /**
  *  Attribute contains the brand of the company car
  */
  String brand;
  int remainingOperatingTime;
  /**
  * Constructor builds a new object of class
  * CompanyCar.
  * @param brand Manufacturer and Type
  * @param usefulLife Number of days of useful life
  */
  CompanyCar(String brand, int remainingOperatingTime){
    this.brand = brand;
    this.remainingOperatingTime= remainingOperatingTime;
  }
  /**
  *  Method returns the useful life of the company car.
  /*
  public int getRemainingOperatingTime() {
    return this.remainingOperatingTime;
  }
  /**
  * Method calculates the useful life of the company car
  * @param life redefines the useful life of
  * the company car
  */
  public void setRemainingOperatingTime(

  int remainingOperatingTime) {
```

```
        this.remainingOperatingTime= remainingOperatingTime;
    }
}
```

HTML Tags Use HTML tags only for simple text formatting. Do not use <a> tags for links, as there is a special doc comment tag for this purpose ({@link}). You should also consider that *javadoc*, a documentation generator that is part of the development environment, can integrate the doc comments to form a more complex HTML document, to which special conventions apply.

Doc Comment Tags Doc comment tags all begin with the at symbol (@). *javadoc* transforms them into HTML tags internally. The following tags are supported:

Tag	Arguments	Meaning
`@author`	Name	Name of the author. Should be specified before class and interface definitions, but not before methods or attributes. If an object has more than one author, the authors' names should be listed in chronological order, each preceded by `@author`.
`@version`	Number	The version number. Should be specified for every class/interface definition.
`@param`	Name, description	Parameters of a method or constructor. Doc comments for methods must use `@param` to document every parameter. The comment sequence must correspond to the sequence of parameters used in the signature.
`@return`	Description	Return statement in methods with return value. Should be used before every method with a `return` statement; do not use in doc comments before classes, interfaces, or attributes.
`@exception`, `@throws`	Class name, description	An exception that is handled within a method. Contains the name of the exception and a description of the handling. If several exceptions are handled, use multiple `@exception` tags. Do not use this tag before classes, interfaces, or attributes.
`@see`	Reference	Adds a reference to other documentation in a separate section. References in printed form are set in double quotes. You can use <a> tags to set references to other digital documentation. You can also refer to packages, classes, methods, and fields in the Java source text itself with the following syntax: `@see characteristic label`

Table 4.16 Doc Comment Tagss

Tag	Arguments	Meaning

		`label` is optional and places a name over the actual reference. Characteristic can be:
		`Package name`
		`Class name`
		`Class name#Method name`
		`Class name#Method name(parameters)`
		`#Method name`
		`#Method name(parameter types)`
		`Class name#Attribute name`
		`#Attribute name`
		`#Method name` can be used only for non-overloaded methods in the same class. You can use `#Method name(parameter types)` for overloaded methods in the same class. The `class name` can also be an interface.

`{@link}`	Reference	Similar to `@see`, except that *javadoc* does not create a separate section, but instead inserts the reference directly in the text. This tag can be used anywhere in doc comments. The curly brackets are required to set the tag apart from any surrounding HTML tags.
`@deprecated`	Description	Indicates obsolete elements that should no longer be used. Its description should contain the reasons why the element is obsolete and refer to a more suited class. The Java compiler recognizes this tag and issues warning messages if the element is used in the program.
`@since`	Version	Version number of the API from which the element is included. It should appear before every class and interface definition, as well as before any subsequently added methods and attributes.
`@serial`	Description	Should appear before every attribute whose class implements the `Serializable` interface and for which `transient` does not exclude serialization. The text should describe the function of the serialized attribute.

Table 4.16 Doc Comment Tagss (cont.)

5 Development Tools and Objects

Because the origins and paradigms vary widely for ABAP and Java, their development tools differ as well. To use both languages efficiently, you need to know the optimal tools for ABAP and Java.

5.1 ABAP

This section is a brief introduction to the ABAP development environment and to programming with ABAP. As in Chapter 4, here, too, we don't intend to teach you ABAP; we simply want to refresh your memory of ABAP before comparing it to the equivalent functions in Java.

History

We will first present a brief history of the development of the SAP System, particularly the development track of the user interface.

Two different approaches existed within SAP's product range in the 90s: the mainframe-based R/2 System and the client/server technology of the R/3 System. Both approaches were aimed at developing robust, open, autonomous business software. The SAP GUI (graphical user interface) was introduced as the presentation layer starting in R/3 Release 3.0. This new user interface boasted a host of novel features, such as pushbuttons, table controls, and more.

Internet Capability

The R/3 System has been Internet-capable since Release 3.1. This enables end users to communicate directly with an R/3 application through a Web browser, providing an efficient method for communication among enterprises, customers, and vendors. From the technical perspective, an Internet layer was integrated between the application and presentation layers. In particular, the following components, which were introduced in this release, deserve special mention: ITS (Internet Transaction Server), IAC (Internet Application Component), and BAPI (Business Application Programming Interfaces).

Release 4.0 does not provide any new features for the frontend. Instead, the ABAP programming language was enhanced to support object-oriented language constructs, the ABAP Objects.

EnjoySAP

SAP began adding new application functions again starting in Release 4.6. EnjoySAP altered the appearance of the GUI. The control technology (tree and grid controls) now enables simpler navigation using tree controls (like in the Microsoft Explorer), while the ALV (ABAP List Viewer) displays lists in a user-friendly format. This does not mean that developers will have to spend an enormous amount of time on new developments; instead, SAP supplies general, reusable functions as reuse components. Users can now also create a list of their favorites—functions and applications—in personal menus.

MVC and BSP

In Web Application Server 6.20 and later, the focus was on separating the application from the presentation layer more consistently. This concept is called MVC (Model View Controller). The Business Server Pages (BSPs) were introduced as the new development components for the presentation layer.

Java Release 6.30

We should add that the Java Release 6.30, which was never released for general use, did not implement any new features in the ABAP area. However, it did provide a new way to develop SAP applications—a new, Java-based integrated development environment (Java IDE) that provides many of the new features that are already recognizable from the ABAP Workbench. New ABAP development tools were added in Release 6.40. In particular, a conversion tool is available to convert conventional screens (dynamic programs) into Web Dynpros.

5.1.1 The ABAP Development Environment

The ABAP Workbench integrates all tools for developing programs, function modules, ABAP Dictionary objects, and other development objects. It covers all the phases of a development project, including management of organizations, transports, and versions.

The ABAP Workbench has many useful features, including:

- Simple navigation to different development objects; a list of favorites can also be defined.
- Clear display of all components (events, subroutines, data elements, and so on) that belong to a development object. This makes for a well-defined structure of the developed program, function group, etc.
- You no longer have to use the earlier, unwieldy transaction codes to access the different development tools.
- Central development of all major components required for a software project.
- Components for organizing software projects, such as a transport system and versioning.

The development environment has a wide range of functions, the most important of which are introduced briefly below (they are discussed in more detail in later sections):

Development Environment Functions

- **ABAP Dictionary**
  A tool for maintaining and defining ABAP Dictionary objects, such as database tables, views, data types (simple data types, structures, table types), search help functions, and lock objects
- **Data Modeler**
  Development tool for creating and modeling data models
- **ABAP Editor**
  One of the main software development tools, for creating and editing ABAP programs, module pools, reports, and so on
- **Function Builder**
  Development environment for creating and editing function modules; also provides a test environment for function modules
- **Class Builder**
  Development environment for creating, editing, and testing global classes and interfaces
- **BAPI Explorer**
  You use the BAPI Explorer to develop BAPIs (Business Programming Application Interfaces), which are used as interfaces for different applications (Internet applications, methods for Business Workflow, and so on). The BAPI Explorer consists of two areas: the hierarchy area, to display components, and the navigation area, where you can access the other tools in the Workbench.
- **Reuse Library**
  A library of reusable functions, with example coding. Examples of reuse components include the ALV (ABAP List Viewer), customer containers, and trees.
- **Modification Browser**
  Modification wizard for changing or enhancing the SAP browser
- **User interface**
  A tool for developing user interfaces
- **Business Object Builder**
  An environment for creating, changing, and displaying business objects
- **Transport Organizer**
  A set of tools used to manage transport requests/tasks

- **Runtime analysis**
  A test environment for transactions, programs, and function modules
- **SQL trace**
  A program used to manage and analyze SQL logging

Additional tools also exist for documentation and for translating application texts.

Object Navigator

The Object Navigator is central to development, and therefore to the entire software cycle as well. To start it, enter Transaction code SE80 or choose menu path **Tools · Overview · Object Navigator**.

The Object Navigator is divided into several sections: the browser view, the object view, and the tools. These views are described individually below:

- **Browser view**

  For navigation to the corresponding results lists. You can select the following objects directly:

  - MIME Repository
    List of MIME (Multipurpose Internet Mail Extensions) objects
  - Repository Browser
    The Repository objects (application hierarchy, packages, program, function group, class/interface, Internet service, BSP applications, BSP extensions, inactive objects, local objects) are displayed in an object list.
  - Repository Information System
    Used to search for objects in the SAP System. The object types are arranged in a hierarchy list.
  - Tag Browser
    Displays tags for Web applications. A selection of templates and wizards for HTML business functions, BSP extensions, and BSP directives.
  - Transport Organizer
    Displays transport requests and the objects assigned to a request. The Transport Organizer displays all Workbench and Customizing requests for the user. You can also display individual transport requests and tasks.

- **Object view**
  - Object list
    The corresponding object types for the selected browser area are displayed.
  - Object list selection
    Different views are available for each browser area. The search function is supported only for the Repository Browser and MIME Repository.
- **Tool view**
  Displays the individual tools, such as the ABAP Editor, Function Builder, and so on.

5.1.2 ABAP Dictionary and Data Modeler

ABAP Dictionary

The central development tool is the ABAP Dictionary (Transaction code SE11 or menu path **Tools · ABAP Workbench · Development · Dictionary**). The most important functions performed by the ABAP Dictionary are managing data definitions and creating and changing user-defined types, which can be used in programs, screens, and interfaces of function modules. The tables and views that are defined in the ABAP Dictionary are then saved in the database. Because the ABAP Dictionary is actively integrated in the development and runtime environments, changing the definition of a data element also affects the programs and interface definitions that use it.

The different object types that you can create and maintain in the ABAP Dictionary are introduced below.

Data Types

You define data elements by specifying the data type, length, and (possibly) number of decimal places. Data elements describe semantic characteristics in a business context, and are used to maintain field labels, flags for writing change documents, and—through the documentation—the **F4** help.

Structures consist of components, which can have any type.

Table types describe the internal structure of a table. We differentiate between the different table types depending on how they are accessed:

- Standard table
- Sorted table
- Hashed table
- Index table

These table types are used in reports and screens, as well as for typing interface parameters in function modules.

Database Tables

Nearly all technical and commercial information in the SAP System is saved in database tables. Therefore, defining and maintaining database tables are primary tasks of the development environment.

To create a table, proceed as follows: In the initial screen of the ABAP Dictionary, enter a name in the database table field and click on the **Create** button. Make sure your chosen name lies in the customer namespace. The **Maintain Table** screen then appears. You now have to enter a short description for the table, along with technical information regarding the delivery class and for subsequent maintenance. Then, select the **Fields** tab to maintain the fields, assign data elements, and specify the primary key. You can define foreign key relationships to create links to other tables. After you save and activate the settings, the table is known in the runtime environment.

You can also copy and delete existing tables from within the initial screen of the ABAP Dictionary.

Views

Types of Views

The system features four different types of views that you can create in the ABAP Dictionary:

- **Database view**
  Database views can represent multiple tables. You define them using the relational operations selection, join, and projection. You are not allowed to insert, change, or delete information in this view.
- **Projection view**
  Projection views let you hide or rename some of the fields in a table. You can insert, change, and delete information.

- **Maintenance view**
  Maintenance views help to simplify user maintenance of table contents.
- **Help view**
  Help views select the value sets for the **F4** help.

Domain

Unlike a data element, which contains the semantic information of a data field, a domain defines its technical characteristics—such as data type, field length, and (possibly) number of decimal places. You also define the output characteristics here. Domains provide information about the value range, which is defined as fixed values. You can create a domain directly in the initial screen of the ABAP Dictionary.

Search Help

There are two different types of search help—elementary search help and collective search help:

- **Elementary search help**
  Defines the selection and display of value sets for a data field or screen field.
- **Collective search help**
  A grouping of several elementary search help functions, which creates several different search paths for the user.

Lock Object

You can create lock objects to avoid concurrent, inconsistent access to the same object by different users. These objects enable you to set and release business locks.

5.1.3 Development Objects

This section introduces the most important development objects of the SAP Web Application Server (SAP Web AS). It also covers the new concepts that were implemented in Release 6.20.

Package

The concept of development classes was fundamentally revised and replaced by the package concept in Release 6.10. Packages are an enhancement of development classes, with extended semantics. A package is used for technical modularization, encapsulation, and decoupling. The packages group the development elements together—function modules, BAPIs, classes, ABAP programs, types, and so on. Contrary to development classes, packages can also be nested in a hierarchy.

Reports and Programs

You can display and edit programs in the editor of the ABAP Workbench. The editor is the main tool for editing program texts. Alternatively, you can also use Transaction SE38. The following development elements can be processed with this tool:

- ABAP program source coding: reports, include modules, module pools, and so on
- Screen flow logic
- Logical databases
- Function groups
- Global development elements for ABAP Objects: interface pools and class pools
- Modifications to standard SAP programs. A special Modification Wizard is integrated in the ABAP Editor for this purpose.

The program coding of an ABAP development object is defined in the database of the R/3 System, along with the generated runtime objects. The ABAP program editor is a fully integrated tool within the development environment, which means when other objects are included or declared, you can refer to them directly.

Checking and Testing Programs

The ABAP Editor features several different functions for checking and testing the developed programs:

- The *syntax check* verifies that keywords use the correct syntax.
- Certain checks are not performed during the standard check due to runtime limitations. These checks can be carried out using the *extended program check*, which also checks interfaces against external program sections that can cause runtime errors.
- The *code inspector* targets any potential problems. In particular, it checks performance criteria such as index access, table buffering, and so on.
- The *debugging* function is an integrated test tool in the ABAP Workbench. Developers use this tool to check the program logic and local-

ize errors in the source coding. The debugging function lets you execute single steps in an ABAP program, one after another, checking the processed logic and results of each individual statement. You can also use it for *Business Server Pages* (BSP). There are different ways to start the debugger: You can either start the program in debugging mode or set a *breakpoint* in the appropriate place in the program.

- A technical limit applies to the generation of an ABAP program. This limit can be displayed by the *generation limit*. If this limit is exceeded or in a critical range, the program cannot be generated or executed.
- The *runtime analysis* measures the CPU times for the program, especially the processing time of the passed coding and the table accesses.
- The *performance trace* records database accesses, locking activities, and remote calls from reports and transactions in a trace file. The file is output as a list. You can define a filter to limit which data is recorded in the performance trace. This allows you to record individual accesses to the database, for example.

The ABAP Editor also has other features that make coding easier (Pretty Printer, add patterns, and so on).

Screen Painter

The *Screen Painter* and *Menu Painter* tools are used to design screens and their flow logic. The *Screen Painter* consists of four components:

- The **Characteristics** define the attributes, such as screen type, next screen, and other settings.
- The **Element List** displays all the fields and field attributes.
- The **Layout** lets you display all the elements of a screen in a graphical user interface. The graphical elements of a screen include the following objects: text fields, input/output fields, radio buttons, checkboxes, pushbuttons, frames, table controls, custom controls, and tab strips. Wizards are provided for creating table control and tab strip elements.
- The **Flow Logic** is the main component of the screen definition; the flow logic of the screen is implemented here.

The technical term "dynpro," or "dynamic program," refers to the combination of a screen and its flow logic. Screen Painter uses a procedural programming language that differs from ABAP. This language is interpreted by a screen processor, not the ABAP processor.

The Menu Painter is the tool for creating and maintaining user interfaces for ABAP programs. It is independent of the screen, which means different user interfaces can be used for the same screen and vice versa. The user interface is defined by the components GUI status and GUI title. The user interface contains the following elements:

- Title bar: The top screen line contains the window title for the displayed component
- Menu bar
- Standard toolbar: Contains the standard icons
- Application toolbar: Contains all the possible icons and pushbuttons defined by the developer

The menu bar, standard toolbar, and application toolbar can be defined with function key settings. These elements are defined by the GUI status. Not all elements of the user interface are always required, for example, only the application toolbar and function key settings are required to create a dialog window.

Function Groups and Function Modules

Function modules are generally available routines that all programs can use. They are saved centrally in the Repository and are therefore available systemwide. Like subroutines, function modules encapsulate the program coding, while also providing a well-defined interface for exchanging data. Every function module is assigned to a function group. Each function group, *<functgrp>*, has a main program called *SAPL<functgrp>*. The main program contains references to the include objects, where the global data and program text of the individual function modules are defined. In general, function modules that are related to one another should be saved together in function groups.

The Structure of Function Modules

Each function module is divided into the following components in the ABAP Workbench:

- **Administration information**
  Name of the function module, short text to describe its function, membership of a specific function group, process type (regular function module, remote-capable module, update module), and development class
- **Interface parameters**
  Elementary data objects, data types, and so forth are available for the import, export, changing, and table interfaces. You can also define optional interface parameters. You can use exception parameters to catch errors and pass them on to the calling program.

- **Source text**
  You can select the **Source Text** tab to start the ABAP Editor and enter the program text. Place the program text between the `FUNCTION` and `ENDFUNCTION` keywords.
- **Documentation**
  You can save documentation for the individual interface parameters and the function module.

Once the function module has been saved and is active in the Repository, it can be called from within any program. To do so, the appropriate actual parameters have to be passed on and any exceptions must be caught.

You can also create remote-capable (RFC-capable) function modules. These functions make it possible to access the R/3 System where the function module is located from within a Java application or a different R/3 System, for example. To do so, the function module must be defined as RFC-capable in its process type.

You can also set the process type to **Update Module** in the characteristics for the function module. Update modules only have an import interface. Exception parameters and export parameters are not allowed. The function module is given all the information needed for the database change through the import interface.

Class/Interface

ABAP Objects

SAP extended the ABAP vocabulary to include ABAP Objects starting in Release 4.0. Object orientation, or object-oriented programming (OOP), is a problem-solving method that maps actual business objects within a software model. The concepts of OOP were already discussed in the Java context (see Section 4.2.2).

As in Java, the basic object types in ABAP Objects are classes and interfaces. These object types can be defined locally in a program text, which means they are visible only in that program's context, or can be saved in the Repository, where they are visible globally. Any program can use global classes and interfaces.

You can use the Class Builder to define and maintain global ABAP classes and interfaces. The Class Builder performs the following tasks:

- Tool for creating, testing, and managing global classes and interfaces
- Generation of the main program
- Management of the includes where the program text is saved

Structure of the Class Builder:

- **Basic data maintenance**
  Defines the object types and corresponding components.
- **Class Editor**
  Takes you directly to the ABAP Editor, where the methods are implemented.
- **Class Browser**
  Simplifies navigation via the class library, sorted by application component.
- **Test environment**
  Enables you to test the developed class outside of a specific program context.

Internet Service

Web-Capable Applications

The Web Application Builder tool enables you to create Web development objects within the ABAP Workbench. Existing R/3 transactions need these objects to run them as Web transactions in the Web browser (inside-out approach). You can also use the Web Application Builder as an IDE for MiniApps (outside-in approach).

The Web Application Builder is a development tool that is fully integrated in the ABAP Workbench. The Web development objects defined here, such as service files, HTML templates, and MIME objects, are created in the R/3 Repository and integrated with the Transport Organizer.

Its functions include:

- Creating Internet services for existing R/3 transactions
- Creating MiniApps and defining administration data for workplace integration
- Creating and implementing Web applications based on the flow logic
- Generating HTML templates for screens of transactions (these templates contain standard HTML and HTMLB statements, which emulate the screen layout)
- Editing the generated HTML template with the HTML and HTMLB vocabulary, to enhance them further
- Creating independent objects for JavaScript files
- Including MIME objects (icons, graphics, Java applets, animations, and so on) as additional layout design objects

- Creating language-specific texts (language resources)
- Creating language-specific MIME objects
- Publishing the services or individual service components on the Internet Transaction Server (ITS)
- Running the complete Web application, launched from the ABAP Workbench
- Connecting to the Transport Organizer

BSP Applications

An independent Web server was integrated in the SAP Basis starting in Release 6.10. The server supports BSP (Business Server Pages), the new tag language developed by SAP to make it easy to design and program dynamic Web content. BSP is similar to other server-side tag languages like JSP, ASP, and PHP. The special thing about BSP, however, is that it uses ABAP as its integrated programming language, in contrast to Java and Visual Basic for JSP and ASP, respectively. The integration of ABAP gives it a significant advantage over the previously used ITS technology. The close integration between Web server, tag language, and ABAP runtime (where all application logic runs in the SAP System) is reflected in the name of the system itself—the SAP Web Application Server.

The Web Application Builder has been introduced as a new development tool for BSP applications. Web development is integrated completely in the Repository Navigator. Consequently, BSP applications can access Repository objects such as function modules, classes, BAPIs, or database objects, and are also embedded in the SAP Transport and Correction System.

Functions of the Web Application Builder

The Web Application Builder features the following range of functions:

- Creating and changing BSP applications and the corresponding BSP pages
- Layout editor for BSP pages in HTML and the scripting languages ABAP and JavaScript
- Integration of an event handler in ABAP (for data retrieval, for example)
- Definition of page-related data
- Integration of MIME objects

BSP applications are independent Web applications with defined presentation, flow, and application logic. Therefore, BSP applications meet the requirements of the MVC design paradigm. The controller technology provides for separation between the presentation logic and the application logic of the BSP application.

The presentation level, where the data is actually displayed, consists of a certain sequence of Web pages, each of which contains different elements:

- **Static Web page**
  Contains only HTML coding; no server-side scripting languages are used.
- **Dynamically generated Web pages**
  These pages are requested by the application server at runtime and integrated in a Web site.
- **MIME objects**
  Integrates specific elements in the Web pages, including images, icons, and so on.

In order for a Web application to run on the client, several components have to work collectively. The individual components that are responsible for the control and flow of such BSP applications are introduced below.

Components of a BSP Application

A BSP application consists of all or some of the following components:

- **Application class**
  A BSP application has a series of different development objects, one of which is the *application class*. The application class is a regular ABAP Objects class. As such, it can possess any methods, attributes, and events the developer chooses. A typical task that the developer must perform is to save and present data across BSP pages as attributes, while encapsulating the logic used in the BSP application in methods. Consequently, multiple BSP applications can easily reuse the same application class, to create a single business application with multiple user interfaces (each specialized for a different device, for example), without having to replicate the business or application logic.
- **Controller**
  The controller is a component of the MVC design and the connector between model and view. The controller is responsible for handling events such as initialization and request processing. The controller

must also manage and transfer data, and direct the data to the various views.

- **Business Server Pages**
  Business Server Pages are the basis of the content displayed in Web pages. BSPs consist of static HTML coding and dynamic server scripts, which permit the dynamic creation of Web content. A BSP implements the complete life cycle of a Web page, combining options for event handling, data retrieval, and data display in a single component. *Page attributes* make it possible to use the same data globally in a BSP. When defined as *automatically fillable*, they can copy form data or URL parameters directly, saving developers from having to do so manually.
- **Navigation**
  The navigation structure is used to define navigation requests. They describe the beginning and end of a request—that is, the navigation from the start page to the next page. This page assignment in navigation requests results in a strictly formal description of the navigation diagram within a BSP application. This makes it possible to change the flow control of a BSP application without changing the coding.
- **MIME objects** (Multipurpose Internet Mail Extensions)
  MIMEs are extensions of the original Internet e-mail protocol that make it possible to exchange different types of data over the Internet. The data formats vary widely and include audio, video and image data, cascading style sheets (CSS), application programs, and ASCII files. The object types are processed by either plug-ins or integrated applications. Each new BSP application creates an identically-named MIME directory, which is used to store all the application-specific MIME objects. The MIMEs are managed centrally in this repository.

  Another concept involves *themes*, which serve as definitions that replace MIME objects. Consequently, the appearance of BSP applications can be changed later on without having to change the presentation logic. This makes it possible to replace the MIME objects with objects in the local file system. The theme concept enables subsequent layout changes to BSP applications, along with customization to individual demands. A theme is created as an independent development object in the Web Application Builder, and serves as a container for all the defined replacements.

- **Views**
  Views are responsible for only the layout (or visualization) of the application data. They are similar to pages, but don't have event handlers or automatic page attributes. Regular page attributes are possible, and are filled by the controller. The controllers route the views' calls and communicate with a model. A view's life cycle is determined by its corresponding controller. When a view knows the type of controller class (see the **Properties** tab of the view), the view can access the attributes of that controller class.
- **Event handler**
  The event handler is part of the flow control, which determines the temporal and logical flow of an application. Event handlers are executed at defined times in a defined sequence during the life cycle of a BSP page. The event handler is implemented in ABAP Objects and allows access to certain objects at BSP runtime. A series of events are processed in a specific sequence during page processing. Individually, we differentiate between: `onCreate`, `onRequest`, `onInitialization`, `onLayout`, `onManipulation`, `onInputProcessing`, and `onDestroy`.

Stateful Versus Stateless

Two state models are available for use in BSP applications. We differentiate between the stateful (context-oriented) and stateless models. The functions are provided by the ICF (Internet Communication Framework). An active BSP application is referred to as a "BSP session."

A stateful BSP application (comparable with a conventional SAP transaction with screen change) is executed in a single context across all user interactions. Therefore, the application context is held beyond the response. During further execution of the application, a corresponding context is rolled into the work process. As a result, data entered by the user or calculated by the application over the course of the process can be held over the entire life cycle of the session. Data retention is implemented through the application class, which is provided by the SAP Web Application Server.

Stateful mode has both advantages and disadvantages. In general, data is retrieved only once and then buffered as attributes in the application class. This data can be accessed simply in the subsequent pages, which avoids frequent database reads. Of course, this improves performance on the server side. In turn, this produces another advantage: Fewer requests to the back-end system means a lower network load. The disadvantage of this approach is that the corresponding context has to be saved for each session, which generates a commensurately higher load on the SAP Web AS.

In contrast to the stateful model, the stateless model does not block contexts on the SAP Web AS for an unnecessarily long time. As soon as a request is processed, all assigned resources are released immediately, which means the resources are occupied only as long as it takes to process the request itself. The disadvantage of this approach is that the application context has to be created frequently, so you pay for the advantage in memory with a disadvantage in runtime.

Life Cycle of BSP Applications

The following steps take place when you start a BSP application: First, a URL is entered in the address bar of the Web browser. It defines the BSP application to start. Various URL parameters can be set to define the response of the application, and are saved in the characteristics of the BSP pages. Entering the URL sends a request to the BSP application. The runtime environment on the Web Application Server (BSP Engine) determines the requested application and the corresponding BSPs. This may or may not be followed by a logon to the SAP Web AS, depending on the configuration.

The requested BSP page is now processed within the BSP runtime environment, the components run, and the processing steps in the program logic are performed. The result is a Web page that is sent back to the caller as the response process. This generation involves different phases. The events mentioned above are processed in a defined sequence, limiting a programmer's response options. The events correspond to the event handlers, which process various tasks at different times. The processing flow of a BSP application, and therefore, the order in which the different event handlers are processed, is affected by the state model, which can be either stateless or stateful. The state can be defined in the characteristics of a BSP application or be overridden dynamically at runtime (the `runtime` object is provided for the latter).

Event Handler Sequence

When a BSP is called, the runtime environment determines whether a page object has already been supplied for this page. If not, event `onCreate` is called, which creates an instance of the generated class assigned to the BSP. The developer can use the event handler to initialize data or generate any required objects. This event occurs only once in stateful mode, while the page object is generated anew each time in stateless mode.

After this step, event `onRequest` is processed. This event takes place each time a page is requested. The internal data structures are restored during this process.

The next step depends on whether the user made an entry. If so, event `onInputProcessing` is performed; if not, `onInitialization` is carried out.

Let's first examine the case without user interaction.

The `onInitialization` event is used to retrieve data, which can come from different sources. The data is collected either directly from the database or via a call of a function module or BAPI.

Once the data is available to the application, event `onLayout` is processed. This step defines the design and the presentation of the data and other involved page objects, which determines the pattern of the requested BSP page. A page consists of static (HTML) and dynamic (server-side scripting) elements. The server-side scripting can consist of both ABAP and JavaScript.

The `onManipulation` event makes it possible to intervene in the outbound data flow. It is processed after event handler `onLayout`. In stateless mode, the created page object is now destroyed; event `onDestroy` is available to process the data afterwards.

Reaction to Input

But how does the BSP application respond to a user input or navigation? Just because it can display a page does not mean the application is fully functional; users also have to be able to enter data, make selections, or simply navigate from one page to the next. To enable this, certain user actions have to be received and processed in the appropriate manner. Depending on the program logic, the result can be a new Web page, an update to the current page, or an error message. These user inputs are processed by the `onInputProcessing` event.

The `onInputProcessing` event handler is used to verify the validity of inputs, forward attributes, and define the next page for navigation. If no next page is defined, processing continues with event `onInitialization` of the page (navigation within the same BSP). If a next page has been defined, the program navigates to this new BSP. The next page can be determined from the navigation structure or specified in the program coding. The requested page is then created (using the procedure described above) and output in the user's browser. Another user interaction can now take place and the processing flow starts over. The underlying page objects are destroyed after each navigation to trigger event handler `onInputProcessing`.

The processing flow is similar in both the stateful and stateless modes, such that we only have to highlight the difference between the two models: The main difference is that the page objects are retained over the entire session. The first time a BSP is called, the `onCreate` event is executed exactly once. If navigation takes place within the BSP application, the page object remains and `onCreate` is not carried out again.

BSP Extensions

The BSP extensions concept makes it possible for you to develop your own tags for BSPs.

A BSP extension is represented by a special development object in the Workbench. This object comprises a set of related BSP elements with their corresponding attributes, and also includes references to the respective element handler classes. Each BSP element is assigned to exactly one element handler class, which implements the specific functions of that element.

Advantages

BSP extensions have the following advantages:

- You only have to develop the HTML coding once. Any changes apply to all of the assigned elements. This applies across application boundaries, which increases reusability.
- The assigned ABAP class can also contain logic for creating browser-dependent HTML coding.
- The style sheet assignments are also included in the element class. Consequently, the generated HTML coding can reference the style sheets. Global settings for style sheets are used automatically by all referencing BSP extensions, guaranteeing a standardized look and feel.
- The standard XML syntax can be checked at generation time, which means the error checks are performed at design time, and do not have to be handled as exceptions at runtime.

In particular, the strict separation between context-independent components for layout display, like the BSP extensions and their composition and then script-free BSP pages, minimizes the effort required to localize errors and implement centralized changes in projects of all sizes.

MIME Repository

Each BSP application has its own MIME repository. It can be configured with any folder structures, which are used to import the MIME objects. These objects can be referenced in the HTML coding in the BSP application, integrating them in the Web application.

All MIME repositories in all BSP applications can also be accessed centrally in the Object Navigator.

Active and Inactive Objects

Development objects are generally inactive when they are being edited; this means when a development object is included in an executed program, only the last active version is used. The newer, inactive versions of the programs that usually exist are not ignored in the program flow. Objects must be activated before they can be used. During the activation process, the coding is checked for syntax errors and, if none are found, compiled. The current version of the development object is then available for program execution.

Because inactive objects usually require additional development or correction, the developer's current worklist can also be checked for inactive objects, to access any pending developments directly. You can display a list of these objects in the Object Navigator with **Environment/Inactive Objects**.

Active Versus Executable

We should point out that an active object is not necessarily an executable object, because objects can be activated even if they have syntax errors. This makes sense, for example, when certain parts of the coding that contain syntax errors are not executed in a test case. This can be guaranteed by an ABAP language construct such as an `IF` statement that contains a condition that can never arise.

Local Objects

Objects that are needed only in the development system and not intended to be transported to the development system can be declared as local objects when they are created. Objects of this type are used primarily for the automatic generation of test data, temporary testing of development objects, or for training purposes.

5.1.4 Transport System and Versioning

If new objects are required in the R/3 development environment or the ABAP Dictionary due to business needs, they are created on demand and based on a specific request. The requirements of these new objects can change over time. There are two ways to keep up with changing requirements: You can either delete the objects and create them again, or adjust and modify the existing objects. Modifying Dictionary objects creates new object versions. The following changes are considered to be modifications: Number and type of table fields, secondary tables for aggregates and objects, different or new fields for matchcode IDs, and so on. Changes to table entries are not considered modifications.

A new version number is created for each change saved for all modified Dictionary objects that do not belong to a local development class (`$TEMP`).

Version Catalog

The version catalog is a tool in the SAP System that lets developers compare old and new versions of an object, and even restore an old version for errors. Version management also allows you to modify existing objects without activating them. Only one version is active in the SAP System; when changes are made, version management creates a temporary version that does not affect current operations. Version management also functions as a change history for modified objects and developments.

You can display the object versions using the menu in all object maintenance and display transactions. Choose **Utilities · Versions · Version Management** to call the object catalog, which contains the aforementioned functions. Figure 5.1 shows an initial screen of a modified SAP object.

```
Retrieve   Request text on/off   REMOTE comparison

Versions: Function Module /SNP/BM03_RDE_XXXXXXSQLEXEC

Version Cat Fla SAP Rel. Arch Request     Project   Date        Time     Author
Version(s) in the development database:
[x] activ           620       W01K900398            18.03.2004  16:37:26 DWITTENBECK
Version(s) in the version database:
[ ] 00017           620       W01K900421            27.02.2004  16:29:23 BNOLL
[ ] 00016           620       W01K900363            21.11.2003  14:28:26 GKRAUSS
[ ] 00015           620       W01K900350            21.11.2003  10:48:55 ASCHUENGEL
[ ] 00014           620       W01K900309            12.11.2003  09:53:03 BNOLL
[ ] 00013           620       W01K900305            12.11.2003  09:11:48 BNOLL
```

Figure 5.1 Version Catalog

We differentiate between the following types of version creation:

- " ": Version was created on request release.
- "I": Version was created by an import (status after import).
- "S": System request; a version was created based on a system request (for example, for a backup copy before opening a correction/repair or before an import).
- "U": User request; the user created an intermediate version by saving the object at any time. The next time the request is released, all existing "U" versions are summarized and replaced by a regular " " version. "U" versions can also be created for private local objects.

The **Fla SAP** column indicates the source of the versions:

- "X": Version generated or delivered by SAP.
- " ": Version created directly in a customer system.

In the initial screen of the version catalog, you can use the **Display**, **Compare**, and **Restore** functions for the individually selected object versions. You can display or hide the request texts for the relevant transport requests. You can also use RFC to compare different objects across system boundaries. Figure 5.2 shows a simple example of a version comparison.

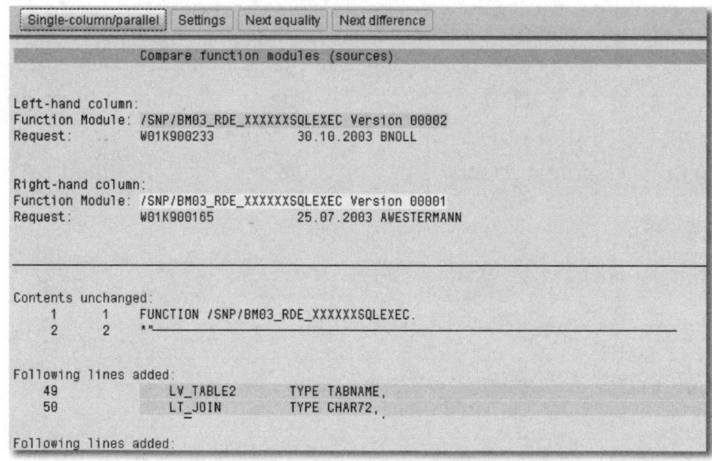

Figure 5.2 Delta Comparison with Single-Column Display

You can toggle the view between **Single-column** and **Parallel**. You can also save certain settings, such as full display or display changes only, as the defaults. Use the **Next equality** and **Next difference** buttons to navigate to the next section.

If you want to restore an older object version as the active version, you do so in object change mode. Choose **Utilities • Version Management** to call the object catalog. After you select the version to restore with the radio button on the left side of the screen and start the **Restore** function, a dialog box appears with a message indicating that the selected version will be used as the new revised version. After you confirm, you must activate the object so it is listed as the active version in the version database.

Changes to the Repository and to Customizing settings are generally recorded in change requests in the SAP System, enabling you to take advantage of the following SAP software logistics functions:

- Change history at object level
- Summary of project-specific changes to various objects
- Distribution of changes, settings, and modifications across system boundaries

Transport Layers

Transport requests are distributed along defined *transport layers*. All development projects that are carried out in an SAP System and transported to the target system(s) over the same transport routes are grouped together in one transport layer.

You define transport layers before you start your first development project, in the transport route editor of the Transport Management System (TMS). This transport layer is assigned to the development system as the default transport layer ("ZDEV" in Figure 5.3, for example). The objects delivered by SAP belong to transport layer "SAP." Typically, you need additional transport layers only if you add new development systems to your SAP system group.

We differentiate between two types of *transport routes* (see Figure 5.3):

- **Consolidation routes**

  A consolidation path is required in every transport layer to make changes transportable. The source of these consolidation routes is the development system; the transport target is the quality assurance system (or, in a two-system landscape, the production system).

  Changed objects for which a consolidation route has been configured are grouped together into transportable change requests, and can be imported into the consolidation system after the transport administrators release the requests.

  When objects are changed for which there is no consolidation path from the current SAP System, these changes are automatically saved in local change requests (or in Customizing requests without a transport target). The objects cannot be transported into other SAP Systems in this case.

Only one consolidation path can be defined for each SAP System and transport layer.

- **Delivery routes**

  After the developments have been imported into the quality assurance system, they must be transported to the production system or into multiple SAP Systems (additional training systems, for example). To do so, you must define delivery routes. Delivery routes have one source and one target system.

  By configuring a delivery route, you ensure that all change requests that are imported into the source system of a delivery route are automatically flagged for import into the target system of that delivery route.

  Depending on the structure of your system landscape, you can configure multiple delivery routes with the same source system and different target systems (parallel forwarding) or in a chain one after another (multilevel forwarding).

DEV	=	Development System
QAS	=	Quality Assurance System
PRD	=	Production System
ZDEV	=	Standard Transport Layer
SAP	=	SAP Transport Layer

Figure 5.3 Transport Routes

Transport Control

The transport control program in the Change and Transport System (CTS) ensures that all requests that are exported from the development system are flagged for import into all other SAP Systems in the same order in which they were exported. Because the same Repository object or the same Customizing settings can be contained in different requests from different stages of development, this avoids overwriting a new version with an older version.

We differentiate between the following request types, depending on the characteristics of the modified object and the transport itself:

Request Types

- **Workbench requests**
  Workbench requests are used mainly to record changes to Repository objects in the ABAP Workbench and to cross-client Customizing. They can also record changes to client-specific Customizing.

  The system settings determine transport capability and the target system. Whether changes to Repository objects are transported is contingent on a transport route from the current system having been defined for the development class of these objects.

- **Customizing requests**
  Customizing requests record the client-specific Customizing settings from a single client (= source client of the request). Customizing requests are created whenever Customizing settings are changed in a client where automatic recording of Customizing activities is active.

  In contrast to Workbench requests, the transportability of Customizing requests does not depend on which objects are recorded; depending on the system setting, all changes are either transportable or local. You define the transportability and the target system in the standard transport layer, although manual changes are possible.

- **Transport of copies**
  Use this request type to transport specific objects to another SAP System. The objects are transported in the exact version available in the current SAP System. The original location of the objects remains unchanged. The objects are not delivered to any other SAP Systems.

- **Relocation without changed development classes**
  Use this request type if object development is to take place temporarily in a different SAP System, for example, for special developments that you don't want to interrupt regular developments for and therefore have to be performed in a separate SAP System.

  A relocation without a change of development class essentially carries out the same function as the transport of copies, except that the original location of the objects is moved to the target system.

- **Relocations with changed development classes**
  Use this request type when you want to permanently change the development system of individual objects. The original location of the objects is changed to the target system at the same time the development class of the objects is changed.

If you change the development class automatically, the objects will have the desired transport characteristics immediately after being imported to the target system, and can be processed in transportable change requests there without any other configuration effort.

- **Relocation of complete development classes (with change of transport layer)**
  Use this request type when you want to permanently change the development system of complete development class.

  This request type can convert the transport layer of the development class automatically. The object list of the request is created automatically and contains all the objects in the development class. If you change the transport layer automatically, the objects will have the desired transport characteristics immediately after being imported to the target system, and can be processed in transportable change requests there without any other configuration effort.

You can assign different tasks for different project team members within a single transport request. Members can release their assigned tasks after completing their individual work; once all the tasks have been released, the request owner can release the overall transport request.

Import Variants

If you use the *import queue* for transports, when you release the modified objects summarized in the object list of the transport request, they are all imported to the queue of the consolidation system via the consolidation layer. Transport management features different ways to import transport requests into the consolidation system:

- **Mass transport**
  All requests pending for import are imported together. The requests are imported into the target systems in the same order in which they were exported from the source system. This minimizes the risk of errors occurring because requests were imported in the wrong order, or because objects are missing because they are contained in requests that have not been transported yet.

  Mass imports are especially well-suited to the quality assurance system and for production systems during the implementation phase of a project.

- **Single transport**
  A subset of the requests is selected from the import queue and imported into the target system. Other requests remain in the import queue and can be imported later (or not at all). Single transports give

you a high degree of flexibility, but usually require greater administrative effort.

Single transports are especially well-suited to maintenance and upkeep of production systems.

To simplify transport administration, the transport system can be workflow-controlled or project-driven. In the first case (workflow control), releasing a request starts a workflow automatically. This workflow controls the transport process, determining the correct processor for each step and giving these individuals a work interface in which they can perform their assigned tasks.

In the second case (project control), the developments and Customizing activities are planned in the project structures of IMG project management. Changes that are independent of one another can be divided into different projects and imported into the downstream systems autonomously.

SAP provides various tools to ensure correct, error-free transports.

Transport Organizer

The *Transport Organizer* provides functions for creating, documenting, and releasing change requests during the Customizing and development process, and for reorganizing the development landscape. The Transport Organizer tools are intended for development teams and the managers of development and implementation projects.

You can call Transaction code SE09 or SE10 directly to display the Transport Organizer initial screen. From within the ABAP Workbench, you can display the overview of requests in the Transport Organizer by using the menu path **Goto · Transport Organizer (Requests)**.

To display one user's requests, based on the specified selection criteria, choose **Display** from the Transport Organizer's initial screen, which is typically the **Selection** screen for most transactions. You can adjust the default selection as necessary.

The status selection for the requests is also applied to the tasks by default. Select **Settings · More Settings...** to change the default selection.

The right side of the initial screen contains cross-system information about the status of transports and repairs, and an option to go to the transport task queue of the transport workflow.

Extended View of the Transport Organizer

To reach the initial screen of the *extended view* of the Transport Organizer, call transaction code SE01 or select menu path **Goto · Transport Organizer (Extended View)** from within the Transport Organizer. The extended view provides additional transport types to address special requirements:

- Piece lists
- Client transports
- Delivery transports
- Individual display

Unlike Workbench and Customizing requests, the transport types defined here do not have automatically assigned transport routes. Therefore, these requests don't follow the configured delivery routes.

Because some of these request types have their own naming conventions and the owner is not a logical selection criterion for all request types, the extended view of the Transport Organizer consists of the various selection screens and tab pages.

Select the menu path **Request/Task · Requests** to search and select specific requests and tasks.

This path also corresponds to one of the functions of the *Transport Organizer tools*. This collection of tools—which you can access directly with Transaction code SE03 or by using the menu path **Goto · Transport Organizer Tools**—provides various functions for finding, analyzing, and managing change requests.

Transport Management System (TMS)

While the Transport Organizer supports development teams during the development process up to the release of a change request, the *Transport Management System* (TMS) supports administrators in importing the requests into the target systems. You use Transaction code STMS to start the TMS.

The TMS helps you organize, execute, and monitor transports between the different SAP Systems. Because all required information and functions are modeled in the SAP System, user intervention at the operating-system level is no longer required in most cases.

The TMS has the following features:

- Graphical editor for configuring the transport routes
- Display of import queues for all SAP Systems within the transport domain

- Import of all requests in an import queue
- Import of all requests for a project
- Import of individual requests
- TMS quality assurance
- Transport workflow
- Transports between SAP Systems that don't share a transport directory

5.1.5 Testing

The complexity of modern business applications makes errors inevitable. Comprehensive testing is required to localize and correct these errors. The extended computer-aided text tool (eCATT) tools are SAP's comprehensive test environment for inspecting business applications. eCATT helps you check both interactive components, such as screen transactions, and non-interactive components, such as function modules.

Support for Teamwork

eCATT helps the development team define and categorize the test cases, process these test cases systematically, and document the results.

In a realistic scenario, several teams will be involved in the testing process:

- The developers of the application or software component to be tested
- The authors of the test cases
- The testers, who process the test cases and analyze and document the results
- Test managers, who create the test packages, assign testers, and monitor the progress of the testing

Various objects are available to model the testing process; they're maintained and integrated in the transactions of the Test Workbench. You can maintain these objects using Transaction code SECATT and the transactions in the Test Organizer.

System Data Container

The system data container defines the system where the tests will be performed. Tests can also be performed on satellite systems through an RFC connection; all necessary data is saved in the system data container.

Test Scripts

The test script defines the steps to be performed. Test scripts are recorded in a simple, interpreted scripting language, which consists of statements for executing transactions and function modules, simple logical branches, and loop constructs. eCATT also enables you to manipulate typed data and assign it to parameters of function modules and transactions, which makes it flexible enough to carry out even complex tests. An import interface also makes it possible to reuse tests: You can parameterize the test scripts through this interface, which lets you use a single script for several different tests.

Test Data Container

The test data container is used for parameterization of test scripts, as mentioned above. The container stores variables that can be transferred to the script through its import interface. A container can have several sets of import variables, which are called *variants*.

Test Configuration

The combination of system data container, test script, and test data container (possibly with several variants) defines a test configuration. The system data container is optional; if it is not specified, the tests are performed in the current system.

5.2 J2EE

Now that we have summarized several important aspects of ABAP development, the remaining part of this chapter deals with one of the key topics of this book: the world of J2EE development.

Since the collapse of the dotcom bubble, the market for Web-based business software has entered a consolidation phase. Costs have to be cut, and any new developments have to be future-proof. In this situation, the J2EE architecture—which was developed by Sun and is supported by many other vendors—is a suitable platform for a wide range of distributed Web-based applications.

Requirements

Applications that are based on the J2EE infrastructure don't have to implement essential business functions such as transaction management, authorization system, distribution, and persistence themselves, but can instead fall back on standardized Java technologies. An architecture based on distributed applications supports robust scalability from the start. J2EE is a cross-vendor standard, although Sun developed the specification. This fact both ensures that software components can be reused, once developed, and makes it easier to integrate software, such as ERP systems from different vendors.

The fact that vendors other than Sun also support the J2EE standard—including IBM, SAP, and JBoss—has helped to ensure its continual evolution and adaptation to meet new requirements. Web services have become a fixture of the architecture, for example, along with other HTTP-based and XML-based technologies. Ultimately, however, the Java programming language itself is largely responsible for the success of J2EE.

5.2.1 Architecture

J2EE applications are based on a multilayer programming model that can be divided into layers for presentation, business, and data retrieval logic. This corresponds to the conventional view—also common in SAP Systems—of scalable applications, in which the different layers can be implemented by separate physical systems. The presentation layer, for example, is typically processed on a client (a PC or a workstation). The most common methods are Web browsers or dedicated user interfaces such as the SAP GUI. The business logic is located on the application server, and this centralization helps reduce maintenance and distribution effort. The data, in turn, is contained in *Enterprise Information Systems* (EIS), which consist of databases, file systems, document management systems, and *Enterprise Resource Planning* (ERP) systems.

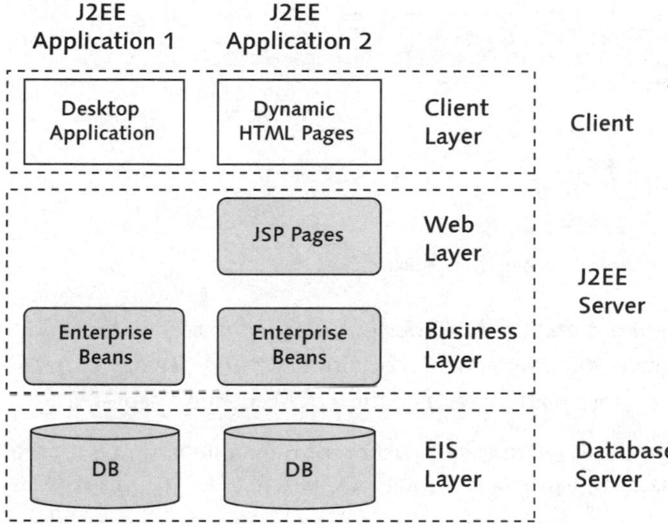

Figure 5.4 Four-Layer Model Under J2EE

Clients

There are three typical occurrences of clients that present application data under J2EE:

Web Clients/ Browsers

Web clients—which are often called *thin clients*, because they do not access application components like JavaBeans or *Enterprise JavaBeans* (EJBs) themselves, but instead function as a graphical interface to the user—require the Web layer on the server side (already mentioned above) to format the data from the application appropriately for the client, often in a markup language such as HTML.

MVC The separation between presentation of data, recording user inputs, and integration with the application are implemented through the *Model View Controller* (MVC) design pattern. This pattern originated from the Smalltalk language, and represents the successful attempt to decouple user interaction (control), display (view), and the business logic (model) in the background. Simply put:

In the MVC context, the browser outputs the data to the user, representing the view, but also contains elements—such as forms, hyperlinks, and buttons—that enable user input (control) and routes this input data to the application (the model).

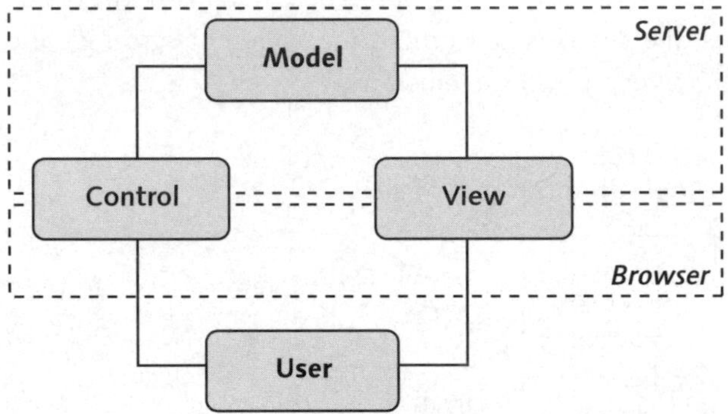

Figure 5.5 Model View Controller Design Pattern

We should point out that the MVC design pattern is implemented on different platforms in different variants, occurrences, and degrees of detail. For a complete, cross-platform explanation of MVC, see Chapter 7.

Applets Applets that are displayed in the browser represent a departure from thin client technology towards rich clients. Applets have a life cycle that is independent of the Web site that they are embedded in, and can theoretically access functions in the application layer directly. Technically, they run in an instance of the *Java Virtual Machine* (JVM) on the client, although they are embedded in the context of a Web page.

This latter aspect, however, means applets do not completely satisfy the MVC pattern for interacting with the application via Internet/intranet. They also place certain demands on the client, such as the existence of a JVM in the browser or configured security guidelines, that have caused user acceptance to diminish in the past. On the positive side, however, they represent a way—in the potentially heterogeneous environment of the Web—to exploit the more advanced display capabilities of applets in comparison to HTML rendering.

Rich clients include desktop applications that have rendering mechanisms such as Swing or AWT in addition to their homogenous display methods. They do not require a Web layer on the server side. They can either access the application functions directly or be connected via a MVC.

Desktop Applications

As browser-based applications become easier to distribute, however, this type of client has forfeited much of its importance in recent years. Because applications are intended to serve the largest possible range of potential users, Web pages are really the only suitable means of the application's presentation layer.

Components

In addition to the entities described above, which are considered components of the J2EE architecture on the client side, there are several other components on the server side:

Web Components

Web components are embodied in the J2EE world by servlets or *Java Server Pages* (JSPs). The latter is a type of servlet that developers without specialized Java skills (but who know the basics of HTML) can create and maintain. The presentation logic that is implemented in the methods of a class in the servlet can be encapsulated in separate tags in JSPs or formulated in short blocks with Java coding as *scriptlets*. JSPs are compiled internally as servlets, but should be used only for output (view) in the MVC, while the servlet represents the controller. The controller is responsible for taking inputs that come from forms or links of a JSP page and converting them to the appropriate control data for the model, and using this data to address the business logic (as Enterprise JavaBeans).

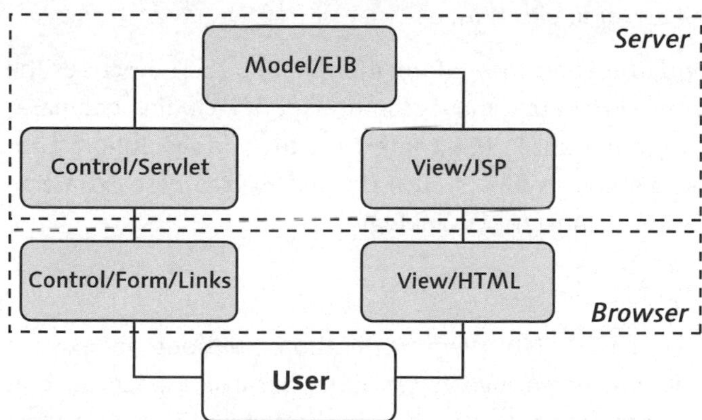

Figure 5.6 MVC Using Servlets/JSPs and EJBs

Business Components The business logic in J2EE is encapsulated as EJBs. They are divided further into three specific subtypes, each with a dedicated area of activity. Session beans model the business logic in the true sense and can be linked together to form transactions under the container architecture. There are stateful and stateless session beans. The former can be implemented to retain certain status information across several requests, while the latter does not support this feature. Communication with session beans is usually synchronous, which means the engine waits for the return parameters from method calls to session beans to arrive before it continues processing the program. Because beans can also be used as remote modules on remote systems, this characteristic can impede system scalability. To avoid this potential problem, *message-driven beans*, which can communicate with their environment asynchronously, were introduced in the EJB 2.0 specification.

Entity beans represent a data object held persistently by the data store, which should be addressed only in the context of session beans and the business logic they contain. The internal logic of an entity bean ensures that the bean status is always consistent, even if transactions are terminated or communication between server and client breaks down.

Support for Web services has been implemented in Version 2.1 of the EJB specification for stateless session beans, which enable an EJB-supported system to communicate via Web services.

The regular JavaBeans have been freed from the EJB specification and now serve only as an optional extension to the Web layer for communicating with the business logic, or as navigation targets from desktop applications to a server application.

Enterprise Information System In the J2EE world, the Enterprise Information System (EIS) describes the components of the system that manage information, including databases and ERP systems. Important in this context are the various options provided for accessing existing systems, such as the JDBC database extraction layer and the various connector technologies.

Containers

Developing server-based thin client applications without an existing application model can be an involved process, because aspects such as transactions, message distribution, and system scalability and robustness have to be developed from scratch. These characteristics, which are critical for any business application, are provided through the container architecture in J2EE.

Container Services

Containers handle these low-level functions and model them in a platform-independent environment. The individual components have to be used in containers during distribution (the deployment process). In the process, they are configured in a distribution-specific manner with XML descriptors, depending on their specific purpose.

If a component is to be used for messaging purposes, for example, it makes sense to use it as a replicator at several places in the system, improving the scalability of the application. An external interface should have tighter access privileges for the component than an object within the system, to prevent unauthorized use of the provided services by third parties.

Another example of the different configuration of components during their deployment to different containers involves their naming. If you want these components to be found later with a naming service, such as the J2EE JNDI lookup service, they must have unique names, which you can specify here.

The transaction model also specifies the relationships between individual methods of specific objects or components that can be executed only atomically in this context. This powerful function is integral to the multi-user operations in enterprise environments.

The settings for remote use of the components rounds out the list of the most important configuration values for a container. In this case, a component is addressed by a remote system and used as if it belonged to that remote system. This characteristic of components makes it possible to seamlessly scale entire system landscapes via hardware enhancements.

Typically, components can have different responses in different environments (containers). This is an argument in favor of reusing components, as it does not require any extra programming effort, even though configuration can often be just as difficult.

J2EE Server

The J2EE server provides the runtime environment for components and the two container types described below. In addition to the runtime environment, the J2EE server also includes a dispatcher, which can forward various requests to certain handlers (such as a Web server), and a deployment service that lets you import applications to the server.

EJB Container

The EJB container is a component of the J2EE server that manages the life cycle, retrieval, and deployment of Enterprise JavaBeans. The life cycle includes activating and deactivating EJBs. The EJB container also manages the connection between the entity beans and a data store in the deployment information.

Web Container The Web container supplies servlets and JSPs. It ensures that the received requests are processed properly and manages the life cycle of servlets and JSPs.

Contrary to the above containers, the application client container runs on the client, not on the J2EE server. It provides the runtime environment for desktop applications on the corresponding client computers and—in contrast to browser-based thin client applications—the application client can establish and manage stateful connections to the J2EE server.

Applet Container For the applet version of browser-based applications, the Java browser plug-in serves as the runtime environment for applets, along with the corresponding instance of the JVM or the Java runtime environment integrated in the browser. Stateful connections to the application server can be established here as well, in contrast to thin client-based applications.

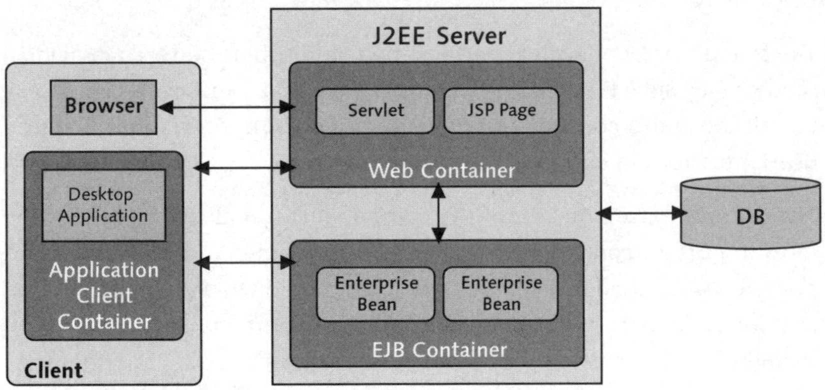

Figure 5.7 J2EE Container Structures

Packaging

J2EE projects consist of components that should be loosely coupled by design, to enable them to be recombined and integrated in any J2EE server for a specific use. As mentioned above, this approach involves using containers.

To simplify their transport, components can be grouped together to form distribution packages or *modules*. The J2EE specification defines four types of modules, each of which has a specific purpose. Each module is described and configured for specific use by a deployment descriptor—one or more files in XML format.

Enterprise JavaBeans Archives

The business logic that is encapsulated in Enterprise JavaBeans can be grouped together in EJB modules with the file extension *.jar*. In this case, the corresponding deployment descriptor primarily contains information for locating EJBs through the Java Naming and Directory Interface (JNDI) and, when entity beans are involved, information as to how they are saved and retrieved in a data store, such as a relational database.

Application Client Archives

The classes for application clients can also be transported using files with the *.jar* extension. The classes are required whenever an application is to be used by a Java-based client, such as an applet or desktop application. They contain the interface between the clients and the application logic on the J2EE server.

Web Archives

The presentation logic that is implemented in JSPs and servlets, as well as MIME objects such as images and HTML files, are grouped together in Web modules with the file extension *.war*. In addition to authentication directives, the deployment descriptor also contains information about URL mapping—that is, which URL has to be used to reach a specific servlet or JSP. It can also contain information for locating EJBs used in the context.

Resource Adapter Archives

Archives with the file extension *.rar* (resource adapter archive) contain all interfaces, classes, and system-dependent libraries; together with the deployment descriptor, they represent the implementation of the J2EE Connector architecture. Resource adapter archives make it possible to link a J2EE project with its back-end systems, such as ERP systems.

Enterprise Archives

All of the above modules can be combined to create an *Enterprise Archive* (EAR), which represents a complete, specific application, because all configuration information is contained in the individual modules. The enterprise module can also be configured using a deployment descriptor. According to the deployment theory, an enterprise archive can be added to any J2EE server without additional effort. In practice, however, to avoid additional effort, the J2EE server must comply with the specification standards; the application cannot use any extended features of a specific J2EE server; the system landscape (such as data stores or ERP systems) must be sufficiently compatible; and there must be no overlapping namespaces between the named applications and URLs. Therefore, transferring a distribution within a heterogeneous system landscape will probably involve difficulties and require additional planning effort.

J2EE Specifications and APIs

In contrast to programming Java desktop applications, you will have relatively little contact with low-level functions (such as direct access to the file system) when developing J2EE applications. Therefore, we recommend that you introduce the programming interfaces and specifications that you will be using at this point. They are primarily higher-level interfaces that intentionally conceal low-level, system-specific operations from developers in order to make projects more easily transportable and scalable. The low-level work is undertaken by the corresponding containers, which contain configuration information for the deployed modules in their deployment descriptors.

The specifications can be divided into three major groups:

- Component model technologies
  - Enterprise JavaBeans specification
  - Servlet specification
  - Java Server Pages specification
  - Java Naming and Directory Service
  - Java Message Service
  - J2EE Connector architecture
- Web service technologies
  - Java XML API
  - Java XML-RPC API
  - SAAJ API
  - JAXR API
- Other technologies
  - JDBC API
  - Java Transaction API
  - JAAS
  - Java Mail API

Enterprise JavaBeans Specification

The Enterprise JavaBeans specification defines the Enterprise JavaBeans architecture, already introduced above. It defines a transactional, distributed, object-based programming model that hides the system-specific, persistence-related, infrastructure-based aspects of the model from application programmers, without limiting their flexibility. The Enterprise JavaBeans—not to be confused with the JavaBeans components—represent the components of a system based on business logic. There are three general occurrences of EJBs:

1. Entity beans, which represent business objects saved persistently in a data store (see Section 6.1.2 for more information)
2. Stateful and stateless session beans, which encapsulate business logic in the true sense, and generally access entity beans
3. Message-driven beans, which support synchronous and asynchronous communication between services

Session beans and message-driven beans are part of the business layer, and are described in detail in Section 6.3.2.

Enterprise JavaBeans are a central component of every J2EE application, as they usually encapsulate the complete application logic and deploy it to clients and servlets in standardized forms.

EJB Container

As previously mentioned, the infrastructure-related aspects of the architecture are covered by the EJB container used in the J2EE server. It isolates the received EJBs from direct external access. Instead, all access must take place through the container, which is one of the infrastructure-related tasks of the J2EE architecture and does not concern the application programmer. The *Java Naming and Directory Interface* (JNDI) provides a global, standardized interface for accessing various containers.

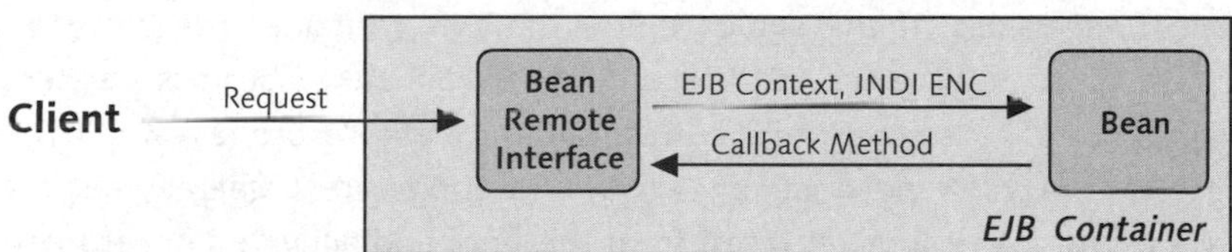

Figure 5.8 External Access to an EJB

Because the EJB container usually manages a wide range of EJBs simultaneously in a production environment, but some thought also has to be given to preserving system resources, some types of EJBs—such as the persistent entity beans—do not create a new object during every access; instead, a free instance is supplied from a pool of EJBs that have the requested type. If a bean has not been used for a longer period of time, it is removed from the memory of the J2EE server and written back to the permanent store. The client of the process has no idea about the life cycle of an EJB in the EJB container, nor does it have to: As far as the client can tell, "its" bean is always available with the expected result.

Controlling the Life Cycle

Several options are available for the container to communicate efficiently with the bean, to manage this life cycle. Callback methods, implemented either automatically or manually, for example, let the container inform the bean of a status change and initiate the appropriate steps, such as loading from or saving to a persistent storage medium. In turn, the EJB context is available to the EJB. It provides a direct reference to the container where the bean is located and can be used to query environment variables or information actively. The bean's clients use the JNDI mentioned above to locate another bean in a container and make it available either locally or remotely. The clients of an EJB can be other beans, servlets, applets, or desktop applications, which use the business logic encapsulated in a session bean, for example, satisfying the most important paradigm of object orientation: the reusability of coding.

The life cycle of a bean can be written to the bean in a state machine, by calling the callback methods. Therefore, Figure 5.9 schematically illustrates the sequence of method calls to an entity bean, whose mnemonic names make it easy to track the individual states.

`setEntityContext()` makes it possible for the bean to access the container, which is especially relevant where JNDI is used. At the same time, it is loaded into the object pool of the EJB container, to be available more quickly. `ejbCreate()` creates a data record in persistent memory, `ejbLoad()` loads it and sets the entity bean as an object with the corresponding values. If the values differ, the EJB container triggers `ejbStore()` to update the data record. When an entity bean is deleted, `ejbRemove()` removes the corresponding data record as well. The `ejbActivate()` and `ejbPassivate()` methods are triggered, respectively, when a bean is retrieved from the pool and activated or returned to the pool because the client no longer requires it.

EJB Architecture

Enterprise JavaBeans are remote-capable modules that are available to other applications in a client/server-like communication. In a cursory comparison, they could be considered to be the equivalent of a function group from the ABAP world. *Remote-capable* means that an EJB can provide a local interface and a remote interface, which the clients can use to access the EJB, in addition to its actual implementation. Because there is one interface each to locate and create an instance, and one each for the provided business methods, each EJB can have a maximum of four interfaces.

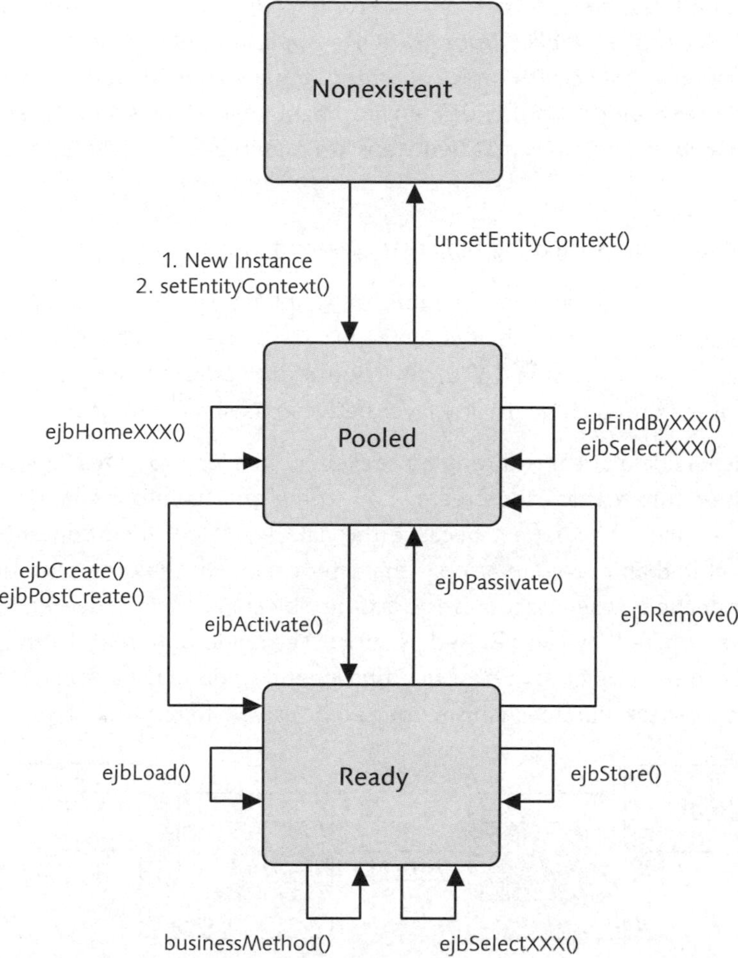

Figure 5.9 State Machine—Life Cycles of an Entity Bean

Remote refers to all EJBs that are not located in the same instance of a JVM. The interface makes it possible to generate objects on the client that appear to be local, offering the bean's functions on the client. In fact, the process involves relatively simple objects, which merely forward the queries they receive over a network connection through sockets, and send the returned results back to the client. The counterpart to these *stubs* on the server side is the *skeleton* (see below). It monitors the appropriate sockets for inbound requests, analyzes them, and forwards them to the correct instance of the addressed EJBs.

Transport Protocols

The EJB container is fairly flexible with regard to selection of the transport protocol, although each vendor supports a different mix. Most vendors support both *Java Remote Method Protocol* (JRMP) and CORBA's *Internet Inter-Object Request Broker Protocol* (IIOP). Application developers don't have to worry about which protocol is used, because the EJB container is used to access objects in the J2EE environment anyway. The only difference to a *normal* object is that two steps are required to instantiate it:

1. Locating the EJB with JNDI
2. Creating an instance using the create method in the stub

Internally, IIOP acts as a modified form of simplified Java RMI. The RMI-IIOP layer ensures compatibility between the two layers and handles the necessary type conversions. You can choose any transport protocol, as long as it features a compatibility layer between itself and Java RMI.

Serializing Objects

To transport data streams through a socket connection, you must transform them into a character stream. Converting objects into a character stream is called *serialization*, because the data types and their contents are structured and saved in a serial character chain. On the other end of the connection, *deserialization* restores the objects in their native environment, where they can be used as such. We should note that it is not possible to serialize all Java classes. Consequently, you may be forced to provide a serialization mechanism yourself or use a different data type.

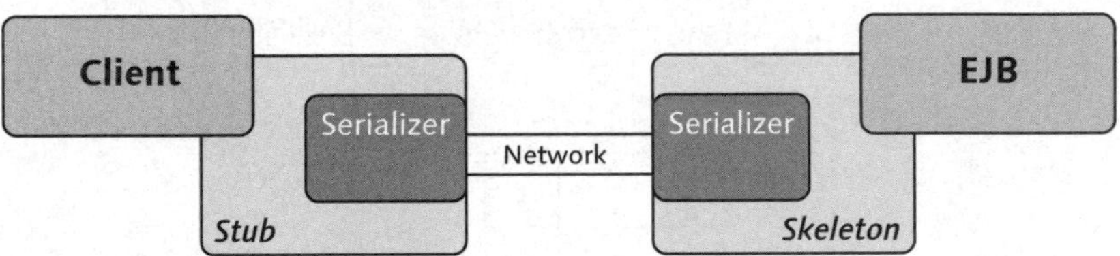

Figure 5.10 Stub/Skeleton Architecture

Stub/Skeleton

The stub/skeleton architecture involves an architecture with an intended loss of information regarding the complete structure of the EJB. It enables you to choose which methods are visible to—and can therefore be accessed by—a potential client on a local or remote interface. With very few exceptions, this involves the business methods primarily, which are not required in the interface description. Special finder methods must be provided to locate an EJB, however, just like create methods to create an instance on the client; otherwise, the EJB will not be remote-capable. Finder methods exist for only persistent entity beans, and make it possible to locate the corresponding data record in the database. You do not necessarily have to implement these methods yourself in many cases, however, as described further below. The create methods of an EJB create an object that does not exist yet in the database, even though this only has to be implemented manually for entity beans.

There are two ways to save entity beans. In the first method, you let the EJB container perform the data retrieval and storage tasks, including the initial creation of the object, rolling EJBs into and out of memory, location, updates, and deletion. The advantages of this approach are the low implementation effort and the low error rate. However, you pay a price for these advantages—the functions of the entity beans managed in this way are limited, and the configuration effort is much greater. The latter includes increased communication requirements in projects where the developer and deployer are two different individuals, although these requirements can be reduced as experience is gained over time. CMP

The degree of support for *Container-managed Persistence* (CMP) varies from J2EE to J2EE server. Therefore, you may encounter complications when transporting applications from one vendor's system to another, although, in theory, they are compatible. The current implementation of SAP Web AS 6.30 supports only container-managed entity beans in one table, for example. Multi-table entity beans are possible in SAP Web AS 6.40 and later.

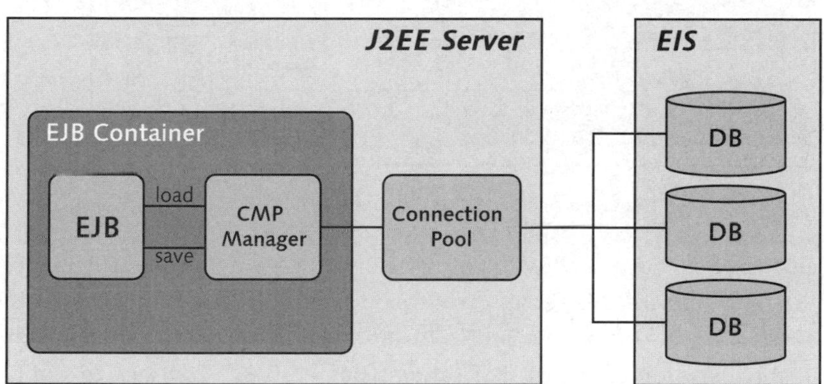

Figure 5.11 CMP-Managed Access to the Database

A much greater degree of flexibility is required to develop complex business objects. The use of *Bean-managed Persistence* (BMP) gives you this flexibility. In this approach, the entity bean itself takes care of establishing the connection to the database (usually through a connection pool), the roll-in and roll-out mechanisms, instantiation, deleting objects from the database, and serializing the data types to be transferred. BMP

As you will see in the examples below, we will need an entity bean, with its own persistence management, even for a simple application like ResMan. The greater the effort that you put into development, the less the configuration effort required later. However, there is a direct functional dependence between the bean and the underlying data sources, which the configuration would otherwise have abstracted with XML descriptors. This fact promotes neither reusability of the entity bean in a different context nor its transportability to other systems, as every time the data structure changes, all entity beans are potentially subject to that change. In such cases, you cannot use the well-documented configuration like you can with CMP-managed beans, but instead have to change the implementation of the bean itself. This can require a significant additional effort, depending on how clean and simple the bean is implemented.

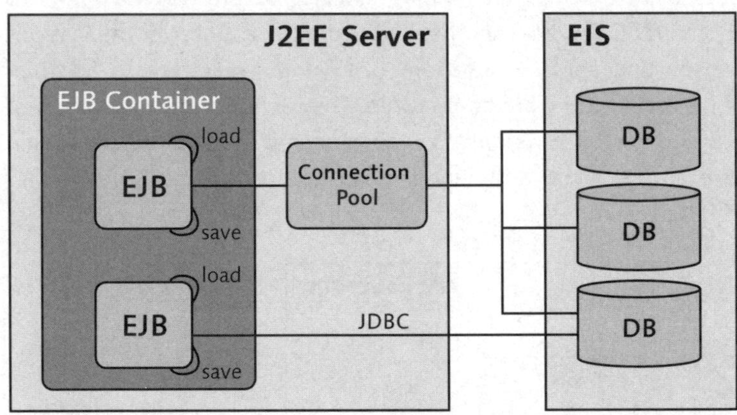

Figure 5.12 BMP-Managed Access to the Database

Session Beans

Now that we have dealt with entity beans in some detail, we will devote the remainder of this section to session beans. They serve primarily to encapsulate business logic, which can then be deployed to client servers in their environment just like other types of EJBs. Contrary to entity beans, however, session beans aren't used to manage persistent data. Instead, they provide the process flows that allow global access to this data. This makes it possible, for example, to publish session beans as Web services and use other programming languages to access the logic they contain. In turn, session beans can behave internally as clients for other session beans or entity beans, use Web services, or provide stateless logic such as simple arithmetic operations or character string formatting.

This statefulness is a primary advantage and decisive capability of session beans, which make it possible to hold status information for a client session in memory in the environment of HTTP-centric Web applications—without requiring any additional programming effort. You can open connections to remote resources through client queries, for example, or hold contents from such resources in memory. The resulting advantages are readily apparent: improved resource management and reduced network load, which can otherwise easily become a bottleneck in distributed systems. Stateless session beans are also possible. They present a smaller load on the J2EE server end and can be used when the program logic does not contain any stateful information.

This does not change the general remote capability of the bean. Session beans also have two pairs of interfaces for local and remote access. Again, one interface makes it possible to create an instance of the bean on the either local or remote client, while the other interface provides the business methods of the beans. Of course, the finder methods that are required for entity beans to select a data record for certain criteria aren't needed, as a transient session bean cannot be represented by a data record in a persistent data store. Therefore, the `ejbCreate()` and `ejbRemove()` methods don't create or remove data records, but instead can be considered constructor and destructor of a bean and implemented with equivalent functionality. When a stateful session bean is used, `ejbPassivate()` and `ejbActivate()` make it possible to define status changes manually when submitting a bean for user by a client. The `setSessionContext()` context is the equivalent to `setEntityContext()` in the session bean and, together with `getSessionContext()`, enable you to access the session context actively from within the bean. The stateful values of the bean can be stored there, and, even after a repeated activation, are still there and can be retrieved.

Session beans also support the transactional concept. The callback methods `afterBegin()`, `beforeCompletion()`, and `afterCompletion()`, which use the Boolean parameter values `true` and `false` to indicate a commit or rollback, enable you to control transaction-related characteristics of a session bean manually.

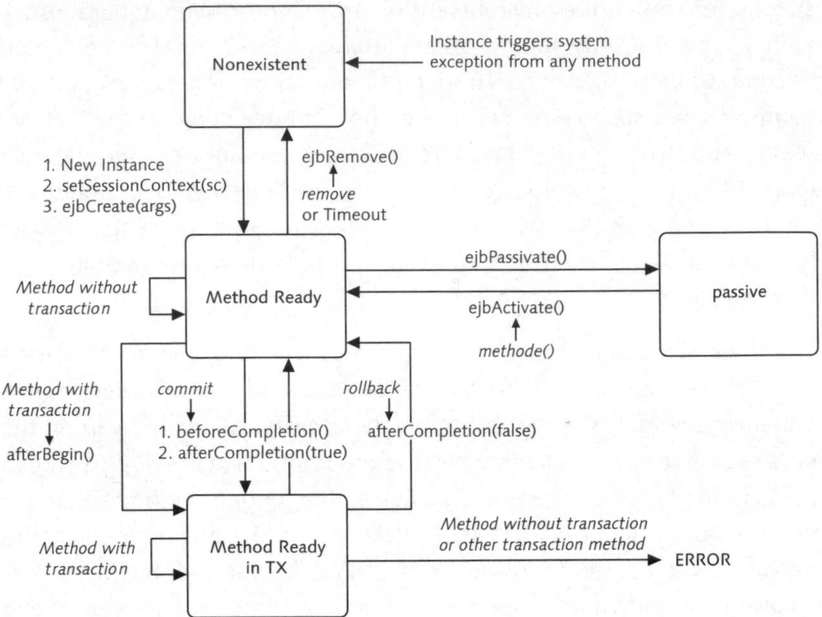

Figure 5.13 State Machine—Life Cycle of a Stateful Session Bean

Deploying EJBs

Once the implementation part of the EJBs is complete, it has to be integrated in the EJB container. This deployment process requires additional information, which is provided by XML descriptors. The container requires this declarative mechanism to automatically perform tasks such as automatic persistence, transaction management, access control, and others. You can generally create, maintain, and integrate them in the *JAR* file—the distribution package for EJBs—manually. The SAP NetWeaver Developer Studio features a graphical user interface, however, to minimize this effort. We will not go into the details of the deployment descriptor for EJBs here; instead, refer to the corresponding tutorial in Section 6.3.2.

There are fixed rules that define the exact structure of these XML files, however, just as there are for other XML terminologies, defined as a document type definition (DTD) at the following URL:

http://java.sun.com/dtd/ejb-jar_2_0.dtd

A descriptor can consist of several beans and defines the class paths to all interfaces and implementations, in addition to their names. It also references the corresponding data sources and objects used from the JNDI, as well as access privileges. When CMP-managed entity beans are involved, it also contains data-mapping information, such as the contained fields, table names, and selection criteria.

Servlet Specification

Although servlets are generally used in the context of an HTTP service, they can also be used in other ways to respond to any type of request. The `HttpServlet` class, which is typically used, provides methods such as `doPost()` and `doGet()` from package `javax.servlet.http` to respond to the corresponding HTTP requests. Typically, in order to generate the desired response, the application programmer must implement the servlets as interfaces.

The life cycle of a servlet is determined by the Web container used for its distribution. In this perspective, a query received by the dispatcher that refers to a specific servlet triggers the following actions:

1. If the Web container does not contain an instance of the servlet:
   - The servlet class is loaded.
   - An instance of the servlet is generated and called with the servlet's `init()` method. It is used to reserve resources (such as network connections) or read configuration information.
2. The service method for the request, such as `doGet()`, is called. Servlets forward `Request` and `Response` objects to their service methods, which are required to read request-specific information (such as form contents) and generate output for the browser.

Thanks to the request-independent life cycle, variables are retained in the servlet across multiple requests. This makes it easier to deal with data that has to be retained through various requests by one or more users.

Sessions

To deal with user-related session variables, the stateless `Request` object also contains a session object, which can save stateful information. The `getSession()` method is used in this context to either generate an object with type `HttpSession` or get it from the `Request`, to fill it subsequently with variables and objects that are then available in the session object automatically during the next request. To link this object with a specific user despite the statelessness of HTTP, an automatically generated key is used in the background and passed on either through cookies or in the URL.

If the container is instructed to destroy the servlet—by shutting down the J2EE server, for example—the `destroy()` method is called first and can be used here to release occupied resources (such as network connections). To guarantee a clean shutdown of the servlet, do not release any resources until all the queries have been processed. You can do this, for example, by implementing a counter for open requests as a servlet variable. The `service()` method, which should not usually be overwritten, is suitable for implementing the response in this particular case. When a request is received, it calls the service methods of the servlet implicitly:

```
public class RequestCounterHttpServlet extends
  HttpServlet {
   private int counter = 0;
   protected synchronized void openRequest() {
      counter++;
   }
   protected synchronized void closeRequest() {
      counter--;
   }
   protected synchronized int countOpenRequests() {
      return counter;
   }
   protected void service(HttpServletRequest req,
                          HttpServletResponse res,)
                          throws ServletException,
                                 IOException {
         openRequest();
         try {
            super.service(req,res);
         } finally {
            closeRequest();
         }
   }
}
```

Listing 5.1 Counter for Public Requests on a Servlet

Java Server Pages Specification

Although Java Server Pages (JSPs) ultimately generate services as their product, they stem from a different motivation. Their original intent was to make it easier for developers without Java skills to create dynamic Web pages. JSPs are basically text-based documents that generate content—usually HTML—automatically. Therefore, the tools are designed with HTML designers and Web programmers in mind.

You can use self-defined and implemented tags (elements of a markup language) to trigger server-side interactions. For differentiation purposes, these tags use an XML namespace, which is linked in the page context with a *TagLib*, or tag library. TagLibs are generally arranged by subject and make it possible, for example, to access JavaBeans and XSLT processors or database connections from directly within a JSP. TagLibs are the J2EE equivalent to BSP extensions. In contrast to BSP extensions, however, various ready-to-use TagLibs are already available for JSPs and can be easily integrated in the respective JSP context, as shown in the following example:

TagLibs

```
<%@page contentType="text/html"%>
<%@taglib prefix="txt"
          uri="/WEB-INF/MyTxtTagLib.tld" %>
<html>
   <head>
      <title>JSP Example</title>
   </head>
   <body>
      <txt:headline size="large">
         My example JSP page
      </txt:headline>
      <txt:paragraph>
         This is an example paragraph
      </txt:paragraph>
   </body>
</html>
```

Listing 5.2 Example of a JSP Using TagLibs

One important JSP TagLib is the *Java Standard TagLib* (JSTL). It links the most common elements of the presentation logic in tags. It consists of four parts:

JSTL

- The core library, which provides tags for controlling the program flow and presentation logic, such as query blocks, loops, and the integration of external sources
- A library for using XML, for analysis, generation, and transformation
- A format library for localizing texts and formatting date values and numbers
- Lastly, a library for database access that is based on SQL rounds out the JSTL

Scriptlets In addition to the TagLib technology, you can also use scriptlets to integrate Java coding directly in a JSP. A script block, which starts with <% and ends with %>, can execute the full functions of the standard procedural Java code. It quickly becomes apparent, however, that using scriptlets makes servlets more unwieldy to maintain, which is why scriptlet functions that belong to the business logic are encapsulated in enterprise beans, while functions that belong to the presentation logic are encapsulated in tags.

Life Cycle of a JSP The life cycle of a JSP basically corresponds to that of a servlet. A JSP is compiled as a servlet the first time it is called, however, which has implications for translating JSP code into servlet code:

1. The directives that start with <%@ represent information as to how a JSP is converted to a servlet and how that resulting servlet will be execute, namely, the *page attributes*.
2. Scriptlets are inserted in the implementation of the servlet class to be generated, as mentioned above.
3. Separately defined tags are converted to calls of the corresponding methods for the tag classes.

Note that errors can occur in both the translation phase and the execution phase; however, users will not see these errors until the page is initially displayed.

Error Handling These internal errors (error code: 500)—as well as other errors such as "access denied" (error code: 403)—are designated in the user's Web browser. In many cases, however, you want to display an *HTTP error page* in such cases to mask an error in the production application, to prevent potentially unauthorized access to data in the listing, or, in the development environment, to give the user detailed debugging information, and to help localize and correct the error.

The instruction <%@ page errorPage=«<file_name>« %> routes the Web container to another JSP if an error occurs. This page provides an object with type javax.servlet.jsp.ErrorData, which makes it easier to process and display error and debugging information. You can access the JSP without using scriptlets by using the expressions formulated below:

```
${pageContext.errorData.statusCode}
${pageContext.errorData.uri}
${pageContext.errorData.servletName}
${pageContext.errorData.throwable}
```

In turn, the last object gives you several options for retrieving more specific information to determine the probable cause of the error. For more information, see the Java documentation under

http://java.sun.com/j2ee/1.4/docs/api/javax/servlet/jsp/ErrorData.html

Buffer Control

One page attribute for configuring the output control for the requesting client is the so called buffer control. It specifies how many characters are placed in an internal buffer at first before they are sent to the browser. As we already mentioned, you configure this control with a page attribute that you can define as follows:

```
<%@page buffer="none" %>
<%@page buffer="1024kb" %>
```

Buffer control is particularly important in the context of the transport protocol used for client-server communication. The header data of a protocol always has to be output to the client before the user data. Therefore, if a piece of data—such as the dynamic specification of a media type—cannot be determined until a JSP is processed, the user data should first be held in a sufficiently large buffer. If the buffer overflows, the data it contains is automatically forwarded to the client and the opportunity to send header data is gone.

Media Types and Encoding

The media type provides the user's browser with information, instructing it as to how to display the contents of a page. The contents of a JSP are sent as `text/html` by default. You can also set the media type dynamically, however, to send other text-based formats, such as XML, SVG, and WML. You specify the media type as follows:

```
<%@ page contentType="text/xml" %>
```

A list of all registered media types can be viewed free of charge at Internet Assigned Numbers Authority (IANA). You can also define the encoding of the output stream dynamically. Because this involves setting an HTTP header for the browser, developers are subject to the same rules defined in the corresponding W3C specification on this subject, which you will find at the following URL:

http://www.w3.org/Protocols/rfc2616/rfc2616.html

JavaBeans Components

Access to JavaBeans components (not to be confused with Enterprise JavaBeans, which we already discussed) is also standardized in Java Server Pages. The bean components provide for structured, reusable access to application components. In general, these components enable you to retain and process attributes over a certain period. The life cycle of a JavaBeans component depends on the variable scope where it is used. When implemented as a class, it must adhere to certain conventions to be addressed by the tags:

1. An attribute can be readable or writable in any combination.
2. An attribute can contain or index atomic value types, that is, it can be implemented as an array. Its actual type does not matter as long as the automatic conversion can generate it from a string literal in a constructor call.
3. A given attribute of a class, `XYZ`, must have implemented `get` and `set` methods, `getXYZ()` and `setXYZ()`.
4. A JavaBeans component must contain a constructor without parameters.

The implementation of a simple JavaBeans component—whose task is to store the name of the last visitor to a page and return it at any time—looks like this:

```
package statistics;
public class UserStatistics {
   public UserStatistics() {
   }
   public void setLastUser(String user) {
      this.lastUser = user;
   }
   public String getLastUser() {
      return this.lastUser;
   }
}
```

Listing 5.3 JavaBean Component for User Statistics

To use this component in a Java Server Page, you have to use certain predefined standard tags to address it:

```
<jsp:useBean id="user"
             class="statistics.UserStatistics"
             scope="application">
```

```
    <jsp:setProperty name="user" property="lastUser"
    value="CurrentUser"/>
</jsp:useBean>
```

Listing 5.4 Using the JavaBean Component in a JSP

The `id` parameter of the `jsp:useBean` element must agree with the parameter name of the `jsp:setProperty` element to establish a unique assignment between the individual actions to JavaBeans components. The `scope` parameter determines the variable scope where the JavaBeans component is used. Possible values are `application` (every user of the application across multiple requests), `session` (a single user of the application across multiple requests), `request` (a single user for a single request), and `page` (every user of the page across multiple requests).

There are several ways to gain read access to the attributes of a JavaBeans component:

```
<jsp:getProperty name="user" property="lastUser" />
${statistics.UserStatistics.lastUser}
```

The latter type of access in a single expression is the most widely used and propagated form.

Includes

Reusability of existing coding is one of the central paradigms of object-oriented programming. Java Server Pages feature several such mechanisms, one of which you have already learned: The ability to define your own tags and encapsulate them in TagLibs. Another option is to add parameterizable *includes* of other JSPs in the context of a higher-level Java Server Page. Because includes are processed when the JSP is initially translated, and are ultimately considered a temporary forwarding of the request to another JSP, whose generated output is integrated in the higher-level page in place of the include, you may ask yourself which parameters can be passed on in the actual request. An include has the following structure:

```
<jsp:include page="/reservation.jsp">
   <jsp:param name="title" value="Reservation_page" />
</jsp:include>
```

If you want to forward to another JSP instead of including its output, you can use another standard element from the JSP specification:

```
<jsp:forward page="/reservation.jsp" />
```

Note that you cannot send any output to the browser prior to forwarding—this can occur, for example, when the buffer defined as the page attribute has been configured too small. Because `jsp:forward` involves only redirecting the client to a different page, based on the HTTP header, the header must be sent before the actual user data as previously stated.

Because includes have to be entered manually in every page they use, they can prove difficult to handle in larger projects. Thus, once your application reaches a certain degree of complexity, we recommend that you learn about template technologies (which are not dealt with at this point).

Java Naming and Directory Interface

The *Java Naming and Directory Interface* (JNDI), already mentioned several times in the context of EJB and connection pooling, provides a standardized interface to many name and directory services, including LDAP, DNS, RMI, and CORBA. Thanks to its open architecture and standardized interface definition for both application developers and vendors, it represents a consistent, future-proof usage within Java applications.

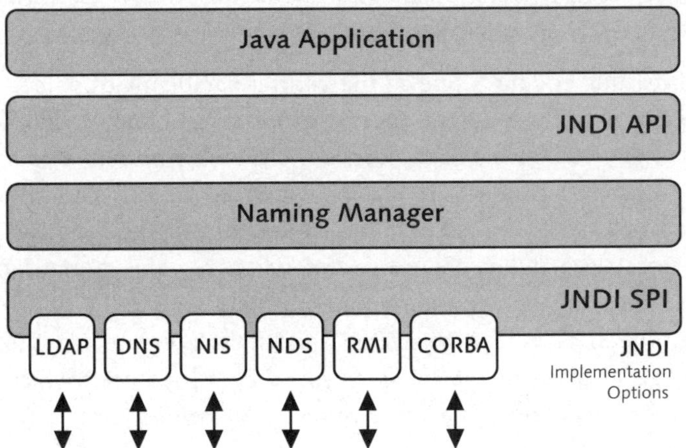

Figure 5.14 JNDI Architecture

Generally, the third-party naming and directory interfaces make it possible to address and use specific objects—either directly by name or through a filtered search. Ideally, these names will be readable for application developers, who can associate them with a certain object or object type. A *binding* links names with objects on the technical side. The JNDI architecture makes these objects available to application programmers using a driver architecture familiar from JDBC. Because the object term is kept abstract, you can generally address anything that has been registered in a certain type of naming service. Remote interfaces of EJBs are usually located using a JNDI, for example:

```
InitialContext context = new InitialContext();
ResManBeanHome resManBean = (ResManBeanHome)
context.lookup("java:comp/env/ejb/ResManBean");
```

Another popular application case is the retrieval of a database resource from a pool:

```
InitialContext context = new InitialContext();
DataSource src = (DataSource) context.lookup

("java:comp/env/jdbc/MyJdbcConnection");
Connection con = src.getConnection();
```

Contexts

You already learned about two different contexts—`EntityContext` and `SessionContext`—in the framework of EJBs. The context represents a series of bindings, which it manages. A context follows certain naming conventions. Objects in a DNS context, for example, are addressed differently than objects in a directory management context: In the former case, you address objects by their DNS names (such as *www.domain.com*), whereas you address file objects on a UNIX platform—as in the latter context—by path (such as */etc/ResMan/config/resources*).

Contexts can be arranged hierarchically into subcontexts, which have to follow the same naming conventions as the higher-level context. If no specific context (like the `EntityContext` or `SessionContext`) is available, you can use an object with type `InitialContext` to retrieve an initial context. You can then use this object to locate and use other contexts or objects that are located directly in the namespace of the `InitialContext`.

Java Message Service

In the highly modularized world of enterprise applications in general—and J2EE applications specifically—the general objective is to keep interdependencies between components and modules to a minimum, to sustain a scalable, extensible, flexible architecture. This is where the *Java Message Service* (JMS) comes in, by enabling loosely-coupled, message base communication between the applications. In particular, JMS makes two new features available in the J2EE framework:

1. In EJB specification 2.0, JMS enables message-driven beans for asynchronous communication.
2. Messages can be employed as distributed transactions within the *Java Transaction API* (JTA) described further below. This enables you to access an EIS that is integrated through the J2EE Connector architecture asynchronously, avoiding potential bottlenecks that synchronous communication with such systems could create.

JMS is an integrated component of the architecture in J2EE specification 1.3 and later. As such, developers can use and take advantage of the corresponding APIs in any J2EE environment that supports this standard. In particular, this includes the factors of asynchronous communication and graduated, reliable communication, which becomes critical whenever a message has to be received exactly once without relying on a synchronous or firmly coupled messaging infrastructure.

In a practical example, imagine you want to trigger several complex, long-running reports on a remote server and analyze the results on the client. In this case, it makes perfect sense to use asynchronous, parallel processing to boost performance.

JMS is also the foundation for messaging between two components from different vendors, which do not "know" each other and therefore require loose coupling.

The Java Message Service is based on three concepts. To help you understand the internal functions of the J2EE architecture, we will briefly examine all three concepts here.

JMS Architecture

Vendors of J2EE servers are required to implement their own JMS provider architecture since J2EE specification 1.3. A mere interface definition is no longer sufficient in the latest version. This component of the overall JMS architecture is used for internal management of the message system, along with the administrative and controlling system components. JMS clients can use the message system to create or receive messages, which are specific objects that are exchanged between the various clients. As you can see, JMS is not based on the conventional client/server architecture, but instead on peer-to-peer communication. It seems as if only clients communicate with each other. Aside from clients based on JMS, there are still clients that have proprietary interfaces, as they stem from pre-1998, before the first JMS specification was defined.

Administration Objects

Administration objects, such as *connection factories* and *destinations*, are supplied by the JMS provider. Their name comes from their administrative management, in contrast to technical program management. A connection factory is an entity that a client uses to create a connection with predefined values. These values belong to classes `QueueConnectionFactory` or `TopicConnectionFactory`, whose meaning is explained further below, in the context of communication modes. On the other hand, a destination describes the source or target of a communication. Both object types are usually addressed through a JNDI lookup within JMS, to create an object with type `Topic` or `Queue`:

```
Topic someTopic = (Topic) cnt.lookup("SomeTopic");
Queue someQueue = (Queue) cnt.lookup("SomeQueue");
```

As you can see, JMS uses JNDI to localize distributed objects. The `connection factory` and `destination` objects are assigned to a namespace by JNDI in advance, where they can be instantiated by a client at a later time.

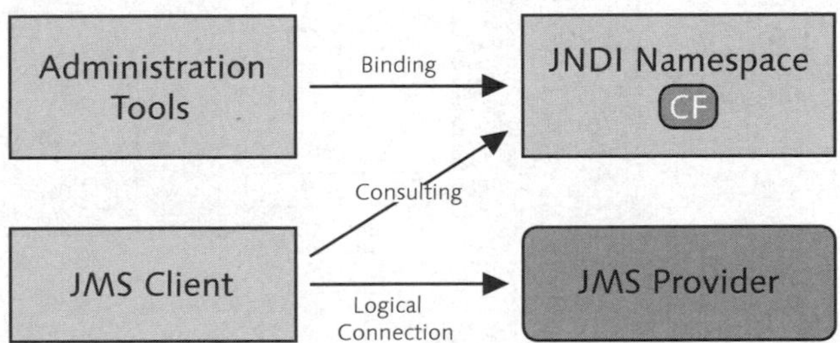

Figure 5.15 JMS API Architecture

The Java Message Service basically implements two types of communication modes, which adopted previous conventional concepts of previous proprietary implementations of messaging systems and added one more concept to them.

Point-to-Point Model

The point-to-point model is based on the concepts of queues, senders, and recipients. Each message is addressed to a specific queue, which the receiving client can process sequentially. A message is retained in the queue until it is removed for processing or expires. In this model, each message has exactly one recipient, which is not subject to time constraints for processing the message and therefore confirms its receipt.

Figure 5.16 Point-to-point Communication Model

Publish/Subscribe Model

In the publish/subscribe model, a message is sent to a hierarchically structured topic, which receives it. In this communication model, the sender and recipient are always anonymous and exist in a potential n:n relationship. The system handles message receipt and distribution, and retains a message only until all recipients have received it. Contrary to the point-to-point model, there is a temporal dependency here, because messages can be received only after a *subscription*, which must be renewed after a message receipt. This deficiency of conventional topic-based message systems is eliminated by the JMS API, which supports permanent subscriptions.

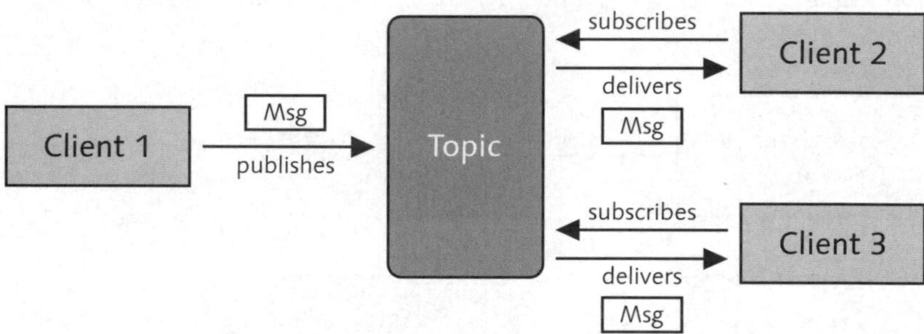

Figure 5.17 Publish/Subscribe Communication Model

While message dispatch is asynchronous in both models, the JMS terminology differentiates more finely between communication types. In synchronous processing, the client uses the `receive()` method to retrieve a message from a `topic` or a `queue`. This can block the further program flow until a message is received, or until a timeout terminates the retrieval process. During asynchronous process, the receiving client is passive until the system calls its callback method, `onMessage()`. This event signals a message receipt.

J2EE Connector Architecture

Existing enterprise information systems have to be integrated in existing heterogeneous system landscapes in order to protect past investments. The J2EE Connector architecture was developed to connect a J2EE server with any proprietary enterprise information system. It enables applications that run on a J2EE server to access enterprise information systems. J2EE Connector architecture 1.5 and later also supports the reverse case, enabling enterprise information systems to access the resources of the J2EE server.

Similar to JDBC, the interface architecture uses a driver-oriented approach. Each EIS has a resource adapter that can be connected to any J2EE server, which has the appropriate version of the J2EE Connector architecture, providing the system with a standardized interface. Aside from the J2EE server, independent clients can also use an interface, the *Common Client Interface* (CCI). As you can imagine, a simple driver architecture is not sufficient to manage connections, transactions, and security aspects. Resource adapters—packages of drivers and interfaces—are used to connect the EIS. In the J2EE Connector architecture, the unidirectional connection from one source to another is established via packages of guidelines called *contracts*.

You can use the following contracts to connect the J2EE server and Java clients to an EIS, starting with Version 1.0 of the specifications.

Connection Management

Connection Management on the J2EE server gives components (such as EJBs) a pool of connections to access the EIS, similar to JDBC. This method saves resources and bandwidth because a minimum of connections is kept open.

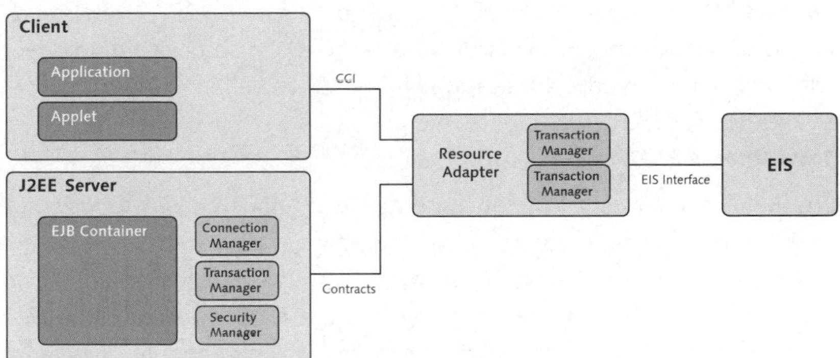

Figure 5.18 J2EE Connector Architecture

Transaction Management

A contract for transaction management enables the integration of EIS resources allocated by the EIS resource manager. The J2EE system manages the transactional context. All necessary communication with the enterprise information system's resource manager is automated here, which eliminates the need for an external transaction manager.

Security Management Data protection for the connection to an external EIS is realized through a separate contract, which provides a secure environment for applications that use EIS resources and reduces potential security risks for information and resources.

Security in the opposite communication direction—connections going back into J2EE or initiated from the opposing EIS—is supported starting in Version 1.5 of the J2EE Connector architecture, giving EIS resources secure access to J2EE applications and components.

Transaction Management If an EIS uses a J2EE software component, that component must be integrated in EIS transaction management. This also involves more far-reaching transaction control, such as providing a restore call to ensure the ACID (Atomicity, Consistency, Isolation and Durability) that typo probably came in on the original translation characteristics of the imported transaction.

Message Management A contract for inbound messages is required to enable systems—that are connected via the resource adapter—with the ability to provide a message service such as Java Message Service (JMS) or Java API for XML Messaging (JAXM). This contract lets external message systems connect to the J2EE engine via a resource adapter, thus participating in messaging directly.

The J2EE Connector architecture is also extremely valuable for third-party vendors. The CCI mentioned earlier not only allows J2EE components access to heterogeneous EIS landscapes as part of a component architecture; in theory, any Java application can do so as well.

Java XML API

The API for processing XML documents (JAXP) under J2EE supports not only the two typical modes of XML processing, *Document Object Model* (DOM) and *Simple API for XML* (SAX), but also the transformation of one XML vocabulary into another language through XML Stylesheet Language Transformation (XSLT). The validation of XML documents (containing a specific vocabulary) with XML scheme or Document Type Definitions (DTD) is also possible. As you would expect, JAXP can be used the same regardless of the implementation of the actual XML parser, making it an abstraction level for XML processing in J2EE.

Java XML-RPC API

In recent years, the Simple Object Access Protocol (SOAP) has become the industry standard XML-based protocol for executing platform-independent methods and function calls, thanks in large part to support by Microsoft and SAP. It is now supported by almost every platform and programming language. In the SAP Exchange Infrastructure (XI), SOAP has even assumed the role of central information broker, together with XSLT. Together with J2EE and SAP (or Java and ABAP), SOAP provides an alternative method to the otherwise RPC-dominated function calls. It also makes it possible to connect to other platforms, such as Microsoft's .NET.

HTTP, SSL, TLS

Despite its theoretical independence of protocols for its XML payload, the transport protocol used for SOAP messages is HTTP. The Java API for XML-Based RPC also supports this popular transmission option through Secure Sockets Layer (SSL) and Transport Layer Security (TLS).

SOAP is inherently capable of accessing Web services. JAX-RPC also makes it possible to create interface descriptions automatically, as Web Service Definition Language (WSDL) files for components to be published as Web services, as well as generate Web service clients automatically by the same means.

SOAP with Attachments API for Java (SAAJ)

Because two basic SOAP styles are used—either *XML-RPC*, optimized for function calls, or *document*, optimized for attachment-based document transmission (for use in email or workflows)—the transmission of attachments with a SOAP call described in the SOAP specification 1.1 has to be mapped as a MIME document. This requirement is covered by the *SOAP with Attachments API for Java* (SAAJ), which is not used by application developers directly, however, as it is part of JAX-RPC.

Java API for XML Registration Services (JAXR)

The *Java API for XML Registration Services* (JAXR) is provided to make Web services easily detectable in public directories, such as the ebXML Registry and Universal Description, Discovery, and Integration (UDDI), after their creation. It ultimately encapsulates use of the two registration services, saving you from having to deal with two separate APIs.

JDBC API

Although they are fully automated under container-managed persistence (CMP), and usually implemented through resource pooling even under bean-managed persistence (BMP), the option to manage database access manually should still be made available. To this extent, Java Database Connectivity (JDBC) provides a programming interface that permits access to databases from nearly any vendor. Similar to the ODBC concept, this is based on a form of SQL that represents the least common denominator among all database vendors. Driver packages, also implemented in Java, ensure that the connection option is truly platform-independent. The use of vendor-specific features, such as object-relational SQL, is not possible in this architecture due to its abstract approach.

Because the database-specific driver is not usually integrated in the code with an `import` statement, but instead loaded at runtime, this often proves problematic if the J2EE engine does not find the driver, because it was not added to a distribution package correctly.

In addition to establishing the connection and its vendor-independent approach to query design, JDBC also features a programming interface for processing the returned results of a query. This generally involves an iteration of the resulting set, which is encapsulated in an object with type `ResultSet` and may also use metadata from an object with type `ResultSetMetaData`.

JDBC as Basis for Other APIs

As a relatively low-level API, JDBC is itself an excellent basis for higher-level APIs that make it easier to use databases or automate them more. In the EJB environment, entity beans provide such an object-based mechanism for partially or totally automated data management. An increasingly popular alternative to beans are *Java Data Objects* (JDO), which implement persistent objects in a database that are independent of the architecture level where they are currently located.

JDBC ultimately forms the basis for all SQL embedded in Java code, such as that created for *SQL for Java* (SQLJ). Because JDBC receives the statements as strings, generating them in Java requires some additional effort—native Java types have to be formatted correctly before they can be inserted in the string. Consequently, SQLJ employs a preprocessor that translates the SQL embedded with native Java data types in the Java code into JDBC-compliant calls prior to the actual compilation process.

JDBC Versus ODBC

Despite first impressions, the *Open Database Connectivity* (ODBC) promoted by Microsoft should not be considered to be the opponent of JDBC, but instead thought of as a complementary technology that can even serve as a base for JDBC. Specifically, the JDBC implemented in Java is linked with the ODBC on Windows, Solaris, and Linux implemented in

C++ through the JDBC-ODBC Bridge. It is entirely possible to address ODBC from Java; however, this comes at the expense of platform dependence and therefore is not the preferred option. Therefore, JDBC is not simply a Java-specific shell for ODBC; it is a separate technology that uses only ODBC as an optional driver—as an alternative to the native database drivers—to ensure platform independence. Addressing ODBC directly causes architectural problems—Java handles all memory management internally, while memory management is the programmer's responsibility in C++. Moreover, JDBC provides an approach that is based on the needs of business logic, and which conceals the complex mixture of high-level and low-level components in the ODBC API from developers. Furthermore, we should mention that JDBC, in its highly developed Version 3.0 specification, boasts features—like SQL99 data types, automatically generated keys, and check pointing for transactions—that far exceed anything that is available in ODBC.

JDBC Driver Types

JDBC uses a driver architecture to transform calls made through the API into calls for the corresponding database. This creates an abstraction level that provides for the often-cited platform independence of the Java programming language in general and JDBC specifically. You have to create only one new driver to enable all JDBC-based programs to connect to a data source. In most cases, you have to map only the correct driver, without making any modifications to the coding.

According to the JDBC specification, drivers can be divided into four categories:

1. **JDBC-ODBC Bridge – ODBC driver**
   This driver, which Sun Microsystems ships with the Java SDK, enables you to access ODBC data sources from within JDBC. Note that this involves a client in binary format, compiled for the appropriate operating system, which must be available on every computer that plans to establish a connection via ODBC. Therefore, this constellation is suitable for only homogenous, manageable system landscapes, in which consistent distribution to the clients is ensured, or a multilayer client/server architecture such as J2EE, in which only the J2EE server or computers in the corresponding cluster have to be equipped with the driver.
2. **Native API – partial Java driver**
   This type of driver converts JDBC calls into calls for the native, proprietary database clients and executes them. The distribution and central-

ization problems discussed under the preceding driver type are also applicable here.

3. **JDBC-Net – pure Java driver**
   Calls that are sent through this type of driver are converted to a vendor-dependent protocol, which the corresponding server software in turn converts to native calls and processes. This type of driver is the most flexible of all categories, as all vendors of network-capable database solutions have to provide a control protocol of this type strictly for architectural reasons. Whether this protocol is suitable for an Internet solution, aside from intranet solutions, will depend on the implemented security mechanisms, firewall compatibility, and other typical Internet-related pitfalls.
4. **Native protocol – pure Java driver**
   This type of driver converts calls directly into calls of the underlying network protocol. This performance-boosting approach is the preferred type for intranets, because it ensures optimum collaboration with distributed systems without the additional effort of security guidelines.

The central starting point to find JDBC drivers that support the corresponding JDBC specification, and are equipped with aspects like connection pooling or distributed transactions, is the Sun Microsystems Web site:

http://industry.java.sun.com/products/jdbc/drivers

JDBC Architecture

In this context, the JDBC architecture corresponds to a three-tier model (see Figure 5.19). A Java application that uses JDBC communicates with the driver manager or a data pool to receive an instance of a connection. The calls placed with the JDBC API are forwarded to the mapped driver, which processes them using the mechanisms described above and passes it on to the appropriate data source. If SQL `SELECT` statements and objects with type `RecordSet` are used, the returned results are packed and can be processed in the application.

Java Transaction API

The specification of the *Java Transaction API* (JTA) describes the interfaces between the transaction manager and vendors who write transactional software. For this reason, and being cognizant of the fact that the EJB container performs this task in the J2EE architecture—and that transactional contexts are configured in the descriptors of a bean definition—you don't require a profound technical understanding of the material.

Nonetheless, it makes sense to examine the architecture of such a system and to possess at least a fundamental awareness of the subject.

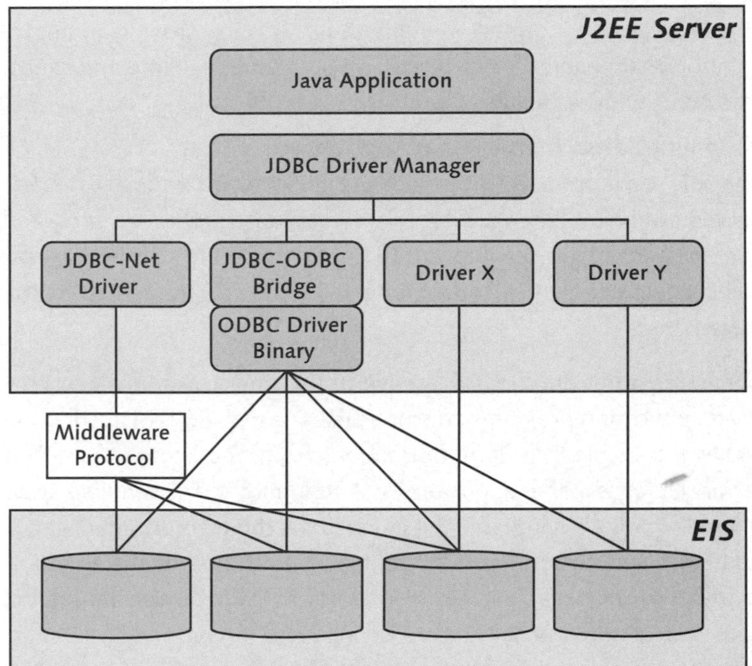

Figure 5.19 JDBC Architecture

In general, the architectural approach for transaction-capable systems involves four components. Each of these components has dedicated tasks, which collectively give the system its transactional capability: **Architecture**

1. **Transaction Manager**
   Responsible for the following transaction management tasks: functions and services that cover the transaction isolation, resource management, synchronization, and management of transaction-capable contexts. If the application programmer is tempted to take over transaction control, it can use these functions and services in the JTA.
2. **Application Server**
   In the J2EE environment, this is the J2EE server—or more precisely, the EJB container—that provides the runtime environment for transaction-capable applications or components (EJBs). The application server typically oversees the associated transaction management.

3. **Resource Manager**
   The resource manager can allocate resources under transactional aspects and make them available to the application, using access points defined in the J2EE Connector architecture. It must provide an implementation that enables the transaction manager to execute and cancel transactions with resources.
4. **Component-Based Transactional Application**
   In the J2EE environment, this role is usually played by the EJBs, especially session beans. The configurable characteristics that are anchored in the XML descriptors enable you to configure settings in the transactional context where they appear, which are then implemented by the EJB container.

In this manner, and from the perspective of the transaction manager, JTA itself is an application programming interface at a high level of abstraction that makes it possible to isolate transactions from one another, and thus create transaction-capable applications. A mapping to the industry standard X/Open XA is also available, which enables the resource manager to participate in a transactional context that is administered by the independent transaction manager. An API also exists to control the Transaction Manager; its use is built into the core of the J2EE server.

Java Authentication and Authorization Service (JAAS)

JCA

The *Java Authentication and Authorization Service* (JAAS) gives all Java access to technologies for data protection, through a vendor-independent interface. JAAS is available in the framework of the extensible *Java Cryptography Architecture* (JCA), which defines standardized interfaces for application programmers on one hand, and vendors of security-related applications, or *Java Cryptography Extensions* (JCE)—cryptographic algorithms, certificate management, and so on—on the other hand in its Service Provider Interface (SPI). Three groups are defined for these dedicated services in SPI:

Cryptographic Services

A cryptographic service describes an engine that represents certain functions in the form of an abstract class. The `Signature`, `MessageDigest`, and `KeyPairGenerator` classes defined in JDK 1.2 make it clear that they are entities for performing specialized tasks, such as generating a signature or a message digest. Which algorithm is used in which case is determined by the implementation of the vendor's derived class.

Certificate Interfaces

The three abstract classes `Certificate`, `X509Certificate`, and `CertificateFactory` describe an interface for the generic response of a certificate, along with access methods for attributes defined in the X.509 specification. The latter interface defines the behavior of an object generation class, based on the factory design pattern, that generates certificates and certificate-revoked lists.

Key Management Interfaces

The abstract `KeyStore` class describes an interface for implementing a key management organization, such as a trust center.

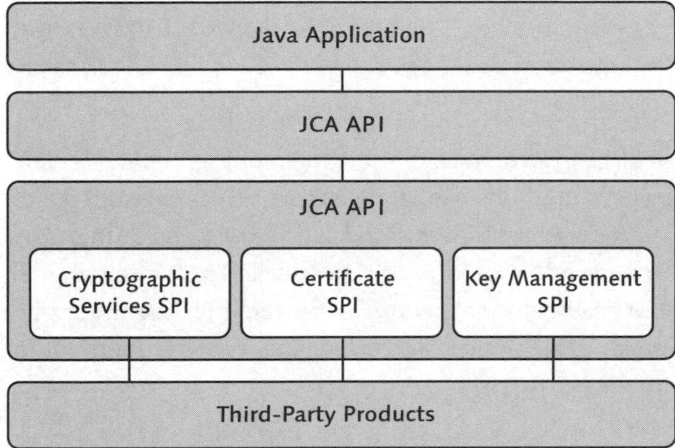

Figure 5.20 JCA Architecture

While JCA was developed at Sun Microsystems, the concept for JAAS does not come from the Java inventor itself. Instead, JAAS is a Java-specific implementation of the PAM *(Pluggable Authentication Module)* framework. JAAS also makes it possible to announce subject-related access restrictions for resources, which are defined in security guidelines. Accessing a resource requires a two-phase protocol.

Authentication

Because users are often dependent on services that require authentication, and these services can request other services under the same principle, the users and services that have to identify themselves are called *subjects* in the JAAS context. To distinguish between subjects, they are assigned a series of characteristics, or *principals* (such as a name), that are not identical to any other subject's principals. They are linked after a successful authentication, enabling the system to carry out certain privileged actions with a subject.

Authentication is performed using a fact or statement that requires knowledge that only its corresponding subject can possess (such as a password). To check such a claim, JAAS introduces *credentials*, which can be seen as security aspect-specific properties of a subject. The difference to principals is that access to these characteristics is not public in all cases. Credentials, which in Java can be recognized by any object assigned to a subject as a credential, are divided into public and private groups. The two differ in their handling, in that several security settings are checked before private credentials are accessed.

Two additional classes are now required to perform authentication: The finalized class of `LoginContext` runs the standard flows of the authentication, based on one or more `LoginModules`. This abstract class controls the process, using the methods `login()`, `logout()`, `commit()`, and `abort()`.

The process takes place in two phases: In the login phase, the `LoginContext` calls the `login()` methods of all the `LoginModules` registered after a configuration. If the user is authenticated for all modules of this class, the `commit()` methods of the modules are now called in the same order. If only one module fails authentication, however, the `LoginContext` responds by terminating the process and calling the `abort()` methods for the registered modules.

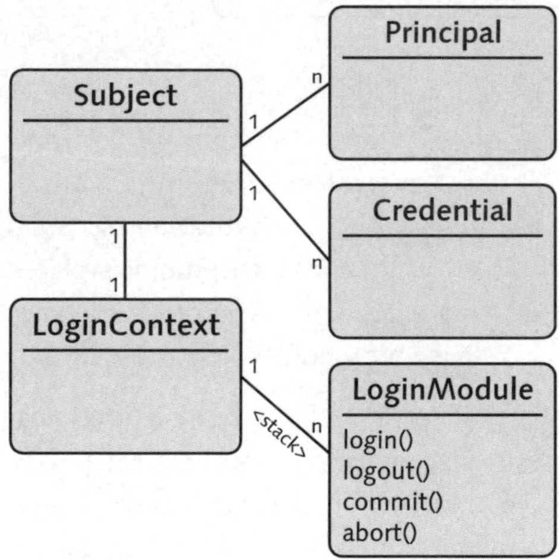

Figure 5.21 Authentication Model Under JAAS

Authorization

As soon as authentication is completed properly, JAAS enables principal-based access controls. These control contexts are called *security policies* and, in the current version of the technology, are saved in text-based files.

The following example shows the simplest possible security policy, which—in typical JDK 1.1 style—gives code from domain `res-`

man.abap2java.com read permission for system directory *resources*, including its subdirectories.

```
grant Codebase "http://snp.de", Signed by "snp" {
   permission java.io.FilePermission
     "/resources/-", "read";
}
```

Because policies that are this simple will not be adequate enough to ensure subject-based or role-based authorization, you can also design them to be principal-specific, in which case the roles are treated as principals for the subject.

In the following example, a subject, webuser, with a principal webuser.Role with value "administrator" is given permission to read and write to system directory "/resources/masterdata/-".

```
grant Principal webuser.Role "administrator" {
   permission java.io.FilePermission
     "/resources/masterdata/-", "read, write";
}
```

Java uses an instance of SecurityManager for access control, which, in turn, delegates this responsibility to an object with type AccessController. It first creates a copy of the current AccessControlContext, which runs with the authorizations in the standard coding by default. During the authorization process, the status of the AccessControlContext may change, based on the underlying security policy.

JAAS supports this architecture by providing the doAs() method for the respective subject. Calling this status method triggers the corresponding authorization checks, which enable the AccessController to make decisions based on the subject's principals:

```
public final class Subject {
...
// links the subject with the current
// AccessControlContext, then performs the action
   public static Object doAs(Subjects,
     java.security.PrivilegedAction action) { }
}
```

Listing 5.5 The Static "doAs()" Method of the Subject

Now that you have read this brief explanation of the authorization procedure and JAAS, the following rough model should give you a final overview of the topic (see Figure 5.22). Although the model lacks the quality of an authorization model that would be implemented, it illustrates the major agents involved in a JAAS authorization process.

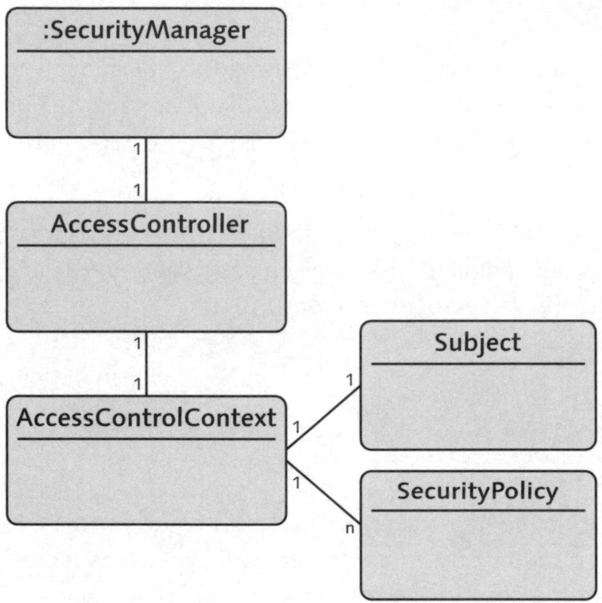

Figure 5.22 Authorization Model Under JAAS

Java Mail API

J2EE applications can use the Java Mail API to send email messages. It also consists of two parts: one API for the application programmer and one API for providers of email services under J2EE. This latter service provider interface (SPI) is filled by default by the Java Mail component.

Summary

J2EE as Architecture

The J2EE architecture features numerous standardized interfaces that allow for both application developers and third-party product vendors to develop products with a high degree of reusability and interoperability. This approach to modularized software development enables vendors of integrated solutions to deploy or invest in the capabilities of external tools, and thus external knowledge, and even swap out these capabilities without having to modify the proprietary code. This ability to swap out software components shifts the pressure to evolve from customer to vendor, because a change of providers is no longer associated with major effort or expense. This greatly reduces the customers' dependency on a single software vendor.

J2EE as Platform

As a platform, J2EE features a complete framework for developing distributed—and therefore scalable—applications based on component technology. It saves application developers from having to design and implement the infrastructure-related aspects of their applications, freeing them from low-level tasks. This reduces the implementation time and allows developers to concentrate more on the business logic. Although J2EE has a fairly steep learning curve for beginners, due to its comprehensive architecture and modularized structures, its ability to support application-independent, cross-project expertise is compensation enough and well worth the initial effort. SAP NetWeaver Developer Studio features a wide range of supporting, productivity-increasing tools, to flatten out this learning curve and enable a fast, intuitive start with J2EE.

5.2.2 Development Environment

SAP NetWeaver Developer Studio is the sturdy, versatile, and flexible development environment for J2EE and Web Dynpro projects on the SAP Web Application Server 6.40. Although its basic approach is somewhat different from the ABAP Workbench, this is due to the history and architecture of J2EE-based projects and the architecture of the development environment itself. We should point out in advance that SAP NWDS is not intended to model the ABAP Workbench in the Java environment.

The advantages and special features of SAP NWDS will be illustrated in detail in the examples and exercises that appear later on in this chapter.

Project Life Cycle

SAP NWDS covers the entire life cycle of a project and offers effective workarounds for known weaknesses from the J2EE world. The general approach is both project-oriented and modularized. Generally, all developments are considered projects, which, in turn, can reference other projects, promoting the cross-project reusability of coding. Specifically, referencing one or more existing projects in a new project makes all the existing classes and packages in the referenced projects available in the new project. *Assembly projects* involve grouping existing projects together to form distribution packages, as well as configuring them with visual tools for use in the respective target container (deployment). Without the appropriate tools, deployment itself can be a complex, time-consuming process in the J2EE world. SAP NWDS features a full range of efficient tools to save developers from this manual work.

Another drawback of J2EE is inherent in its deployment-driven development cycle, which prevents effective code debugging prior to deployment. Although the integrated debugging environment in the SAP NetWeaver Developer Studio cannot eliminate this drawback completely, it does help considerably. The applied paradigms are not that different from those used for HTTP debugging in the Object Navigator.

Speed

The true strengths of SAP NWDS become evident in the context developing EJBs and—especially—Web Dynpros. You can create component interfaces, such as local and remote interfaces of EJBs or the complex class structures of a Web Dynpro, fully automatically. Similarly, maintenance characteristics (like the continuous update of method signatures) are minimized to a minor share of the development effort. In addition to a refined reporting system that indicates coding errors during the development phase and suggests improvements automatically, there are also many automatic options for restructuring existing coding automatically—to respond to spontaneous changes of requirements.

Quality

The defined *refactoring* methods, which greatly simplify code restructuring (needed due to changing requirements), ultimately also improve the readability and quality of the resulting coding. They also promote "good programming style" of the development environment, by providing developers with information about unnecessary coding blocks, incorrect return values, inconsistencies in method values and signatures, and automatic completion of calculable source coding. The same applies to the typical source text documentation with Javadoc, which SAP NWDS also supports. For example, a menu item is available to create the appropriate comment blocks and fill them with the extractable attributes in the coding automatically.

Absence of Forward Navigation and Where-Used Lists

The forward navigation known from the ABAP Workbench and the option to create where-used lists for development objects are not yet available in SAP NetWeaver Developer Studio. While these features have the most effect on development novices, because it makes it easier for them to learn about existing infrastructures, J2EE projects are highly standardized anyway. As long as you have sufficient knowledge of the J2EE architecture and clean project implementation—which is enforced by the development environment—you will be able to derive the necessary infrastructure-related information about a project. Of course, this theoretical approach to starting a project is no replacement for the information provided by forward navigation and where-used lists.

SAP NetWeaver Developer Studio is based on the Eclipse IDE platform from IBM. Eclipse is an open, extremely extensible development environment that focuses primarily on Java. Technically, Eclipse consists of an extremely lean core that hosts a comprehensive plug-in architecture. This process is controlled completely by the Java API that is provided, which plug-in vendors can use to develop IDE extensions. **Eclipse as Basis IDE**

The freely available standard distribution of Eclipse already includes plug-ins for the workspace (to display project trees) and workbench (which provides the basis for the GUI). Eclipse can also be extended in any direction: There are plug-ins, both purchased and free of charge, for UML-based software design, for designing Web interfaces with the Drag&Drop technique, editors for other programming interfaces, RDBMS, and more. Therefore, SAP NetWeaver Developer Studio, based on Eclipse, represents a collection of plug-ins that make it possible to work with J2EE, Web Dynpro, and Java Dictionary projects—which are not covered in the standard scope. Other aspects, such as the refactoring capability mentioned above and consistency checks within the coding, are performed by SAP NetWeaver Developer Studio inherently through the plug-in for Java development, which is included in the standard distribution of Eclipse.

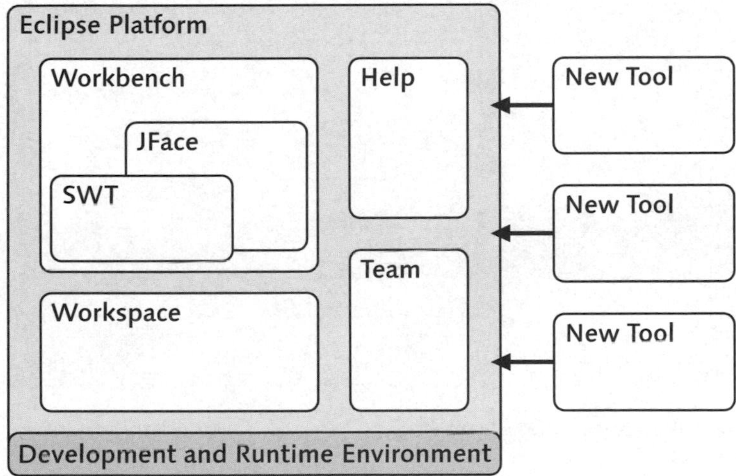

Figure 5.23 Eclipse Architecture

To provide an introductory overview to the user interface of the development environment, Figure 5.24 shows the main components of the SAP NetWeaver Developer Studio. **User Interface**

1. **File bar and toolbars**
   As in any other application, the IDE contains the familiar tools for saving, printing, and so on. Worth noting are the options for saving metadata, which are required to automatically generate the Java class model and the associated update in metadata-based projects such as the Java Dictionary and Web Dynpro. You can also start debugging and test runs with program sections here.
2. **Perspectives**
   The perspectives mentioned above open a view of projects of a certain type. Aside from the standard view for class trees, special views are available for J2EE, Web Dynpro, and Java Dictionary projects. Other non-project-related views, such as the debugging view, are also available.

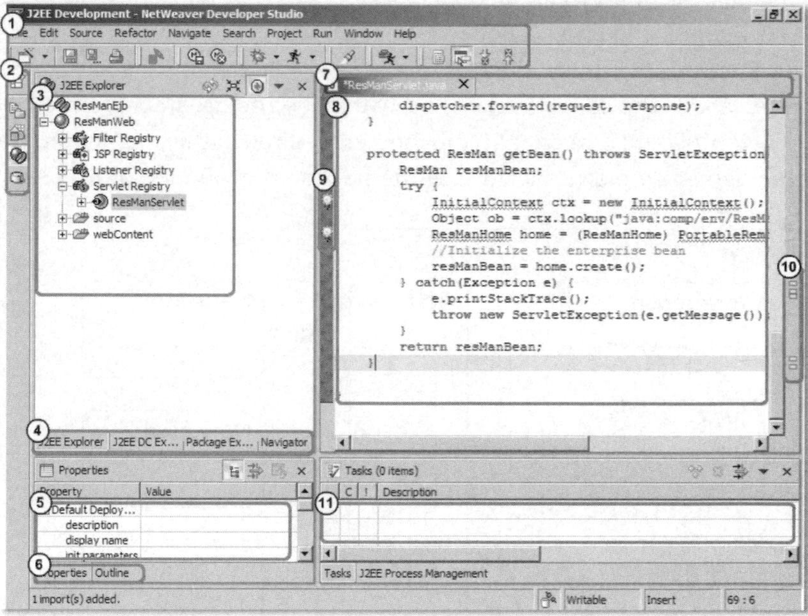

Figure 5.24 SAP NetWeaver Developer Studio

3. **Project tree/Workplace**
   The project tree has a different appearance, depending on the selected perspective. In general, all projects of a certain type are listed here, along with their underlying development objects.
4. **Different workplace views**
   Extended views, such as the "Package Explorer," which are relatively free of the current perspective but are included only when they make

sense for the project type in question, appear in the tabs at the bottom of the Workplace.

5. **Characteristics and excerpt view**
   This view displays the characteristics of the selected project or development object, along with its current values. Alternatively, you can also select the excerpt view for the respective development object; where Java classes are involved, this extends navigation to the methods and variables in the class.

6. **Characteristics/excerpt view selection**
   You can toggle between the characteristic view and the excerpt view by clicking the inactive tab.

7. **Open documents**
   This tab displays all currently open documents. You can change the current document in the work area by clicking the corresponding tab. Documents that have been changed since they were last saved are flagged with an asterisk (*) next to their names.

8. **Work area of current document**
   The work area in the regular development view has space for one document. Other objects, such as configuration masks, can also be displayed here, depending on the development object involved. The visual design/layout environment for Web Dynpros and JSP previews are also available here.

   Syntax highlighting and error detection are used in the development view itself, as well as in the other elements of the development environment.

9. **Warning and error display**
   Warnings and errors due to syntax errors, structure violations, and missing class integration are displayed in the left side of the work area, next to the corresponding line. When you click the mouse on the respective icon, the development environment provides a potential solution (or several alternative solutions in many cases) automatically. The solution is often implemented automatically or semi-automatically, through user dialogs.

10. **Warning and error navigation**
    Because the source text of a class is not always completely visible in the work area, the development environment provides navigation targets to the individual error locations within the active document. When you click on one of the bars, the work area automatically scrolls to the error and its surrounding coding.

11. **Tasks list**
    The two navigation mechanisms introduced above cannot model errors of a cross-document nature. To deal with this, the Tasks list provides a view of all errors and warning messages across all documents and projects. Double-clicking on an error opens the corresponding document and positions the cursor on the error.

As you will notice in the examples later on, the user interface can vary widely depending on the selected project and development object. In most cases, however, it is only the view of the work area that changes, to give you the optimized, most sensible edit options for the respective development object. A rough overview of the user interface in the SAP NetWeaver Developer Studio should suffice to give you an initial impression of the development environment at this point.

Development Paradigm

There are major differences between the development paradigms in ABAP and J2EE, either historical in nature or due to the evolutionary, parallel development of both architectures. The central objective for developing SAP NetWeaver Development Studio was to rejoin these two development tracks without alienating either of the two developer communities; it was implemented accordingly. In most cases, this involved adapting the J2EE environment to the development paradigms familiar from the ABAP world.

Developments from the Java and J2EE environments generally run on the local developer's computer and are deployed to the server upon completion. This approach offers greater development speed, with regard to server load and testing. It also corresponds to the philosophy of loosely-coupled application components and their autonomous development. On the other hand, J2EE developers do not have development objects like a central repository of data types, or knowledge from other products. The inevitable result is a certain redundancy in the set of developed solutions. While a defined terminology and design patterns at least standardize these solutions, they demand a great deal of discipline during development.

The integrative code-checking in the ABAP environment is just such a mechanism, which activates (comparable to deployment) modules to prevent incorrect references, enabling a code check based on globally-defined data types and structures. This is possible because ABAP developments are server-based and integrated, in contrast to the typically client-based, modularized development under Java.

SAP NetWeaver Developer Studio was intended to bridge these differences at a level that benefits both sides, to create the most value for both the architecture of the overall system and for developments. Six main areas requiring harmonization were identified.

Graphical User Interfaces

The GUIs were to be developed based on the Model View Control (MVC) design pattern, to take advantage of the features of decoupling—the ability to swap out one entity without having to modify the other. Existing technologies, such as JSP, BSP, and SAP GUI for HTML, do not have these features. Similarly, the conventional dynpro (screen) is not suitable for Web publishing. The first two technologies would make an MVC-based implementation possible; however, this approach would demand a great amount of discipline from the developers. Changes to existing implementations are error-prone and require considerable effort.

The alternative is the new Web Dynpro technology, a level of metacode on top of the actual implementation that provides for the necessary abstraction in the programming model. In practice, this means creating a user interface with Web Dynpro usually involves only the planning and design aspects, while the actual implementation is provided by a code generator, which generates the platform-dependent coding in a target language and ensures implementation of the MVC pattern.

Database Independence

In J2EE, JDBC ultimately represents the technological basis for database access. Due to the driver architecture, hard-coding the driver path is often helpful for test purposes, but not an option for portable code. While using data pools to manage connections from the J2EE service reduces the direct dependence on a given driver, it poses the problem that not all database vendors have implemented SQL equally. Therefore, any use of advanced features will result in unwanted database dependencies in the coding.

The next logical step is to use CMP-managed entity beans. This technology further encapsulates the dependencies by fixating them in the deploy descriptors, which can quickly reach their limits when complex objects become involved. To overcome this, we have to fall back on BMP-managed entity beans, which, in turn, have to be linked to the corresponding database through JDBC, once again risking platform-dependence. For experienced ABAP developers, switching to JDBC and its associated restrictions and pitfalls will pose an additional burden. In this context, an alternative to the integrated use of SQL within Java—similar to the Open SQL embedding of SQL in ABAP code—would be useful, even if it does contribute to promoting a bad design.

SQLJ provides this type of translation between the two languages. Because SQLJ is not understood by the Java compiler, however, and therefore cannot be translated, a preprocessor has to be integrated in the IDE at this point to convert from SQLJ to JDBC at compile time. Consequently, from an integration perspective, SQLJ is not integrated in Java as seamlessly as Open SQL has been implemented in ABAP. (See Section 4.1.4 for examples.)

Business Logic The creation of J2EE business logic elements, EJBs, is completely supported in SAP NetWeaver Developer Studio. If it weren't, generating and maintaining the individual interfaces of an EJB would be a time-consuming, error-prone process. You would have to ensure that method signatures are consistent between remote and local interfaces, for example, and that the client can address the corresponding business methods. In addition, the IDE also supports the generation and maintenance of JSPs, servlets, and all three types of assembly projects, which are responsible for the creation and configuration of the files that are deployed later.

The cross-platform solution here is Web services. In fact, it is simple to generate and publish Web services from existing Enterprise Java session beans. Once again, the integrated environment automatically guarantees consistency between the different interface descriptions.

Java Dictionary The Java Dictionary in the SAP NWDS models the data structures at a persistent level, equivalent to the ABAP Dictionary in the ABAP. It is only a meta structure, however, which is not created in the respective database until the deploy process. You can use any native Java and JDBC data types in the standard system. You can also define your own data types based on existing types. Therefore, if you always build data structures based on ABAP data types, you will have to include the effort required to create these ABAP data types in the first place.

The primary difference between ABAP and J2EE with regard to their view of data is that the latter completely lacks domains, table types, and other typical ABAP constructs. It has only field types in tables, which are based on simple types, without taking a "detour" through concepts like domains, structures, or table types. A data definition is not necessarily incomplete without this information, however; you can restrict data types with regard to value set, value domain, pattern, and so on.

Infrastructure for Centralized Development The ABAP Workbench uses a server-centric approach to provide a centralized infrastructure. All components, source coding, and so forth are checked out directly from the server, edited, and checked back in. All developers use the same documents and there are no inconsistencies due to interdependence. When a specific object is activated, the system performs a consistency check first, and activates the object only after the check is passed.

This type of work organization is impossible in an environment like J2EE, because developers work in different client-based environments (as mentioned above) and because versioning is usually performed by the tools on the clients' file systems. Reproducing the ABAP model in a J2EE environment would inevitably require the integration of proprietary extensions to the J2EE server, which the specification prohibits. Therefore, a different method has to be found in order to provide ease of use for developers while ensuring a consistent code base.

The targeted solution involves the *Design Time Repository* (DTR) and the *Component Build Service* (CBS). Every development object (see Section 5.2.3 for a classification) is assigned to a development component when it is created, just like ABAP Workbench development objects are assigned to a package. The components can be nested to model complex structures. All development objects within a component that are used by different development objects in other components have to be declared "public." Projects that are structured in this way are centralized, easier to maintain, and have many of the same positive features as the activation methodology from the ABAP Workbench. When a new component is set up, the integrated reference checks the CBS to ensure that the completion of the build process is considered successful only when all of the contained development objects are free of all errors. Only then can a component be deployed to the adjacent J2EE server.

The DTR assumes the task of centralized development object management. To transport these development objects to the client, you must have checked them out of the repository using the WebDAV protocol.[1] WebDAV works on the Repository server file system, which can handle the version history internally and independently, based on the received WebDAV commands.

1 WebDAV represents an extension to HTTP that implements additional methods, such as `PUT` and `DELETE`.

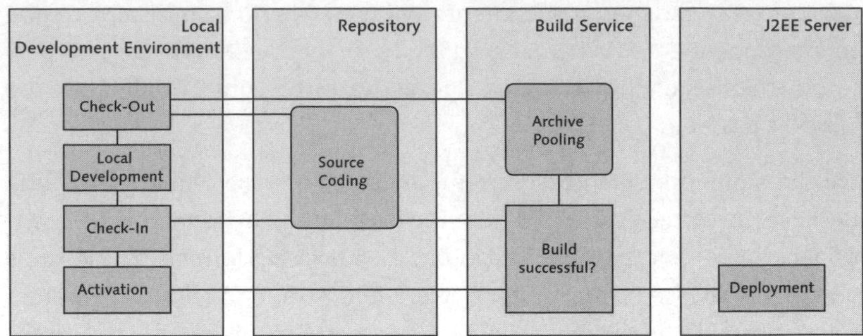

Figure 5.25 SAP Development and Deployment Process

Uniformity of the Development Environment

The method described above makes it possible to manage and edit documents centrally. Incompatibilities can still arise, however, because the archives used for development (*JAR* files)—which are used especially to ensure the correct display, syntax checks, and type checks in the local development—do not necessarily agree with those on the J2EE server. One example already mentioned, though not critical, is the use of different JDBC drivers. For this reason, you must ensure that the development environment is synchronized with the production server with regard to the archive files used for the repository.

5.2.3 Development Objects

The development environment for the SAP Web AS 6.40 is used primarily to develop three types of projects: J2EE, Web Dynpro, and Java Dictionary. These project types overlap and complement one other in some areas, with regard to their objectives and location in the typical three-tier software architecture.

Web Dynpro

Web Dynpro is a typical example of an application at the presentation level of the application architecture. Its ability to quickly develop graphical interfaces—and the corresponding connections in any application model—successfully implements the MVC objective of separating display, user interaction, and application model.

J2EE

J2EE applications span the complete spectrum of the application architecture, but can also be examined in its component parts. Although Java Server Pages (JSPs) and servlets belong to the presentation layer, they don't support fast development cycles and aren't abstract enough to provide planning flexibility and restructuring options. Therefore, they don't represent an alternative to the Web Dynpro technology in SAP Web AS

6.40. At the business logic level, enterprise beans—specifically session beans—add much more value to the existing infrastructure. Because they are executable on distributed systems, they support the modeling of business processes and the "software as service" approach.

For entity beans, the persistence level of the application architecture would also be covered. Even if it would be nice to have automatic support for complex persistence among multiple tables with CMP, the use of BMP-managed beans supports this feature now, even though it demands a greater implementation effort.

Which technology you ultimately use in the BMP context is an open, strategic decision. JDBC is flexible enough to implement BMP completely, and promotes a clean implementation, but doesn't approximate the ease of use implemented by Open SQL under Java. The preprocessed macro language SQLJ serves this purpose under Java, even though it is not part of the actual Java syntax, like Open SQL in ABAP. Java Data Objects (JDO) represent another alternative. Their automatic persistence models one aspect of EJBs, but does not cover features like distributed objects or the transactional concept. Accordingly, they will be of only limited use for J2EE applications. Nevertheless, JDO is an optimal way for vendors of EJB containers to implement CMP.

As far as Web services are concerned, their automatic generation from session beans is fast and simple. For this reason, they represent an excellent platform-independent option—alongside the platform-dependent EJBs and BAPIs—of making a system accessible in a controlled manner, expanding the component-based service concept across all platforms.

Java Dictionary

In the three-tier system architecture of SAP Web AS 6.40, the Java Dictionary is located in the data persistence layer. By creating and deploying data structures and data types, it provides for transparency of the data model used for the development environment on the client. Among other things, it uses CMP-based entity beans as the basis for creating the data mapping and persistence conditions, and SQLJ for type checks and conversions.

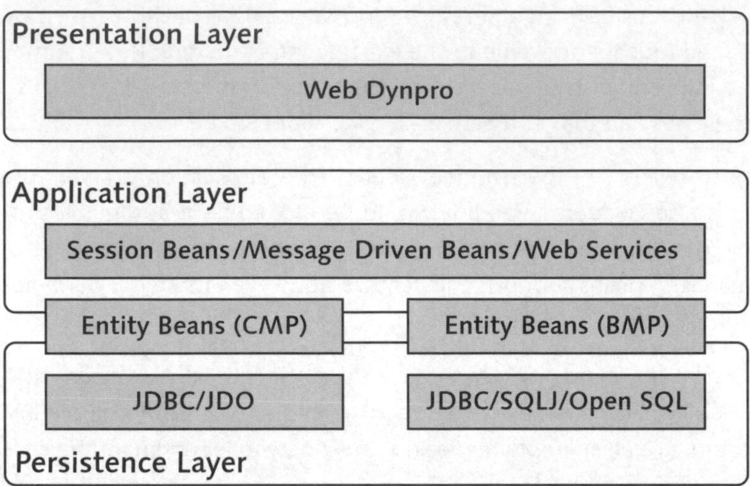

Figure 5.26 Development Architecture of the Java Personality Under Web AS 6.40

Perspectives

Dividing the user interface into perspectives in SAP NetWeaver Developer Studio gives you a better overview of a certain type of project. Because the development objects are contained as entities in the individual projects, they are explained below in reference to their structural assignment. The development objects are described in further detail in the tutorials in this chapter and the next chapter in order to help you put your knowledge to practical use.

As mentioned above, projects from the J2EE environment cover the full field of software developments. Accordingly, this perspective is equipped with a wide, rich range of development objects that you can use when in doubt. As such, it is no surprise that there are already six different basic types of projects in the J2EE environment, which can be nested and ultimately tied together to form a distribution-capable *enterprise application project*.

Web Project A Web project contains all the development objects and entities from the presentation layer, including connections to the business logic objects—EJBs. Because there are some overlaps regarding the ability to implement certain sets of development objects, the MVC structure cannot be implemented as consistently in the standard development as a Web Dynpro project. The application perspective is also different, and is much more complex. In general, this type of project demands much greater discipline and experience from developers than the Web Dynpro projects described above, but it offers much greater freedom as well. As far as ease of development is concerned, it lies far behind its internal SAP NetWeaver competition, because you, the developer, are fully responsible for the implementation of the project.

JSP

Java Server Pages are one way of designing browser-based user interfaces. To achieve abstraction, encapsulation, and reusability, you use TagLibs exclusively within a JSP and avoid scriptlets. This makes a JSP free of maintenance-intensive Java coding. It is used for display only, and not for data retrieval. Because JSP does not offer much support regarding the separation of business/control and presentation logic, scriptlets enable you to introduce business/control logic into your JSPs. This is why developers require discipline to promote this separation.

Servlets

In the MVC model, servlets perform the tasks of the controller as an intermediary between the queries sent by the user and the outputs sent to it. They can also be used to implement the view component, although this compromises a clean realization of the MVC model. In fact, JSPs are nothing more than specialized servlets, whose simpler notation serves this specific purpose.

Filters

Servlets can be equipped with *filters*, which were introduced in Version 2.3 of the servlet specification. Filters can be used to modify an HTTP request placed with a servlet or the response sent back to the browser. They can be considered as a preprocessor for a servlet for an HTTP request, and a postprocessor for an HTTP response—whose answers are processed again after they are generated. For a practical example, consider the following scenario: A servlet for accessing ResMan is responsible for retrieving the data from the available resources and representing it platform-independently in XML. The output that comes from the servlet (as a filter for the HTTP response) is sent to an XSLT-based postprocessor, which converts the XML into a readable output format (such as HTML or WML) for the target platform (Web browser, PC, mobile device).

Listeners

Listeners represent another modifier for servlets. They register for events that are triggered during the life cycle of a servlet—such as receiving a request or starting and stopping a servlet—and can then respond accordingly. According to the event listener model, which the observer design pattern extracts as a concept, listeners have to act themselves—to determine their anticipated reaction—once notification of an event is received.

Web Application Project

Web projects are not executable alone. Although they contain the implementation of the presentation logic, they lack the configuration data for production use in the Web container of the J2EE server, which, as previously mentioned, is stored in XML descriptors. You can group one or more Web projects together in Web application projects and provide them with these descriptors.

XML Descriptors You define all the major settings for your Web projects in the XML file *WEB-INF/web.xml*. Due to the large number of possible settings, however, only the most important are listed below, with references to the corresponding tutorials in the next chapters. It is possible, for example, to define alternative URLs for JSPs and servlets where they can be accessed with a Web browser, or even use URL patterns to create a mapping. Also, you can define the authentication procedures for the individual servlets here, as well as other security settings. Information regarding the use of external resources—database connections, database pools, or components like EJBs—is also critical. Another descriptor file—*WEB-INF/web-j2ee-engine.xml*—contains other possible settings to configure the runtime response of the container in connection with a Web application.

Web Archive The result of a Web application project is always a Web archive, or *WAR* file, which encapsulates all the data needed to deploy a Web application. Do not confuse this archive type with the enterprise application project, which also contains the business logic components contained in a Web application project, in addition to the presentation components

EJB Project A project begins at the lowest level as an Enterprise JavaBeans (EJB) project, which implements these components and deploys them together. EJBs play a central role for the business logic and data retrieval logic in the J2EE architecture. In fact, they represent the only supported method of modeling this architecture. Direct access to data sources, which is possible under JDBC, is frowned upon, for example, and allowed only in entity beans that use bean-managed persistence (BMP). Therefore, any EJB project you start will deal mainly with this component model, which has already been described in detail.

The project handling provides support in dealing with the local and remote interfaces of a bean. Semi-automatic functions make it easier for you to perform tasks such as comparing method signatures through the corresponding interfaces.

Entity Beans In the specific implementation of entity beans, you also receive support from a graphical user interface that you use to define container-managed persistence (CMP) characteristics. Because it currently supports persistence only over one table, as mentioned above, you cannot circumvent BMP to work with complex examples. Any difficulties that occur in this development cycle—such as creating non-primitive primary key classes that can be serialized for network transport, or connecting EJBs to data pools—are opposed in the necessary places.

Session Beans

With session beans, in addition to automatic generation of the basic classes and the ease of use of not having to compare the method signatures in the individual interfaces manually—as one would do with entity beans—the IDE also provides support. This is important when you are preparing to publish a session bean as a Web service, as user dialogs are provided to help you create an interface description in WSDL, creating the Java proxies for accepting SOAP requests, and so on. You'll see examples of these cases in the tutorials in this chapter and in Chapter 6.

EJB Assembly Project

You need an *EJB Assembly Project* to group one or more EJB projects together for distribution. In addition to the data from the individual EJB projects, it also contains the necessary XML descriptors, which configure the EJBs for their use in the EJB container on the J2EE server. You can also distribute single session beans as Web services at this point. Contrary to the two XML deployment descriptors available in the Web project area, there are four of these data types available for EJB projects. Because they are responsible for the bottom two tiers of the three-tier application architecture, they also have to assume more responsibility for descriptions.

XML Descriptors

Besides the parameters for defining the runtime environment in file *META-INF/ejb-j2ee-engine.xml*, the successful distribution of EJB components is primarily the responsibility of the descriptor file *META-INF/ejb-jar.xml*. It contains parameters that apply to all EJB types, such as connections to external JNDI resources like data pools or use of other EJBs in a nested structure. This latter characteristic is extremely important, because there is no other way for EJBs to access one another other than from the EJB context addressed through JNDI. The reason for this is obvious, in light of the possibility of scaling such components by distributing them to physically separate computers.

The configuration of the container-managed persistence, mentioned several times above, takes place in the descriptor for CMP-managed entity beans: *META-INF/persistent.xml*. The values are mapped to the appropriate database tables in the Java Dictionary here. This mapping is essential to decouple the structure of an entity bean from its physical manifestation in the database, to enable modifications to the data structures in the EIS (Enterprise Information System) without requiring modifications to the application logic.

To deploy Web services successfully, you need a configuration of the service descriptor *META-INF/ws-deployment-descriptor.xml*. As with all other descriptors, SAP NetWeaver Developer Studio features input templates to configure these values, instead of working directly with XML. You can select the methods of the session bean to be published, as well as define the URL endpoint—the physically defined URL of the Web service.

Java Archive

Once again, the result of this project type is an archive file with type *JAR*. It merges all the Enterprise JavaBeans and their descriptors into a file that is deployable and can be used in the EJB containers of the J2EE server. When a complete business application is involved, it is packed into an enterprise application project together with a Web archive, where it is tied into an enterprise archive. Because EJB assembly projects don't have a visual representation, this display is performed in most cases by a Web application project, which acts as a client for the Enterprise JavaBeans it contains. Exceptions to this pattern are the components that are published as Web services. SAP Web Application Server 6.40 already provides a Web page for each Web service—accessible through its endpoint URL—that you can use for comprehensive testing; the interface descriptions are also to be retrieved here as WSDL files. Independent application clients can use the *JarClientAPI* to access EJBs.

Enterprise Application Project

The J2EE architecture features enterprise application objects in order to unify Web applications and their representation, the Web archive, and EJB assembly projects and prepare them for distribution to any J2EE server. They use additional descriptors to consolidate several of the aforementioned archive types and generate an enterprise archive, which contains all the necessary data. As long as none of the components in an archive violates the J2EE specification—and the J2EE target server is implemented in accordance with the standard—the application can theoretically be transported anywhere. This theory often fails to deliver in actuality, however, because the J2EE servers must be configured identically, for example, to provide data pools.

Web Service Client Project

Just as session beans can be made available to other applications as a Web service, they can also be made to act as clients for a Web service.

To do so, you can generate a Java proxy class, building on a WSDL-based interface description, and use it as an object instance (similar to a Java object). Communication is internal and uses the stub/skeleton pattern, which you were already introduced to in our discussion of EJBs.

5.2.4 Java Dictionary

Now that you've had an overview of the contents, functions, and structures of the SAP NetWeaver Developer Studio, you will run through the development cycle of a Java Dictionary project, based on the example ResMan project. All the activities involved in creating and deploying data types and data structures are depicted in comprehensible examples. Your objective is to create the necessary data structures for ResMan, transport these data structures, and fill them with data properly—to gain practical knowledge of how to work with Java Dictionary projects in the SAP NetWeaver Developer Studio.

The Java Dictionary is based on the concepts of independence of data structures and their reusability in different contexts. Specifically, the Java Dictionary addresses three facets of the application design directly.

Content Independent of Implementation

As you recall, the MVC model separates structure, layout/design, and data on the frontend. The Java Dictionary and the data types it contains do the same thing for separating data and implementation. Therefore, all data is contained in one or more repositories and is referenced in the implementation. Linking data directly with an implementation—for example, taking literals for status texts directly from the coding—will create a direct dependency between two layers of the system architecture that are supposed to be kept separate. Consequently, redundancies will inevitably arise, the program will become more difficult to maintain, and the knowledge of an application is tied to a single developer. All these factors drastically reduce the flexibility with which the application can be managed, and, above all, cause extra costs.

If you take this idea one step further, it also applies to the description of data types and structures within the implementation. While it is often possible to convert data types at runtime, this is associated with a considerable programming effort, as well as diminished performance. The alternative is the data types and structures that are generally defined outside the coding in the Java Dictionary, which are included in the coding at compile time through a declarative framework such as Web Dynpro, and can be integrated via mapping configurations there.

So, a descriptive framework like Web Dynpro generates the code that is required to execute the actual program, which is based on structured metadata (XML) at design time. The data types are also included and optimized according to the mapping at this point. This enables you to generate clearly structured coding in any target language (such as Java), helping you to conceal complicated implementation concepts from the application programmer. Therefore, you can make the descriptive framework platform-independent, because any target language can be used.

To now enable one or more of these frameworks to access data types, you must be able to enrich the data types themselves with meta information that can be used or ignored in different contexts. The Java Dictionary supports this as well, for example, by defining labels or field lengths for the Web Dynpro input templates. You can generally divide this method into two categories: In the first category, which we have already mentioned, is the GUI. In the second category, there is another interface for other metadata. Value restrictions, for example, can be used by both the client and the server to validate user inputs, depending on which end processes the validation.

Developers from the SAP world, who have already used the ABAP Workbench and are familiar with the screen and ABAP Dictionary in the SAP System, will recognize these concepts. Until now, however, such declarative frameworks were nonexistent in the world of Java.

Standards for Describing Data Types and Structures

In order to address metadata through the respective interfaces from various places, a common standard has to be found. Because the information made available in the respective interfaces is different, but the contents have to be managed centrally and uniformly, we recommend that you use the storage format of the metadata as the common standard. This information is always managed in XML in the Java Dictionary. The basis is the descriptive language for XML vocabulary formulated in XML itself: the XML scheme. This makes it possible to define simple and complex data types, as well as restrictions to contents and relations. In addition to these typing characteristics of the XML schema, additional meta information is provided for the interfaces through an extension of the XML schema definition.

With this foundation, XSLT or other transformation procedures make it relatively simple to generate a different XML format that is understood by the respective framework—which ultimately uses the data. For Web services, which, in turn, describe themselves with WSDL using XML vocabulary, you can reuse the data types and data structures from the Java Dictionary elsewhere as well.

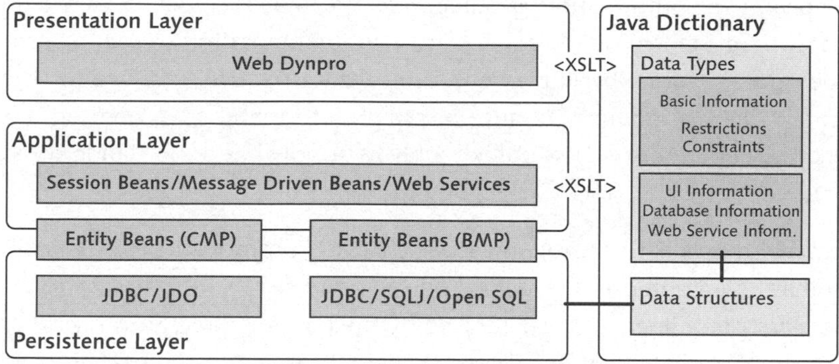

Figure 5.27 Java Dictionary Integration with Other Parts of the System

Data Types

You can divide data types into a category with multiple categories, like the illustration in Figure 5.27, in which the lower-level components inherit their attributes from the higher-level components. You can also expand this hierarchy further, creating any number of further specialized, user-defined data types.

You can generally divide data types into scalars and complexes. This categorization should be sufficiently familiar from the definition of an XML schema, and their names should indicate what they do. Scalar data types are divided further into *built-in* types and simple types. The former category involves derivatives of the basic data types from Java, which are taken either from the standard language scope or from the JDBC data types. Simple types are always user-defined types, such as the SAP NWDS, which does not provide any preconfigured simple types. They can be based on either a *built-in* type or another simple data type and specialize it further—which satisfies the inheritance principle of object orientation.

The opposite side is represented by the complex data types, which as you would expect involve a structure of *built-in* or simple data types. They can generally be divided into structures and lists, although flat (list-like) structures are also possible.

Services for Data Types

As mentioned above, the metadata defined in the data types can have different meanings in different contexts, and each data type requires different meta information. As an example, think again of the values for field labels, which GUI environments like Web Dynpro use to automatically fill the labels for the input fields.

Supplying this information is called a *service* that is attached to a data type. Therefore, to use this service as the implementation to use the provided data, it must be implemented by the respective interface for the context. This is required because the same information can be used differently, dependent on its context. Only its supply has to be standardized by the data type (XML).

To make things easier here, however, while still promoting the extensibility that is anchored in the data type definitions, several standard interfaces are predefined and can be used by the context directly and without a separate implementation. These standard interfaces can be categorized by the pattern in Table 5.1.

Category	Service	Input Parameters
Type-based	Formatting	Data source, language
	Validation	Data source
	Simple value sets	Data source, language
	Complex value sets	Data source, language
	History	
	Standard/default values	
General	Field labels	Language
	Column labels	Language
	Value description	Language
	Brief information	Language
	Help texts	Language
	Documentation	Language
Generic	Access to general metadata	Language, ...

Table 5.1 Existing Services for Data Types

Tutorial: Creating a New Java Dictionary Project

Objective In the project used in this book, ResMan, the data structures used must be defined in the Java Dictionary for various reasons. The data structures can then be reused elsewhere, for example, by Web Dynpro components. You also have to create a way to build data structures automatically on the underlying database server.

To define data structures and data types, you first have to create a Java Dictionary project. The necessary steps are listed in the following tutorials. Once you have worked through them, you should be able to create your own projects.

Requirements

- The SAP NetWeaver Developer Studio is open.
- You are familiar with the basic structure of the SAP NetWeaver Developer Studio from the previous sections.

Process

1. Choose **File · New · Project ...** to open the user dialog for creating a new project.
2. Choose **Dictionary** as the project category on the left side and **Dictionary Project** to select the project type on the right side. Now click **Next**.
3. In the next screen, you have to enter specific information for the project. Enter "ResManDictionary" as the project name, and either check the **Use default** checkbox or enter a directory path. Click **Finish** to create the project.

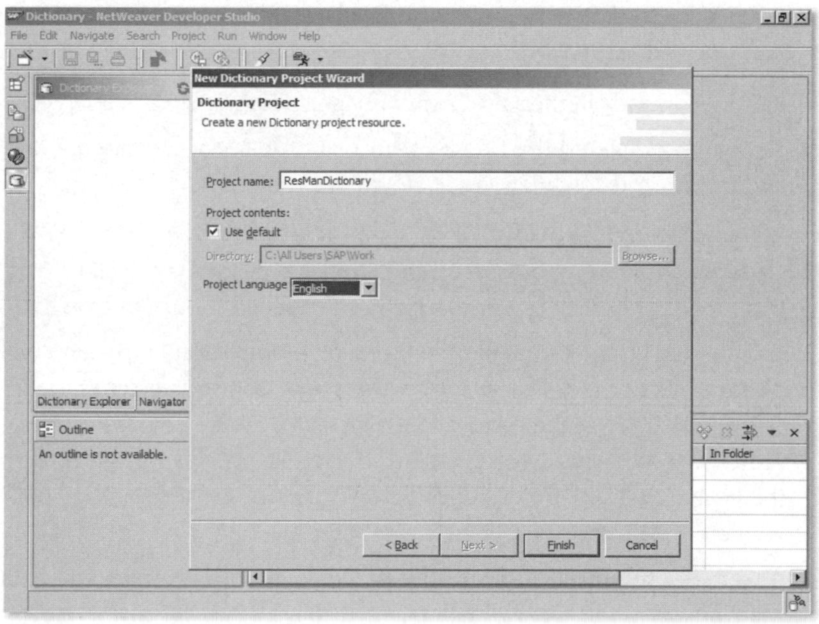

Figure 5.28 Creating a Java Dictionary Project

Result

You have created a Java Dictionary project, where you can now define the data types and data structures. The directory structure of the project was created at file level, and contains all the local files that belong directly to the project. The directory path is defined by the basic project setting that you just defined.

You now see the project structure in the Workbench as soon as you select the Java Dictionary perspective and the **Dictionary Explorer** from the tabs at the bottom of the screen. In its current state, the project does not have any specific entries yet, merely the sub-node **Dictionary**, which, in turn, has two empty sub-nodes, **Data Types** and **Database Tables**.

Tutorial: Creating Data Types

Objective Data types in the Java Dictionary help promote redundancy-free reusability across data structures. Changes to data types affect all structures, which is desired in the vast majority of cases. While you can fall back on the predefined, scalar types, or built-in types, they do not permit any value restrictions, helpful descriptive data, or any other constraints, nor can you validate them manually in the business logic; instead, you have to use the service concept for data types.

To prepare you for the later steps in the application, you will now create a series of simple data types, which you will use in table structures repeatedly in the next tutorial.

Requirements

- You are currently in the Java Dictionary perspective of the SAP NWDS.
- You have completed the previous tutorial properly and created a Java Dictionary project named *ResManDictionary*.

Process

1. Completely expand the project tree for the *ResManDictionary* project.
2. Click the right mouse button on the **Simple Types** node to call its context menu. Click **Create Simple Type** with the left mouse button.
3. You are now in the user dialog for creating a simple data type, and will create a data type that represents the possible resource types. Enter "ZRM_RESTYPE" as the name and assign java package `com.sap.resman.dictionary.datatypes` to the new type. In accordance with the Java model, an equivalent directory structure for the package path is created, with the file type as an XML type.
4. If you are prompted to create the package, confirm the prompt with **Yes**. You have now created data type "ZRM_RESTYPE" and can select it in the project tree.
5. You can now select from several templates at the bottom of the work area to define the data type and all its metadata completely. First complete the **Definition** screen as described below:

Field	Contents	Explanation
Built-in type	string	Basic data type that builds on this simple data type. Alternatively, you can also extend an existing data type.
Description	Resource ID	Information regarding the contents of a data type
Maximum length	2	Maximum number of characters
Minimum length	1	Minimum number of characters

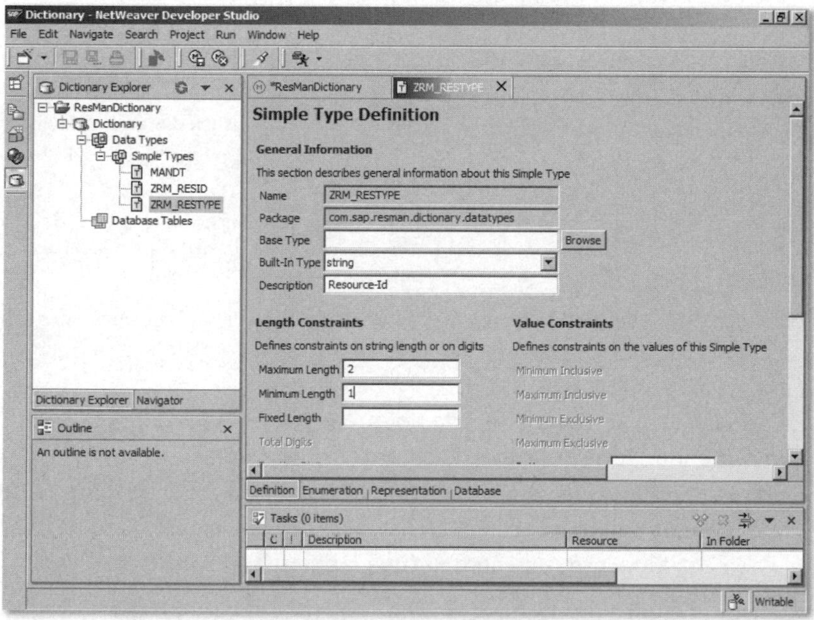

Figure 5.29 View of Definition of Data Type "ZRM_RESTYPE"

6. Switch to the **Enumeration** tab to specify all the values that this data type can contain. These values are used by Web Dynpros to generate value lists, for example, to simplify value entry for users. Web services also use these values to represent the restrictions in their interface descriptions described in WSDL. Click **New** once each time to create a new value with the following pattern:

Enumeration Value	Enumeration Text
A	Automobile
R	Room
P	Projector

7. Enter labels, formats, and lengths for the data type in the **Representation** tab. Web Dynpros also use this information for display purposes to automatically derive field labels for input fields or column labels for lists. Complete the template as indicated in the following list:

Field	Contents	Explanation
Field label	Resource type	This representation is used for a GUI that uses the data type as a label for an input field within its model.
Column label	Resource type	This representation is used for a GUI that uses the data type as a column header to output a list within its model.
Quick info	Type label of resource	This text appears as a tool tip when you move the mouse over an object.

8. The last tab, **Database**, is intended for recording database-specific information. To ensure that each entry in the database is assigned a corresponding value, verify that **Not Null** is selected. Because the value will be represented in a selection list, a value will be generated anyway when a data record is created in the graphical user interface.

Result You have created a user-defined simple data type "ZRM_RESTYPE," which limits the type of a resource to the following values: "A" for automobile, "P" for projector" and "R" for room. This type already includes all the settings you need to create the other data types for the ResMan project. For a complete list of all the data types required for a project, please visit the Web site that accompanies this book, *www.sap-press.com*.

Tutorial: Defining Database Tables

Objective Creating database tables within a Java Dictionary project serves primarily to define structures. You can then transport these structures to a database and create them there, for example, or, you can help an Entity Enterprise JavaBean define its CMP behavior. You will learn about this and other examples for dealing with integrated data structures in the SAP NetWeaver Developer Studio in this book.

In this example, you will create a table that contains the master data of all available resources. This data structure—"ZRM_RES_MASTER"—uses the user-defined data types that you defined in the previous step by using them as field types. We will forego the alternative of using the predefined simple data types at this point in order to keep any changes to them central and targeted.

Requirements

- You have created the *ResManDictionary* Java Dictionary project.
- All data types have been defined properly.
- You have expanded the tree of the project down to the second level and can see the **Database Tables** node.

Process

1. Click the right mouse button on the **Database Tables** node to display the context menu, and choose **Create Table**.
2. Name the table "ZRM_RES_MASTER" and click **Finish**.
3. You have created a new table in the Java Dictionary and are now in the template for defining it completely. Enter a description of the table's function in the **Description** field. In this case, table ZRM_RES_MASTER contains master data for the resource catalog.
4. You have to perform the next step iteratively for each column you define in the table. The MANDT column, which describes the client, is used as an example of the complete column definition.
   - Enter "MANDT" as **Column Name**.
   - Set the checkbox in the **Key** field to include this in the key definition.
   - The next three steps define the data type. You can use either a built-in type or one of the user-defined types. Due to the above arguments, we will use the latter option. Therefore, click **...** in the **Simple Type Selection** column and select data type "MANDT" in package `com.sap.resman.dictionary.datatypes`. The other columns are filled in automatically, based on the values and metadata specified in the data type—ease of use that is not available with the built-in types. In addition, changes to the referenced inclusion are completely transparent: If you change a central data type in the repository, these changes are updated automatically in the tables that use these types.
   - In the last step, which is optional, you can enter a description of the purpose of this field in the **Description** column.

5. As mentioned above, repeat the above step for all subsequent field descriptions.

Column name	Key	Data type	Description
MANDT	Yes	MANDT	Client
RESID	Yes	ZRM_RESID	Resource ID
RESTYPE	No	ZRM_RESTYPE	Resource type
DESCRIPTION	No	ZRM_DESCRIPT	Description
INV_NUMBER	No	BF_INFNR_ANLA	Inventory number
LOC_ADDRESS	No	AD_ADDRNUM	Address key

6. You can create and maintain indexes for a table in the **Indexes** tab. This process is intuitive and enables you to define a logical name for an index that is separated from the indexes in other projects through a namespace convention, and then assign columns in a certain order. Click **New** in the left-hand column and create an index called "ZRM_RES_RESTYPE"; then, click **New** in the right-hand column and assign it field **RESTYPE**. You can ignore the other options, such as defining the singularity of values with **unique** or not installing indices for some database types.
7. You can configure the buffering of requests for this table in the **Table Buffering** tab. Due to the manageable size of the project, however, you don't need to use this feature.

Result Now that you've performed these steps, you have a complete table definition for the resources master data table in the ResMan project. As you can see from the project's data model, however, you will need several more tables to complete the pattern. All other table definitions, for which you will repeat the above steps to create, are listed in the Web site for this book.

Once you have performed all the steps as described above, your screen should look like Figure 5.30.

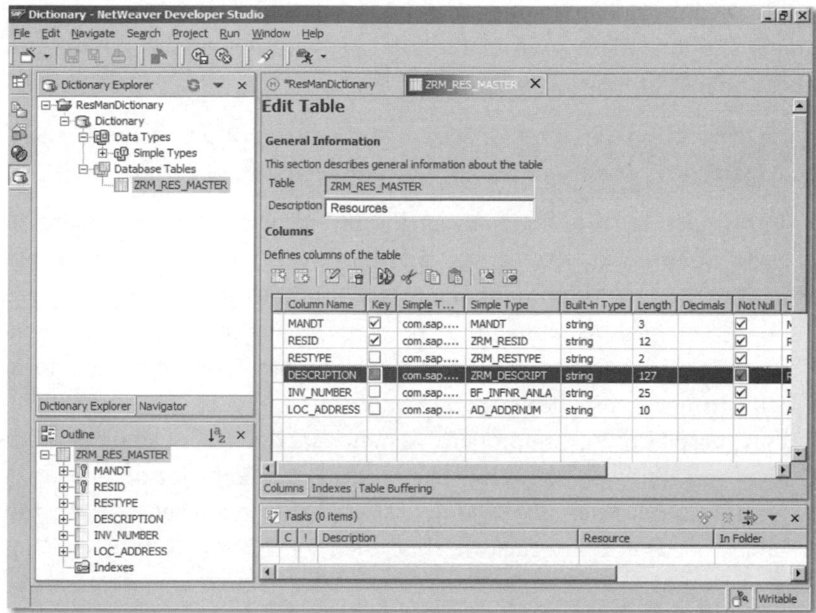

Figure 5.30 Full Definition of Table ZRM_RES_MASTER

5.2.5 Deploy Process

This section is intended to perform one aspect of deployment for the data structures you created. All other practical examples related to deployment are located in the sections that deal with EJB, JSP, and Web Dynpro.

Tutorial: Deploying the Data Structures

Objective

To make table definitions available in the database, where the corresponding processes can be filled with data or queried, the structures from the Java Dictionary first have to be established in the target system. The step required to do so usually represents the first practical part of deployment during a project. This is an iterative process, as you will see if you determine that the dataset requires an extension. In the following tutorial, you'll use the tools available in SAP NetWeaver Developer Studio to carry out the first practical deployment process according to the steps that we have outlined in our tutorial above.

Requirements

To expedite this part of the deployment process, the Software Deployment Manager (SDM) must be executable as a J2EE server component. To verify this, call **Window · Preferences** to display the settings for SAP NetWeaver Developer Studio, and then select **Software Deployment Manager** from the list on the left. Enter the server and port of the target system and click **Check connection** to ensure that the SDM is working properly. If the function works and the SDM is running, you should see a screen similar to the one in Figure 5.31.

If the connection fails, you'll have to verify the SDM process in the SAP Management Console and restart the J2EE server if necessary.

Process

1. To transport a Java Dictionary to the underlying database initially, or update existing structures, you first have to ensure that your current dataset in the development environment is consistent and correct. To do so, you have to rebuild the complete project in the first step. Fortunately, SAP NetWeaver Developer Studio provides tools to perform this process automatically. You can generate the data iteratively at any time, based on the comprehensive metadata definitions that are available. You will learn about and use similar procedures for other project types. You now start a *rebuild* by calling the context menu for the top project node in the project tree and then select **Rebuild Project**.

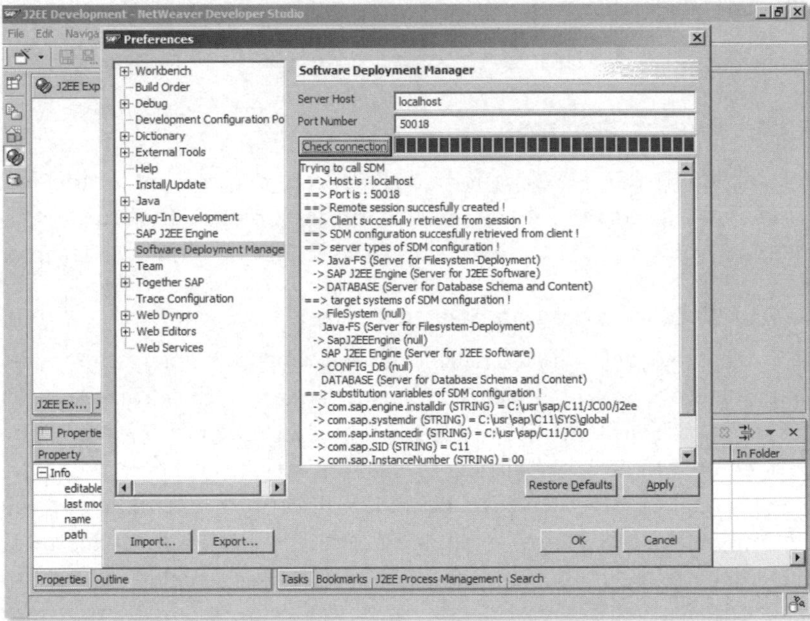

Figure 5.31 Successful Test of the Software Deployment Manager

2. Once you have rebuilt the code base and dealt with any problems in the task list, you now have to generate a transportable archive from the metadata. To do so, call the context menu for the top project node again and select **Create Archive**.

3. The last step involves the actual deployment of the data structures and the generation of tables this deployment initiates. If you have not already done so during your preparations, please make sure the Software Deployment Manager is functioning properly, as described above. Now call the context menu for the top project node one more time and select **Deploy**.

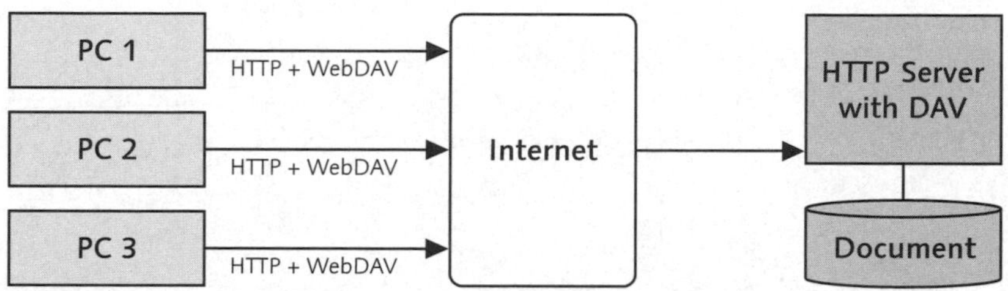

Figure 5.32 Deployment of the ResManDictionary Project

Result

At this point, the SDM takes care of creating tables, data types, and structures in a platform-independent manner—tasks that are otherwise largely manual in J2EE development. If any problems occur during the deployment process, the SDM informs you automatically and provides you with information to solve them. You have now transported the *ResManDictionary* project to the database server and can begin filling the data structures in the next tutorial.

Tutorial: Creating Data in SQL Studio

Objective

As yet, SAP NetWeaver Developer Studio does not provide options for maintaining data structures directly, to correspond to the table maintenance view (Transaction code SM30) from the SAP world. Instead, the SQL Studio is part of the development environment. This tool makes it possible to maintain data in native SQL, using the Data Manipulation Language (DML). We assume that an appropriate plug-in will soon be available for the development environment, replacing this inefficient, error-prone procedure with an integrated data maintenance function. Nevertheless, at this time, it makes sense to learn about SQL Studio as the tool for native data manipulation because it lets you access data directly more than any other tool. In the next tutorial, you'll use SQL to fill the data structures with values that can be used by the ResMan application that you will create in the upcoming chapters.

Requirements

- SQL Studio is installed on your client.
- The database instance that you use to test the examples in the book is available, and you have the necessary access privileges.
- You have at least rudimentary SQL skills.

Process

1. Start the SQL Studio and use the appropriate data to log on to the database that you defined with data structures in the previous tutorial.

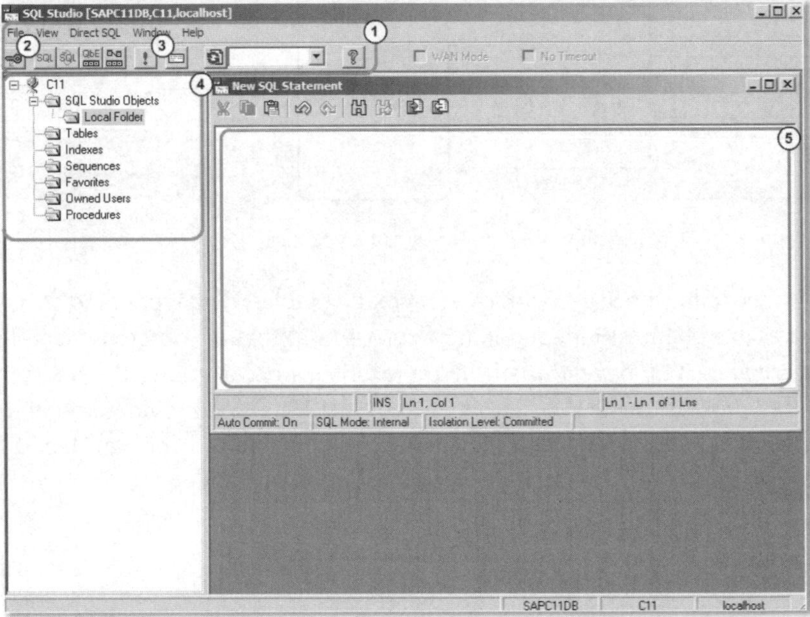

Figure 5.33 SAP SQL Studio

2. Getting around SAP SQL Studio:
   - The menu bar and application toolbar (1) contain the general and specific functions, as in any other Windows application.
   - Click the icon (2) to log on or log off from the system.
   - Use the appropriate icon (3) to execute the SQL statements in this tutorial.
   - The tree structure of the database objects (4) contains all the entities—tables, indexes, procedures, and the like—that were defined in the database.
   - To submit SQL statements, you must enter them in the appropriate window (5) and then click on the icon (3) to execute them.

3. The Web site for this book contains the SQL statements that you'll need to create the initial dataset. Execute these statements in sequence to fill the data structures of the individual tables.

Result

You have filled the database tables for the ResMan project with data that the application can now use accordingly. To check whether the tables now have contents, simply execute a `SELECT` statement and verify the results, which are output in table form.

5.2.6 Collaboration Tools

Team Collaboration

Because Java does not provide any central development objects, in contrast to ABAP development in SAP Systems, complications can multiply in J2EE-based programming. As team collaboration becomes more important, inconsistencies can always occur in the system when several developers work on Java projects together. A development environment whose instance was used by only one developer in the past is now faced with the challenge of providing an infrastructure for dealing with team projects to solve these very difficulties. The role model here is the ABAP Workbench and its centralized datasets for both development objects and user data. When SAP elected to implement Java, it was clear that the existing Java development environments did not provide the customary ease of use, nor meet the demands of working in large teams. SAP defined its objective of building a reliable, efficient, equivalent system for the Java world. The Developer Studio already covers many of these demands. In continuation, the *SAP Java Development Infrastructure* (JDI) was developed as part of the SAP Web Application Server.

Java Development Infrastructure

JDI addresses these very problems. It contains tools to support Java developers within the SAP world and is intended to simplify team-based software development. To optimize this, it is integrated directly in the SAP NetWeaver Developer Studio. This infrastructure is available in SAP Web AS 6.40 and later. Versioning, change management, and automated deployment are just a few of its features.

The infrastructure is an attempt to link central and local developments. Java developers will continue to program locally, while a central development environment provides the necessary synchronization for teamwork. JDI represents the main difference between the Developer Studio and other Java IDEs. It makes it easy for developers to collaborate and enables the Developer Studio to support hundreds of programmers within a project. To access the JDI functions, the individual developer simply imports the deployment configuration file. This import enables collaboration in all the JDI components described below, and makes all necessary source texts and libraries directly available to the developer. Almost all the tasks within and between components are performed automatically.

Design Time Repository

The primary component of the JDI is the Design Time Repository (DTR). It manages development objects such as tables, Java classes, and Web Dynpro project files centrally. This approach enables versioning of all project components and synchronization among developers, while guaranteeing that all programmers are working on the same code base. The central DTR server on one side saves and manages all the versioned files. On the opposite side, developers use the local Developer Studio, which contains the DTR client and communicates with the DTR server to provide access to files, making it possible to check files in and out, compare versions, and so on. As such, this flexible environment also makes it possible to synchronize project components and other related project data between the repository and the local file system.

In addition, the DTR can manage different versions of a development object. In fact, several developments can even make changes to the same object. The DTR has new capabilities such as change management and distributed multiuser development. Replacement of old files with new files is performed centrally, and a version history is managed. In large, complex projects, developers can work with several DTRs in parallel. In this case, the DTRs themselves have to be synchronized. Ultimately, the DTR is a novel approach to distributed development that boosts productivity while cutting costs.

Component Build Service

Like the DTR, the *Component Build Service* (CBS) is a database-supported J2EE application. The difference is that instead of version management and change management, the CBS handles all the Java archives that are created and used. To do so, it creates a *buildspace* for each software component that contains these archives. You can initiate a central *build* (the process of composing, compiling, and preparing projects for deployment) in the CBS, which includes only changed files and their references. Incremental builds let you correct errors step by step, providing for shorter troubleshooting cycles. If archives are changed during a build, a rebuild is created automatically with the new version. Also, when an object is changed, its references are also rebuilt. A request within the IDE initiates this process.

After the successful completion of the build process, the CBS automatically releases the source texts and archives for other developers. Because the current versions of all archives are available centrally in the CBS, it represents the ideal source for querying and updating libraries in the local file system. Faster build cycles reduce development costs, development times, and errors, especially in large projects.

Software Logistics

Once development work is complete, you are done with the lion's share of activities, but some tasks are still pending. These tasks can include application deployment, corrections, hand-off to the customer, or maintenance, for example. In large development teams and when many end users are involved, central management of these tasks is needed. This demands an efficient infrastructure—*Software Logistics* (SL). You can consider this component to be the basis of the DTR and CBS components. The JDI is provided centrally, by importing the development configuration file. The transports are handled centrally during the switch from the development to the correction phase.

Software Logistics consists primarily of the *Change Management Service* (CMS) and the *Software Delivery Manager* (SDM). The CMS manages software versioning, while the SDM is responsible for deploying the Java applications.

Developing with the JDI

You first have to import the development configuration file into the Developer Studio. You can then synchronize the local system with the DTR and the CBS. The usual development process now takes place, with local application development, local build process, and local testing. JDI now performs synchronization and deployment to the test environment automatically. After a successful test, the objects are checked in to the DTR. Once the central build of the archives is run, they are automatically loaded to the CBS. The build now starts and the elements are activated automatically if it succeeds. Software Logistics oversees the deployment to the central test environment. The last step is the release for further changes.

Conclusion

In summary, you have learned the following: The infrastructure has a centralized organization. A simple file import makes the project development objects available centrally. You can transfer these objects to your local environment, creating a flexible development. The centralized storage in DTR makes centralized build processes possible. Old versions are not overwritten; instead, a version history is created. Similarly, all the Java archives are centralized in the CBS, which ensures that only the latest versions will be used. Comprehensive tests can be performed at early stages of development, avoiding ugly surprises later on. CBS enables incremental builds and shorter life cycles. It provides more security in the use of archives. Any changes to the archives automatically trigger a rebuild of the dependent components. When the centralized build is successful, the elements are released.

All of these measures simplify reusability and maintenance. Control of distributed versions with simultaneous access to resources facilitates the management of large, geographically distributed projects.

5.2.7 Versioning

Document Management Systems

When you examine the trend in programming project sizes, it's clear that quantum leaps have been made in recent years. While a single 1.44 MB diskette could hold a project in the early 90s, today's projects require many CD-ROMs containing 700 MB each. Of course, the ever-increasing size of programs and their source coding means that software development has to be a team effort, in which several individuals from different areas work on the coding together. Accordingly, this demands a procedure that allows multiple, independently working programmers to work on the same document without creating conflicts. Document management systems such as WebDAV and CVS can help solve these problems.

WebDAV

WebDAV, which stands for *Web-based distributed authoring and versioning*, provides functions to promote collaboration with documents and their management. WebDAV extends HTTP and gives applications write protection for specific contents. The primary functions of WebDAV include updating data, managing multiple users, and supplementing files with additional meta information (such as author and creation date). WebDAV can exchange data between a server and the local PC, similar to FTP.

Several new functions, some of which are based on HTTP, have been introduced to implement WebDAV. Therefore, one decisive advantage of WebDAV is that it operates over HTTP.

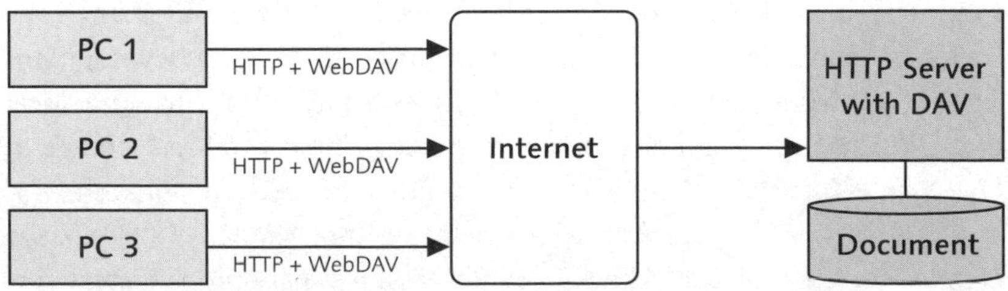

Figure 5.34 WebDAV

Problems due to protected ports are rare because WebDAV uses port 80, which most administrators enable.

The basic HTTP functions include:

- **POST**
  Send data to the server.
- **GET**
  Request resources.
- **PUT**
  Write resources.
- **DELETE**
  Delete a resource.
- **HEAD**
  Similar to the GET function, but does not return the message body.
- **TRACE**
  Used to check and diagnose the request/response.
- **CONNECT**
  Reserved for tunneling by proxies.
- **OPTIONS**
  Request communication-related information without performing an action.

The WebDAV extension adds three more concepts, which were not contained in HTTP, namely:

- Namespace management
- Overwrite protection (locking)
- Metadata (properties)

Namespace management enables you to depict data in hierarchical form. It's comparable to a conventional data system with the familiar namespaces (packages) of Java specifications, except that these resources are not organized physically in WebDAV, but instead they are organized only *virtually*. Three methods are available:

- **MKCOL**
  Creates a new namespace (collection) using the path specified in the URI.
- **COPY**
  Copies an existing namespace.
- **MOVE**
  Moves a namespace.

Another WebDAV function is *overwrite protection*. The main benefit of this function is to lock documents that are currently being edited on the server in order to maintain data consistency. You should be familiar with this concept from the ABAP environment, which is illustrated in Figure 5.35.

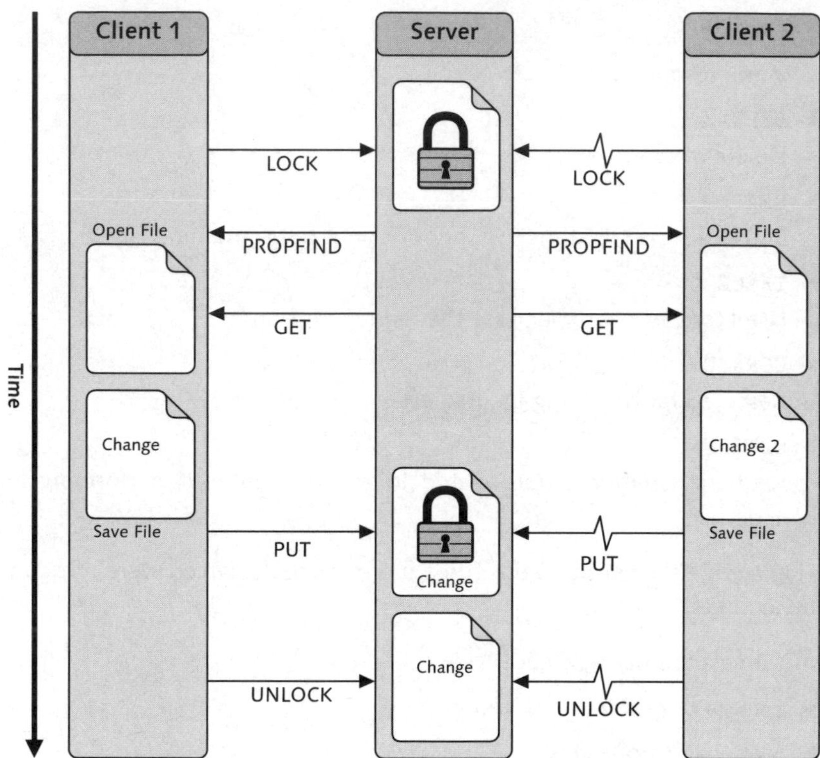

Figure 5.35 WebDAV Locking

Two methods are available:

- **`LOCK`**
  Sets write protection for a resource.
- **`UNLOCK`**
  Releases a previously locked resource.

We differentiate between exclusive lock, in which only one processor is authorized to change an object, and shared lock, which allows several processors to work on the same document. Typically, a protected document is read only, until it is released again or a timeout is reached.

The last extension in WebDAV is *metadata*. This major new feature adds status information to the documents. The following commands are defined:

- **PROPFIND**
  Reads existing metadata for resources or namespaces.
- **PROPPATCH**
  Changes the existing metadata.

These characteristics are described by their assigned names and values. The names are strings, while values are described as XML expressions. The following metadata is defined by default in the WebDAV protocol:

- **createtime**
  Date/time the resource was created
- **displayname**
  Resource display name for the user
- **getcontentlanguage**
  Language of content
- **getcontentlength**
  Length of a resource
- **getlastmodified**
  Time/date resource was last changed
- **getetag**
  Entity tag
- **lockdiscovery**
  Active write protection
- **resourcetype**
  Resource type
- **source**
  Resource source address
- **supportedlock**
  Lock capability supported

In general, version control—which was added later, under the name *DeltaV*, over the evolutionary development of the protocol—is considered to be the most important aspect of WebDAV. DeltaV also represents an HTTP extension; it adds the following methods:

- **`VERSION-CONTROL`**
  A file that is not versioned yet is subjected to a version control.
- **`BASELINE-CONTROL`**
  Creates a consistent copy of a collection of resources. Both versioned and non-versioned resources can be placed under control to create a configuration. A new baseline is created as the overall version after every check-in and check-out.
- **`CHECKOUT`**
  Starts the editing process for a resource.
- **`CHECKIN`**
  Ends the editing process.
- **`UNCHECKOUT`**
  Interrupts the editing process.
- **`REPORT`**
  Returns the version history.
- **`LABEL`**
  Adds a version label; it is used to uniquely identify a resource.
- **`UPDATE`**
  Updates a current resource with a newer version.
- **`MERGE`**
  Merges the histories of several concurrent users.
- **`MKACTIVITY`**
  Lets you group several check-outs or check-ins together.
- **`MKWORKSPACE`**
  Creates a new workspace, where one person can work in isolation from other users and their changes. The client side receives a copy of all the resources that belong to a project and saves them on a local data medium. Each processor has his or her own separate work area on the server side.

CVS Another version system is the *Concurrent Versions System* (CVS). You can use it to record development steps during programming and trace them later. It also makes it possible for several users to edit the same files simultaneously, and deals with the related problems such as reciprocal overwriting, inconsistencies, and the various types of code drift. These functions are achieved through *revisions*, *merging*, *branching*, and *tagging*.

In CVS, all resources are first placed in individual repositories, which are located in an area within the file system and represent a hierarchical structure like in WebDAV. The repository is therefore the central location for the project data, and also contains information for restoring prior versions. It is located on the CVS server.

Version Control

Version control saves the source files together with the corresponding metadata about the changes made. In a typical constellation, the developer uses version control to check a version of one or more source files, verifies the changes for potential conflicts, and returns the revised, consistent file to the repository, where a new version is saved. This makes it possible to manage all developments within a project centrally and track changes.

Revisions

All implemented changes are divided into *revisions*. Each version of a file is assigned a number by the system. This version number is sub-versioned automatically during the branching process (which is explained further below) and incremented by one in the last version position.

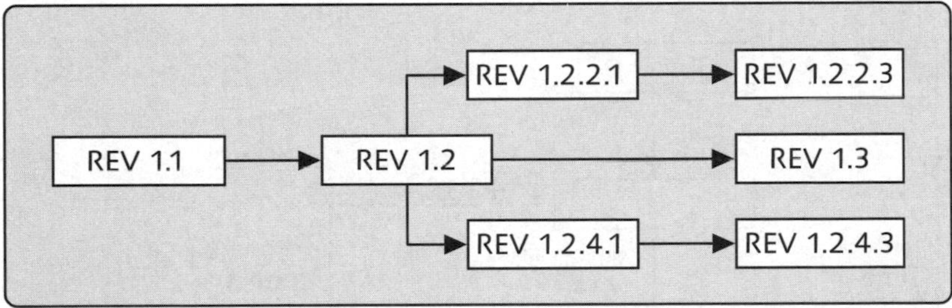

Figure 5.36 CVS Versions

Collision Control

Another CVS feature is its *collision control* mechanism, which makes it possible to merge two different versions in one file. This is achieved by using the *diff algorithm*, which compares the changes in a file line by line. If inconsistencies exist, the developer is informed in cases where clear assignment and problem resolution are not possible—if the same line has been changed in both files, for example. Otherwise, versioning takes place as usual.

Branching

As mentioned above, CVS also supports *branching*. This makes it possible to create separate development branches. A separated branch of a file can be versioned further through a sub-revision, and exists independently of its parent—the version of the file from which the branch was originally spawned. One possible situation for using branching is when several developers want to work on different aspects of a file at the same time. Once the two branches work independently of one another, the changes will be merged again at a later time. Another case for justifying branching is a release. This approach often involves a strategy in which a release is held in a separate branch and release-specific bug fixes are performed in a separate branch, while the root is used to develop additional features.

```
/** @merge workspace: Changes in the Workspace */
  /**
   * Extra property
   */
  private String sample = null;

/** @merge repository: Changes from the Repository
  /**
   * Sample property
   */
  private Object sample = null;

*/
```

Figure 5.37 CVS Merge

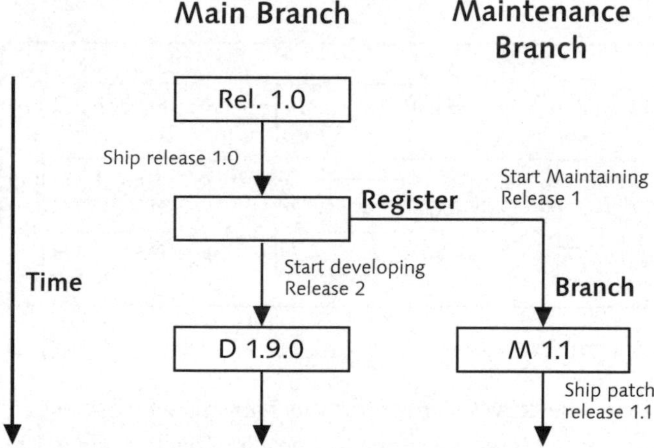

Figure 5.38 CVS Branch

As indicated above, *diffing* is the basis of version control. It involves the character-based comparison of two file versions. This makes it possible to localize changes at any time between any versions of a file. This type of comparison is depicted in Figure 5.39.

Tagging The last noteworthy CVS feature is *tagging*, which involves linking files within a project to a project version. It makes it possible to create a new release from different source files (see Figure 5.40).

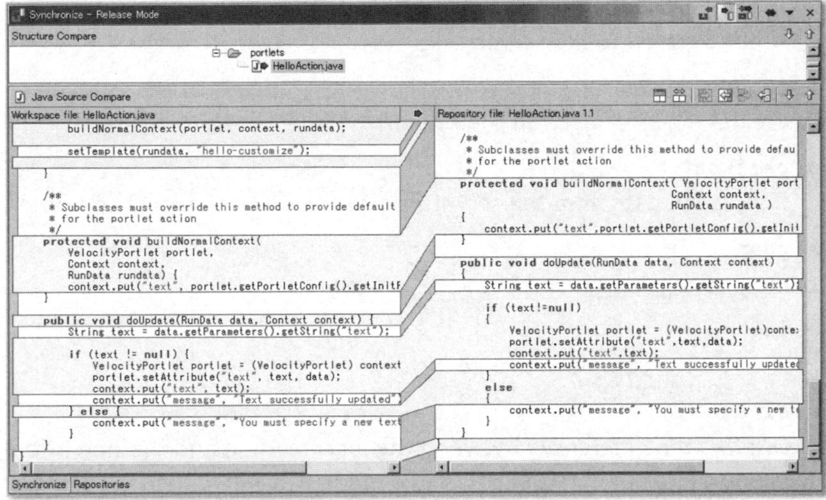

Figure 5.39 CVS Differences

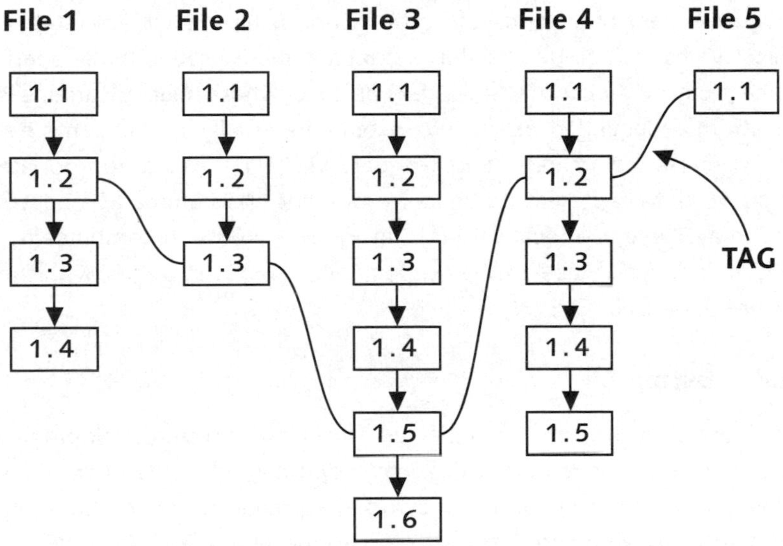

Figure 5.40 CVS Tag

The following commands have been defined for these features in the CVS log. They are not described in any detail, because they are not required for the SAP NetWeaver Developer Studio. Nonetheless, you could benefit from knowing about them:

- **`login`**
  Used to log on to the server.
- **`import`**
  Creates a new project on the server.
- **`checkout`**
  Checks out data from the server for processing on the local computer.
- **`commit`**
  Local changes are saved in the Repository.
- **`log`**
  Displays the complete change history.
- **`diff`**
  Displays the differences between the local revision and the one in the Repository.
- **`add`**
  Adds new files to the Repository.

As you can see, both kinds of version control have their advantages. While CVS has established itself as a standard and is used in many open-source projects, WebDAV is still a new protocol whose main advantage is its platform independence. The two systems are usually used in combination: WebDAV commands send the data via HTTP to the appropriate server, which translates it into the corresponding CVS commands and has it made available in a local CVS repository. This approach combines the platform independence and Web capability of WebDAV/DeltaV with the advance features of CVS.

5.2.8 Testing

Testing is a critical, yet often neglected aspect of software development. Exhaustive testing is required to discover and correct errors in complex software products. The JUnit framework has proven to be an extremely useful tool for automated testing of Java developments. You should always conduct unit testing after every deployed operation, to ensure that the changes made do not cause errors in some remote part of the system.

The JUnit test cases are *self-verifying*, which means they can be repeated automatically. JUnit has also been integrated as a plug-in for the SAP NetWeaver Developer Studio, which makes it much easier to use. JUnit tests program units in isolation from all other units that are required in the overall context of a program. Test options are available for individual methods and classes, as well as complete components.

Extreme Programming

This supports a model of programming in which tests are integrated into the development process from the start. The fundamental idea that drives the philosophy is this: Before the functions to be tested are actually designed, the requirements of these functions must be defined and tested. This approach automatically focuses attention on clear requirements, and keeps the resulting components lean from the start, because developers concentrate on meeting the requirements of the test, instead of performing daring architectural feats. The basis for this is the *Extreme Programming* (XP) methodology—an agile software development process aimed at improving product quality by subjecting the individual software components to repeated standardized tests. The result is a product that has a low error quotient and is therefore more durable. The interaction between these methods creates an efficient, flexible procedure model for software development that meets demands for ease of use, transparency for developers and customers, and compatibility with existing tools. This pragmatic approach makes the software development process more flexible. The development process undergoes several iterations, with the goal of keeping the software as error-free as possible.

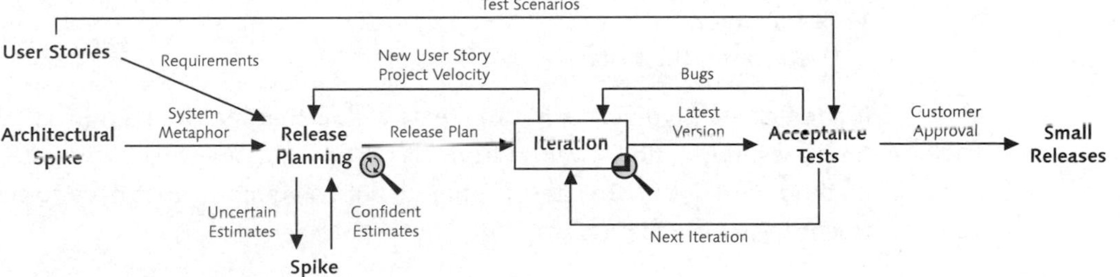

Figure 5.41 Extreme Programming

JUnit was published under IBM public license and can be downloaded from *http://www.junit.org*.

Unfortunately, developers often neglect these tests due to tight schedules or a disinclination to conduct comprehensive tests in addition to their programming work. This is shortsighted because they miss the opportunity of developing a clear idea of the function required, which would help them get off to a more efficient start to the design phase.

Two methods for testing a program are usually considered. The first method involves analyzing an error that has occurred with a debugger, which is integrated in a Java IDE like the one in SAP NetWeaver in most cases. The second method involves outputting information to the respective output medium.

Both methods have a decisive disadvantage, however: They require active thought and exact knowledge of the software and its interface in order to rank the errors or determine why they occur. Moreover, the default output is often filled quickly, which means the most important information is lost. JUnit provides the solution to these problems.

JUnit Import the JUnit Java archive into the SAP NetWeaver Developer project. Once you do, all the classes you need for testing are available in package `junit.framework`. The most important classes are:

- **`TestCase`**
  Used to enter a test case.
- **`TestSuite`**
  Lets you group individual test cases together.
- **`Assert`**
  Defines a condition.
- **`Test`**
  The interface that merges the TestCase and TestSuite.
- **`TestRunner`**
  Used to run the tests.

In the first step, you use JUnit to create a class that represents the actual test cases. It inherits its values from class `TestCase` and then overwrites method `runTest()`. This test routine defines statements that have to be true for the tests to pass.

Class `junit.framework.TestCase` defines the methods for the tests that you have to implement yourself. The following methods are relevant for you, the developer; you should implement them as necessary:

- `setUp()`
- `runTest()`
- `tearDown()`

Each of these methods is executed during a unit test. The `setUp()` method is performed to prepare the test environment. In one example, this could involve requesting a database connection, which would be followed by the `runTest()` method to conduct the actual test series. The `tearDown()` method is performed in conclusion and is responsible for cleanup tasks, such as terminating the database connection. You don't necessarily have to implement these methods, however, since all methods that start with the `test` prefix are also performed.

If a test fails, error messages are transferred to provide information about the test run. To demonstrate the use of JUnit, consider the `Factorial` class in the example below. This class contains the mathematical algorithm for calculating the factorial of a given number.

The factorial, $F(n) = n!$, is defined for $n > 0$ as

$$F(0) = 1$$
$$F(n) = n \cdot F(n-1) \quad \text{for} \quad n > 0$$

An example Java class that implements this algorithm appears below:

```
/**
 * Factorial.java
 */
package de.snp.abap2java.math;

public final class Factorial {
  public static int fac(int i) throws
                                   ArithmeticException {
    if (i < 0) throw new IllegalArgumentException();
    switch (i) {
      case 0 :
        return 1;
      case 1 :
        return 1;
    }
    try {
      int j = fac(i - 1);
      int k = i * j;
      if (k / i != j) throw new ArithmeticException();
      return k;
    } catch (StackOverflowError e) {
      throw new ArithmeticException();
    }
  }
}
```

Listing 5.6 Class That Calculates Factorials for Testing

As specified in the function definition, the argument for the factorial function must be greater than 0. This results in the first test case, which triggers an `IllegalArgumentException` if a value less than 0 is passed on.

A second test case determines whether an `ArithmeticException` occurs. This exception should occur whenever the result of the factorial exceeds the defined magnitude of data type `int`. This occurs as soon as a factorial of 13 or more is calculated because data type `int` can no longer represent the result of the factorial (the value range wraps).

Additional test options use the factorial values to test the results of the `fac()` method:

```
/**
  * JUnit Test Case - Factorial.
  */
package de.snp.abap2java.perf;
import junit.framework.TestCase;

public class FactorialTestCase extends TestCase {
  public void testInvalidArgument() throws

ArithmeticException {
    try {
      Factorial.fac(-1);
      fail("Excepted IllegalArgumentException");
    } catch (IllegalArgumentException e) {
    }
  }

  public void testOverflowException() throws
                              IllegalArgumentException
  {
    try {
      Factorial.fac(1000000);
      fail("Excepted ArithmeticException");
    } catch (ArithmeticException e) {
    }
  }

  public void testZero() throws Exception {
```

```
    assertEquals(Factorial.fac(0), 1);
  }

  public void testOne() throws Exception {
    assertEquals(Factorial.fac(1), 1);
  }

  public void testTen() throws Exception {
    assertEquals(Factorial.fac(10), 3628800);
  }
}
```

Listing 5.7 Test for the Factorial Cass

JUnit provides three interfaces for executing the test cases: Graphical user interfaces with Swing and AWT, or direct output of the results in the console.

To execute the respective tests, enter the following commands in the command line:

```
javaw junit.swingui.TestRunner packagename.TestCase
javaw junit.awtui.TestRunner   packagename.TestCase
java  junit.textui.TestRunner  packagename.TestCase
```

or run them directly from the SAP NetWeaver Developer Studio.

6 Application Layers

Conventional applications from both the ABAP and Java/J2EE worlds can be described as three-tier models. Each application contains a certain proportion of data handling, business logic, and presentation logic. In this chapter, we will examine all the layers for both sides—ABAP and Java—of the application.

6.1 Retrieval Logic and Persistence

The data retrieval logic and persistence layer is responsible for providing data to the downstream business logic, which then has to process this data. The goal of the retrieval logic for the business logic is to establish a certain amount of abstraction for the countless resources that can be accessed—including databases, files, remote calls, and services—to fully standardize access in the best case (or at least greatly simplify it) and hide the technical details that aren't relevant for the business logic.

The next sections introduce the options for dealing with the different types of resources available on both platforms.

6.1.1 ABAP

Open SQL

SQL (Structured Query Language) is used for relational databases. It is available for nearly every RDBMS (relational database management system), although in different, vendor-specific versions. The SQL standards of ANSI (American National Standards Institute) and ISO (International Standards Organization) generally serve only as guidelines, which the database vendors more or less follow.

Aside from querying data from the database, SQL also supports changes to table contents, modification of structures, configuration of user authorizations, and settings for system security. SQL is divided into DML (Data Manipulation Language) for reading and changing data, DDL (Data Definition Language) for creating and managing tables in the database, and DCL (Data Control Language) for authorization and consistency checks.

A subset of the SQL statements called *Open SQL* is implemented in all widespread database systems and is available fully in ABAP. This enables standardized access to all databases supported by SAP, making ABAP developments nearly independent of specific database products, as long as Open SQL is used exclusively.

Native SQL Open SQL contains only DML commands, however, which were described in detail in Section 4.1.4. In cases where these commands are not sufficient to meet a specific requirement, ABAP also permits database-specific commands. To do so, the *native SQL* statement is placed between the ABAP statements EXEC SQL and ENDEXEC:

```
EXEC SQL.
    CREATE TABLE BUILD_COMP (
             CLIENT CHAR(3) NOT NULL,
             BUILD  CHAR(9) NOT NULL,
             COMP1  CHAR(6) NOT NULL,
             COMP2  CHAR(6) NOT NULL,
             PRIMARY KEY (CLIENT, BUILD)
                          )
ENDEXEC.
```

Listing 6.1 Example of a Native SQL Statement Embedded in ABAP

The statements embedded in the ABAP coding are forwarded directly to the database system. As such, native SQL lets you use the full range of functions provided by the database-side interface.

On the ABAP side, every work process on an application server contains a database interface with a vendor-dependent layer, which hosts all communications between the ABAP side and the database.

When native SQL statements are used in ABAP programs, switching to a different database product will be costly—because database commands generally differ, you will have to find and adjust all the involved coding manually. Moreover, you should not execute any DDL operations in application programs anyway; instead, use the ABAP Dictionary to create and maintain tables. Lastly, the SAP System does not perform any additional checks of database-specific commands. For these reasons, you should avoid using native SQL in ABAP whenever possible.

Logical Databases

A *logical database* is simply an ABAP program. However, logical databases are special programs that can supply an application program with data for processing. They are most commonly used to read data from database tables and link them with an executable program. They can also be called with function module LDB_PROCESS, which makes it possible to call several logical databases—with the correspondingly complex nesting—within an executable program.

The logical database implements database access using Open SQL access from outside of the application program. It reads the information from the database line by line and supplies it to the executable program at runtime.

Logical databases have a hierarchical organization because many tables are interrelated through their foreign keys.

Tasks

Logical databases can execute the following tasks:

- They can be used in multiple executable programs.
- They can provide a uniform selection screen for all the programs that use a logical database.
- The authorization check is saved centrally in the logical database.
- Changes aimed at boosting performance will affect all application programs that use a given logical database.

Components

The logical database is basically divided into three objects: The *structure definition* defines the data view of the logical database, the *selection* defines the user interface of the executable program, and the *database program* executes the statements for reading the data and passing it on to the calling program. The call has the following structure:

```
GET <table_header>.
...
GET <table_item>.
...
```

Listing 6.2 Theoretical Call in an Executable Program

Persistent Objects

Persistent objects belong to the *object services*, which supply applications with various central services that cannot be represented by ABAP Objects language elements directly. SAP currently provides two such object services, the *Persistence Service* and the *Transaction Service*. The Persistence Service helps ABAP developers use object-oriented data in relational databases.

Transient and Persistent Data Data can generally be differentiated in two different categories: transient and persistent data. Put simply, *transient data* exists only during program runtime, while *persistent data* is durable, for example, in a database. Persistent data can also be found as content in the application and presentation layers. In object-oriented programs, data is usually portrayed as attributes of objects. Methods also define and use local data, of course, but we will overlook that here. In object-oriented programming, an object exists only during program runtime, between the creation and deletion of a program session. To work with persistent data in objects, accesses to the data store must be programmed within the class methods.

The logic behind using persistent objects is that the data of an object is saved in the database transparently for the developer, and is retrieved during the initialization of the object, to allow a program to continue processing the same objects that another program left behind in a certain state. Therefore, the Persistence Service is responsible for providing ways to save the attributes of an object persistently and mapping them to the correct class.

To use the Persistence Service for objects, their classes have to be defined as *persistent classes* in the Class Builder. The Persistence Service manages these objects and their states. The objects in such a class are not created using the `CREATE OBJECT` statement in an ABAP program, but instead with a method of the Persistence Service, which also ensures that the initialization is accurate. In addition to the unique ID, the persistent classes can contain key attributes to identify the object uniquely. The Persistence Service manages the persistent objects and oversees the connection between object and database.

Tutorial: Persistent Class

Objective This tutorial shows you how to create a simple persistent class for a database table. Its objective is to show developers the details of developing persistent classes to compare them to the Java equivalent, the *Java Database Object* (JDO), later in this chapter.

Requirements You should be familiar with the basics of the ABAP Workbench and also have had some contact with ABAP Objects.

Process

1. To create the persistent class, you use the Class Builder (Transaction SE24) or the Object Builder (Transaction SE80).
2. Enter the name for the persistent class as `ZCL_<dbtab>_PERSISTENT`.
3. In the properties for the class, be sure to select class type **Persistent Class**.

4. The created class implements the methods of interface IF_OS_STATE, which manages the object status.
5. Other classes are now generated automatically for the new persistent class: ZCB_<dbtab>_PERSISTENT and ZCA_<dbtab>_PERSISTENT.
6. In the persistence map, assign class database table <dbtab> to class ZCL_<dbtab>_PERSISTENT. To display the persistence map, choose menu path **Goto · Persistence Map**.
7. You can define the mapping for database table DBTAB here.
8. Save and activate the persistent class.
9. The following coding should give you an impression of how persistent classes are used within a context, such as a report. Reference table agent is used to assign a reference to the persistent class, ZCL_<dbtab>_PERSISTENT. Method GET_PERSISTENT is used to check whether an entry exists in the database. If no entry exists, an exception is raised. The program then attempts to create an object within this CATCH block. The entry does not exist in the database until after the COMMIT WORK. If no commit work is performed, the generated object exists only during runtime.

```
DATA: connection TYPE REF TO zcl_<dbtab>_persistent,
      agent      TYPE REF TO zca_<dbtab>_persistent.

Agent = zca_<dbtab>_persistent=>agent.
TRY.
  Connection = agent->get_persistent(
           i_key1 = wa_<dbtab>-key1
           ...
           i_keyn = wa_<dbtab>-keyn ).
CATCH cx_os_object_not_found.
  TRY.
    agent->create_persistent(
            i_key1 = wa_<dbtab>-key1
...
            i_field1 = wa_<dbtab>-field1
... ).
  CATCH cx_os_object_not_found.
    ...
  ENDTRY.
ENDTRY.
```

6.1.2 Java

To analyze the complex architectural details of the Java personality of the persistence layer on the SAP Web Application Server, we first have to examine the interdependencies of data retention within the SAP context. In the pure SAP world that you have dealt with so far, all data is saved in a centralized database. ABAP programs access the database directly, using the mechanisms described above. Why shouldn't it be as easy to implement this in Java? We would assume that new tables would be created in the ABAP Dictionary and accessed at some point in the Java coding.

While this approach may seem simple and logical at first glance, it harbors several disadvantages. The most serious of these is the fact that this approach does not comply with defined J2EE standards, as it would require the existence of an ABAP instance—which is extremely unlikely for a pure J2EE environment, which are used widely in enterprise projects outside of SAP Systems. Moreover, merging ABAP and Java tables would require Java developers to follow ABAP conventions that ensure data consistency, such as those for lock management or update requests.

Design Objectives

Nonetheless, a central database for the Java personality of the Web AS also has enormous advantages. The central instance of the Web AS builds on a central database instance that behaves similarly to the corresponding ABAP instance—Customizing and configuration data is saved along with the application tables. To enable this, SAP's design objectives pursue the following goals:

- **Strict separation of ABAP and Java persistence**
  Each personality has its own isolated database schema, characterized by two logically—or even physically—separated databases. No transaction can extend over both schemas; a Java application can access ABAP data, but not at the database level. In other words, table accesses between the ABAP and Java stacks are not possible. Instead, they are performed at the business logic level or its encapsulating middleware, for example, via Remote Function Call (RFC) by means of the Java Connector (JCo). Therefore, the collaboration has to take place at component level at this point.
- **Minimization of database administration effort**
  To keep the effort required for installation and administration to a minimum, despite the necessity of separating both database schemas, it is possible to realize both schemas within a single database. This means

an ABAP transaction accesses the ABAP schema and a Java transaction accesses the corresponding Java schema, but in the same physical database.

- **Extension of Java persistence technologies**
  Familiar features and concepts from the ABAP world, such as caching statements and support for table buffers, have been transferred to the Java world.

The object orientation of the Java language is another aspect that has had a major impact on the persistence layer architecture on the Java side. While most conventional SAP applications are still based on relational persistence and procedural code—making it relatively simple to model business data in tables—Java forces you to think in terms of objects. For this reason, SAP supports both options for accessing data, which generally must be considered separately: relational and object-based data retention. The two methods also differ in the way developers use and manipulate the data.

Open SQL for Java

Framework for a Standardized Data Access Layer

Just like Open SQL provides standardized access to databases in an ABAP environment, Open SQL for Java creates a database access layer for Java applications. This layer provides performance-boosting mechanisms, such as table buffers and statement pooling, and at the same time enables portable access to many different databases, including Oracle, IBM DB2, Microsoft SQL Server, MaxDB, and others. You don't have to modify the applications under this method, because the SQLJ subset balances out the differences between the databases, which means applications can run on different databases without requiring modification.

All the programming models that SAP covers for the supported databases are part of this *Open SQL for Java Framework*. Application developers have various options for accessing data in the persistence layer. All access options within Open SQL for Java are based on the lowest instance—the JDCB API described in Section 5.2. SAP then builds various abstraction layers on top of this programming interface—each of which exists and can be used independently of the others—and offers various functions within its own hierarchy level, each with its own advantages and disadvantages.

JDBC

As you can see in Figure 6.1, JDBC represents the lowest abstraction level. Ultimately, all the higher layers generate JDBC calls that the vendor-specific JDBC database drivers process as SQL statements—based on the Java JDBC API—and send directly to the database. JDBC's extreme popularity is due not least to the wide variety of example coding that is publicly available.

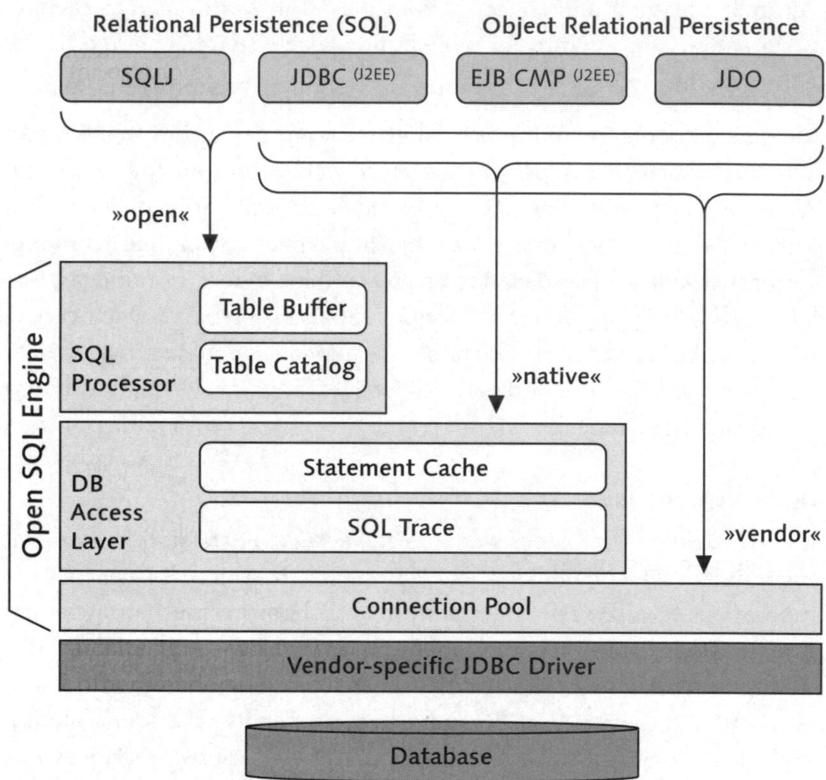

Figure 6.1 Open SQL Framework—Database Access Layers

Native JDBC

Using native JDBC alone does not guarantee database independence; however, ultimately, how the JDBC calls are executed depends on the JDBC driver implementation and the semantics of the underlying database. Note that if you use native SQL or native JDBC explicitly to implement database access, the JDBC API will not provide any framework for inspecting or validating SQL statements. Therefore, you will not be able to verify whether your application coding can be executed on other database platforms.

To avoid potential portability problems with JDBC and SQL, SAP has defined a subset of SQL statements to ensure database independence—at least for the databases that SAP supports. Here, Open SQL for Java is an equivalent to the known Open SQL on the ABAP side, and solves the related problems associated with nearly every programming language.

The core of the Open SQL for Java framework is the Open SQL Engine, which consists of three layers that build on one another, with each higher layer providing more functions. The lowest layer is the connection pool, which is the foundation for the database access layer, which, in turn, is the foundation for the top layer—the SQL processor layer (see Figure 6.2).

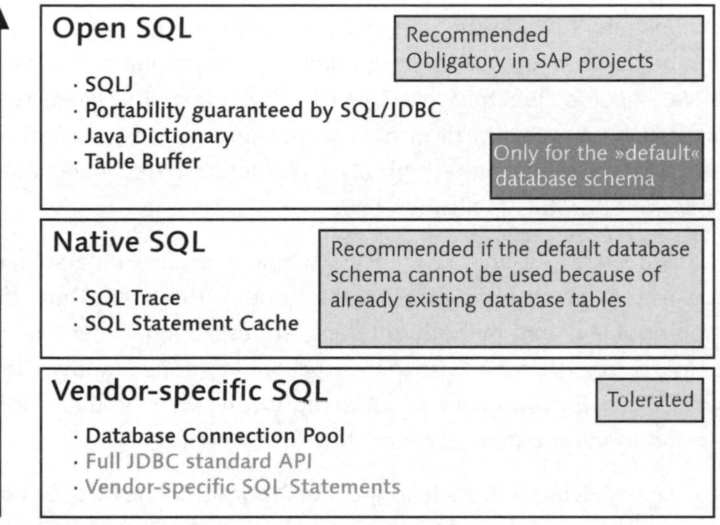

Figure 6.2 Open SQL Engine—Layer Model

Relational and Object/Relational Persistence

As mentioned above, SAP supports various programming models for accessing data. You can differentiate between relational and object/relational persistence and choose between different approaches for implementing each model. Within the relational model, we differentiate further between the SQLJ and JDBC persistence scenarios. For object-oriented persistence, Java provides two possible implementations, using either enterprise entity beans or Java Data Objects. The individual programming models are described in detail later in this chapter. For now, all you need to know is that every model can be built on any of the three layers within the Open SQL layer model (aside from SQLJ, which is based on the highest layer of the Open SQL Engine), which means a connection to the lowest layer is an essential prerequisite. Accordingly, SAP separates these groups into "open," "native," and "vendor-based" connection models. All three layers of the Open SQL Engine are described below.

Connection Pool – Vendor SQL

The lowest layer is the connection pool, which builds directly on the vendor-specific JDBC driver. As you are already aware, creating and providing database connections is a complex process, and an expensive undertaking—from a system resource perspective. The connection pool saves connections to the same data sources in a *pool*, allowing you to create connections without any time delay. The pool also enables access to the default database schema, which is already predefined in the connection pool and does require adjustment.

Once administrators create the connection pools centrally on the J2EE server, the pools are referenced through only logical, unique names from the Java Naming and Directory Interface (JNDI) context. This keeps sensitive data, such as authentication data or maximum loads, away from developers, and prevents these typically architecture-based parameters from being shifted to the application logic.

Applications declare resource references to the pool as a data source. They receive and return their connections through the pool. Thus, the connection pool is shared by both different requests and different applications. Aside from the performance aspects mentioned above, this approach also provides you with a central repository where you can both configure and monitor database connections and accesses.

As you can see in Figure 6.3, each connection approach at least builds on this layer, which means all the functions in the layer are always available.

Vendor SQL or JDBC

When applications access data in a relational database directly, JDBC is used. Although using abstraction models such as enterprise entity beans or JDOs hides this fact from the developer to a certain extent, these object-oriented models also rely on JDBC. Therefore, if you build on this lowest level, you can use the proprietary capabilities of the individual databases, but will lose all the benefits afforded by Open SQL—portability, table buffering, and SQL statement cache, to name just a few. Because this approach involves working directly at the vendor-specific layer of the database, SAP calls this approach "vendor-specific" or "vendor SQL/JDBC."

SAP specifies persistence based on this third layer as "tolerated." Therefore, you should develop at this level only if your applications absolutely require the database's proprietary capabilities.

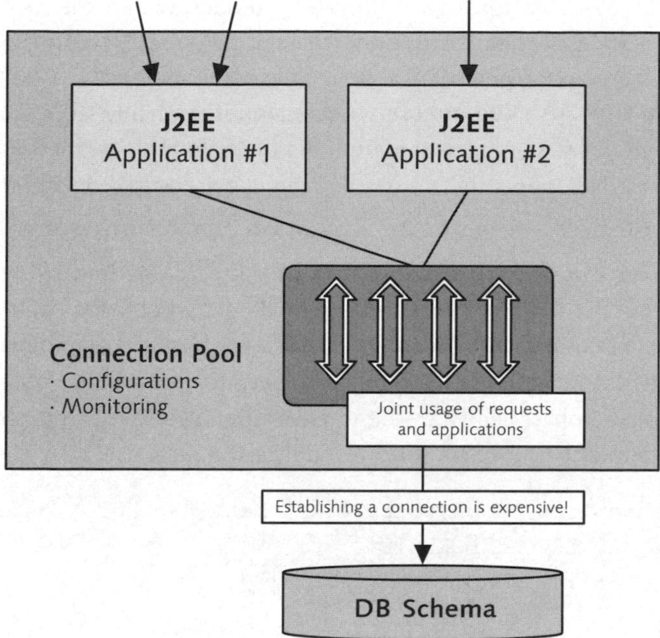

Figure 6.3 Connection Pool

DB Access Layer—Native SQL/JDBC

The second layer for database access builds on the connection pool layer—in accordance with the layer model—to enhance certain functions. Like the vendor-specific layer, this layer gives developers all the functions of the underlying proprietary database system, but again at the cost of portability and table buffering.

Native SQL or JDBC

All method calls are sent to the underlying JDBC driver directly and unchanged. Basically, the implementation of the Native JDBC API is a simple wrapper around the vendor-specific JDBC driver, but with two decisive enhancements regarding the speed and ease of maintenance of the J2EE engine—SQL trace und statement pooling.

SQL Trace

The SQL trace is available on demand to trace all SQL statements submitted to the database and executed using methods of this layer or the higher layer of the Open SQL Engine—the SQL processor layer. You can activate and deactivate the SQL trace dynamically in the Visual Administrator. The trace format is database-independent. Aside from the actual SQL statements, the log entries contain information about the time of a statement, its duration, its input parameters, and its results (where relevant), along with context information.

The SQL trace is available through a browser interface within the SAP Web AS and is particularly helpful for performance analyses. It reveals the causes of errors and poor persistence designs quickly and easily, especially the higher-level APIs that are used create an unreasonably large set of SQL statements. The SQL trace can also be a big help at development time, as it shows developers which SQL coding is generated from their JDOs, JSPs, servlets, and EJBs.

Statement Pooling

Statement pooling improves runtime performance by caching frequently used SQL statements. A buffer helps the engine detect whether an identical request has been recently placed. You can save a significant amount of CPU time because frequently used requests have to be prepared only once (in the prepare phase) and can then be executed repeatedly, which reduces the total number of parse routines sent to the database.

```
PreparedStatement ps = con.prepareStatement("SELECT *
FROM ZRM_RES_MASTER WHERE RESID = ?");
ps.setInt(1, 256);
[...]
ResultSet rs = ps.executeQuery();
[...]
ps.close();
```

Listing 6.3 Life Cycle of a SQL Statement

You should note that this source code fragment can be part of a servlet that is executed several times within the J2EE application, but with different `empl_id` values. The resulting SQL statement would have to be prepared and sent to the database each time that the servlet is executed. Preparing the SQL statement—which means the database has to parse it and create an optimized execution plan—is an extremely cost-intensive process on most systems, and represents a significant performance overhead in the long term.

Prepared-Statement Object

Statement pooling lets the application reuse a statement object that is already prepared (`PreparedStatement` object), similar to the approach of reusing database connections under connection pooling. This reuse is completely transparent for the application. When an application uses a `PreparedStatement` object, whether or not that object participates in statement pooling is immaterial. No coding changes are required. When an application closes a `PreparedStatement`, it can reuse it again with the `Connection.prepareStatement()` method.

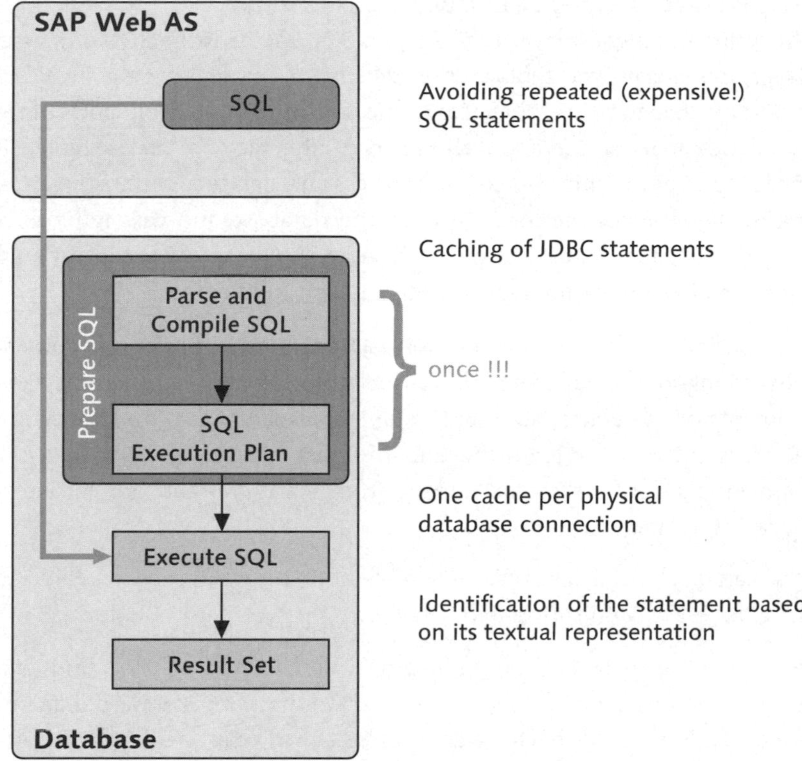

Figure 6.4 Statement Cache

A statement pool instance is associated with a physical database connection and caches `PreparedStatement` and `CallableStatement` objects that are created for this connection. Each time a `prepareStatement()` or `prepareCall()` method is called for a specific connection, the native JDBC driver automatically searches the associated statement pool for a suitable statement. The following criteria are relevant for the developer:

- The statement text must be identical to the statement in the cache (case-sensitive).
- The call type must be the same (`prepared` or `callable`).
- The scrollable type of the result set of the call must be the same (`forward-only` or `scrollable`).

If a suitable statement is found in the pool, a new `PreparedStatement` object is created and passed on to the calling program. Otherwise, the prepare call is parsed initially to create a new object. Each of these new objects is pooled when its `close()` method is called.

SQL Processor—Open SQL/JDBC

The third and highest layer of the Open SQL Engine is the SQL processor layer. It manages the table buffer, which is another building block for boosting efficiency. The objective of the table buffer is to hold parts of the database tables on the application server after they are first accessed in order to avoid multiple accesses to the same datasets within the database. This reduces the load on both the database and the network. A buffer exists for each database schema and Web AS instance, although one buffer can work for several connections simultaneously.

This buffering can be configured for each table individually, and you can also configure the buffering granularity—to buffer only some of the table contents or the entire table. Buffering is transparent for the application: The first buffer access loads the data into the buffer implicitly so that subsequent accesses are served directly from the buffer and don't have to access the database.

Visual Administrator

You can display statistics regarding table buffer usage in the *Visual Administrator*, in the **Monitoring Services** tab.

While the native SQL/JDBC approach, which builds on the second layer of the Open SQL Engine, should be selected only if no standard database schema can be used (because data tables already exist, for example), the Open SQL approach is generally the first choice. The roles at development time are clearly structured in this model, and the Java Dictionary is included in the process explicitly.

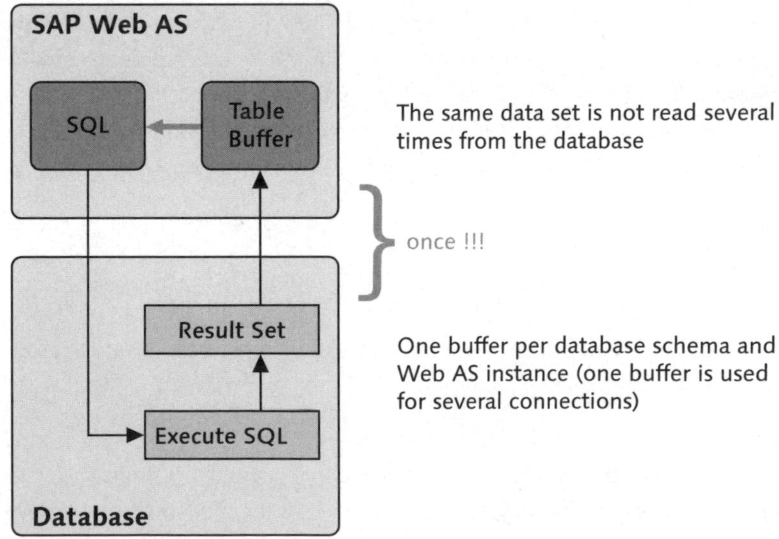

Figure 6.5 Table Buffer

Fully integrated in SAP NetWeaver Developer Studio, the Java Dictionary is used to manage the life cycle of the database object, that is, definition, creation, and modification. It is available only to those developments passed on the top layer of the SQL engine. As is true for ABAP, DDL operations should be executed only within the Dictionary.

Java Dictionary

Requests and DML expressions are handled by the Open SQL Engine, which performs a dual role in this model. It also handles all database connections, SQL statement processing, table buffering, statement pooling, and SQL trace.

In addition to these performance optimization features, the SQL processor level rounds out the concept of the Open SQL Engine by offering functions that make a new programming model possible within the Java persistence. Ultimately, all of the programming models introduced so far (JDBC, EJB, JDO)—regardless of which layer they are built on within the Open SQL Engine—use the JDBC driver to generate the finished SQL statements.

It's also evident that the Open SQL Framework for Java is generally quite similar to its ABAP counterpart, but with one major difference: The syntax of pure JDBC requests (including derived requests) cannot be analyzed until runtime; therefore, errors cannot be detected at design time, making the overall development process more complex. To avoid these difficulties, SAP has developed another abstraction level for persistence—SQLJ.

SQLJ

SQLJ defines a syntax for embedding static SQL expressions in Java source code—in contrast to JDBC, where SQL statements are passed on as string arguments of a JDBC method.

Because the Java compiler cannot handle these expressions, source code files with SQLJ elements are saved with file extension *.sqlj*. An SQLJ translator in the Open SQL processor replaces these elements with calls to the SQLJ runtime environment in a preprocessor step. It is then possible to compile the resulting Java source text.

SQLJ was initiated by Oracle, which founded an SQLJ consortium that grew to include Oracle, IBM, Microsoft, Sun, Sybase, Tandem, and Informix. Oracle then developed the reference implementation and standardized it as an ISO/IEC specification (number 9075–10).

The API used for SAP's Open SQL for Java Framework was derived from this specification. This SAP implementation ensures that the syntax is always compliant with the Open SQL grammar, which results in maximum database portability—since the Open SQL syntax is a subset of the SQL syntax that all leading database vendors support. Consequently, you cannot use SQLJ to process any database-specific SQL calls.

Open SQL Grammar

The Open SQL grammar is based on Entry Level SQL and is specified by ISO/IEC 9075 (Third Edition, November 1, 1992). It also supports the following SQL constructs:

- Joined tables
- Dynamic parameter specification

Open SQL supports the following subset of SQL statement sets:

- Queries
- Data Manipulation Language (DML)

Syntax

The SQLJ syntax is extremely simple to read: In SQLJ, SQL expressions start with the directive `#sql`. The precompiler skips the Java coding and processes only the SQL coding directly, with an initial syntax check. If no errors are found, the translator generates the Java source code, converting the SQLJ expressions into the necessary JDBC calls.

The SQLJ translator is seamlessly integrated in SAP NWDS. When the SQLJ source files are saved, the corresponding Java classes are generated automatically. The original SQLJ source files are displayed and edited to debug the application.

The objective of this API, which is defined at a higher level than JDBC, is to create simpler, more compact, more robust programs. Although the programs are certainly more robust—because syntax, semantics, type validity, and portability are checked at development time, and not after deployment at runtime—we cannot say that the SQL commands and source coding have become much less complex.

Nor is the test phase necessarily shortened, because the additional precompiler cycle shifts this phase forwards to before the deployment operation. SAP is working to mitigate these effects, however. Because the development environment supports the resolution of SQLJ statements, you can already test at design time.

The code is not any less complex; in fact, it can now be even more confusing due to the resulting mixture of languages and syntaxes. For example, variables are addressed in SQLJ with `:varName`.

While the SQLJ model represents a simplification for practiced ABAP developers, it is similar to the embedding of Open SQL in ABAP coding. But, because the SQL statements are hard-coded in the Java source text, and the syntax check doesn't support dynamically generated statements, SQLJ lets you use only static SQL functions contrary to Open SQL in ABAP, which, to a certain extent, supports the dynamic generation of SQL statements.

SQLJ Development

SQLJ statements start with directive `#sql` and finish with a semicolon. In addition to the reserved Java keywords, the `iterator`, `context`, and `with` keywords are also reserved within SQLJ expressions. Like Java coding, SQLJ statements are case-sensitive.

The actual SQL statement is contained within curly brackets, { and }, and is case-insensitive. Host variables have a colon (`:`) as a prefix.

```
#sql context Ctx with (dataSource = "jdbc/SYS");
String var;
#sql [ctx] { Select col into :var FROM tab };
```

You can use the following comments within an SQLJ source file:

- Java-like comments (`/* ... */ or //`)
- SQL-like comments (`/* ... */ or --`)

The SQL comments can be used for only the SQL parts of the source coding; you have to use Java comments outside of the SQL fragment:

```
/* #sql context Ctx with (dataSource = "jdbc/SYS");*/
// String var;
#sql [ctx] {
        --Select col into :var FROM tab
};
```

Host Variables

Java host variables are used to exchange data between Java (the host language) and SQL (the embedded language). They have the following syntax:

```
<host expression> ::= (IN | OUT | INOUT)?
  ':'( <java variable> |
       '(' <java expression> ')' ).
```

Host variables and expressions can be used anywhere in an embedded SQL statement where the Open SQL grammar permits the use of dynamic parameters. To use a Java variable as a host variable, you must preface it with a colon (:). Moreover, the variable names within the Java part must be identical to the names in the SQLJ part of a source file, including case sensitivity:

```
String res_id = "1";
       #sql [ctx] { DELETE FROM ZRM_RES_MASTER
                         WHERE RESID = :res_id };
```

Host Expressions

Like variables, complex Java expressions can also be embedded in SQL statements as host expressions. Host expressions must be enclosed with :(and). Host expressions are evaluated from left to right as they appear within the statement.

In the following coding example, two Java expressions are embedded in a SQL statement: ref.getKey() is an IN parameter, while values[++i] is an OUT parameter. Both expressions are evaluated after the statement is executed.

```
String[] values = new String[5];
MyClass ref = new MyClass();
int i = 3;
#sql [ctx] { SELECT col
                      INTO :(values[++i])
                      FROM dbtab
                      WHERE key = :(ref.getKey()) };
```

Parameter Mode

To determine the parameter mode of a host variable or expression, you can use one of the optional parameter mode indicators "IN," "OUT," or "INOUT" (all directions are from the database perspective). While this aids comprehension of the source coding, the system actually recognizes and executes the data flow automatically. The IN parameter indicates that data is passed from the Java variable to the SQL statement, while the OUT parameter shows that the result of the SQL statement is passed back to the Java application. INOUT defines a data flow in both directions, as illustrated in the following source text:

```
#sql [ctx] { SELECT col
                      INTO :OUT var
                      FROM dbtab
                      WHERE key = :IN (ref.getKey()) };
```

You should exercise caution when using host expressions, as they are evaluated at specific times: OUT expressions are evaluated after the SQL statement is executed, while IN expressions are evaluated beforehand.

Database Connection Context

Database connections are identified in SQLJ through a defined *connection context*, which specifies the target database, the session, and the transaction. All SQLJ expressions or DML statements have to use an explicit connection context. This means such expressions have to contain a label to determine the connection context object where the expression is executed. Simply put, the connection context object represents a database connection.

The SQLJ translator substitutes this connection context declaration with the declaration of a specific Java connection context class, which implements the `sqlj.runtime.ConnectionContext` interface. Because the generated class contains static variables, a connection context can only be declared as a global or static inner class.

The connection context class, in contrast to the object, does not represent a database connection, but instead a data source and a logical catalog (at design time); the latter is discussed later in this section.

We differentiate between two types of data source connection contexts: The URL connection context has constructors that make it possible to instantiate a new connection context based on a URL. In contrast, the data source connection context makes it possible to create an object based on a data source.

Connection Context with Data Source

The declaration of a connection context can contain a `with` clause that specifies the value for the data source. This case involves a connection context with data source: The data source is linked and can be found under the specified name in the JNDI directory. The default constructor generates an instance of this context class, which contains a JDBC link to the associated data source. If a `with` clause is not specified, a URL connection context is involved. The following coding illustrates a connection context with data source:

```
#sql context SysCtx
with (dataSource = "java:comp/env/jdbc/MyDB");
 [...]
       SysCtx sysCtx = new SysCtx();
       #sql [sysCtx] { DELETE FROM dbtab WHERE key = 17 }
;
```

```
[...]
            sysCtx.close();
```

SQLJ in the IDE The SAP NetWeaver Developer Studio models the entire development process of the persistence of a Web AS J2EE application.

Java Dictionary Before you create a new project, all the tables you need must be defined in the Java Dictionary. The Java Dictionary is integrated completely in the NetWeaver Developer Studio. When you create new tables, metadata for the tables is initially created only on the client side (the developer's workstation) and then generated in the respective database during the deployment process. Because the procedure for developing with the Java Dictionary was described in detail in the corresponding tutorial in Chapter 5, we will only address the major SQLJ issues here.

Tutorial: SQLJ Development

Objective You have to create the SQLJ source files. You can either create completely new files or convert existing pure Java source code into SQLJ source code and them embed SQL statements within them. As described above, the SQLJ translator generates Java classes from the SQLJ files automatically as soon as you save your work. For this reason, you should always use the SQLJ layer, and never the Java files directly, as you will otherwise create inconsistencies because the Java classes will be overwritten the next time the corresponding SQLJ files are saved.

Requirements

- You are working in the SAP NetWeaver Developer Studio.
- A project already exists.

Process Use the wizard to create new files:

1. Choose **File · New · Other** ...
2. Select **Persistence** on the left side of the screen and then **SQLJ Source** on the right side.
3. Choose **Next**.
4. Enter the required information, as you would do so for a Java file.

To convert an existing Java source file, proceed as follows:

1. Create a Java source file—if you have not done so already or do not have a usable file.
2. Click on the Java source file with the right mouse button and choose **Convert to SQLJ** from the context menu.

You now have a SQLJ file and a Java file with the same name. Never edit the Java file, as it contains only the generated code.

Result

The SQLJ Checker is integrated seamlessly in SAP NetWeaver Developer Studio. When the SQLJ files are converted—which is performed automatically as soon as the data is saved—the checker runs through the embedded SQL statements. The checks validate compliance with the Open SQL grammar and also test the schema against an offline catalog provided by *.gdbtable* files. These files were created when you created the Java Dictionary project and contain all the metadata, which was also used in the deployment process.

Validation—SQLJ Checker

To perform this schema check, the SQLJ converter has to know the path of the *.gdtable* file that contains the offline catalog. Therefore, you must associate this file with your project:

Procedure

1. Select the project.
2. Select **Properties** in the context menu.
3. Select **SQLJ Translator**.
4. Select **XML Source** and enter the path for the *.gdtable* file.
5. Click on **OK**.

Once you associate the offline catalog description, the SAP NWDS allows you to localize SQL errors at design time. Conversion errors and Java compiler errors are displayed directly. Options are also available to navigate directly to the relevant part of the SQLJ source file, as well as set breakpoints in it.

Debugging

Although you should not use debugging on the pure Java code that is generated, you can activate it for the SQLJ source files at any time. Otherwise, the debugging is exactly like debugging for Java source files: Breakpoints are set within the Java files, the source text is analyzed step by step, and the values are checked. You cannot set breakpoints for SQLJ statements.

Procedure

To activate SQJL debugging, proceed as follows:

1. Choose the menu path **Window · Customize Perspective ...**
2. Select **Other**.
3. Select **SQLJ Debugging**.
4. Click on **OK**.
5. SQLJ Debugging is added to the **Run** menu.
6. Choose **Run · SQLJ Debugging**.

Result

SQLJ debugging is now active for the current session.

The procedure for writing the actual SQLJ source texts almost always involves the following steps:

1. Declare a database connection context object, for example:

   ```
   #sql context SysCtx with (dataSource = "jdbc/myDB");
   ```

   This object is based on the connection context class.
2. Create a connection to the database by instantiating the object (connection context).
3. You can now use this connection to send SQL statements and process the results.
4. Close the connection.

Combination of SQLJ and JDBC

To develop dynamically generated statements, you can use JDBC on the relational persistence side to implement dynamic SQL requests and statements. Because SAP recommends using Open SQL (SQLJ) to implement the Java persistence—and even requires it explicitly for internal developments—you may ask how you can combine these two models.

You can combine SQJL and JDBC to use dynamic and static expressions together in the same application. JDBC connections and SQLJ connection contexts are mutually convertible, as are SQLJ iterators and JDBC result sets.

Exchange Connections

Because Open SQL and SQLJ are converted to JDBC requests at runtime, by using the Open SQL Engine, both of them can employ the same database connection and transaction. Conversely, SQLJ cannot use the same connection or transaction as native SQL/JDBC or vendor SQL/JDBC, because the latter don't run the full stack of the Open SQL Engine.

Using the JDBC Connection with SQLJ

All connection context classes have a constructor that contains an existing JDBC connection as an argument. The SQLJ connection created using this constructor shares the underlying database connection with the JDBC connection from which it was created. When the SQLJ connection context is closed with the `close(boolean closeConnection)` method, the underlying JDBC connection is also closed. If the Boolean value `true` is passed on an argument, however (or, for better readability, as constant `ConnectionContext.KEEP_CONNECTION`), the `close()` method call merely disassociates the SQL connection context object from the underlying JDBC connection, which means the former is not closed.

In the following coding example, an SQLJ connection context, `ctx`, is created by the JDBC connection `conn`. `ctx` and `conn` now share the same database connection. The `INSERT` and `DELETE` statements are both performed for this connection and share the same transaction.

```
#sql context MyCtx;

//...

Connection conn = ... ;
Statement stmt = conn.createStatemnt();
stmt.executeUpdate( "INSERT
    INTO ZRM_RES_MASTER
      (MANDT, RESID, RESTYPE, DESCRIPTION,
      INV_NUMBER, LOC_ADDRESS)
  VALUES (100, 1, 'R', 'Conference room 1st floor',
                  null, '0000100100')");

MyCtx ctx = new MyCtx(conn);

#sql [ctx] { DELETE FROM ZRM_RES_
MASTER WHERE RESID = 1 };
```

Listing 6.4 Connection Sharing from JDBC to SQLJ

JDBC Connection from SQLJ Context

The `getConnection()` method of the `ConnectionContext` interface makes it possible to receive a JDBC connection from an underlying SQLJ connection context. In the following example, the JDBC connection that underlies the `ctx` SQLJ connection context is made available to the pure Java coding, outside the SQLJ coding. `ctx` and `conn` then share the same database connection. The `INSERT` and `DELETE` statements are both performed for this connection and share the same transaction.

```
#sql context DemoCtx with (dataSource = "jdbc/DEMO");

// ...

DemoCtx ctx = new DemoCtx();
#sql [ctx] { INSERT
  INTO ZRM_RES_MASTER
```

```
    (MANDT, RESID, RESTYPE, DESCRIPTION,
     INV_NUMBER, LOC_ADDRESS)
  VALUES (100, 1, 'R', 'Conference room first floor',
                     null, '0000100100') };

Connection conn = ctx.getConnection();
Statement stmt = conn.createStatemnt();
stmt.executeUpdate(
       " DELETE FROM ZRM_RES_MASTER WHERE RESID = 1");
```

Listing 6.5 Connection sharing from SQLJ to JDBC

Exchanging Result Sets/Iterators

Result sets and iterators can be shared—like database connections—and are mutually interchangeable.

JDBC Result Set to SQLJ

It's easy to convert a JDBC result set to an SQLJ iterator, using an SQLJ CAST statement. You can apply the CAST statement to any result set iterator in the current viewing area in Open SQL/SQLJ. To ensure compatibility with SQLJ translators from other vendors, you should apply only the CAST statement to public result set iterators. Once the SQLJ ResultSetIterator object has been created, you should use the results of this method to handle all data retrieval operations.

In the following example, JDBC result set rs is converted to an SQLJ result set iterator with the CAST statement.

```
#sql iterator NamedIterator (String name);

//...

NamedIterator namIter;
Connection conn = ...

Statement stmt = conn.createStatement();
ResultSet rs =
       stmt.executeQuery("SELECT RESID FROM
                          ZRM_RES_MASTER"
);

#sql namIter = { CAST :rs };
```

```
while (namIter.next()) {
        System.out.println(namIter.name());
```

Listing 6.6 Converting a JDBC Result Set to a SQLJ Result Set Iterator

Iterators from SQLJ to JDBC

You can use SQLJ results records within JDBC in a similar manner. Every `ResultSetIterator` object has the `getResultSet()` method, which is used to retrieve the underlying JDBC `ResultSet` object. As this example once again clearly demonstrates, SQLJ merely hides the underlying JDBC layer from the user.

Conversely, once the JDBC `ResultSet` object is created, you should use this specific object instance to transfer the data to the surrounding Java program—instead of going to the additional (redundant) effort of instantiating a SQLJ `ResultSetIterator`.

In the example below, the `getResultSet()` described above is called for the SQLJ `ResultSetIterator` object, `namIter`, and returns it as the JDBC `ResultSet`.

```
#sql iterator NamedIterator (String name);

//...

NamedIterator namIter = null;
#sql [ctx] namIter = { SELECT RESID FROM
                       ZRM_RES_MASTER };

ResultSet rs = namIter.getResultSet();
while (rs.next()) {
        System.out.println(rs.getString(1));
}
```

Listing 6.7 JDBC Taking Over a SQLJ Iterator

Object/Relational Persistence

In the previous chapters, we mentioned the object orientation of the Java language several times, but didn't elaborate on any details of Enterprise Java Beans. Now, we'll examine the entity beans more closely.

Subjects of Business Processes

Entity beans model business concepts that can be expressed as subjects. This general model helps developers decide whether a business concept is suitable for implementation as an entity bean. Unlike session beans, entity beans aren't business processes; rather, they are business objects or actual entities. They describe the state and the behavior of objects in the real world, and enable developers to encapsulate the data and business rules that belong to a specific concept. Therefore, these beans represent data in the database, which is why changes to the beans automatically result in changes to the database.

There are many advantages to using entity beans instead of accessing the database directly. The data is molded into object form, providing a simple mechanism for accessing and changing it, which a method employed by the beans themselves. In a sense, the developer doesn't communicate with the database, but instead, he or she communicates with objects by using the method, `PersonObject.tellMeYourName()`. If used properly, this method simplifies the implementation and makes the coding easier to understand (think of the countless SQL statements, many of them nested, that you would otherwise have to deal with). It also increases your chances of writing reusable software. However, you must ensure that an entity bean holds all the functions to ensure data consistency and simplicity for the developer.

When a new bean is generated, a new data record has to be added to the database, and a bean instance linked with this data. If the bean is used and its state changes, these changes have to be synchronized with the data in the database: adding, changing, or deleting entries. Therefore, the communication between the application and the database still takes place, but is transparent to the developer. This communication process of coordinating the database with the data represented by a bean instance is called *persistence*.

We differentiate between two types of entity beans, which implement this persistence using two different concepts: container-managed persistence and bean-managed persistence.

Container-Managed Persistence (CMP)

Under container-managed persistence, as the name implies, the persistence is managed automatically by EJB containers. These containers know how the bean's instance attributes are mapped to the database (or the table fields within it) and take care of inserting, changing, and deleting the data for the entities in the database.

Developer Perspective

From the developer's perspective, CMP entity beans are easier to program, because they enable you to focus on implementing the business logic by delegating responsibility for persistence to the container. When you implement a bean of this type, you define a mapping to specify which fields the container will manage and how they are mapped to the database. Once defined, the container generates the necessary logic to save the state of the bean instance automatically.

Fields that are mapped to the database are called *container-managed fields,* and can contain any primitive Java types or serialized objects. The advantage of CMP is that the bean can be developed independently of the underlying database that saves its state later. Container-managed beans can be used in both relational and object-based databases. The bean's state is defined independently, increasing flexibility and therefore, possibilities for reuse.

A general disadvantage of CMP is that it requires complex mapping tools to define how the fields are mapped to the database. In some cases, however, it will suffice to map each field in the bean to a column in the database or serialize it in a file. But, there are also much more complicated cases; for example, a bean's state could be defined based on a complex relational database join. Even so, the SAP NetWeaver Developer Studio features many different functions for defining the mapping.

O/R Mapping

SAP calls this type of mapping *O/R mapping* (object/relational mapping). This concept involves certain O/R mapping rules that determine which Java data types can be mapped to which JDBC types. If you create the O/R mapping in the SAP NWDS, these requirements are fulfilled automatically; if you deviate from this schema, the Developer Studio also features O/R mapping verification.

O/R Mapping Rules

Enterprise Bean Requirements

Each entity bean class corresponds to a separate table in the database. To ensure data integrity, you cannot map different bean classes in the same table.

Rules for the CMP Fields

A CMP field, which represents a basic attribute, is mapped to a single column. The following JDBC types are accepted for the corresponding CMP fields:

Java Data Type	Possible JDBC Data Types	Default JDBC Data Type
`java.lang.String`	VARCHAR, CHAR, LONG-VARCHAR, CLOB	VARCHAR
`byte[]`	VARBINARY, BINARY, LONG-VARBINARY, BLOB	VARBINARY
`java.lang.Byte[]`	VARBINARY, BINARY, LONG-VARBINARY, BLOB	VARBINARY
`Short`	SMALLINT	SMALLINT
`java.lang.Short`	SMALLINT	SMALLINT
`Int`	INTEGER	INTEGER
`java.lang.Integer`	INTEGER	INTEGER
`Long`	BIGINT	BIGINT
`java.lang.Long`	BIGINT	BIGINT
`Float`	REAL	REAL
`java.lang.Float`	REAL	REAL
`Double`	DOUBLE, FLOAT	DOUBLE
`java.lang.Double`	DOUBLE, FLOAT	DOUBLE
`java.math.BigDecimal`	DECIMAL, NUMERIC	DECIMAL
`java.util.Date`	TIMESTAMP	TIMESTAMP
`java.sql.Date`	DATE	DATE
`java.sql.Time`	TIME	TIME
`java.sql.Timestamp`	TIMESTAMP	TIMESTAMP
`java.sql.Clob`	CLOB	CLOB
`java.sql.Blob`	BLOB	BLOB
`Boolean`	SMALLINT	SMALLINT
`java.lang.Boolean`	SMALLINT	SMALLINT
`Byte`	SMALLINT	SMALLINT
`java.lang.Byte`	SMALLINT	SMALLINT
`java.io.Reader`	VARCHAR	VARCHAR
`java.io.InputStream`	VARBINARY	VARBINARY

Table 6.1 Rules for Mapping CMP to JDBC

Relationships are implemented as references between primary key columns and foreign key columns. **Rules for Reference Fields**

You define one or more different foreign key column(s) for each relationship. If n connections exist between two beans, then n mappings have to exist between the primary and foreign key columns as well. The foreign key and primary key both must have the same JDBC data type.

In addition, a column with type "unique key" cannot be part of a foreign key. For that reason, you cannot define a foreign key column as "unique," because the corresponding primary key would be "unique" automatically.

1:1 Relationship When you implement a 1:1 relationship, the foreign keys are contained in one of the two tables involved in the relationship.

1:n Relationship In a 1:n relationship, the foreign keys are located in the table that belongs to the bean, which represents the n side of the relationship.

n:m Relationship To define an n:m relationship, you have to implement an intermediate table that contains the foreign keys for both primary keys of the objects involved in the relationship. The columns must have the same JDBC type as the primary key columns.

Restrictions The validation functions in O/R mapping cannot detect and handle the following errors:

- A column is defined as a logical foreign key, but is not a true foreign key.
- A column is a primary key, but is defined as a foreign key.

CMP is often referred to as *declarative persistence*. It is very easy to use, even if the object model of the persistent data is complex. You don't have to program any SQL statements—you can generate the O/R mapping, the corresponding tables, and the SQL statements automatically within the development environment.

Tutorial: Creating a Container-Managed Entity Bean

This tutorial describes the procedure for using the wizard in the SAP NetWeaver Developer Studio to create an entity bean. You can also create enterprise beans, using the context menus of the relevant project.

Requirements An EJB module project already exists.

Process

1. Choose the menu path **File · New · Other**.
2. Choose **J2EE · EJB** on the left side of the first wizard page and then **Enterprise Bean** on the right side.

3. Click on **Next**.
4. Enter a name for the new entity bean in the **EJB Name** field.
5. Select the name of the project where you want to create the bean in the **EJB Project** field.
6. Choose **Entity Bean** in the **Bean Type** field.
7. Specify a package in the **Default Package** field or, if none exists yet, create a new one.
8. Choose **Generate default interfaces** or specify which interfaces will be generated and used, as shown in Figure 6.6.

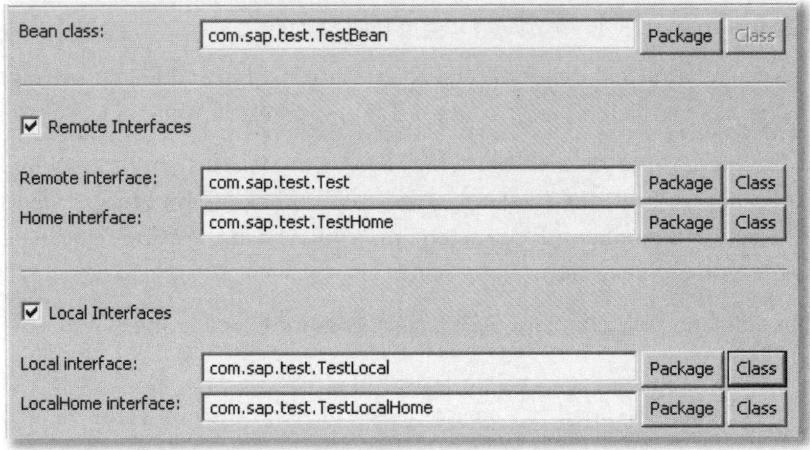

Figure 6.6 Selecting Bean Interfaces

9. Click on **Next**.
10. Select the persistence type, **Container-Managed Persistence** or **Bean-Managed Persistence**—select **Container-Managed Persistence** in this case. You can now add and remove persistence fields (and any time later as well).
11. Click on **Next**.
12. Add superclasses (if necessary) and click on **Next**.
13. Add the methods (which you can also do at any time during the development phase). For each method, choose the method type and click on **Add**. Enter the names and return types of the methods and specify the parameters.
14. Click on **Finish**.

Result The J2EE Explorer in the SAP NWDS resembles Figure 6.7.

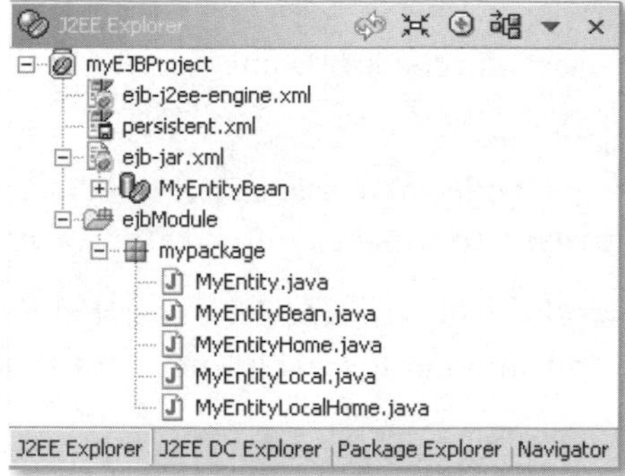

Figure 6.7 Result in the J2EE Explorer

You can now edit the entity bean in the source code and create the fields for container-managed persistence (CMP fields).

Process

1. In the J2EE Explorer window, select your project, then ejb-jar.xml, and finally the enterprise bean whose fields you want to create.
2. Select **Open** in the context menu; the bean properties appear in the right-hand window.
3. Select the **Fields** tab.
4. Select **Persistent Fields** and click **Add**. A new persistence field appears as a sub-node within the **Persistent Fields** tree structure.
5. Enter the following data in each of the fields listed below:

    - **Name**: name of the field. The SAP NetWeaver Developer Studio uses this name to create the corresponding get and set access methods. In accordance with Java conventions, the first letter of the field name is uppercase, prefaced by set or get.
    - **Fully Qualified Name**: the fully qualified name of the field type, which also must contain the package name.
    - **Array**: Choose this option to specify that the persistence field represents an array of the specified type. Enter the dimension of the array in the field that appears after you select **Array option**. You must enter values between 1 and 9.

Result

The persistence fields are now described by the corresponding *ejb-jar.xml* deployment descriptor file. Its O/R mapping was automatically written to the SAP J2EE Engine-specific deployment descriptor, *persistent.xml*. This file configures the EJB container to take over the container-managed persistence, by setting the following values and properties in the *persistent.xml* file:

- Data source and database vendor
- Type and method of lock mechanisms for the entity beans
- The O/R mapping
- The deployment properties of the finder and select SQL methods, which the container uses to optimize performance of the entity beans

During the deployment process, all the necessary code is generated by the EJB container, based on the information in the deployment descriptors.

As a result, developers no longer have to implement the access logic; they only have to declare and configure attributes and relationships.

Bean-Managed Persistence (BMP)

Bean-managed persistence is much more complicated than container-managed persistence, because you—the developer—have to program the persistence logic explicitly in the bean class.

This means you have to implement the SQL statements completely yourself. Consequently, this model makes you highly flexible in defining how the state is managed between the bean instance and the database. Entity beans that are defined through complex joins, a combination of different database systems, or other resources (such as legacy systems) generally benefit from BMP. Even though O/R mapping of the abstract schema does not meet the project's requirements, this programming model can still help.

Container-managed persistence lets you map objects to only one table, which is relatively restrictive when it comes to true distributed objects—which aren't held in just one table, but instead can be composed of multiple attributes from different data sources. Bean-managed persistence offers many more possibilities and greater flexibility in such cases.

The disadvantage of BMP is that a lot more work is required to define the beans. You have to understand the database structure and develop the logic to generate, update, and remove the data associated with an entity. You have to be very careful when dealing with the generic bean methods, especially `ejbLoad()` and `ejbStore()`. You even have to develop the search methods defined in the bean's home interface, along with the mapping of the bean attributes to the database, explicitly and manually.

A bean-managed application is not as database-independent as a container-managed entity, but is better suited to dealing with complex data.

You can use both pure vendor-specific JDBC and the native form, as well as Open SQL (SQLJ) to ensure the greatest possible database independence.

Even so, SAP recommends always using CMP (or JDO, which are described below) within object-related developments. Accordingly, we will not describe BMP in further detail here. If you would like to learn more, see the specific Java or J2EE literature.

Java Data Objects (JDO)

Java Data Objects are SAP's second recommended method for implementing object/relational persistence.

The JDO standard is a very promising technology for implementing persistent Java objects. Although JDO is one of the many Java standards and is usually mentioned in the context of J2EE, it is not included in the J2EE 1.3 or 1.4 specifications. Java Data Objects is implemented in the SAP Web AS, however, due to the many advantages it offers compared to the EJB concept.

While EJB entity beans are based on the component model of the J2EE architecture, the JDO standard tries to keep as close as possible to the Java object model. JDO lets you make almost any Java class persistent directly, independently of the architecture layer where the objects are contained. Accordingly, JDO does not require the container model of the J2EE environment, but instead adds persistence directly to the Java language.

JDO also enables you to access nearly any type of data store—relational databases, object/relational databases, or even file-based formats.

JDO is based on a byte-code transformation of the classes to be made persistent. An XML-based mapping file has to be created for each class that you want to save persistently. This file describes how the class attributes are mapped to the database tables, similar to the CMP approach. The *byte-code enhancer* then overwrites the access methods of the class and replaces them with the required SQL statements.

JDO features a Persistence Manager, which manages the life cycle, transactions, requests, and identities of the persistence objects. The query language is JDOQL *(Java Data Objects Query Language)*.

JDO can be combined with JSPs, session beans, and entity beans (BMP)—but not with container-managed entity beans (CMP)—within a J2EE environment.

Tutorial: JDO Development Cycle

Objective For the developer, developing a persistent object is an extremely structured process, with a defined procedure. The JDO development tools are not yet integrated in the SAP NetWeaver Developer Studio, however, which means all the steps have to be performed manually. This tutorial describes the development cycle for an employee object, implemented by the class `Resource`:

Process

1. Define the database tables.
2. Create the pure Java classes that you want to make persistent.

   The classes that will implement the persistence must be created and implemented in the SAP NetWeaver Developer Studio, just like any other Java classes. Ultimately, each of these classes defines objects that will be saved in a database and can be retrieved from the database.

   To create the classes, choose **New • Java Class**. Enter "Resource" as the class name.

   The new Java files open automatically and you can enter the coding. The following coding excerpt illustrates an example of such a class; it is limited to three attributes of the resource object at this point.

```
public class Resource {

   // Class attributes: the persistent fields
   //                   of a resource.
   // Also defined inside the file Resource.jdo
      private int resId;
      private String resType;
      private String description;

   // Required: a no-args constructor
   public Resource() {
     this.resId = 1;
     this.resType = "INITIAL";
     this.description = "INITIAL";
   }

   // Constructor where the ID is set
```

```
    public Resource(int resId) {
      this.resId = resId;
      this.resType = "INITIAL";
      this.description = "INITIAL";
    }

    // Implement the getter methods of the class
    public int getResId() {
      return resId;
    }

    public String getResType() {
      return resType;
    }

    public String getDescription() {
      return description;
    }

    // Implement the setter methods of the class
    public void setResType(String type) {
      resType = type;
    }

    public void setDescription(String desc) {
      description = desc;
    }
}
```

3. Define the object identity.

   JDO provides for an identity class for each persistent object, which ensures that an individual JDO instance is associated with a persistence manager that represents a specific data store object—the database.

   While the JDO standard describes three types of identity—application, data store, and nondurable identity—SAP's JDO implementation supports only the application identity. In this form, the application manages the JDO identity and holds it in the data store. In most cases, the instance identity is the primary key.

   To implement the identity, you have to create a special object identity class for each persistent class, which is defined as `static public` inner class ID of the corresponding persistence class. The object identity class has a corresponding public instance field for each primary key field, with the same name and data type.

The object identity class has a constructor without arguments, like the persistent class. It also has a string constructor, which returns an instance as a string (like a toString() method).

It also has to implement a hashCode() method, which returns the primary key, and an equals() method, which uses a Boolean return value to check the instance or check which instance a given object belongs to.

The following coding illustrates the identity class for the resource object as an example:

```
import com.sap.jdo.SAPJDOHelper;
static public class Id {

// public field corresponding to the primary key of the
// PC class
public int resId;

static {
    // establish the relation: Resource$Id
    // class is the identity class for the
    // PC class Resource.
    SAPJDOHelper.registerPCClass(Resource.class);
}

public Id() {
 //required: a no-args constructor
}

public Id(int resId) {
      this.resId = resId;
}

public Id(String string) {
// required: a string constructor
// defined as the counterpart of toString()
              resId = Integer.parseInt(string);
}
```

```
public int hashCode() {
// required: implement hashCode()
            return resId;
}

public String toString() {
// required: toString() defined
// as the counterpart of the string constructor
            return Integer.toString(resId);
}

public boolean equals(Object that) {
// required: define equals()
            if (that == null || !(that instanceof Id))
                  return false;
            else
                  return resId == ((Id) that).resId;
}
}
```

4. Define the JDO metadata.

   You can now define the XML metadata for the JDO objects. To do so, each persistence class is assigned a corresponding **.jdo* file, which must be located in the same directory.

   - Choose **New · File**.
   - Enter the directory where you want to save the file and enter the same file name as the corresponding Java class file, but with extension *.jdo*.
   - You can now enter the definitions. The following listing shows the coding for the preceding Java class as an example:

```
<?xml version="1.0" encoding="UTF-8"?>
<!DOCTYPE jdo SYSTEM "jdo.dtd">
<jdo>
  <package name="temp.persistence.gettingstarted.jdo">
<class name="Resource"
        identity-type="application"
        objectid-class="Resource$Id">
     <field name="resId"
```

```
                persistence-modifier="persistent"
                primary-key="true"/>
            <field name="resType"
                persistence-modifier="persistent"/>
            <field name="description"
                persistence-modifier="persistent"/>
        </class>
    </package>
</jdo>
```

5. Define the O/R mapping for the persistence classes.

   You can now create the mapping, using another XML file that you also save under the same name in the same folder, but with file extension **.map*.

   The format of this class is defined by the JDO mapping metadata Document Type Definition (DTD).

   You create this file just like the **.jdo* file; the mapping for this example is demonstrated below:

```
<?xml version="1.0" encoding="UTF-8"?>
<!DOCTYPE map SYSTEM "map.dtd">
<map version="1.0">
  <package name="temp.persistence.gettingstarted.jdo">
    <class name="Resource">
      <field name="resId">
        <column name="RESID" table="ZRM_RES_MASTER"/>
      </field>
      <field name="resType">
        <column name="RESTYPE" table="ZRM_RES_MASTER"/>
      </field>
      <field name="description">
        <column name="DESCRIPTION"
                table="ZRM_RES_MASTER"/>
      </field>
    </class>
  </package>
</map>
```

6. Use the JDO Enhancer to compile the code.

   Now that you have created the appropriate classes and descriptors, use the JDO Enhancer to create the classes that will communicate with the application business logic.

   Because the JDO Enhancer and the validation tools are not integrated in the Developer Studio yet, you have to perform these steps manually. To do so, we recommend using the ANT build tool, which is available as a plug-in for the Developer Studio.

   - Create a new file for your project—using the context menu—with name *build.xml*, and save it in the main directory of your project.
   - Enter the following coding (continuing the above example):

```
<project name="GettingStartedWithJDO" default="enhance"
        basedir="..">

  <property name ="sourceproject.dir"
            value="GettingStartedJDOWeb"/>
  <property name ="dictproject.dir"
            value="GettingStartedPersistenceDic"/>
  <property name ="src.dir"
            value="${sourceproject.dir}/source"/>
  <property name ="bin.dir"
            value="${sourceproject.dir}/bin"/>
  <property name ="catalog.dir"
            value="${dictproject.dir}/gen_ddic
                   /dbtables/"/>

  <property name ="enhancer"
            value="com.sap.jdo.enhancer.Main"/>

  <property name ="utility"
            value="com.sap.jdo.sql.util.JDO"/>
  <property name ="tssap"
            value="C:/Program Files/SAP/JDT/eclipse
                   /plugins"/>
  <property name ="jdo"
            value="${tssap}/com.sap.ide.eclipse.ext
                   .libs.jdo/lib/jdo.jar"/>
  <property name ="xml"
            value="${tssap}/com.tssap.sap.libs
```

```
                   .xmltoolkit
                   /lib/sapxmltoolkit.jar"/>
  <property name ="jdoutil"
            value="${tssap}/com.sap.jdo.utils
                   /lib/sapjdoutil.jar"/>
  <property name ="dictionary"
            value="${tssap}/com.sap.dictionary.database
                   /lib/jddi.jar"/>
  <property name ="logging"
            value="${tssap}/com.tssap.sap.libs.logging
                   /lib/logging.jar"/>
  <property name ="catalogreader"
            value="${tssap}/com.sap.opensql
                   /lib/opensqlapi.jar"/>
  <property name ="classpath"
            value="${jdo};${jdoutil};${xml}"/>

<property name ="classpath.check"
          value="${classpath};${dictionary};${logging};
                 ${catalogreader};${bin.dir}"/>
<target name="enhance">
  <antcall target="enhance.Resource"/>
</target>

<target name="check">
  <antcall target="check.Resource"/>
</target>

<target name="enhance.Resource">
  <java
    fork       ="yes"
    failonerror="yes"
    classname  ="${enhancer}"
    classpath  ="${classpath}">
    <arg line ="-f -d" />
        <arg value="${bin.dir}"/>
        <arg value="${src.dir}/temp/persistence/
             gettingstarted/jdo/Resource.jdo"/>
        <arg value="${bin.dir}/temp/persistence/
             gettingstarted/jdo/Resource.class"/>
      </java>
```

```
    </target>

    <target name="check.Resource">
      <java
        fork       ="yes"
        failonerror="yes"
        classname  ="${utility}"
        classpath  ="${classpath.check}">
        <arg line  ="-v -p" />
        <arg value ="${sourceproject.dir}
                      /checker.properties"
         />
        <arg value ="-c"/>
        <arg value ="${catalog.dir}"/>
        <arg value ="check"/>
        <arg value ="temp/persistence/gettingstarted/jdo
                     /Resource.class"/>
    </java>
  </target>
</project>
```

- Now create a new file called *checker.properties*, again from the context menu of the project, and save it in the main folder for the project as well. Enter the following coding in this new file:

```
com.sap.jdo.sql.mapping.useCatalog=true
com.sap.jdo.sql.mapping.checkConsistency=true
com.sap.jdo.sql.mapping.checkConsistencyDeep=true
```

7. In the Java perspective of the Developer Studio, open the context menu for the *build.xml* file and choose **Run ANT...**
8. If they are not set already, set the **enhance** and **check** objects in the **Targets** tab.
9. Choose **Apply** and then **Run**. The result of the process is output in the Developer Studio console.
10. The generated classes now implement interface `javax.jdo.spi.PersistenceCapable`, which can be used by the business logic.

Figure 6.8 summarizes the development process of JDO persistence. **Result**

Although the JDO development process is quite structured, the fact that the corresponding tools for using JDO are not integrated in the Developer Studio yet is a distinct disadvantage. Therefore, you have to spend a lot of time on tasks that the appropriate tools could perform automatically. Errors are likely in larger projects because developers can quickly lose track of the manually created files.

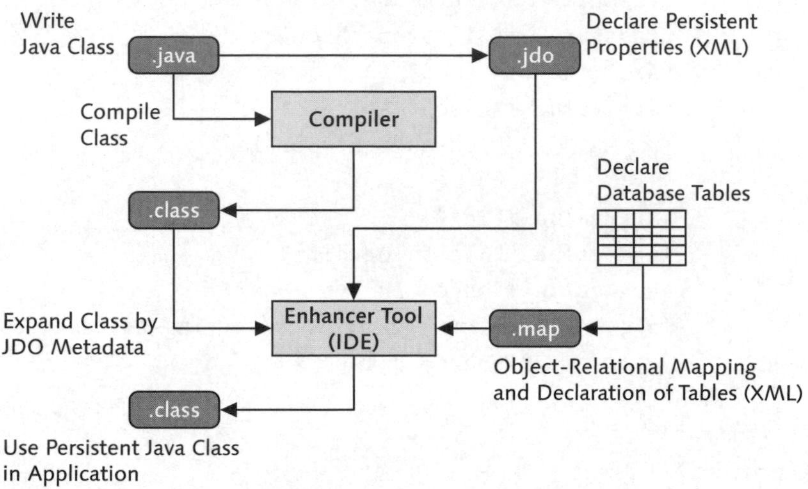

Figure 6.8 JDO Development Cycle

You probably won't be able to leverage the full potential of the JDO approach in SAP environments until SAP adds the necessary extensions to the Developer Studio.

As we already mentioned, SAP recommends using CMP or JDO for object-oriented persistence, instead of using relational-persistence by implementing raw SQL via JDBC bean-managed persistence, which is completely ignored at this time. The following table compares and contrasts the two SAP-recommended approaches and suggests possible uses for each:

JDO 1.0	Entity Beans (CMP) 2.0
Not part of the J2EE standard, that is, it is not supported by all J2EE application servers.	Part of the J2EE standard; the J2EE specifications guarantee support for CMP. CMP features a complete programming model.
Does not support direct remote calls, but they can be implemented using façade session beans.	Although direct remote calls are possible, SAP recommends using entity beans only locally, and delegating remote communication to façade session beans.
No implicit security features are available.	The CMP specifications contain security features.
JDO is available in both managed environments and open Java environments.	Only executable in managed environments such as EJB containers.
Supports inheritance and interfaces, multiple mapping, and mapping to legacy tables.	Does not support inheritance or interfaces. A bean can only be mapped to a single table.
A separate class is required for the primary keys; this implementation is not automated and is therefore time-intensive.	No primary key class is required.
The inter-object relationships are not managed centrally.	The inter-object relationships are managed centrally.
JDOQL permits dynamic queries, which always return objects. JDOQL has a Java-like syntax, however, and is not as powerful.	EJBQL can execute only static queries that return unchangeable datasets. EJBQL has a syntax comparable to OQL and is more powerful than JDOQL.
Faster development cycles.	The deployment processes are very complex and hence, much slower.
Java skills are sufficient to create new implementations.	Using EJBs requires extensive knowledge of object orientation and distributed concepts.

Table 6.2 Comparison Between JDO and Entity Beans

6.2 Middleware: Connectivity Between Applications

Direct access to the ABAP Personality

As we have already mentioned several times, all connectivity between the ABAP and Java personalities has to occur at application level. It is usually not possible for a Java application to access the ABAP instance's database directly—through a JDBC driver, for example. This also applies to ABAP applications when attempting to access a Java instance.

Connections of this type are required simply for data retrieval from a persistence perspective; from the business logic perspective, many projects aim to achieve communication between these two entities to execute business processes. In both cases, information and data is exchanged at the component level, based on a middleware architecture that SAP provides in several aspects within the SAP Web AS.

To do so, SAP developed the Java Connector (JCo), which makes the standard SAP RFC (Remote Function Call) available for Java, enabling high-performance communication in both directions: All *remote*-enabled function modules, as well as Business Application Programming Interfaces (BAPIs), can be called from within Java. Conversely, the methods implemented in Java on the JCo server can also be called from within ABAP programs.

6.2.1 RFC

Remote Function Call is a proprietary SAP communication protocol that enables function calls over a network connection, making it possible to pass on request parameters and receive the corresponding result parameters. The data types of the parameters can be defined freely, letting you transfer even complex structures and tables in both directions. An essential prerequisite for communication between function modules is that these modules be flagged as *remote-enabled*, as only this type of function module can be called through RFC.

RFC supports synchronous, asynchronous, and transactional calls. The terms *synchronous* and *asynchronous* have already been explained. Transactional RFC communication makes it possible to consolidate function module calls to form a transaction, extending transaction security across remote systems.

External (non-SAP) systems usually support only synchronous RFC calls, while the other options are used exclusively for communication between SAP Systems.

6.2.2 JCo

The *Java Connector* (JCo) is a framework based on the *Java Native Interface* (JNI), which SAP has implemented partially in Java and partially in C. You can use it to enable communication between Java and ABAP in both directions—*inbound calls* ("Java calls ABAP") and *outbound calls* ("ABAP calls Java"). The SAP JCo is an integrated component of both the SAP Business Connector, for communication with external Java applications, and the SAP Web Application Server, to link the integrated J2EE server with the ABAP environment as described above. Still, the JCo is a software component that can be installed independently of the SAP System. The installation files are available from the SAP Service Marketplace at *http://service.sap.com/connectors*.

Functionality

The SAP JCo provides the following functions for creating SAP-capable Java applications:

- The RFC middleware of the JCo is based on the JNI.
- The JCo supports SAP Systems with Release 3.1H and later, as well as other SAP components that feature BAPIs or RFMs.
- Both inbound (Java client calls BAPI or RFM) and outbound (ABAP calls Java server) function calls are possible.
- It supports synchronous, transactional, and queued RFCs.
- It enables connection pooling, which is critical for Web servers.

Architecture

Figure 6.9 shows a technical schematic of data conversion within the SAP JCo:

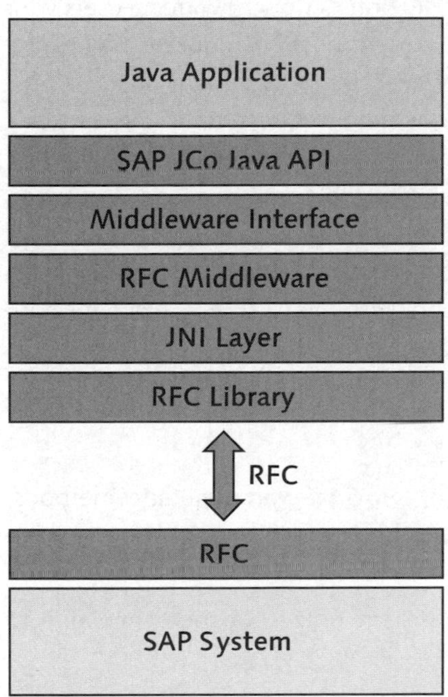

Figure 6.9 SAP JCO Architecture

From the Java client's perspective, a Java application forwards a Java method through the SAP JCo-Java API to another middleware interface for the RFC middleware. Once there, it is converted to an RFC or ABAP call, using the JNI layer and the RFC library, and sent to the SAP System.

Similarly, in the opposite direction, an RFC call is converted to a Java method call and forwarded to the Java application. Both scenarios are described in more detail below.

Java Calls ABAP

In the *inbound call* scenario, a JCo client has to be implemented on the Java side for each function module in the ABAP personality that you want to make available within the Java application.

Two programming models are available for this: direct connections and connections through connection pools. Direct connections can be opened and held as long as necessary. In contrast, connection pools manage the connections and make them available on request. As soon as a connection is no longer required, it is returned to the connection pool, where it can be assigned to another user. You define how many connection objects are available within each pool, which lets you set the maximum number of simultaneous connections appropriately for the server's resources. You should use this model for Web server applications in particular, as you (the developer) generally don't know how many users your system will attract, nor the number of connection requests. If you use direct connections, this option is not available: A JCo client object is generated automatically for every connection request until the system's resources are finally exhausted. Therefore, this model is recommended for only desktop applications with a predictable resource load. Moreover, to save system resources in this model, you have to ensure that all connections that are no longer needed are closed. You can generally use both models in parallel in the same application. We will now examine both models in detail, starting with the direct connection.

Direct Connection

To develop direct JCo connections, a JCo client requires three classes that are contained in package `com.sap.mw.jco.*`:

1. `JCO`—The main class of the JCo; provides various static methods, including the `create()` factory method, which is used to generate a JCo client object.
2. `JCO.Client`—This represents the client object, or the connection to the SAP server.
3. `JCO.Attributes`—These classes contain the attributes of a connection, such as information about the release of the SAP System.

You may wonder why the client and attribute classes are specified as static attributes of the main class. The answer is that the main JCo class is the only public class within the JCo framework; it references all the other subclasses indirectly, all of which are implemented as private ("hidden") classes.

Tutorial: Implementing a JCo Client

Objective

In the following example, you will implement a JCo client to permit access to the ABAP-side business logic from within Java, using function module `Z_RM_BOOK` to do so.

Requirements

- The JCo is completely installed and configured on the J2EE development server.
- You know the access data required to reach the corresponding SAP System.

Process

1. First, every program that uses the JCo has to contain the following import statement:

   ```
   import com.sap.mw.jco.*
   ```

2. In the next step, define a connection variable—the JCo client—to address a defined client in the SAP System:

   ```
   JCO.Client resManBookConnection
   ```

3. You now have to instantiate the JCo client—not using a constructor, but instead the `createClient()` factory method of class `JCO`, which then returns a reference to the client object. The main parameters that you have to provide for this method are the *client number*, a *user name*, the corresponding *password*, the *language ID*, the *application server name*, and the *system number*.

   ```
   resManBookConnection = JCO.createClient(
     "100",          //Client number
     "user",         //User name
     "******",       //Password
     "EN",           //Language
     "host.snp.de", //Name of application server
     "00");          //System number
   ```

4. Creating the JCo client object does not establish a connection to the SAP server yet; you now have to generate it explicitly with the `connect()` method call on the client instance. In general, automatically connecting resources in constructors is not the preferred method,

because it removes the allocation of "expensive" resources from the developer's responsibility.

```
try {
  resManBookConnection.connect();
} catch (Exception ex) {
  System.out.println("Exception occurred: \n"
                    + ex);
  if (resManBookConnection != null) {
    resManBookConnection.disconnect();
  }
}
```

5. You now want to call a function in the SAP System. To do so, you first generate the input parameter list (as an object) and then fill this list. You also have to define a list object for the expected output values. Because ABAP uses different data types than Java, you will have to map the data types. Table 6.3 shows the different data types and their mapping.

ABAP Type	Description	Java Type	JCo Type Code
b	1-byte integer	int	JCO.TYPE_INT1
s	2-byte integer	int	JCO.TYPE_INT2
I	4-byte integer	int	JCO.TYPE_INT
C	Character	String	JCO.TYPE_CHAR
N	Numeric character	String	JCO.TYPE_NUM
P	Binary-coded decimal	Big decimal	JCO.TYPE_BCD
D	Date	Date	JCO.TYPE_DATE
T	Time	Date	JCO.TYPE_TIME
F	Float	Double	JCO.TYPE_FLOAT
X	XString	Byte[]	JCO.TYPE_BYTE
g	String (variable length)	String	JCO.TYPE_STRING
y	XString (variable length)	byte[]	JCO.TYPE_XSTRING

Table 6.3 Data Type Mapping, ABAP—JCo

Therefore, you end up with the following parameter lists for input and output parameters; the name, data type, length, and parameter value are specified for each input parameter.

```
JCO.ParameterList
            input = JCO.createParameterList();
input.appendValue("I_RESID",
                JCO.TYPE_STRING, 12, "3");
input.appendValue("I_DATE_FROM",
                JCO.TYPE_DATE, 8, "20041224");
input.appendValue("I_TIME_FROM",
                JCO.TYPE_DATE, 6, "103000")
input.appendValue("I_DATE_TO",
                JCO.TYPE_DATE, 8, "20041231");
input.appendValue("I_TIME_FROM",
                JCO.TYPE_DATE, 6, "193000")
input.appendValue("I_REMARK",
                JCO.TYPE_STRING, 255,
                "Please re-fill the mini-bar");
input.appendValue("I_MANDT",
                JCO.TYPE_INT, 4, "0100");
```

You also have to create an object for the output parameter list, in which you specify the parameter name, type, and length for each parameter. Because the SAP function module used in this example, Z_RM_BOOK, does not have any return values, the following coding is merely an example for a single output parameter:

```
JCO.ParameterList
            output = JCO.createParameterList();
output.addInfo("RESPONSE",
            JCO.TYPE_CHAR, 255);
```

6. You can now use the execute() method to execute the function on the object:

```
resManBookConnection.execute("Z_RM_BOOK",
                              input, output);
```

7. Once you are done using the connection, you should close it to avoid blocking system resources unnecessarily. To do so, use the disconnect() method of the object. In contrast to connection pools—as you will see below—we don't recommend calling a function and closing the connection immediately afterwards (until the next function call) for direct connections. Instead, unless no further activities are expected

for a longer period, we recommend that you don't close the connection

```
resManBookConnection.disconnect();
```

Result We have now created a direct link from a Java application to an SAP System. Especially when Web applications are involved, however, we recommend using connection pools, as described in the next section.

Connection Pools If you use generic user names to connect to the SAP server from the Java instance, which is usually the case for Web server applications, it makes sense to use connection pools, as all the connections in a pool contain the same information about the system, users, and client. Connection pools also provide several marked advantages when compared to direct connections:

1. They avoid creating overhead during system logon, because the connections remain open and can be reused immediately after logon.
2. The maximum number of possible (concurrent) logons can be limited to avoid wasting resources on the client and server sides.

   You must configure the maximum number of concurrent logons carefully so users are not faced with unnecessary wait times.

Theoretically, the maximum benefit can be obtained from connection pools by having all the pools use the same user ID. Because authorizations within an SAP System are linked with the user, however, this is recommended only under certain conditions, for example, if no security-relevant areas are involved.

Tutorial: JCo Client, Version with Connection Pool

Objective This tutorial is a variant of the previous tutorial to demonstrate the use of connection pools (as opposed to direct connections).

To implement a connection using connection pools, you will need the following specific classes in addition to the main class, `JCO`:

1. `JCO.Pool`—Represents a connection pool.
2. `JCO.PoolManager`—Manages all the connection pools within a Java Virtual Machine (JVM).

As in the previous example, use `import com.sap.mx.jco.*` to include the classes in the corresponding application.

Process

1. You first have to define a pool name. You can select any name you like. However, note that pools are valid only within a JVM; thus, if different

applications run on the same JVM, you should use a clearly structured naming procedure:

```
static final String POOL_NAME = "ResManPool";
```

2. You now have to check whether a pool already exists under this name, and create it if not. The global `JCO.PoolManager` object, which manages all the pools, can be retrieved using method `getClientPoolManager()` of class `JCO`. It uses the `getPool()` method to try to call a specific pool under this name. If no pool exists (`null` is returned), the pool has to be created in the next step:

```
JCO.Pool pool =
  JCO.getClientPoolManager().getPool("ResManPool");
if (pool == null) {
  OrderedProperties logonProperties =
    OrderedProperties.load ("/logon.properties");
  JCO.addClientPool(
    "ResManPool",       //Name of pool
    15,                 /*max. number of simultaneous
                          connections*/
    logonProperties); //Logon data
}
```

As you can see, the `addClientPool()` method is used to create a new pool. Because you cannot increase the maximum number of defined connections subsequently, be sure to select a value that is sufficient, but not too large. The `addClientPool()` method lets you define the logon information in different ways. In this case, a *properties object* is used, which was created from a file using a *utility class* called `OrderedProperties`. The contents of this example file appear below:

```
jco.client.client = 100
jco.client.user   = user
jco.client.passwd = *****
jco.client.ashost = host.snp.de
jco.client.sysnr  = 00
```

3. You can now request and release a connection. You first have to initialize a `JCO.Client` object, as in the model above; but, instead of using the `create()` method for instantiation, you use method `JCO.getClient("ResManPool")` and specify the pool name.

4. Because the function call is identical to the direct connection case, we can skip the example here. After a successful function call, the connection is returned to the pool with the `releaseClient()` method. Therefore, a session begins with a call of `getClient()` and ends with `releaseClient()`. Never use the `connect()` or `disconnect()` methods (from class `JCO.Client`) within connection pool implementations, as these functions are performed automatically by the pool manager. You should call the `release()` method in a `finally` block to ensure it is executed in any case, regardless of whether an `Exception` was thrown. If you don't, and the connection is not released, the connection pool could run out of free connections.

Result You can now take connections from the pool, execute one or more function calls, and finally return the connections to the pool. If all the connections in the pool are assigned and the pool reaches its maximum size, SAP JCo waits for a certain interval (default value: 30 seconds). If a connection does not become available within this period, an exception message (`JCO.Exception.JCO_ERROR_RESOURCE`) is thrown.

If necessary, you can use the `setMaxWaitTime()` method to change the default value for both the pool manager and the individual `JCO.Pool` objects. You specify the value in milliseconds.

Summary You can now call any ABAP function module flagged as *remote-enabled*, as well as any method in the ABAP Repository, from within a Java method. The procedure itself is relatively simple, as soon as you go to the initial effort of configuring the basic JCo functionality (which itself is not a simple task, however).

ABAP Calls Java In contrast, accessing Java objects from within ABAP applications is somewhat more complicated with the JCo. In general, a Java program, which acts as an independent server, has to be deployed to the host, which ultimately receives the inbound ABAP client calls through socket connections. The program can contain several virtual JCo servers, each of which contains different business functions. Whether you choose to use the façade design pattern—which is described in the next chapter—to model the different business functions as a virtual server depends primarily on the logical hierarchy requirements of the system. Both strategies are generally valid. While the latter tends to save resources, it offers a narrower function range at runtime, because the task of locating the service (virtual server) is shifted to the ABAP client.

Tutorial: Implementing a JCo Server

This tutorial demonstrates how you can implement a simple JCo server and make it available to an ABAP client within a Java program.

Process

1. To implement a JCo server, you first need class `JCO.Server`, which is contained in package `com.sap.mw.jco.*` and which you have to `import` into your program context:

   ```
   import com.sap.mw.jco.*;
   ```

2. The server itself is defined as a public, static class that inherits the `JCO.Server` class and all its methods for defining the life cycle.

   ```
   static public class Server extends JCO.Server {
     ... //Server implementation follows
   }
   ```

3. In the simplest case, you can ignore the obligatory class constructor because delegation is performed by the superclass at runtime. Even so, a possible server signature is listed below as an example:

   ```
   public Server(String gwhost,
                 String gwserv,
                 String program_id,
                 IRepository repos) {
         super(gwhost, gwserv, program_id, repos);
   }
   ```

4. The first callback method in the life cycle of the JCo server is `onCheckTID(String transid)`. It has to be overwritten by the inheriting class, and is used to save the transaction ID of the method specified in `transid` in a permanent data store, or restore the context around the transaction. If this is possible, `true` is returned; an appropriate exception is thrown in all other cases.

   ```
   protected boolean onCheckTID(String transid) {
        //Implement data retrieval here
    return true;
   }
   ```

5. The `onConfirmTID(String transid)` method is called after a local transaction step, to release any resources that may have been allocated during that transaction step. This method also has to be overwritten in the inheritance hierarchy. A transaction step consists of an RFC method call, although a transaction can also consist of several calls:

```
protected void onConfirmTID(String transid) {
  //Release any allocated resources
}
```

6. To conclude a successful transaction involving multiple RFC calls and complete any local cleanup tasks, the JCo server has to implement method onCommit(String transid):

```
protected void onCommit(String transid) {
  //Close transaction locally
}
```

7. The alternative branch, which is performed if the transaction fails, is method onRollback(String transid). In particular, a rollback is required for all transaction participants if errors (such as an Exception) occur during the last callback method:

```
protected void onRollback(String transid) {
  //Cleanup activities required after
  //a failed transaction
}
```

8. The handleRequest(JCO.Function function) method is used to process a request from the ABAP client. The transferred object, with type JCO.Function, contains all the call properties required to trigger the corresponding actions. Because the JCo is primarily an element of the application infrastructure, we don't recommend implementing the business logic directly in this class (except for test purposes). Instead, the appropriate business object—which you can determine by applying method getName() to object function—is instantiated and processed. One typical process in the EJB-driven J2EE world is to take a session bean from the JNDI context, based on the requested function name, and access a corresponding business method of the EJB using a naming convention or an interface.

```
protected void handleRequest(JCO.Function function) {
  String name = function.getName();
  System.out.println("received function: " + name);
  if (name != "") {
    //Process the request, e. g. through
    //delegation to an enterprise session bean
  } else {
    //Otherwise create a short dump in ABAP
```

```
        //by returning an exception
        throw new JCO.AbapException("NOT_SUPPORTED",
          "This function has not been implemented");
      }
    }
```

Section 5.2.1 already described how to retrieve an EJB from a JNDI context.

Runtime Environment

You now have to include this example JCo server in a context. Because this is not a J2EE component that can be used in a container environment—like servlets or EJBs—you have to create a separate runtime environment. You do this using a simple Java program that implements a `main()` method, as described in Section 4.2.11. This class, in its role as runtime environment, serves as a listener for certain events on the JCo server, using the methods defined through the interface implementations. Hence, any errors or exceptions in the runtime environment can be communicated, and the system can respond appropriately (with an entry in the error log, for example).

```
public class RunTimeEnvironment implements
  JCO.ServerExceptionListener, JCO.ServerErrorListener {
  ...
}
```

To implement the `JCO.ServerExceptionListener` interface, you use a method with the following signature and example error message:

```
public void serverExceptionOccurred(JCO.Server srv,
                                    Exception ex) {
  System.out.println("Exception on server " +
                     srv.getProgID() + ":\n" + ex);
  ex.printStackTrace();
}
```

Similarly, the implementation of the `JCO.ServerErrorListener` could look like this, where the default output also points out an error, as well as listing the current stacks:

```
public void serverErrorOccurred(JCO.Server srv,

Error err)  {
  System.out.println("Error on server " +
                     srv.getProgID() + ":\n" + err);
```

```
  err.printStackTrace();
}
```

The most interesting part of the runtime environment is its initialization phase, which is implemented in the constructor. The first step within this implementation phase is to create a client pool with the static method JCO.addClientPool():

```
JCO.addClientPool(
  "POOL_A",           //Any logical name for pool
  3,                  //Max. number of simult. connections
  "100",              //Client number
  "user",             //User name
  "******",           //Password
  "EN",               //Logon language
  "host.snp.de",      //Address of server
  "00"                //System number
);
```

You have to use this client pool in order to request type information for the inbound call parameters in the original SAP System (if necessary). Each host system of an ABAP-based JCo client has a standard function module that helps audit certain aspects of the ABAP Dictionary. The results of the request are saved in a repository for easier retrieval, which is generated and associated with a pool:

```
Irepository repository = JCO.createRepository("SYSTEM_A",
                                              "POOL_A" );
```

In the last required step, you must initialize the JCo server, providing it with an IP address, a DNS, the logical system name, and the repository that you just instantiated:

```
Server server = new Server(
  "172.16.255.227",
  "jcosrv.snp.de",
  "SYSTEM_A",
  repository);
```

The following coding lines are required to register the runtime environment methods from the interfaces for error/exception handling with the server:

```
JCO.addServerExceptionListener(this);
JCO.addServerErrorListener(this);
```

Implementing the `JCO.ServerExceptionListener` and `JCO.ServerErrorListener` on the server ensures that the `serverExceptionOccurred()` and `serverErrorOccurred()` methods are available in the runtime environment.

As described above, the JCo server is initialized and started in the `main` method of the runtime environment. While it is possible to include the start process in the constructor, the resulting implicit merge of these two phases is not helpful, because it limits your ability to reuse the runtime environment in a different context.

```
public static void main(String[] argv) {
  RunTimeEnvironment env = new RunTimeEnvironment();
  try {
    env.server.start();
    System.out.println("Server running...");
  } catch (Exception ex) {
    System.out.println("Error during server
                        startup!");
  }
}
```

Communication Model

On the ABAP side, a JCo server is called like a function module on a remote system, with the `DESTINATION` addition. The specified RFC connection points directly to the JCo server. The RFC call contains the appropriate parameters, which are typed by name, but are neither self-descriptive nor do they necessarily have to be coordinated with the server interface. Therefore, when an inbound function call of the JCo server is received, it has to start an RFC call to the SAP System as a client in order to retrieve the metadata for the parameters contained in the original call and save them in the repository. This communication model can be confusing because, in contrast to conventional middleware, ABAP-to-Java communication is not based on the service provider's needs; instead, it is up to the service provider to convert the types according to the requesting client's schema.

Disadvantages

The resulting additional call on the JCo server side results in an additional network load and a dual dependency, despite the repository, which impairs the efficiency of the procedure in at least the latter communication variant, despite use of the binary protocol. For this reason, an advanced procedure for ABAP clients to use remote Java functions based on Enterprise JavaBeans has been established over time.

6.2.3 EJB Proxy Class

Another way to access Java functions from within an ABAP program is to attain a session bean. This involves an ABAP class that is generated automatically based on the session bean, which provides the same methods as its Java equivalent—as a native ABAP development object—to any consumer from the ABAP environment. The procedure is based on the stub/skeleton architecture, with which you should already be familiar. In contrast to calling a JCo server, the interface that will use the function is sufficiently known at design time, and the calls have to be tailored to this interface.

Communication Model

The call itself takes place using the HTTP protocol, a `GET` method, and a set of parameters transmitted as an XML stream. The call is initially sent to a servlet-based J2EE application that is part of the standard distribution of the SAP Web Application Server. This application analyzes the inbound XML, calls a reference to the requested session bean internally, through a JNDI bind, and executes the called business method with the transmitted set of parameters. The return value (if any) or Java exception is serialized in XML and returned to the stub during the cycle of the synchronous HTTP call, which deserializes the result and makes it available to the consumers again as native data constructs.

***Tutorial:* Creating and Using an EJB Proxy Class**

Objective

In the following, you will perform the cycle of integrating an enterprise Java session bean. In the process, you will generate the appropriate proxy class and execute it within an ABAP program.

Requirements

At this point, we assume that a stateless session bean, as described in Section 6.3, is available on the J2EE server and has already been deployed successfully. This session bean contains the familiar business methods `Z_RM_BOOK`, `Z_RM_CANCEL`, and `Z_RM_GETLIST`. Once again, the first method is the most relevant because you want to book a resource within the ABAP program.

Process

1. Create the Java EJB proxy class.

   To create a Java EJB proxy class, use program `BSPJAVABEAN`, which you can run in Transaction SE38.

   As soon as you run this program, you're prompted to enter the connection data to the J2EE server where the session bean was deployed.

All you have to do is specify the server for the build process. You can make the EJB available on another server at any time afterwards.

After you enter the host name and port of the destination J2EE server, you see a list of the available EJBs on the server. If you haven't done so already, you can select any EJB and generate the corresponding proxy class. You can now select a name for the class, which has the fixed prefix CL_EJB.

2. Use the proxy class.

   To implement a business message call in any ABAP program, you first have to type and instantiate the corresponding object correctly:

```
DATA: lo_bean TYPE REF TO CL_EJB_RESMANBEAN.

CREATE OBJECT lo_bean
  EXPORTING
    HOST   = 'host.snp.de'
    PORT   = '50000'.

IF SY-SUBRC <> 0.
*   Perform error handling
ENDIF.
```

   Next, call the corresponding business method in the object instance, which is available transparently:

```
CALL METHOD lo_bean->Z_RM_BOOK
  EXPORTING
    PAR0 = '4711'       "Resource ID
    PAR1 = '20040602'  "From date
    PAR2 = '1000'       "From time
    PAR3 = '20040602'  "To date
    PAR4 = '1200'       "To time
    PAR5 = ''           "Comments
    PAR6 = '100'.       "Client
```

   To save resources, the call is not executed immediately, but instead written to a queue. Consequently, calls that are theoretically not interdependent can first be lined up in the queue. When you want to execute them, a static method of generic class CL_EJB_QUEUE is available:

```
CALL METHOD cl_ejb_queue=>flush( ).
IF SY-SUBRC <> 0.
```

```
*    Perform error handling
ENDIF.
```

Disadvantages

Despite the relative simplicity of the described procedure and theoretical ease of use of the interfaces, the practical implementation as a whole—while possible—is subject to several traps and pitfalls.

1. First, the report used to generate the ABAP proxy class appears to be "incorrect.". The generated class is subject to fixed naming conventions and can be generated only in the SAP namespace, which is not possible without access keys in the specific case. You can generate the class in a different namespace by overwriting the default value for the SAP namespace.
2. Another problem involves using the generated class: The J2EE server specified during the initialization phase has to be characterized by a fully qualified DNS name. Because this name is not forwarded internally as a whole, but up to only the first ".", the server *HOSTS* file must contain the fully qualified name and the short-form DNS name. The use of "." as a separator also prevents the use of IPs, which means you cannot specify just any J2EE server without going to the corresponding administration effort beforehand. SAP recommends addressing only J2EE servers running on the same hardware, for which a fully qualified name should be available as described above.
3. Another disadvantage of the communication is use of the `GET` method for transmission. In contrast to the `POST` method, the `GET` method is not suitable for sending large data quantities to the server, at least in theory, which means data can be lost if the inbound parameters are too long—when transferring a binary file, for example.
4. The last disadvantage worth mentioning is the inconsistency in transferring Java exceptions. A null value is usually transferred at this point, which means the ABAP client cannot determine the success or failure of the call. Therefore, we recommend catching exceptions on the session bean side and sending them back as a different data type. While this procedure results in additional effort at design time and runtime for everyone involved, it is the only way to ensure that errors will be communicated reliably.

6.2.4 More Interfaces

The SAP Web AS contains numerous other interfaces that SAP has developed over the years, including SAPphone, SAPconnect, Application Link

Enabling (ALE), and the DCOM Connector. Ultimately, however, they are all based on RFC; some are additionally based on the IDoc (intermediate document) message format.

6.2.5 Web Services

Web services represent one of SAP's preferred interface technologies for the coming years. As such, it is important to have a standardized Web service architecture. The SAP Web Application Server (SAP Web AS) permits the development and execution of Web services in the ABAP and Java personalities. On the ABAP side, SOAP Runtime provides the functions for building and consuming Web services. In the Java personality, the procedure for using Web services is defined by the standardized Java Web Services Developer Pack from the Java community, which is expanded by a separate Web service toolkit that's equipped with several additional features.

SAP's preferred method for developing Web services involves using the SAP Exchange Infrastructure (SAP XI), which makes later inclusion in integrated, complex business scenarios much easier. Because SAP has promoted equality between the ABAP and Java programming languages since the introduction of Release 6.10 of the SAP Web AS, the construction and use of Web services are equally relevant in both languages. In the following sections, we will address Web services in detail, using practical examples to examine different scenarios and reveal their advantages and disadvantages.

Note that Chapter 2 is a prerequisite for understanding and working through the following sections.

ABAP Web Services

The Problem

The functional scope of the ResMan demonstration project involves various functions for resource management. In this scenario, you want to implement the booking process for a resource using a Web-based user interface. In the process, you will build on the existing components that ResMan already implements.

Users should be able to book a resource through a Web page, and a booking confirmation should be displayed after a successful booking.

Context

You'll use ABAP function module Z_RM_BOOK to implement the booking function and make this function module available to external applications as a Web service.

You'll implement the user interface as a Java Server Page application that adheres to the MVC model. To execute the posting in the system, the Java application accesses the Web service as a consumer.

Therefore, the recipient side is represented by an ABAP application, and the caller side is represented by the Java application.

Recipient Side

The SAP Web AS features SOAP Runtime, a mechanism that lets you access and call RFC-capable function modules as Web services, using the SOAP protocol via HTTP. The parameters required to call a remote component are serialized as an XML stream within a SOAP message and sent over the respective transport protocol. Once a function module is declared as remote-enabled, it is automatically available as a Web service through the Internet Communication Manager (ICM). Although the *service interface* principle is used, the interface and skeleton are generated automatically within the SAP System as soon as a function module is flagged as being remote-enabled. Under SAP Web AS 6.20, developers had no further influence over this mechanism, which was not an ideal solution unless you were willing to put up with the resulting restrictions. In contrast, SAP Web AS 6.40 gives developers much more freedom to develop Web services, and also provides a development environment within the ABAP Workbench.

As a result of this process, the Web Service Definition Language (WSDL) interface description is generated, which you can view using a BSP application on the SAP Web AS or a Universal Description, Discovery, and Integration (UDDI) interface. The language mentioned previously in Chapter 2 is used to describe Web service interfaces; in addition to the available functions, it also describes the permissible communication methods and their parameters.

The automatic Web service generation process, which takes place internally, can be portrayed as follows. Because the request is sent to the Web service via HTTP, it is initially accepted by the ICM. To assign the request, the ICM requires a local handler—generally the skeleton in this case—for each RFC-capable application. Web service handlers are objects of global class `CL_HTTP_EXT_SOAPHANDLER_RFC`, which represents an extension class of the Internet Communication Framework (ICF).

The skeleton that the SAP System generates internally also includes the `SOAPINCS` collection of directives, which means the SOAP classes are also available. Class `CsoapDocument` lets you wrap a SOAP document for the request/response process. All Extensible Markup Language (XML) aspects are concealed from the user; the class takes care of serializing and deserializing the requests and outbound responses in native data constructs or their SOAP-compliant XML representation. A central XML processor in the kernel of the SAP Web AS oversees this process. The serialized data includes both the SOAP header and SOAP body. It is not possible to interpret SOAP headers during deserialization, however, due to the restrictions of the SOAP Runtime. Another class, the SOAP transport class (`CSoapTransportHttp`), oversees the sending and receiving of SOAP messages via the ICM.

Although these classes are outside the direct influence of developers who create Web services in the current Web AS version, Figure 6.10 illustrates how the recipient side is built, to aid your understanding of the internal process flows.

The result of the automatic interface generation is a WSDL description of the service that is available in the SAP System and is created on demand.

Caller Side

The caller side is generally implemented in two sections:

According to the MVC model, the presentation logic with the corresponding data retrieval logic has to be implemented first. Because the caller side is implemented in Java, we recommend that you use a typical JSP/servlet scenario. The JSP (view) is used to present the user interface, which supplies form fields for entering the data and displaying the result from the booking process. An HTML page is then generated from the JSP automatically on the server side and sent to the user's browser. The controller here is a servlet that acts as an agent between the view component and the model (the business logic), by sending the preprocessed request to the model, receiving the data model from the model, evaluating it, and sending the resulting values to the view—which ultimately displays them.

The ResMan demonstration project already implements a scenario of this type; however, an EJB component is used in this conventional case. In this example, however, you want to use the ABAP Web service model. It will not deal with the creation of the JSP or the servlet in any detail, but will emphasize the advantages of object-oriented programming with a component, as it focuses on the changes that have to be implemented in the servlet in order to change the model used, creating a Web service stub from the EJB.

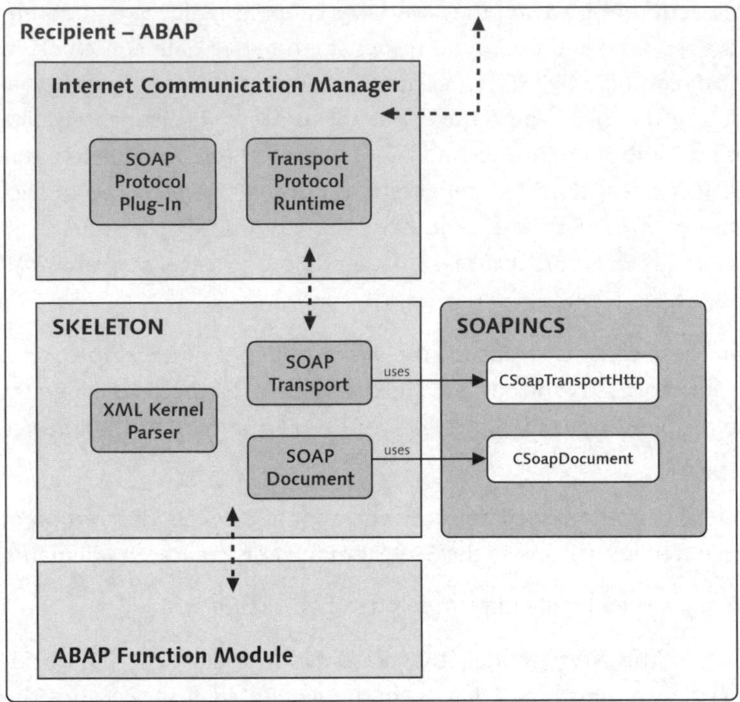

Figure 6.10 ABAP Web Service, Recipient Side

The actual nucleus of the implementation is limited to the creation of proxy classes, which the servlet can use to access the Web service functions. This resulted in the development of the *service gateway* and the *stub*. The Java application—the servlet in this case—provides the stub with the remote methods of the Web service as if they existed locally. The stub must then be made available to the servlet; to do so, the JNDI makes its services available by enabling you to locate the component through a logical, structure-capable identification that is unique throughout the system. To create the proxy classes, the WSDL description of the service in question is required, which can be called from the SAP System on the ABAP side after the service is created.

Cooperation

Now that both parts of the application have been described, we can create a cross-scenario class diagram as illustrated in Figure 6.11.

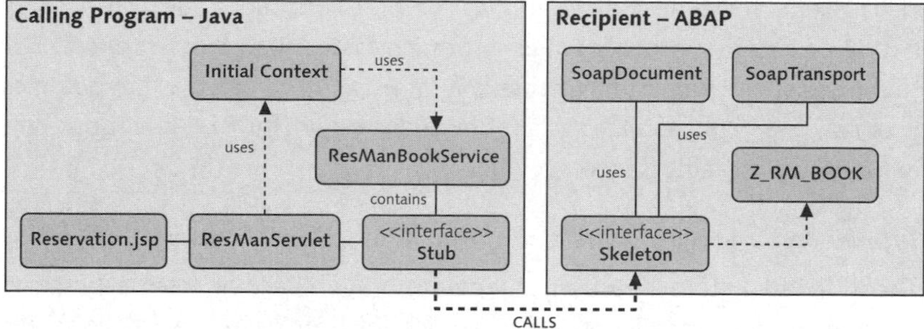

Figure 6.11 ABAP Web Service—Class Cooperation Diagram

With regard to the skeleton on the server side, we should mention that automatic service provision by the SAP System is an extremely complex process that involves the ICM, the RFC infrastructure, and the relevant handler superclasses. Developers cannot determine whether a skeleton class has actually been generated, or whether generic functions in the individual handlers handle inbound processing for the remote queries. For this reason, you should consider the ICM handler to be a skeleton itself, as it masks the functions of other skeletons.

This is not immediately relevant for its practical use, as described above, because the user receives a transparent WSDL description as a result.

Restrictions

This approach to implementing Web service applications is subject to the following restrictions:

If the recipient side (server side) of the scenario involves an ABAP application, SOAP Runtime is responsible for implementing the Web service. SOAP Runtime merely represents an alternative mechanism for synchronous RFCs (Remote Function Calls), and is not a completely generic framework for general SOAP processing. It enables synchronous RFCs, which are otherwise implemented based on the RFC engine in the Web AS Kernel or external RFC library, to be substituted with Web service mechanisms—a typical constellation for cross-platform integration tasks. SOAP Runtime in SAP Web AS now makes it easier to integrate non-SAP Systems, because wrappers are no longer required to create RFCs. In light of increasing support for SOAP and WSDL, external systems will more likely provide Web service interfaces than support for SAP's proprietary RFC interface. In most cases, it takes far less time to integrate systems with Web service technology than it does to implement an RFC interface.

At the same time, however, you should consider whether the reduced effort at design time is not offset by the longer runtime: RFC can be especially useful for time-critical applications (at runtime), because its very nature as a native protocol makes it much faster than Web services. For that reason, the worst imaginable way of using Web service technologies is to consider Web services as a mere replacement for RFC—without taking these other factors into account.

Tutorial: Web Service Generation from a Function Module

Recipient-Side Implementation

The individual steps needed to generate a Web service from a function module are described in detail below. Screenshots from the development environment provide additional information about the respective context.

Process

1. Create and implement the business logic of a function module in the ABAP Workbench.

   You first develop the Web service implementation as a function module, using the Function Builder in the ABAP Workbench (Transaction SE37). To do so, create a function module called `Z_RM_BOOK`, in accordance with the ResMan requirements described in Chapter 3—you enter the input and output parameters and implement the actual business logic.

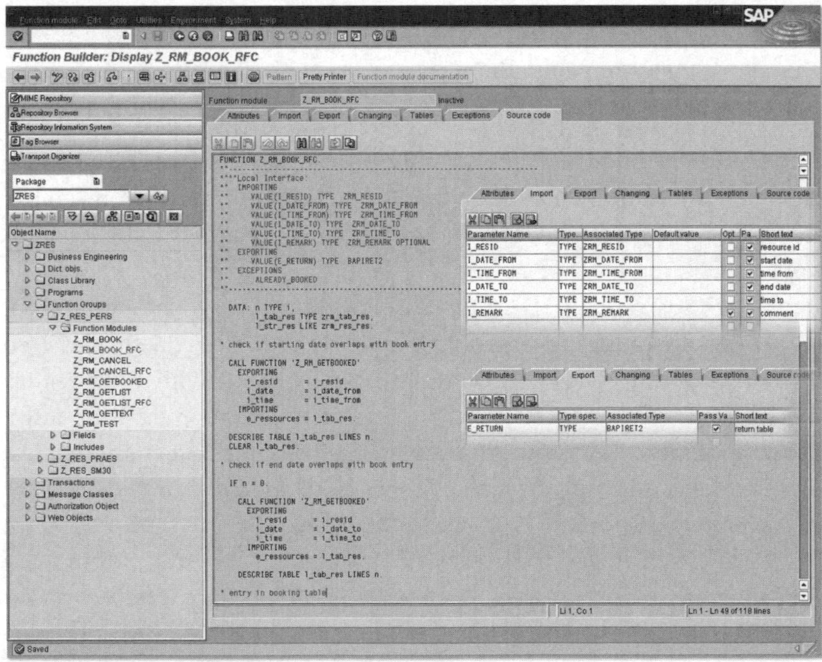

Figure 6.12 Function Module Implementation in the ABAP Workbench

2. Declare the function module as remote-enabled.

   You now declare the function module as remote-enabled, save it, and activate it in the system. From this point on, the function module's WSDL description is available through a BSP application, and you can parameterize it with the name of the function module.

3. Test the function module.

   Test the function module in SE37. Once your application passes the tests, you have finished the implementation on the recipient side.

   An ABAP Web service can be reached using URL *http://<hostName>:<portNumber>/sap/bc/soap/rfc*, where *<hostName>* and *<portNumber>* have to be replaced with the values of the respective instance. In our example, *<hostName>* is "host.snp.de" and the port is "8000". Therefore, the correct URL is: *http://host.snp.de:8000/sap/bc/soap/rfc*.

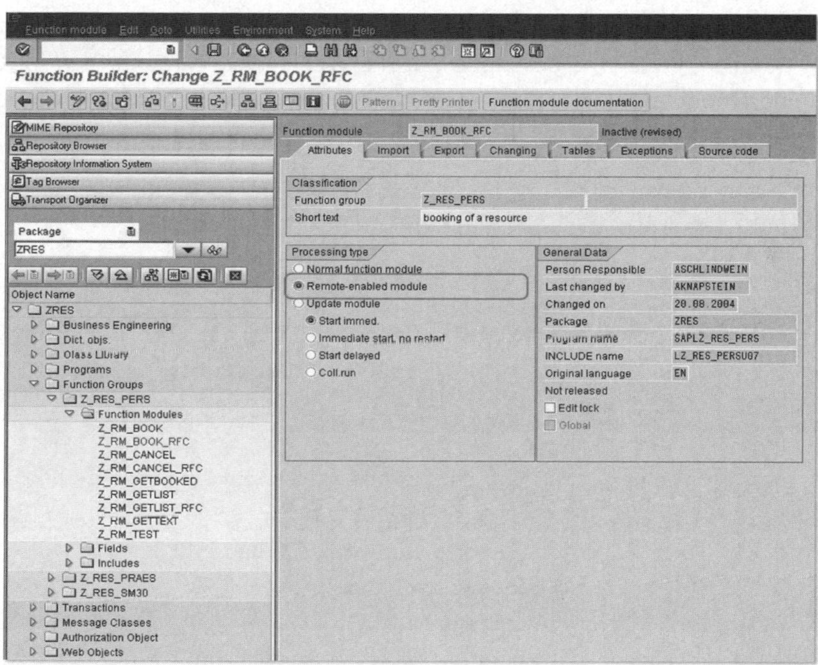

Figure 6.13 Declaring a Function Module as Remote-Enabled

You have now developed a remote-enabled function module whose WSDL interface description is available automatically in the SAP System.

Caller-Side Implementation

To implement the caller side, perform the following steps:

Process

1. Download the WSDL description using the SAP Web Service Browser.

   You can call the descriptions of all available RFC-enabled function modules, and thus all Web services as well, using a BSP application on the SAP Web Application Server.

   This tool—the Web Service Browser—can be reached at the following URL:

   http://<hostName>:<portNumber>/sap/bc/bsp/sap/WebService-Browser/search.html?sap-client=<client>

   Once again, *<hostName>* and *<portNumber>* have to be replaced accordingly; also, the *<client>* placeholder stands for the required client in the SAP System. In this example, the full URL is:

   http://was620.snp.de:8080/sap/bc/bsp/sap/WebServiceBrowser/

   search.html?sap-client=100

   You can display the description of the Web service through the function module of the same name. The following source coding shows an excerpt from the WSDL description of the Web service:

```
<?xml version="1.0" encoding="UTF-8"?>
<definitions xmlns="http://schemas.xmlsoap.org
                            /wsdl/"
[...]
                  targetNamespace="urn:sap-com:document
                                    :sap:rfc:functions">
  <types>
  <xsd:schema
   targetNamespace="urn:sap-com:document:sap:rfc:
                            functions">
       <xsd:element name="Z_RM_BOOK_RFC">
         <xsd:complexType>
           <xsd:all>
             <xsd:element name="I_DATE_FROM"
                                type="s0:date">
[...]
   </xsd:schema>
  </types>
  <message name="Z_RM_BOOK_RFCInput">
    <part name="parameters"
```

```
                element="s0:Z_RM_BOOK_RFC" />
[...]
   <binding name="Z_RM_BOOK_RFCBinding"
                type="s0:Z_RM_BOOK_RFCPortType">
     <soap:binding style="document"
       transport="http://schemas.xmlsoap.org
                  /soap/http"/>
       <operation name="Z_RM_BOOK_RFC">
         <soap:operation soapAction=
             "http://www.sap.com/Z_RM_BOOK_RFC" />
           <input>
             <soap:body use="literal"/>
           </input>
[...]
   <service name="Z_RM_BOOK_RFCService">
     <port name="Z_RM_BOOK_RFCPortType"
              binding="s0:Z_RM_BOOK_RFCBinding">
      <soap:address location=
       "http://host.snp.de:8000/sap/bc/soap/rfc"/>
     </port>
   </service>
 </definitions>
```

Listing 6.8 Excerpt from the WSDL Description of the ABAP Web Service

To use this description to create the client, we recommend saving the XML file on your local computer, as you will need it to create the client in SAP NetWeaver Developer Studio.

2. Create a new project in SAP NetWeaver Developer Studio or import an existing project that consumes the Web service.

   Because ResMan already contains a full implementation of the presentation logic and is available as a project package, you import the individual project packages into the SAP NWDS (see Figure 6.14).

3. Generate the actual Web service client in the form of proxy classes (see Figure 6.15).
4. Save the Web service client (stub) within a JNDI context, to make it available through the JNDI naming service (see Figure 6.16).
5. Make the Web service available within the controller (see Figure 6.17).
6. Deploy the project to the Java server instance of the SAP Web Application Server (see Figure 6.18)

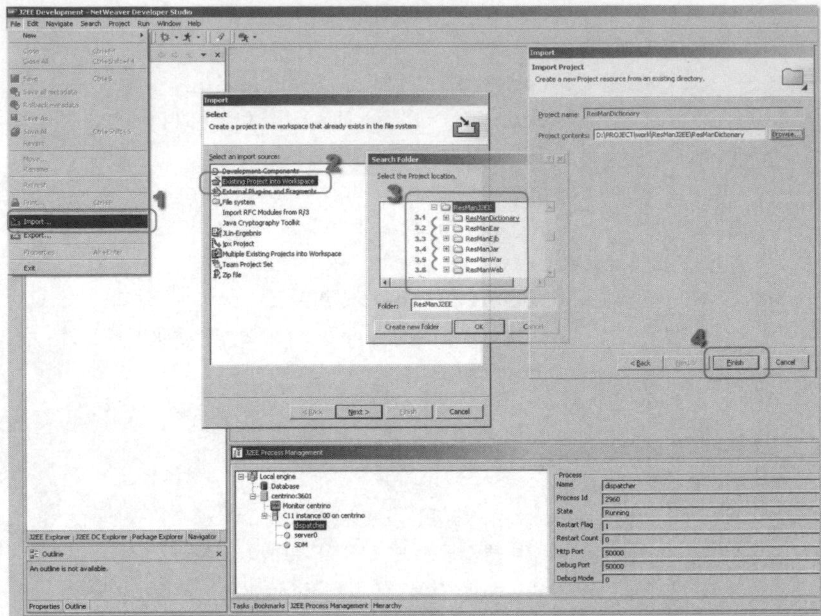

Figure 6.14 Importing Project Packages into the Developer Studio

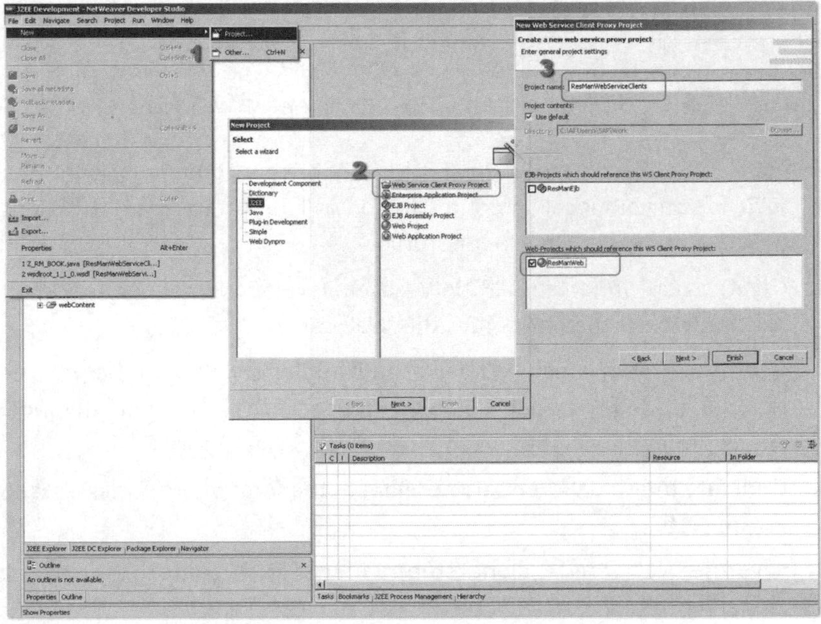

Figure 6.15 Generating Web Service Client Proxy Classes

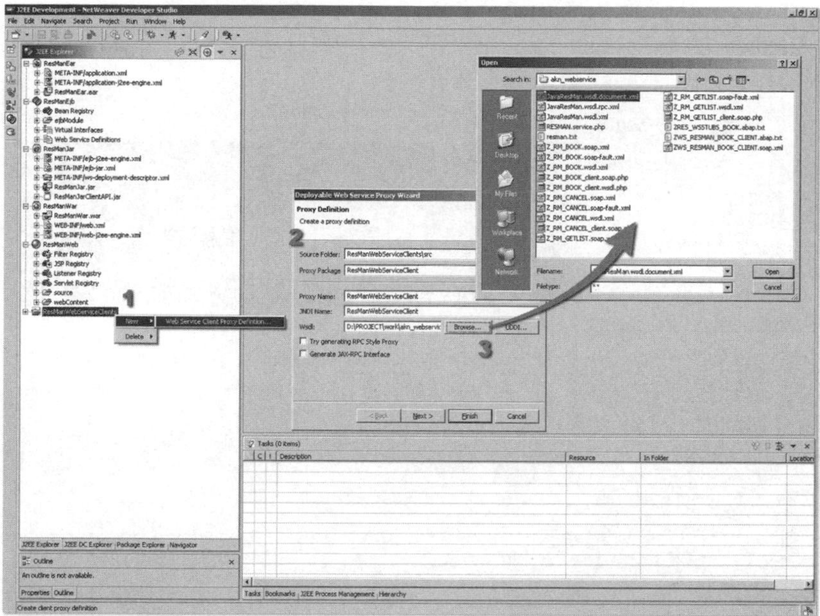

Figure 6.16 Saving a Web Service Client in the JNDI Context

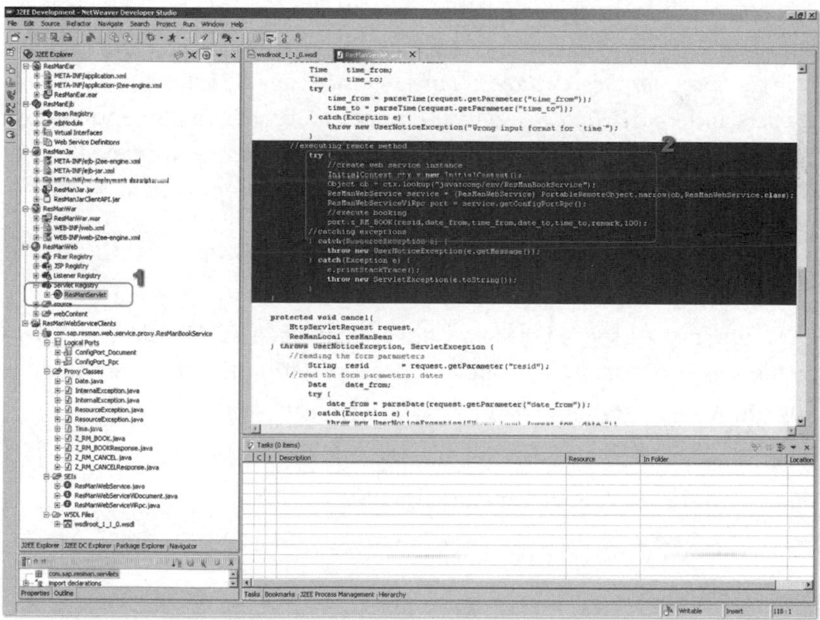

Figure 6.17 Making a Web Service Available within the Controller

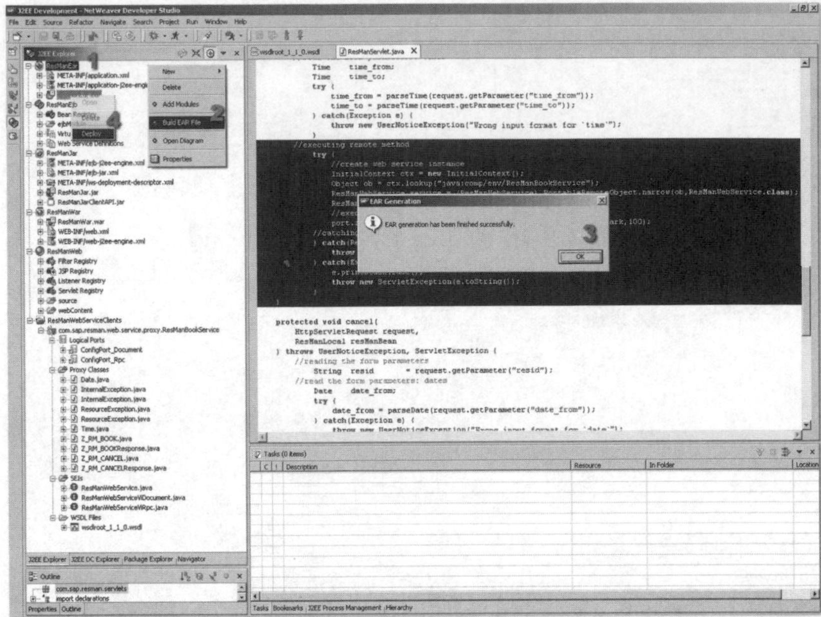

Figure 6.18 Deploying the Project on the Java Instance

Result

After the deployment process, the application is executable and ready for use. The Web page can be reached through the URL *http://<host-Name>:<portNumber>/<projectName>*, once again substituting *<host-Name>* and *<portNumber>* with the appropriate values. JSP applications can usually be reached through port 50000. The *<projectName>* element is replaced by the name you specified during the deployment process—ResMan in this case. So, the full URL is:

http://host.snp.de:50000/ResMan

Now, when the user selects and books a service, a SOAP message is sent to the server to initiate the booking process within the function module. The following SOAP request is sent to the ABAP Web service:

```
<?xml version="1.0" encoding="UTF-8"?>
<SOAP-ENV:Envelope xmlns:SOAP-ENV=
    "http://schemas.xmlsoap.org/soap/envelope/"

    SOAP-ENV:encodingStyle=
      "http://schemas.xmlsoap.org/soap/encoding/"
    xmlns:SOAP-ENC=
      "http://schemas.xmlsoap.org/soap/encoding/"
```

```
        xmlns:xsi=
          "http://www.w3.org/1999/XMLSchema-instance"
        xmlns:xsd=
          "http://www.w3.org/1999/XMLSchema"
        xmlns:saprfc=
          "urn:sap-com:document:sap:rfc:functions">
        <SOAP-ENV:Header>
          <vendor:TransactionID SOAP:mustUnderstand="1">
            ID9234928739829384
          </vendor:TransactionID>
        </SOAP-ENV:Header>
        <SOAP-ENV:Body>
          <saprfc:Z_RM_BOOK_RFC>
            <I_RESID xsi:type="xsd:string">1</I_RESID>
            <I_DATE_FROM xsi:type="xsd:string">
              20040319</I_DATE_FROM>
            <I_TIME_FROM xsi:type="xsd:string">
              103000</I_TIME_FROM>
            <I_DATE_TO xsi:type="xsd:string">
              200400319</I_DATE_TO>
            <I_TIME_TO xsi:type="xsd:string">
              113000</I_TIME_TO>
            <I_REMARK xsi:type="xsd:string">
              Please provide refreshments for
              the meeting. Thanks</I_REMARK>
          </saprfc:Z_RM_BOOK_RFC>
        </SOAP-ENV:Body>
      </SOAP-ENV:Envelope>
```

Listing 6.9 SOAP Request to the ABAP Web Service

The function module receives the request and, if the resource is still available on the requested date, books it. In this case, the following SOAP response is returned to the client:

```
<?xml version="1.0" encoding="UTF-8"?>
  <SOAP-ENV:Envelope xmlns:SOAP-ENV=
    "http://schemas.xmlsoap.org/soap/envelope/">
  <SOAP-ENV:Body>
    <saprfc:Z_RM_BOOK_RFC.Response xmlns:saprfc=
      "urn:sap-com:document:sap:rfc:functions">
      <E_RETURN>
```

```
          <TYPE>I</TYPE>
          <ID>ZRES_MESSAGES</ID>
          <NUMBER>000</NUMBER>
          <MESSAGE>Resource was booked.</MESSAGE>
          <LOG_NO/>
          <LOG_MSG_NO>000000</LOG_MSG_NO>
          <MESSAGE_V1/>
          <MESSAGE_V2/>
          <MESSAGE_V3/>
          <MESSAGE_V4/>
          <PARAMETER/>
          <ROW>0</ROW>
          <FIELD/>
          <SYSTEM>W01CLNT100</SYSTEM>
        </E_RETURN>
      </saprfc:Z_RM_BOOK_RFC.Response>
    </SOAP-ENV:Body>
  </SOAP-ENV:Envelope>
```

Listing 6.10 SOAP Response from the Web Service

If the resource is already occupied, the function module generates a SOAP fault message, as illustrated below:

```
<?xml version="1.0" encoding="UTF-8"?>
<SOAP-ENV:Envelope xmlns:SOAP-ENV=
  "http://schemas.xmlsoap.org/soap/envelope/">
  <SOAP-ENV:Body>
    <SOAP-ENV:Fault>
      <faultcode>SOAP-ENV:Client</faultcode>
      <faultstring>ALREADY_BOOKED</faultstring>
      <detail>
        <rfc:Z_RM_BOOK_RFC.Exception xmlns:rfc=
          "urn:sap-com:document:sap:rfc:functions">
          <Name>ALREADY_BOOKED</Name>
        </rfc:Z_RM_BOOK_RFC.Exception>
      </detail>
    </SOAP-ENV:Fault>
  </SOAP-ENV:Body>
</SOAP-ENV:Envelope>
```

Listing 6.11 Fault Message from the Web Service

The application controller sends the results to the JSP as appropriate for the server response, and the JSP displays it in the browser.

Assessment

Developing the scenario in this context results in an application that is based on a relatively complex architecture, but which is quite fast and easy to implement with the available tools. The result is a small application that uses many of the aforementioned concepts and establishes client/server communication that adheres to the Web service standard.

Positive Aspects: Simplicity

The most positive aspect of this approach is the simplicity of generating a Web service from an application. The SAP System performs all the technical work automatically, making the interface creation process completely transparent. The fact that the detailed inner workings of this mechanism are obscured within the SAP System is more positive than negative, as it eliminates most potential incompatibility problems in future Web AS releases—because developers have no choice but to use the standard SAP implementation process.

Isolation

The implementation of the business logic on the ABAP side is not affected because the skeleton (or ICM handler) is completely detached from the function module.

Flexibility

Applying the MVC pattern makes it easy to integrate the Web service as part of the model, and reduces major changes to the controller logic of the servlet-based J2EE application.

Speed

At design time, the high degree of automation in the ABAP Workbench and SAP NetWeaver Developer Studio environments gives you an advantage regarding the speed at which you can develop your Web service, because developers only have to make manual changes in a few places.

Negative Aspects: Runtime Behavior

The fact that this approach is slower than the native RFC protocol was already mentioned above. Because the data is serialized in a standardized XML format on both the client and server sides, Web service integration will always be slower than connections based on native formats. When choosing between Web service integration and the alternatives, you should always consider the aspects of the network load and delivery time associated with each call.

SOAP Runtime Restrictions

Another shortcoming of the Web service implementation on the SAP Web AS 6.20 is that the SOAP Runtime is not fully compliant with the SOAP 1.1 Specification published by the World Wide Web Consortium (W3C).

The handling of SOAP headers by the Web service is not supported. For that reason, SOAP extensions such as Web Services Security (WS Security) and WS Routing, the SOAP routing client, cannot be provided or used together with SOAP Runtime, which means these functions have to be saved in the body block of the SOAP message. Consequently, the handling for these elements must be implemented manually on both the client and server sides. As such, the handling of infrastructure-related aspects is mixed with the business logic, although it should be clearly separated between handler and function module.

The SOAP actor concept, which permits routing and intermediate processing of SOAP requests across multiple Web services until they reach their final destination, is not supported. Because the recipient side always assumes that it is the sole recipient, you cannot implement any intermediate stops, which are theoretically supported according to the SOAP specification.

SOAP Runtime is also subject to restrictions in the type system: It supports only XSD simple types that can be mapped directly to ABAP data types. As such, the element *normal form* is required, which means XML attributes cannot be used to represent application data, but used instead for only canonical self-mapping. Nor are array types available to map complex, nested structures, and therefore SOAP encoding (which is otherwise optional) is not available.

There is no general transformation mechanism for the XML documents—the structure of the SOAP messages corresponds to the ABAP data types, through the canonical mapping described above. Because RFC does not support references to data or objects, these functions are not available in SOAP either. The *Serialization of ABAP Data in XML* specifications describes how ABAP data types are mapped to XML and vice versa.

Nor can MIME documents be used as attachments. All attachments have to be BASE64 encoded binary data, which is used as function parameters. Although this type of binary data transmission via XML was commonplace prior to the *SOAP with Attachments* specifications, it was never standardized.

Only HTTP and HTTPS are supported as transport protocols, not SMTP or FTP (SOAP transport binding).

Because SOAP headers are not interpreted, caller authentication is feasible only via the ICF mechanisms, while authorization can be enforced only via the RFC mechanisms.

As mentioned previously, SOAP Runtime supports synchronous communication, not asynchronous messaging.

SAP Web AS 6.40

The restrictions and examples described are based on the SOAP Runtime implementation in the ABAP personality on the SAP Web AS 6.20. In addition to the benefits that a J2EE implementation of Web services and Web service clients confers under SAP Web AS 6.40, we should note that the ABAP personality features improved Web service handling in SAP Web AS 6.40, as you will see in the next chapter. Completely new development tools are available in the ABAP Workbench. In addition, several inconsistencies from 6.20 have been corrected.

Java Web Services

The Problem

Our sample application for a Java Web service has the same functional scope as the previous example, but in a different context. Once again, you want to implement the booking process for a resource using a Web-based user interface.

Context

In this scenario, you will implement the booking function using the `Z_RM_BOOK` method of Enterprise JavaBean `ResManBean`. You will implement this EJB completely in Section 6.3.2 and make it available as a Web service.

You will implement the user interface as a BSP (Business Server Page). To book a resource, the BSP application acts as a consumer to access the Web service on the Java side.

Accordingly, the recipient side is implemented as a Java application, while the ABAP (BSP) application represents the caller side in this case.

Recipient Side

The business logic within the Java application is contained in an Enterprise JavaBean that is already available to the ResMan demonstration project, as mentioned above. You now have to create a skeleton for the EJB on the recipient side that the Web service client can use to access the business logic methods.

Because the recipient side now involves a Java application, you use the SAP NetWeaver Developer Studio to develop the skeleton.

In this example, the skeleton is an instance of bean class ResManBean, which implements the actual business logic—with methods `Z_RM_BOOK()`, `Z_RM_CANCEL()`, and `Z_RM_GETLIST()`. It is located inside the EJB container, which, as you are already aware, represents the runtime environment for Enterprise JavaBeans. The EJB container provides four explicit interfaces for each Enterprise JavaBean:

1. Remote interface (*ResMan.java*)
2. Remote home interface (*ResManHome.java*)
3. Local interface (*ResManLocal.java*)
4. Local home interface (*ResManLocalHome.java*)

Figure 6.19 shows the corresponding EJB class diagram.

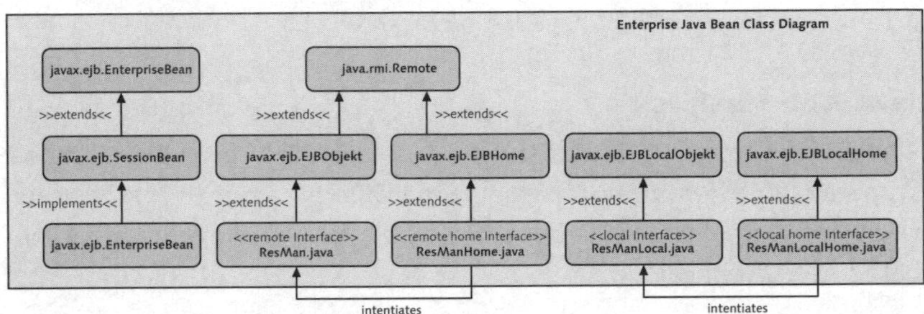

Figure 6.19 Enterprise JavaBean Class Diagram

The two home interfaces merely implement the `create` methods for the respective interface (remote home calls `remoteInterface.create()` and local home calls `localInterface.create()`). If a client calls the create method of one of the home interfaces, for example, that method generates an instance of the EJB object that references a suitably-typed bean instance. As soon as the `create()` method is executed, the respective home object sends a reference to the EJB object that was just created back to the client. This reference is called the *stub*, which the client can use by calling business methods from it.

This model differentiates between local clients and remote clients: Local clients are located on the same server (or the same J2EE server instance), while remote clients are at least on different server instances and probably on remote servers.

This differentiation between local and remote clients is particularly relevant for the model in this scenario, because the client that accesses the Web service is running on a different server instance. It runs in the ABAP runtime environment, while the provider is processed on a J2EE instance in this example.

Because the client request is sent to the Web service via HTTP, a skeleton for the Web service has to be available within the Web container of the

J2EE application, as all HTTP requests are delivered to this container automatically. The Web container in this case is comparable to the ICM from the previous example, as it also has to provide a type of handler to accept and process the request. This handler is now implemented as a servlet that accepts the request and is processed by the business logic of the Enterprise JavaBean. These functions are included in the scope of the platform, as it is not up to the application developer to implement infrastructure-related aspects of the platforms here. At this point, the servlet acts as the skeleton for the ABAP-based Web service client. At the same time, it uses an EJB stub—generated through its local home interface, as it is available on the same server—to gain access to the business methods.

Fortunately, the SAP NetWeaver Developer Studio performs the vast majority of these tasks automatically; nonetheless, you should be aware of the interrelationships involved, as manual changes to some of these components are sometimes necessary.

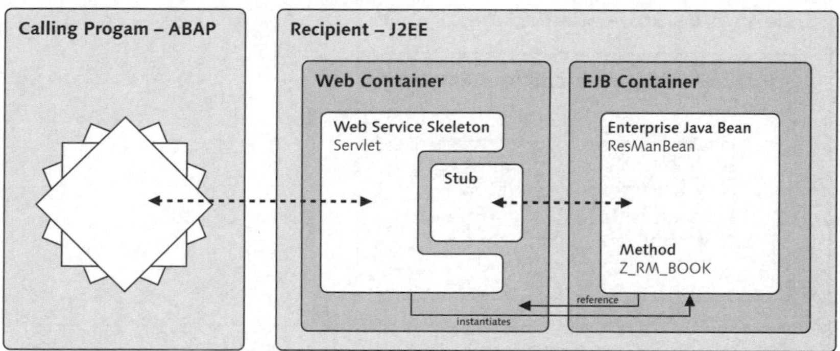

Figure 6.20 Server-Side Components

Caller Side

On the caller side, you first have to implement a BSP application to serve as user interface. The view portion of this BSP page is equivalent to the JSP page in the previous example. The view provides form fields for entering the data, as well as functions for presenting the results of the booking to the user.

The model is the business logic on the Java server, which is accessible via a Web service interface.

The controller acts as intermediary between these two components. Based on the user's inputs, it calls the remote method of the Web service, interprets the Web service response, and sends the results to the view component. Therefore, the controller provides the functions of a broker or service gateway.

ResMan also provides the necessary view logic here; the focus lies on developing the controller in this case.

Because an ABAP application is involved in this case, you use the ABAP Workbench to implement it. Contrary to the previous example, the SAP Web AS 6.20 unfortunately does not have any automatic mechanisms for generating the Web service consumer—the controller—automatically based on a WSDL description. You have to develop it manually. To do so, you implement a function module—the stub—which encapsulates the intrinsic model for the controller logic by routing the controller's calls to itself.

Finally, you have to make the generated controller available to the BSP page. BSP applications are also developed in the ABAP Workbench, using an integrated subprogram in this case. Figure 6.21 shows the components on the caller side.

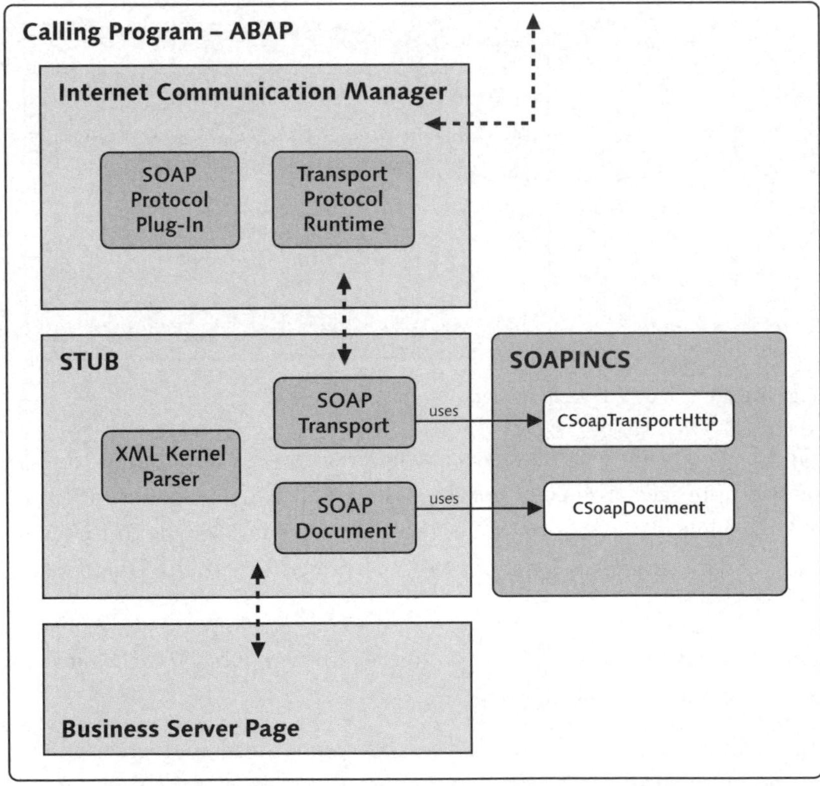

Figure 6.21 Java Web Service Components on the Caller Side

Cooperation

Calls of Web services from within an ABAP application are forwarded by the ICM, as in the above example. To do so, the ICF provides the include program `SOAPINCL`, which endows the application on the client side with the familiar classes `CSoapDocument` and `CSoapTransportHttp` for wrapping and sending a SOAP document respectively.

Restrictions

The restrictions of the SOAP Runtime apply to both the caller and recipient sides, which means only synchronous calls are allowed.

Tutorial: Web Service Generation from a Java Application

Recipient-Side Implementation

The individual steps required to generate a Web service from a Java module are described in detail below. Screenshots from the NetWeaver development environment offer additional information about the respective context.

Process

1. Import the ResMan project into the SAP NetWeaver Developer Studio.

   The J2EE ResMan project consists of several folders, which are contained in a higher-level main folder. The individual folders must be imported in succession, as illustrated in Figure 6.22. The import sequence is irrelevant. Consequently, you may have to adjust some of the paths, especially if the project was originally developed on a different computer that uses other path specifications. The task window provides information about any errors that require correction.

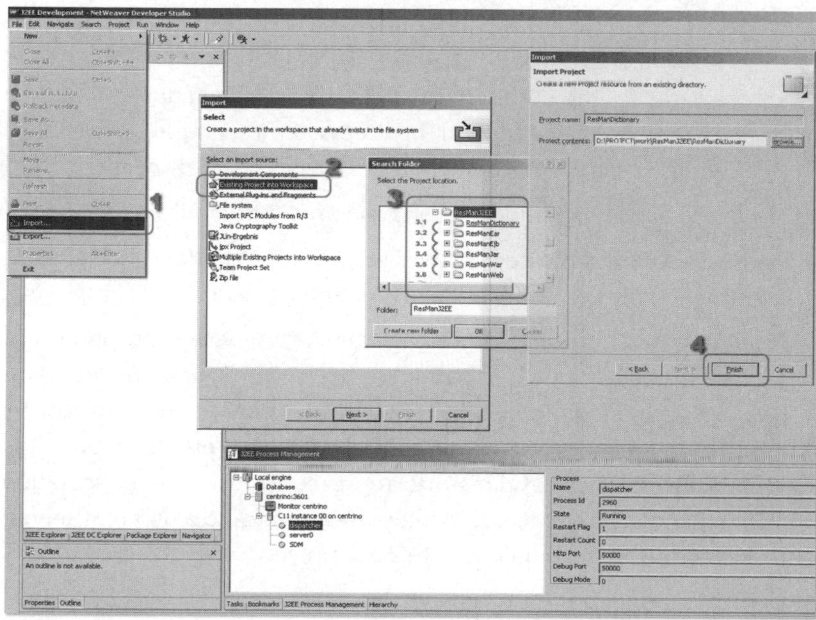

Figure 6.22 Importing the Project

2. Create a Web service for the Enterprise JavaBean `ResManBean`.

   Once you have corrected all the errors, you can create the Web service. To do so, select the `ResManBean` contained in the *ResManJar* file and right-click it to open the dialog (see Figure 6.23).

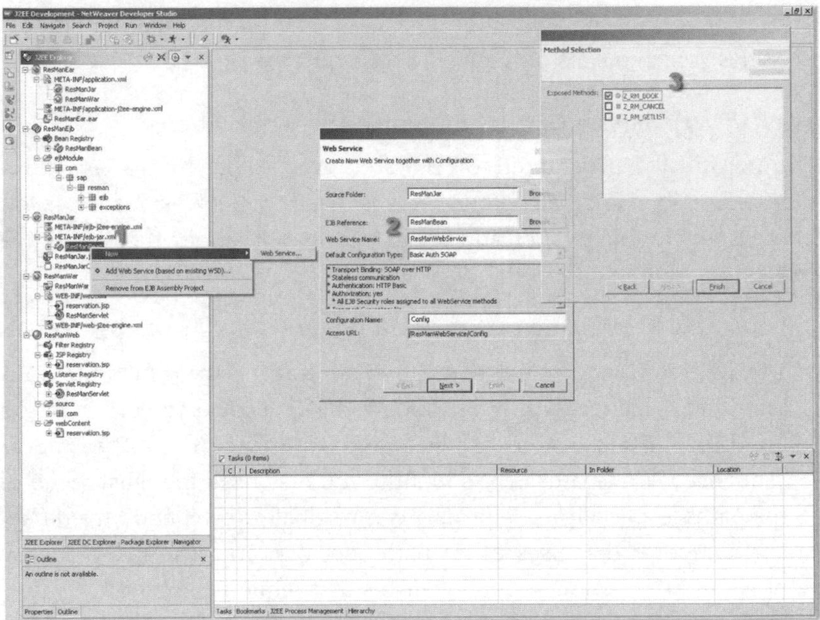

Figure 6.23 Creating a Web Service

   Enter a name for the Web service in the window that appears and then select the methods that that can be accessed through the service interface. In this specific case, only method `Z_RM_BOOK()` is needed.

3. The Web service definition is now generated automatically.

   Figure 6.24 shows the new folder *Web Service Definitions*, which contains the description **ResManBeanWebServiceWsd**.

   The *Config* node is used to configure the Web service description. You can see the relative path to the Web service configuration, */ResManBeanWebService/Config* in this case. In turn, this server path can be used to download a WSDL description, for example, to publish the Web service in a UDDI directory. You can also use the configuration URL to generate a *JAR* file, to deploy the interface to a different server; however, this is not required in this example.

4. Generate (rebuild) the EJB archive.

When you now rebuild the Enterprise JavaBean, the latest versions of all required classes, proxies, and Java descriptors are packed automatically, so the entire project can be deployed to a server.

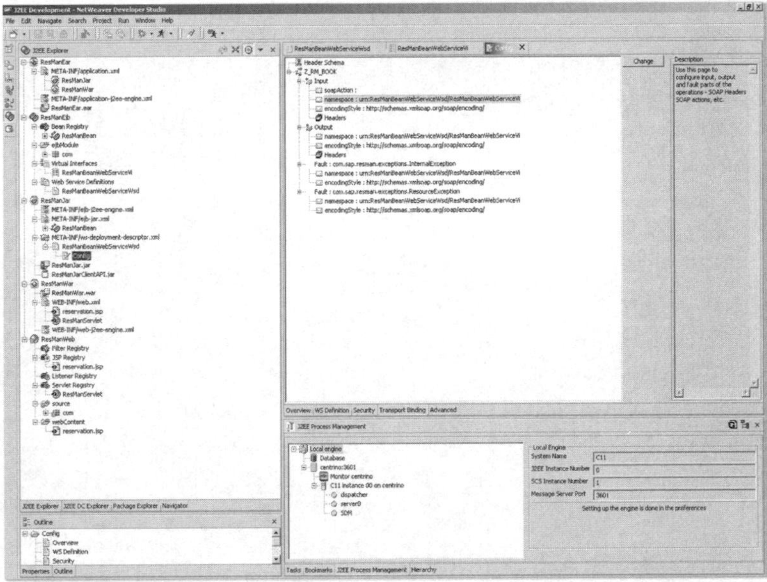

Figure 6.24 Configuration of a Web Service Interface

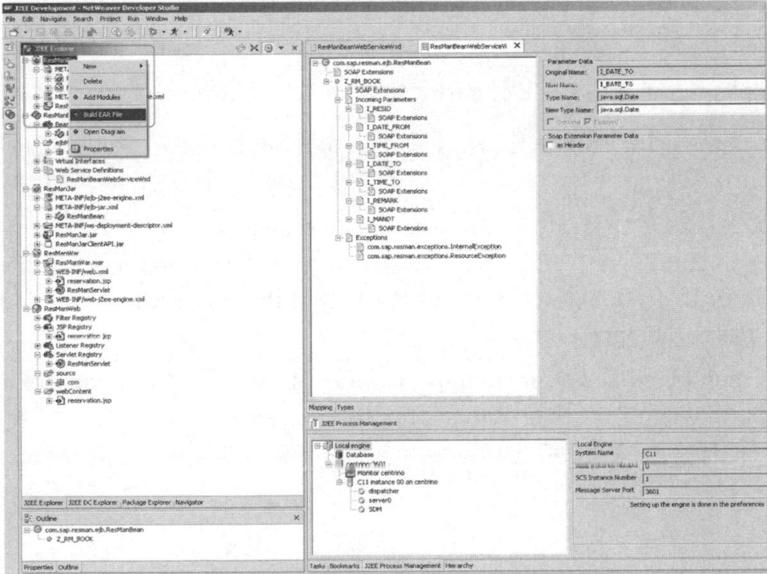

Figure 6.25 Generating the EJB Archive

5. Deploy the EJB archive to the server

   Figure 6.26 shows the deployment process, in which the Developer Studio exports the project to the currently connected server. The receiving side is now executable.

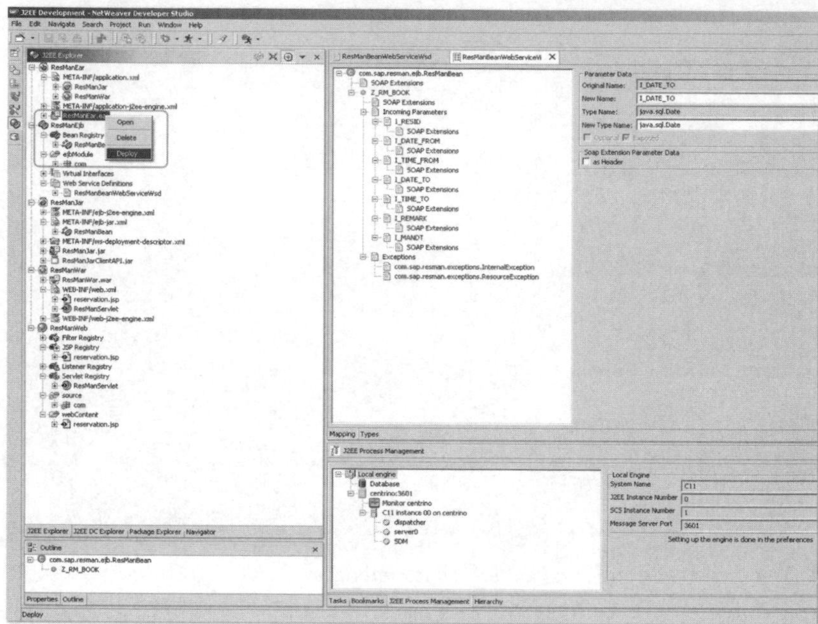

Figure 6.26 Deployment Process

Caller-Side Implementation

To implement the caller side, perform the following steps:

1. Implement the stub as an ABAP function module in the ABAP Workbench.

   You first have to create a new function module within the ABAP Workbench, ZRES_WSSTUBS_BOOK, which accesses the Web service in the role of the model, as the controller within the BSP application, and retrieves the necessary data.

   As mentioned above, include program `SOAPINCL` has to be imported first (in line 001 of the ABAP source coding below).

```
001>  INCLUDE SOAPINCL.
002>
003>  FUNCTION ZRES_WSSTUBS_BOOK.
004>  *"----------------------------------------
005>  *"*"Local interface:
```

```
006> *" IMPORTING
007> *"    VALUE(I_RESID)     TYPE  I
008> *"    VALUE(I_DATE_FROM) TYPE  DATS
009> *"    VALUE(I_TIME_FROM) TYPE  TIMS
010> *"    VALUE(I_DATE_TO)   TYPE  DATS
011> *"    VALUE(I_TIME_TO)   TYPE  TIMS
012> *"    VALUE(I_REMARK)    TYPE  STRING
013> *" EXPORTING
014> *"    VALUE(E_SUCCESS)   TYPE  C
015> *" EXCEPTIONS
016> *"     EX_SOAP
017> *"     EX_SOAPFAULT
018> *"     EX_CANNOTCONNECT
019> *"-----------------------------------------------
020> DATA: soapurl TYPE string VALUE
              'http://host.snp.de/RESMAN'.
021> DATA: soapmet    TYPE string  VALUE ''.
022> DATA: methodname TYPE string  VALUE 'book'.
[...]
```

SOAP Runtime, which is similar to the RFC concept, implements the request using an instance of class `CSoapDocument` and an instance of class `CSoapTransportHttp`. To do so, you have to generate an instance of the document class first (see lines 031 and 056). This instance is then provided with values by first specifying the SOAP method to call (see lines 059 to 063) and then setting the parameters for the SOAP call (see lines 067 ff.). The `direction` parameter specifies the direction of the SOAP parameters; the count constants themselves express the direction with an `_in` or `_out` suffix.

```
[...]
030> *"--- DEFINE LOCAL VARIABLES -------------------
031> DATA: osoap   TYPE REF TO CSoapDocument.
032> DATA: isoap   TYPE REF TO ISoapSerialize.
033> DATA: otransp TYPE REF TO CSoapTransportHttp.
034> DATA: ofault  TYPE REF TO CSoapFault.
035> DATA: soapact TYPE string.
036>
037> DATA: trnEx TYPE REF TO CSoapExceptionTransport.
038> DATA: fltEx TYPE REF TO CSoapExceptionFault.
039> DATA: fmtEx TYPE REF TO
```

```
                         CSoapExceptionDocumentFormat.
DATA: usgEx TYPE REF TO CSoapExceptionUsage.
DATA: resEx TYPE REF TO CSoapExceptionResource.
DATA: intEx TYPE REF TO CSoapExceptionInternal.

DATA: httpFault TYPE REF TO CSoapHttpFault.
DATA: httpCode  TYPE i.
DATA: httpInfo  TYPE string.
DATA: httpBody  TYPE string.
DATA: httpRc    TYPE sysubrc.
DATA: httpMsg   TYPE string.

DATA: mixed TYPE C VALUE 'X'.
DATA: dref  TYPE REF TO data.

*"--- BUILD SOAP MESSAGE -----------------------
  TRY.
    CREATE OBJECT osoap.

*"--- SET THE METHOD NAME ------------------
    CALL METHOD osoap->set_method
      EXPORTING
       nsprefix = 'saprfc'
       nsvalue  =
       CSoapConstants=>sc_rfc_soap_function_ns_uc
       name     = 'book'.
[...]
    GET REFERENCE OF I_RESID INTO dref.
    CALL METHOD osoap->add_parameter
      EXPORTING
        direction = CSoapConstants=>ic_param_in
        name      = 'I_RESID'
        value     = dref.
[...]
*"--- SET THE OUTPUT PARAMETERS ------------
    GET REFERENCE OF E_SUCCESS INTO dref.
    CALL METHOD osoap->add_parameter
      EXPORTING
        direction = CSoapConstants=>ic_param_out
```

```
114>          name        = 'result'
115>          value       = dref.
```

A reference is created to generate the transport class instance (see lines 033 and 034).

After the document class is filled, a call of a factory method generates an instance of the transport class (see line 131 ff.).

```
[...]
129>  * --- create transport and set payload ----------
130>  TRY.
131>    CALL METHOD CSoapTransport=>new_http_transport
132>      IMPORTING
133>        transport = otransp.
134>    CATCH CSoapExceptionResource INTO resEx.
135>      RAISE EX_Soap.
136>    ENDTRY.
[...]
```

The transport object is then supplied with information about the target system (see line 140 ff.). Finally, the finished document class is passed on to the transport instance (see lines 155–157) and the call is initiated (see line 164).

```
[...]
138>  *"--- PREPARE CONNECTION DATA -------------------
139>    TRY.
140>      CALL METHOD otransp->set_destination_by_url
142>        EXPORTING
143>          url = soapurl.
144>
145>      IF soapmet CS 'http://'.
146>        soapact = soapmet.
147>      ELSE.
148>        CONCATENATE soapurl soapmet INTO soapact
          SEPARATED BY '#'.
149>      ENDIF.
150>
151>      CALL METHOD otransp->set_soapaction
152>        EXPORTING
153>          soapaction = soapact.
154>
```

```
        CALL METHOD otransp->set_payload
          EXPORTING
            payload = isoap.
      CATCH CSoapExceptionUsage INTO usgEx.
        RAISE EX_CANNOTCONNECT.
      ENDTRY.

*" --- EXECUTE CALL ----------------------------
      TRY.
        CALL METHOD otransp->request_response.
[...]
```

2. After you activate the module, you can use it.

   The function module is completely implemented and ready for use after activation.

3. The module has to be made available in the BSP page.

   To implement the MVC concept, a BSP page uses event handler callback methods, which are not addressed in any detail here. At this point, you should know that the call of the Web service client, `ZRES_WSSTUBS_BOOK`, takes place within event handler `OnInputProcessing`, which is executed automatically when the user enters data in the Web page and initiates the booking process. The Web service client now has to be called within the event handler, as shown in Figure 6.27.

4. After you save and activate the BSP page, you can access it from within the browser.

   To do so, you must save the BSP application and activate it in the SAP System.

Result The Web page can now be reached from within the browser and you can execute the booking process in line with the requirements. The URL in this case is *http://<hostName>:<portNumber>/<bspProjectName>?sap-client=<sap-client>*, with the corresponding values substituted. The port is "8000" in this example. Accordingly, the full URL is:

http://host.snp.intern:8000/ResMan?sap-client=100

When the user selects and books a resource, a SOAP message is sent to the Java server in the previous example to execute the booking process. Similarly, another SOAP message is used to send the response back to the ABAP client.

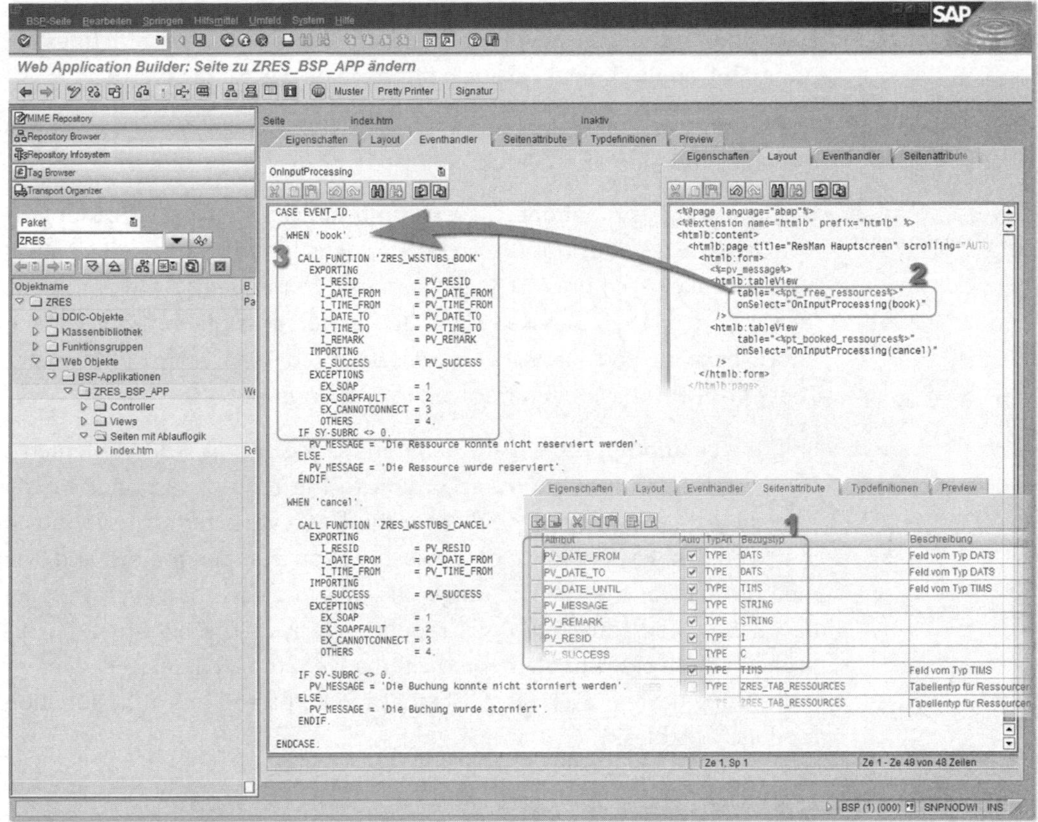

Figure 6.27 Web Application Builder—Creating the BSP Application

Because these messages are not much different from the preceding example, we have omitted the corresponding screenshots here. The functions haven't changed; the sender and recipient have merely swapped roles with regard to the surrounding personality.

Developing this scenario in the given context will result in a robust application with the following features:

Positive Aspects: Simplicity

It is quite simple to create a Web service, despite the component structure on the recipient side, which seems complicated initially and results from the EJBs model. The Developer Studio relieves the application developer of all implementation work. In fact, it was not even necessary to configure the individual components in this scenario. As a result, it seems like implementing a Java application is a simple task, although it is not. Normally, developers have to use various tools to generate the Java coding required for the EJB environments and create the descriptors for deployment to a runtime environment. Contrary to this, SAP NetWeaver Developer Studio is a powerful tool that integrates all the functions for using J2EE applications in a single interface on the SAP Web AS.

Negative Aspects: SOAP Restrictions

The restrictions of the above example also apply to the ABAP part of this example, and are not repeated here.

ABAP Development

Unfortunately, as mentioned several times previously, SAP Web Application Server 6.20 does not feature any options for generating ABAP stubs automatically based on WSDL descriptions. Consequently, the automatic localization of Web services via UDDI is not possible without further effort, because you have to create each Web service client manually. These problems have been resolved in SAP Web AS 6.40.

Still, the creation process is the same in both cases, as ABP implements Web service communication according to the request/response model anyway. As a result, you could theoretically create a template in which you would have to adjust only the input/output parameters and the method calls for the specific usage. In larger projects, however, this can be a labor- and time-intensive, repetitive task that is extremely error-prone. A more easily implemented alternative is to fill parameters dynamically, using flexible parameter lists that can be passed on to the function modules as tables.

6.3 Business Logic

The business logic is the "meaty" part of the application. Ideally, the resources for data retrieval will be abstracted in such a way as to make them completely interchangeable, so that they can come from any third-party vendor; the presentation layers—whether print output, Web, or mobile applications—are too volatile and their requirements are too variable to allow reliance on a tightly-coupled solution.

In contrast, the business logic models processes and data processing in accordance with the service principle defined in SOA applications, and therefore represents the actual application. We don't purport to claim that the business logic isn't subject to changing requirements; however, they have more profound consequences and a greater and direct impact on the (usually critical) enterprise process.

In the following sections, you'll learn about the options and architectural constructs provided by the two platforms that you use to implement the business logic.

6.3.1 ABAP

There are two different types of programs in ABAP. One type is the *executable programs*, which are addressed directly using a transaction code and can start a user dialog or output a report. The other type is the *non-executable programs*, and consists of function modules, classes, and interfaces that cannot be executed directly, but instead serve modularization purposes. At this point, we assume that you, as an experienced ABAP developer, are adequately familiar with the modularization methods used in the ABAP Workbench and know how to implement and use reports, classes, and function modules. Therefore, we will only briefly describe the concepts and objects that play a special role in the ABAP personality.

BAPIs

A BAPI (*Business Application Programming Interface*) is a uniform, standardized interface. BAPIs play a major role in the exchange of business data between different SAP applications, as well as between the various SAP R/3 and non-SAP Systems. The properties of BAPIs make them well-suited for developing integration scenarios.

BAPIs are used in the following different applications:

- **Internet Application Components**
  Individual business functions in the R/3 System are modeled in the Internet/intranet.
- **Component structure**
  Communication between different business applications.
- **External access**
  External clients access the business data and processes directly.

Thus, BAPIs have the following properties: First, they have stable interfaces—that is, the interfaces are frozen and can be called both internally and externally. Secondly, BAPIs do not have a presentation layer; the calling entity has to implement it itself. BAPIs that change data in the database should be called only synchronously and only in an update task. The `COMMIT WORK` call should be implemented only in the calling entity. Technically, a BAPI is a remote-enabled function module (RFM), as described previously in our discussion of ABAP-based Web services under SAP Web AS 6.20.

When a BAPI is used within an R/3 System, the corresponding function module can be called directly. Information about any errors that occur is sent to the calling program as an interface parameter. The function modules for BAPIs don't contain any exceptions or user dialogs; they're intended solely to encapsulate business logic. Each BAPI has an interface parameter called `RETURN`, which contains information about any errors that occur. This exporting parameter always has an ABAP Dictionary type (depending on the release: `BAPIRETURN`, `BAPIRET2`, and so on), Therefore, this structure must be analyzed in the program in order to evaluate potential errors.

BAPIs also permit access to the methods in the BOR (Business Object Repository). The BAPI Explorer provides you with information about the business objects and their corresponding BAPIs. To start the BAPI Explorer, choose menu path **Tools · Business Framework · BAPI Explorer** or enter Transaction code BAPI.

Business Objects

Business objects represent the interface between a workflow and an application, and enable you to access data and business functions. Business objects offer the following benefits:

- **Reusability**
  Because an abstract business object is the foundation for the object types, it can be used in different applications.
- **Encapsulation**
  The full functionality is implemented in one place.
- **Inheritance**
  Object types can be inherited; inherited object types contain all the methods and object types of the original object, along with additional functions.
- **Polymorphism**
  The same functions can be combined from different, specialized objects.

The business object refers to an object type, which contains the implementation of the access to the data and functions. An object type consists of the following components:

- **Key**
  The key uniquely identifies each object instance.
- **Attributes**
  Access to the data for the business model. Data from the database is read and calculated as well.

- **Methods**
  Serve as functions of the business model. We generally differentiate between background methods and dialog methods.
- **Events**
  Can affect the process flow of the application or workflow.

You define business objects in the Business Object Builder, which you call with menu path **Tools · Business Workflow · Definition Tools · Development · Business Object Builder** or directly with Transaction code SWO1. Use the Business Object Builder to test, display, create, change, and delegate an object type.

6.3.2 Java

Overview

Following the detailed examination of the entity beans in the persistence layer in previous sections, you will now learn about session beans and message-driven beans in the business logic layer. This chapter explains the development options that are available for implementing the business logic of enterprise applications on the Java side in the SAP Web Application Server.

Enterprise JavaBeans are a central component of every J2EE applications, as they encapsulate the complete application logic and deploy it to clients and servlets in standardized forms. The SAP Web AS implements the EJBs architecture so it is fully compliant with the J2EE specification.

Effectively, session beans model the business processes in the real world. They can be linked together to form transactions within the container architecture. Note, however, that functions and message exchange are always synchronous, so that a program waits for the return parameters from method calls before continuing its flow. This aspect can hinder the scalability of systems, however, because beans can also be made available as remote system modules.

Ultimately, this was the reason for introducing message-driven beans, which enable asynchronous communication with the environment in EJB specification 2.0 and later.

Session Beans

Tasks

Session beans describe the interaction between beans. They primarily model business processes, and therefore provide business logic. They are not persistent, however, so they don't represent data in the database—in contrast to entity beans. Of course, you could also use session beans directly for data retrieval—using integrated JDBC requests, for example—but this contradicts the logic of the layer model and its implicit way of distinguishing separate concerns. Therefore, you should use session beans with entity beans; the session bean delegates data retrieval to an entity bean in this model.

There are two basic types of session beans: stateless and stateful.

Stateless Session Beans

Stateless session beans usually represent a collection of services, which are represented by the existing methods. Therefore, a procedure is executed. When this procedure has finished, any subsequent access will not have any "memory" of the manipulated data—and therefore, no state is managed. Consequently, the bean is not represented by any data in the client. The client sends a request to the bean, which returns a result, but without any information as to which other requests have been placed previously.

This makes status beans simple and efficient. They present a smaller load on the J2EE server and can be used when the program logic does not require any stateful information. Because they are available for each request, they are not persistent, and not assigned to any particular session client. As a result, the processing logic provided is non-specific and reusable.

Because no persistent data is saved, all necessary information generally has to be passed on as parameters. While this does not prevent the existence of local data or access to resources, this information is not visible to the client and—at least theoretically—is highly restricted by the EJB specification, which forbids the use of IO, JDBC, and threads. Nonetheless, because the specification is only a guideline, some implementations actually do use these technologies.

The descriptor defines an available pool of stateless session beans, which are initialized and then assigned to the clients on request. Therefore, when a client sends a new request, it uses a different bean instance.

Life Cycle of a Stateless Session Bean

The life cycle of a stateless session bean is nothing spectacular. There are only two possible states: *nonexistent* and *method ready*. The client can call the business methods in the second state.

Stateful Session Beans

In contrast to stateless session beans, a *stateful session bean* also contains the user session, which means the bean state—which consists of the saved data—is managed. During each method call, the data for the current user session can be manipulated and saved in the *conversation state*, making it possible to influence subsequent method calls as well.

Stateful session beans are usually scenario-specific. They are used only by a single client. Accordingly, stateful session beans—in contrast to their stateless brethren—are assigned to one client during their entire life cycle. When the user session has ended or a timeout occurs, the bean instance is destroyed.

Statefulness is a significant advantage of session beans and enables status information to be saved from a user session without further implementation effort. It also enables improved resource management and a lower network load.

Life Cycle of a Stateful Session Bean

A stateful session bean has three possible states: *nonexistent*, *method ready*, and *passive*. At first glance, this seems similar to stateless beans. A bean with a *nonexistent* state has not been instantiated yet. There are major differences in the method ready state, however. Unlike other bean types, there is no EJB pool; instead, each instance is assigned to a fixed client. The passive state enables you to make beans inactive, which saves resources until methods are executed for the client. You call the corresponding methods to change the state. A detailed illustration of this life cycle and explanations of the methods are available in Section 5.2.1.

Remote Capability

Enterprise JavaBeans are remote-enabled modules that are available to other applications in a client/server-like communication. In a cursory comparison, they could be considered to be the equivalent of a function group from the ABAP world. Remote-enabled means that an EJB can provide a local interface and a remote interface, which the clients can use to access the EJB, in addition to its actual implementation. Because there is one interface each to locate and create an instance, and one each for the provided business methods, each EJB can have a maximum of four interfaces. The term "remote" refers to all EJBs that are not located in the same instance of a JVM. The interface allows you to generate objects on the client that appear to be local, offering the bean's functions on the client. In fact, the process involves relatively simple objects, which merely forward the queries they receive over a network connection through sockets, and send the returned results back to the client.

Transactional Concept

Session beans also support the transactional concept. The callback methods `afterBegin()`, `beforeCompletion()`, and `afterCompletion()`, which use the Boolean parameter values `true` and `false` to indicate a commit or rollback, enable you to manually control transaction-related characteristics of a session bean.

EJB as Web Service

You can also deploy session beans as Web services. This approach permits you to make the functions available using programming language-independent business logic. Therefore, session beans can address other session beans as Web services, although this approach is recommended in only exceptional cases due to its poor runtime. In contrast, entity beans are not published directly as Web services. Instead, you use a session bean to initiate data retrieval through an entity bean.

The procedure for creating Web services from session beans, to make their services available, was already covered in Section 6.2.5.

Container Management: EJB Containers

As mentioned previously, the infrastructure-related aspects of the architecture are covered by the EJB containers used in the J2EE server. It isolates the received EJBs from direct external access. Instead, all access must take place through the container, which is one of the infrastructure-related tasks of the J2EE architecture and does not concern the application programmer. The Java Naming and Directory Interface (JNDI) provides a global, standardized interface for accessing various containers. Because the EJB container usually manages a multitude of EJBs simultaneously in a production environment, but some thought also has to be given to preserving system resources, some types of EJBs—such as the persistent entity beans—do not create a new object each time; instead, a free instance is supplied from a pool of EJBs that have the requested type. If a bean has not been used for a longer period of time, it is removed from the memory of the J2EE server and written back to the permanent store. The client of the process has no idea about the life cycle of an EJB in the EJB container, nor does it have to—as far as the client can tell, its bean is always available with the expected result.

Tutorial: Implementing Business Logic

Developing Session Beans

We will now examine the next J2EE development of the ResMan application and implement the business logic. To do so, we use a stateless session bean that contains the appropriate business methods. For the sake of simplicity, these methods have the same names as the existing function modules in the ABAP functionality, although this doesn't follow the Java naming conventions. As described in Chapter 3, the following functions are available:

- `Z_RM_GETLIST()`—Retrieve booking data (available, booked, or all resources)
- `Z_RM_BOOK()`—Submit booking
- `Z_RM_CANCEL()`—Cancel booking

The methods implement the business logic and thus represent a connection for data retrieval, for which several different methods are available. One possible alternative, though not recommended for the reasons described above, is direct data retrieval through JDBC. A preferable method is to integrate an entity bean or connect to the SAP System via JCo in order to call the remote function module there. Alternatively, you can also connect to Web services or other session beans.

In addition, the integrated *SessionBean* interface also contains the obligatory standard methods of a session bean, namely:

- `ejbCreate()`—Instantiate the connection or remote objects
- `ejbRemove()`—Terminate the connection or delete the object references
- `ejbActivate()`—Not implemented
- `ejbPassivate()`—Not implemented
- `setSessionContext(SessionContext)`—Set the runtime context

Thus, the session bean class looks like this:

```
package com.sap.resman.ejb;
import java.util.ArrayList;

import javax.ejb.CreateException;
import javax.ejb.SessionBean;
import javax.ejb.SessionContext;

/**
 * @ejbHome <{com.sap.resman.ejb.ResManHome}>
 * @ejbRemote <{com.sap.resman.ejb.ResMan}>
 * @stateless
 */
public class ResManBean implements SessionBean {

  private SessionContext myContext;

  /**
   * Lifecycle Methods.
   */
  public void ejbCreate() throws CreateException {
    try {
```

```
      //Close the database connection (JDBC) or
      //retrieve references to
      //remote objects (Entity Bean, JCo, or Web service)
    } catch(Exception e) {
      e.printStackTrace();
      throw new CreateException(e.toString());
    }
  }

  public void ejbRemove() {
    //Close the database connection (JDBC) or
    //retrieve references to
    //remote objects (Entity Bean, JCo, or Web service)
  }
  public void ejbActivate() { }

  public void ejbPassivate() { }

  public void setSessionContext(SessionContext context) {
    myContext = context;
  }

 /**
  * Business Methods.
  */
  public ArrayList Z_RM_GETLIST(
             String I_FILTER,
             int I_MANDT,
             String I_LANGU) throws RemoteException {
       try {
        /*Retrieve data via database access (JDBC)
          or remote objects (Entity Bean,
          JCo, or Web service)*/
       } catch(Exception e) {
         e.printStackTrace();
         throw new ResourceException("Connection to
                      data source interrupted.");
       }
  }
```

```
  public void Z_RM_BOOK(
           String I_RESID,
           Date I_DATE_FROM,
           Time I_TIME_FROM,
           Date I_DATE_TO,
           Time I_TIME_TO,
           String I_REMARK,
           int I_MANDT) throws RemoteException {
           try {
       //Book via database access (JDBC)
       //or remote objects (Entity Bean, JCo, or
       //Web service)
      } catch(Exception e) {
        e.printStackTrace();
        throw new RemoteException("The resource is
          is already booked or otherwise unavailable
          during the requested period.");
      }
  }

  public void Z_RM_CANCEL(
          String I_RESID,
          Date I_DATE_FROM,
          Time I_TIME_FROM,
          int I_MANDT) throws RemoteException {
           try {
       //Cancel via database access (JDBC)
       //or remote objects (Entity Bean, JCo, or
       //Web service)
      } catch(Exception e) {
       e.printStackTrace();
       throw new RemoteException("The resource is
          is already booked or otherwise unavailable
          during the requested period.");
      }
  }
}
```

Listing 6.12 ResManBean.java

Once you have completed the implementation of the session bean, you now have to define the XML-based deployment descriptor. This object contains declarative configurations, such as security settings or the information that a stateless bean is involved. Although the descriptor is generated automatically in the SAP NetWeaver Developer Studio, the developer can edit it if necessary.

```
<?xml version="1.0" encoding="UTF-8"?>
<!DOCTYPE ejb-jar PUBLIC "-//Sun Microsystems, Inc.//
DTD Enterprise JavaBeans 2.0//EN"
"http://java.sun.com/dtd/ejb-jar_2_0.dtd">
<ejb-jar>
  <description>EJBs for the ResMan project</description>
  <display-name>ResMan EJBs</display-name>
  <enterprise-beans>
  <session>
    <ejb-name>ResManBean</ejb-name>
    <home>com.sap.resman.ejb.ResManHome</home>
    <remote>com.sap.resman.ejb.ResMan</remote>
    <ejb-class>com.sap.resman.ejb.ResManBean</ejb-class>
    <session-type>Stateless</session-type>
      <transaction-type>Bean</transaction-type>
    </session>
  </enterprise-beans>
</ejb-jar>
```

Listing 6.13 ejb-jar.xml

Message-Driven Beans

Although Enterprise JavaBeans technology is already extensive and widespread, development of the J2EE environment—and thus the specifications—continues rapidly.

Asynchronous Processes

As such, the relatively new message-driven beans technology, which was introduced in the EJB 2.0 specification, enhances the existing possibilities and opens new ones: Message-driven beans enable the implementation of asynchronous processes and application cases. The basis of the message-driven beans technology is the Java Message Service (JMS).

Java applications that use JMS are called *JMS clients*, while message systems that forward and deliver these messages are called *JMS providers*.

JMS clients are differentiated between producers and consumers: The producer is the client that sends a message, while the consumer is the one that receives it.

Message-driven beans can send any type of message under J2EE. The corresponding applications or other message-driven beans then process these messages. Of course, an appropriate messaging service also has to be provided. These *message brokers* are exclusively responsible for distributing messages, and ensure that these messages are actually sent and received. Therefore, the application is not harmed when the computer or the network causes an error. The message broker keeps trying to send the message until it receives a confirmation from the consumer process that it has been received. This is especially relevant in today's Internet-dependent world, where notebooks or handhelds can be used offline and networks occasionally fail.

Java Message Service

Each message consists of a header, properties, and a body. The fields in the header contain the identity, as well as the information required to deliver the message. The properties are additional fields that can be determined by the application itself. The data part is the body (or *payload*), which can take various formats. Instead of using RPCs (Remote Procedure Calls), the messages are used. The difference between the two is that messages are queried by the corresponding message-based middleware or by message brokers. Unlike RPC calls, which are always processed synchronously, messaging is generally asynchronous.

One advantage of this asynchronous processing is that it decouples the sender and recipient, preventing logjams during execution of the method—because the sender of the message does not have to wait until the method call is closed. Here, the EJB container provides an environment in which many message-driven beans can run concurrently. The requests are not sent to the message-driven bean directly, but instead forwarded to the EJB server, which then decides which bean will receive a given message. The messages can be requests, messages, or events containing user data.

Topic Queue

Two communication variants are available for messaging:

- Topic
- Queue

Each variant represents a different communication model. Queues are used for point-to-point communication, while topics follow the publish/subscribe model.

In the topic approach, the bean subscribes to messages that involve a certain topic or subject. There are publishers (which send the message) and subscribers (which receive them) for each topic. The main feature of this approach is that a message is sent to all registered clients that have subscribed to the corresponding topic.

The developer has to define in the deployment descriptor whether a subscription is permanent (durable). The difference between durable and non-durable subscriptions is that under the latter, messages are not lost even if the message-driven bean used to send the message is not available at send time. Figure 6.28 shows this procedure.

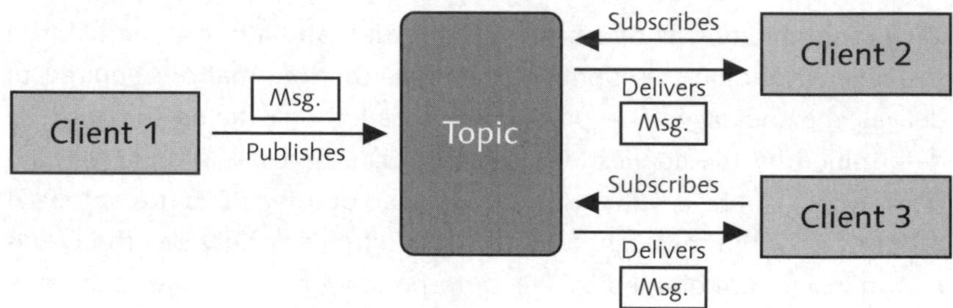

Figure 6.28 Topic

In contrast, the queue works with message queues. A client sends messages to the queue, while the message-driven bean accepts these messages and executes the methods. Subscriptions are permanent; unlike the topic model, differentiation is not possible. This is indicated by the fact that each sent message has exactly one recipient, to which the message is delivered. Even if several recipients have registered for this message type with the message broker, only one recipient receives the message. The broker itself decides which of the registered recipients receives the message.

Figure 6.29 Queue

To find out which messaging model is the right one for you, you have to consider the advantages and disadvantages of each model. The queue model is perfect for communication between two parties in which every message is critical. In the topic model, in contrast, it doesn't matter how many messages are received or which subscriptions are waiting for a message. In addition, it doesn't matter whether a connection is currently active or not.

The reason why two different messaging models exist lies in the origins of JMS and the JMS specifications. They are aimed at integrating existing messaging systems on the market by supporting both *Point to Point* (P2P) and *Publish and Subscribe* (PUB/SUB) models to achieve a certain standardization and level of acceptance from developers.

A JMS connection requires the `ConnectionFactory` object to create a connection between the client and a JMS provider. In turn, these `ConnectionFactories` implement the `QueueConnectionFactory` or `TopicConnectionFactory` interface, depending on which communication model is used. They also provide a session, which acts as a framework for sending the messages. The session handles transaction processing to group a set of send and receive operations together. `QueueSessions` and `TopicSessions` are available, and are also model-dependent. The `MessageProducer` creates each required session, and exists in two versions—`QueueSender` and `TopicPublisher`. The `MessageProducer` doesn't create messages in the sense of generating object instances, however; instead, it sends configured message objects. The last component is the destination (or target) where the JMS message will be sent. Valid destinations are Queue and Topic. Figure 6.30 depicts this object model.

The EJB container usually generates multiple instances of message-driven beans in order to distribute the received messages among them. Each of these beans receives only one message at a time, however. Therefore, it isn't necessary to flag the bean's development as *reentrant* (to start multiple instances). However, you should note that the EJB container delivers the messages asynchronously, and therefore out of order. Thus, it is entirely possible for message three to arrive before message two. So, we suggest that you number the messages to ensure that your application can put the received messages in the proper sequence. To improve performance, the message-driven beans are placed in a pool, as in other EJB models, to provide faster access to the object during a request.

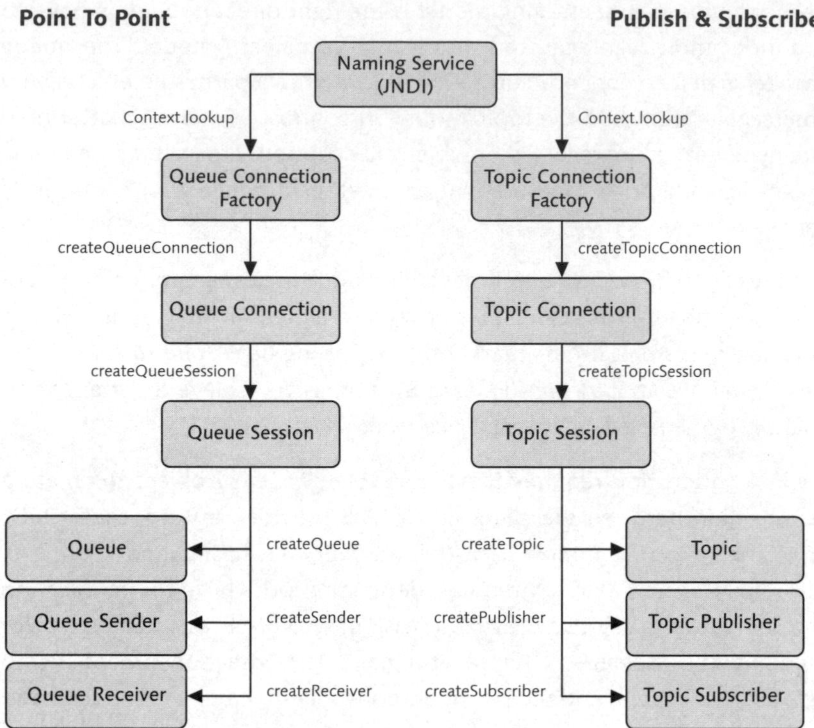
Point To Point
Publish & Subscribe
Naming Service (JNDI)
Context.lookup
Context.lookup
Queue Connection Factory
Topic Connection Factory
createQueueConnection
createTopicConnection
Queue Connection
Topic Connection
createQueueSession
createTopicSession
Queue Session
Topic Session
Queue
createQueue
createTopic
Topic
Queue Sender
createSender
createPublisher
Topic Publisher
Queue Receiver
createReceiver
createSubscriber
Topic Subscriber

Figure 6.30 JMS Model

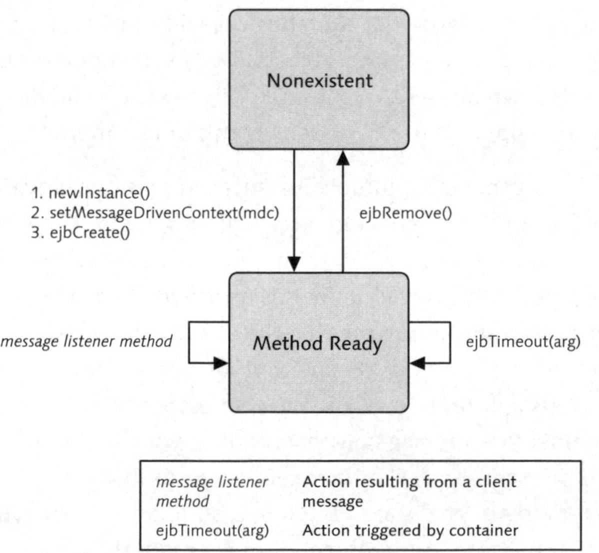
Nonexistent
1. newInstance()
2. setMessageDrivenContext(mdc)
3. ejbCreate()
ejbRemove()
message listener method
Method Ready
ejbTimeout(arg)
message listener method
Action resulting from a client message
ejbTimeout(arg)
Action triggered by container

Figure 6.31 MDB Life Cycle

A deployment descriptor is also needed for message-driven beans. It defines, among other things, whether the container is to take over transaction management. You can also define whether topic or queue should be used at the time of deployment. One possible descriptor is illustrated below:

```
<?xml version="1.0" encoding="UTF-8"?>
<!DOCTYPE ejb-jar PUBLIC "-//Sun Microsystems, Inc.//
DTD Enterprise JavaBeans 2.0//EN"
"http://java.sun.com/dtd/ejb-jar_2_0.dtd">
<ejb-jar>
  <description>ResMan Message-Driven Bean</description>
  <display-name>ResManMDBean</display-name>
  <enterprise-beans>
    <message-driven>
      <ejb-name>ResManMDBean</ejb-name>
      <ejb-class>
         com.sap.resman.ejb.ResManMDBean
      </ejb-class>
      <transaction-type>Container</transaction-type>
      <message-driven-destination>
        <destination-type>
           javax.jms.Queue
        </destination-type>
      </message-driven-destination>
    </message-driven>
  </enterprise-beans>
</ejb-jar>
```

Listing 6.14 Deployment Descriptor of an MDB

You should use message-driven beans in the following situations:

- If a synchronous connection takes too long
- If the target computer is not always reachable
- If the message does not have to be processed immediately

An example of a message-driven bean appears below:

```
package com.sap.resman.ejb;

import javax.ejb.MessageDrivenBean;
import javax.ejb.MessageDrivenContext;
import javax.jms.JMSException;
```

```
import javax.jms.Message;
import javax.jms.MessageListener;
import javax.jms.TextMessage;

public class ResManMDBean implements MessageDrivenBean,
                                     MessageListener {

  private MessageDrivenContext mdc;

 /**
  * Lifecycle Methods.
  */
  public void ejbCreate() {}

  public void ejbRemove() {}

  public void setMessageDrivenContext(
    MessageDrivenContext context) {
    mdc = context;
  }

  public void onMessage(Message inMessage) {
    TextMessage msg = null;
    try {
      if (inMessage instanceof TextMessage) {
        msg = (TextMessage) inMessage;
        //Retrieve reference of session bean
        //through JNDI and method call
      } else {
        System.out.println("Message has wrong type:" +
          inMessage.getClass().getName());
      }
    } catch (JMSException e) {
      e.printStackTrace();
      mdc.setRollbackOnly();
    } catch (Throwable te) {
      mdc.setRollbackOnly();
    }
  }
}
```

Listing 6.15 Example of a Message-Driven Bean

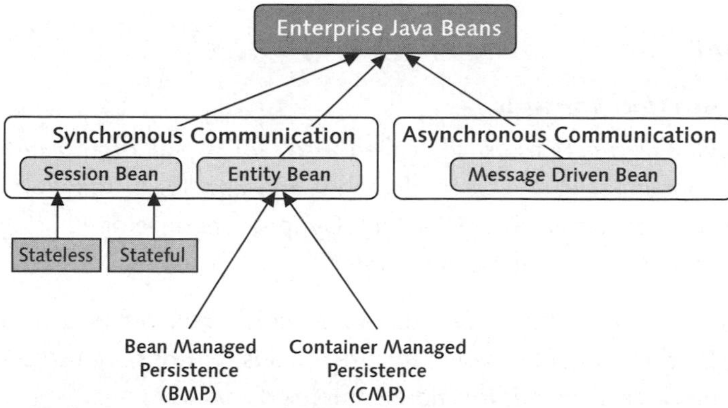

Figure 6.32 EJB Map

The message-driven bean technology has now closed a remaining gap in the communication models within J2EE architectures. Consequently, Java is also moving explicitly towards the vision of service-oriented architectures.

6.4 Presentation Logic

The presentation logic is generally the most temporary of the three application layers. Changing requirements and—as you will see—technologies are easiest to implement in this layer. In contrast, the other two layers of an application are much less volatile. Consequently, any decision regarding which technology to use will have to address the following questions:

- How quickly and efficiently can you implement the end users' changing requirements?
- How open, flexible, and extensible is the technology to architectural change and integration requirements?
- How easy is the technology to distribute; for example, are extensive client rollouts required to deliver the application to the end users?
- How demanding—that is, expensive—is the development of equivalent functionality between the technologies in question?

This section deals with the interface between the application and the end user: the GUI. It will give you an overview of the tools used to implement the presentation logic in ABAP and Java. Here, the currently available technologies—dynpro (screen), BSP, JSP, and Web Dynpro—will be introduced based on an example application.

6.4.1 ABAP

Dynpro & Custom Controls

Dynpro A *dynpro* (*dyn*amic *pro*gram; usually called a *screen*) is part of an ABAP program. It contains screens, screen elements, and flow logic. They form the basis for user dialogs in an SAP System. Dynpros are developed using the *ABAP Editor* and the visual *Screen Painter*.

Each *screen* has various attributes, such as a screen number or a next screen. The Screen Painter lets you define text fields, buttons, input/output fields, and *custom controls* for more complex displays.

The basic events for screens are PBO (*processing before output*) and PAI (*processing after input*). There are also events for *pressing the F1 help key* (POH, process on help) and the *F4 input help key* (POV, process on value help). You assign specific instructions to these events in the Flow Logic Editor, using the ABAP Screen Language. Among other things, you can call dialog modules and subscreens, control data transfer, initiate processing chains, or process tables.

Each dynpro is uniquely assigned to an ABAP program. The program can use specific statements to call dynpros directly or use its elements.

Custom Controls

You can also embed complex display elements—such as tables, lists, tree structures, and text editors—in screens. To do so, you must define areas of the screen as *custom control* in the Screen Painter; these areas are used to embed *controls*. A control is a software component—either an ActiveX element or Java bean, depending on the GUI type—that assumes responsibility for controlling the display element on the client side. The control is addressed by the business logic on the application server. Communication between the application server and the control is saved in classes within the *SAP Control Framework*, while the control is steered by instances of class `CL_GUI_CUSTOM_CONTAINER`, the custom container. Similarly, communication with the control itself is encapsulated by an instance of the corresponding control class. Hence, a control exists as two object instances, one on the SAP GUI (ActiveX or JavaBean) and one as a proxy on the application server.

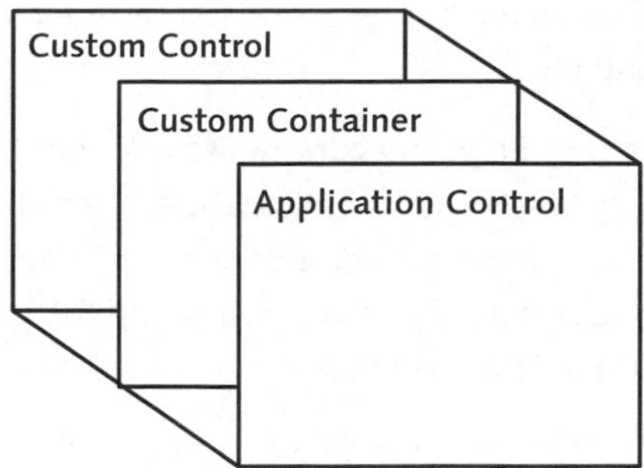

Figure 6.33 The Three Levels of the SAP Control Framework

Selection Screens & Lists

Selection Screens

One special type of dynpro is the *selection screen*, which can contain only certain elements and is defined outside of the Screen Painter. It can be used in only executable programs, function groups, and module pools, and performs two main tasks. First, selection screens enable user inputs as *parameters* (single values) or *selection criteria* (value ranges). Secondly, they act as interfaces for calling programs, which save the corresponding parameters in the input fields when they call an executable program. Each executable program has a standard selection screen; you can also create other, independent selection screens.

You define selection screens directly in ABAP, using use the appropriate statements (`SELECT-OPTIONS`, `SELECTION-SCREEN`, `PARAMETERS`). When the program is executed, the corresponding screen is generated automatically.

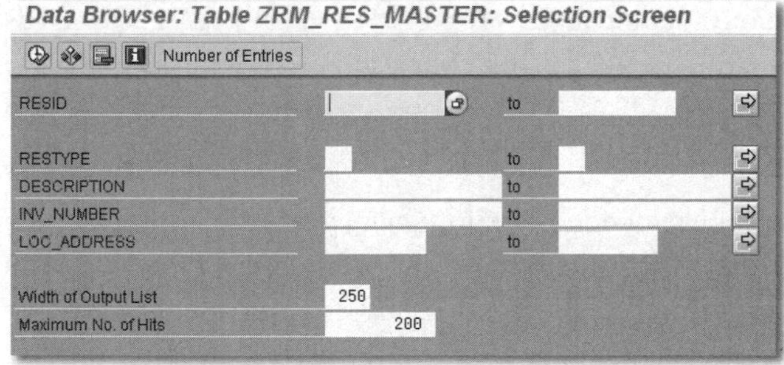

Figure 6.34 ResMan Selection Screen with Various Selection Criteria

Lists

Lists are screens that do not contain any screen elements. Instead, they output texts that are defined by ABAP statements. Lists are saved in *list buffers* in ABAP programs. In addition to the *basic list*, a list buffer can contain up to 20 *details lists*. The individual lists are addressed through a *list index*, which is numbered sequentially.

The output from an ABAP program is written in the current list—the basic list—when the dynpro is called, and displayed by the list processor, which is called either implicitly within an executable program or explicitly with the `LEAVE TO LIST-PROCESSING` statement. Once displayed, the list in the list buffer is closed and can no longer be changed.

You can define *list events* for user interaction with displayed lists. When an event occurs, the list index is increased and a details list is generated and displayed. This makes it possible, for example, to implement branching with an increasing degree of detail.

Lists can also be created as *print lists* and sent directly to the SAP spool system for output in a printer.

BSP

In this section, you will create the ResMan application based on BSP technology. To do so, you'll rely on the information you learned in Section 5.1.3.

Introduction Business Server Pages (BSPs) are an ABAP technology for implementing the presentation logic on the SAP Web Application Server (SAP Web AS). They are server-side scripts that control Web browser-based communication with the user.

The development environment for BSP applications is integrated in Transaction SE80 and is called *Web Application Builder*. BSPs support the following client-side output languages: HTML, XHTML and WML, as well as the XSLT transformation language. The connection to the business logic is implemented by binding ABAP in the appropriate code blocks for the events.

You can also use the client-side markup languages to define server-side markups, or *BSP extensions*, which are also embedded directly in the BSPs. The BSPs are responsible for generating any necessary client-side output. They encapsulate functions with any degree of complexity in classes, and provide them to the layout part of the BSP page as tags.

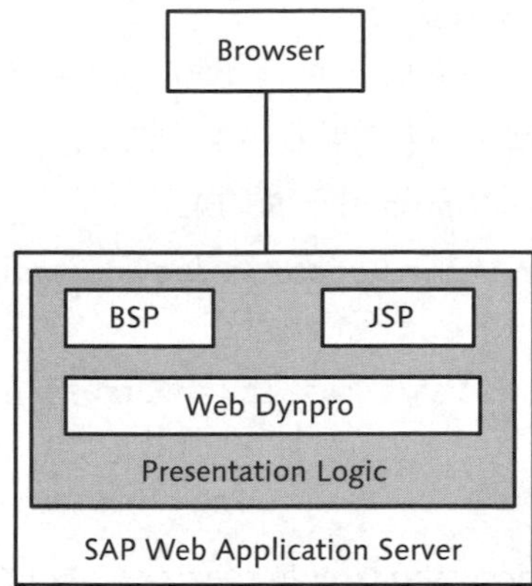

Figure 6.35 Business Server Pages in the SAP Web Application Server

Execution

Therefore, when BSPs are executed, the SAP Web AS converts them to a client-side language like HTML, and the client browser interprets them and displays them in graphical form. Therefore, from the end user perspective, the communication schema of a Web application looks like this:

1. The user enters a URL.
2. The BSP engine generates the addressed BSP object.
3. The BSP Engine detects any predefined events that occur and processes their coding.
4. An HTML page is generated from the script coding.
5. The BSP engine sends the generated HTML page to the browser.
6. The browser displays the HTML page.

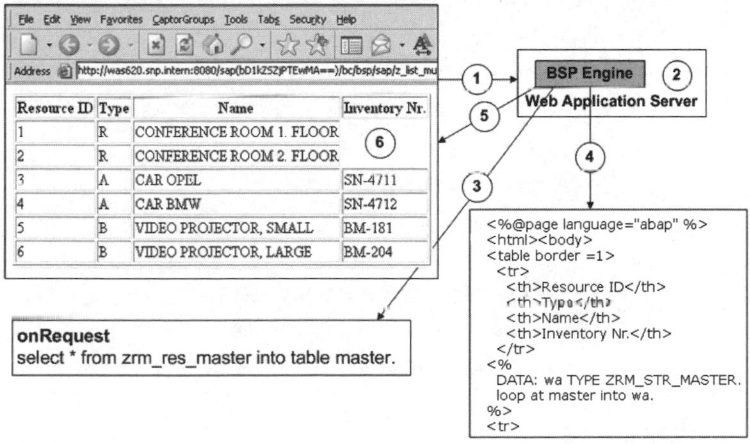

Figure 6.36 Execution of a Business Server Page

Tutorial: Outputting a Table in a Web Browser

Objective In the following example, you will output table ZRM_RES_MASTER in a Web browser, using a BSP with ABAP commands and HTML tags.

Process

1. Open the SAP Web Application Builder (Transaction SE80).
2. Choose program type **BSP Application** in the Repository Browser and enter a name for your application.
3. Enter a short text. Assign the application to a package and a workbench request.
4. Create a page for the application.
5. Define a page attribute, which will be accessed later in the page. In our example: `master` with type ZRM_TAB_MASTER.
6. Assign ABAP coding to the events in the event handler. In this example, when the page is called, you should write the contents of table ZRM_TAB_MASTER to page attribute `master`. Therefore, you have to enter the following coding for event `onRequest`: `select * from zrm_res_master into table master.`
7. Enter the basic structure of the page in the layout area and supplement it with embedded ABAP commands:

```
<%@page language="abap"%>
<html>
  <body>
    <table border="1">
      <tr>
        <th>Resource ID</th>
        <th>Type</th>
        <th>Name</th>
        <th>Inventory no.</th>
      </tr>
      <% DATA: wa TYPE ZRM_STR_MASTER.
         LOOP AT master INTO wa. %>
      <tr>
        <td> <%=wa-resid %> </td>
        <td> <%=wa-restype%> </td>
        <td> <%=wa-description%> </td>
        <td> <%=wa-inv_number%> </td>
      </tr>
      <% ENDLOOP. %>
    </table>
```

```
  </body>
</html>
```

Listing 6.16 Basic Structure of the BSP Page

8. Enter the defined page as the initial BSP of the BSP application.
9. Run the BSP application.

Result The BSP sends the contents of table ZRM_TAB_MASTER, embedded in HTML, to the Web browser.

BSP Extensions

The Web Application Builder enables you to add BSP extensions to BSP applications. A BSP extension is a class that contains various *elements*. It is an abstract tag used to implement the concept of *reusability*. Certain extensions are already available, such as HTML Business for BSP (HTMLB). You can also create your own extensions to address specific requirements. Use the *Tag Browser* in the Web Application Builder to access the tags saved in the *tag library*.

There are several advantages to using BSP extensions:

- The syntax of the page description languages is checked as soon as you translate the BSP extension.
- You enter the coding for the page description languages only once.
- The generated HTML code contains correct links with the corresponding style sheets.
- A uniform look and feel is guaranteed.
- When you develop your own extensions, you can implement additional logic for browser-dependent display directly in the BSP extension.

The logic and language elements of the BSP extension elements are saved in an ABAP element handler class on the Web AS. Various methods can influence the tag responses.

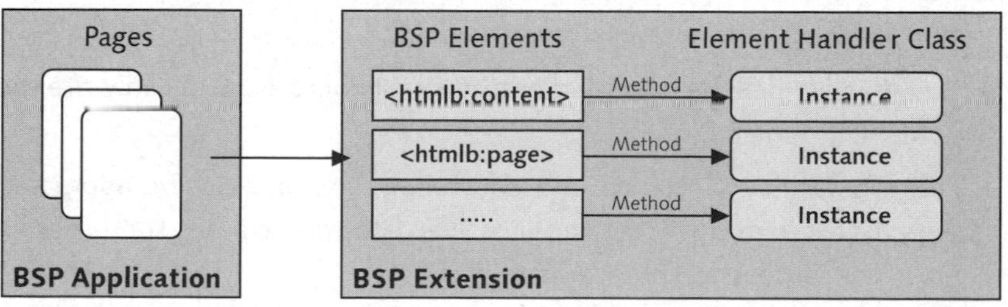

Figure 6.37 Integrating BSP Extensions in a BSP Application

The preceding tutorial for BSP applications can also be implemented using HTML Business for BSP. To do so, you merely have to change the source code in the layout area of the BSP page as follows:

```
<%@page language="abap"%>
<%@extension name="htmlb" prefix="htmlb" %>
<htmlb:content>
  <htmlb:page>
    <htmlb:form>
      <htmlb:tableView id="tab1"
                       table="<%=master%>"
                       visibleRowCount="10" />
    </htmlb:form>
  </htmlb:page>
</htmlb:content>
```

Listing 6.17 The Tags That Start with "htmlb" Are Defined in the Corresponding BSP Extension

BSP with the Model View Controller

In SAP Web AS 6.20 and later, the *Model View Controller* (MVC) design concept can be implemented in BSP. In this design pattern, the display pages are separated from the data model and the program flow is optimized. It also lets you structure views better and group them together as logical entities for use in larger applications.

Using MVC offers the following advantages:

- You can structure the application better, which eases later changes and maintenance.
- The layout can be generated at runtime (as opposed to static HTML page).
- The use of the `<bsp: ... >` extension makes the inclusion of pages more efficient, variable, and resource-friendly.
- Performance is improved because of fewer client-side redirects and, in turn, a lower number of server roundtrips
- You're more flexible in implementing events because you can write the controller yourself.
- A *controller* is an instance of a controller class and can be addressed directly through a URL; it supplies the data, determines the program flow, and processes any events that occur.

- A *view* is responsible for displaying the application data; it does not have its own event handling, and its attributes are filled by a controller.
- The *model* contains all the relevant application data in appropriately defined data structures; it performs all activities involved in reading, changing, locking, and saving data in the database.

A controller can also address multiple views, request data from multiple models, and call other controllers. Therefore, you can implement structures with any level of complexity.

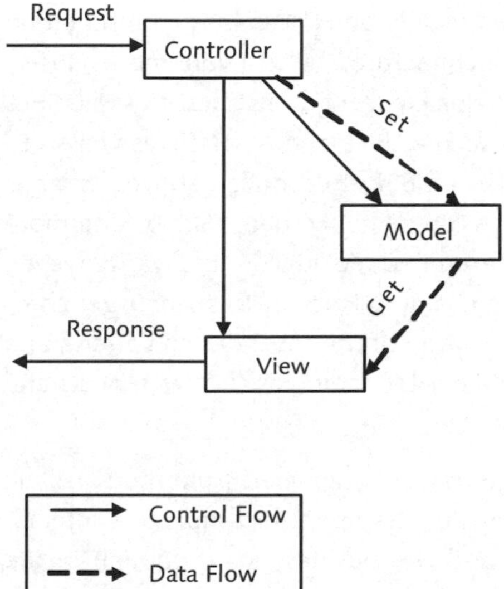

Figure 6.38 Simple Control and Data Flow in a BSP Application Based on the MVC

Web Dynpro

Web Dynpro, a new user interface technology for both the ABAP and Java personalities, represents an entirely new approach to designing SAP application interfaces. Because Web Dynpro for ABAP has not yet been released for general use in SAP Web AS 6.40, we won't describe it in any detail here. The basic concepts, which are generally valid for both personalities, are described in the next section, including information about developing Web Dynpro applications with Java.

6.4.2 Java

There are basically two ways to model the development of presentation logic on the Java side: *Java Server Pages* and *Web Dynpro*. The former is a mature technology from the J2EE world that is used to generate HTML dynamically through Java coding. The full complexity that is usually associated with a J2EE development environment is introduced later in this section.

An extended version of the Eclipse editor, which now specifically supports Web Dynpro projects and their development cycle, serves as the development environment for Java-based projects.

JSP

Overview Java Server Pages (JSPs) are a technology from the J2EE world that enable you to create dynamic GUIs, based mainly on HTML, in the presentation layer of multilayer application architecture. When you more closely examine the coding of a JSP, you'll quickly recognize structural similarities to server-side scripting languages such as PHP and ASP.NET, as well as to application-oriented languages like the BSPs introduced above. As far as the complexity and system architecture is concerned, JSPs belong more to the latter group. The language embedded in JSPs is Java, however, which also implies all the specific characteristics of this language: complete object orientation, implementation of the MVC design pattern, and integration with familiar Java container technologies such as servlets and Enterprise JavaBeans (EJBs).

MVC The Model View Controller design pattern originated from the Smalltalk language, and represents the successful attempt to decouple user interaction (controller), display (view), and the business logic (model) in the background. Simply put:

> *In the MVC context, JSP pages output the data to the user, representing the view, but also contain elements—such as forms, hyperlinks, and buttons—that enable user input, making it possible to route this input data to the application through servlets and Enterprise JavaBeans.*

Servlets Servlets generally give JSPs a way to access the application functionality. They are separate containers that catch the events triggered by the JSPs and associate them with the application. This additional programming layer is especially useful when specifications change in one of the other two layers (JSP und Enterprise JavaBeans). In such cases, you need to modify only the servlet, which minimizes the effort involved because a servlet usually provides access to an application for several different JSPs.

JSPs are processed by the J2EE engine on both the SAP Web AS and other platforms. Aside from other development-relevant aspects, the J2EE engine provides a Java Virtual Machine (JVM) instance for processing the individual components of an application. At this point, we should mention that the J2EE engine treats JSPs as servlets, and compiles them as well. However, this doesn't change anything about the basic architecture, or the associated benefit that JSPs are relatively simple for developers without extensive Java experience to use.

TagLibs

Tag libraries, or TagLibs, perform the same function for JSP as do BSP extensions for BSP. They enable you to isolate the Java coding that is usually embedded in JSPs and encapsulate it further in freely definable tags. Although you have to use an XML namespace to differentiate these tags from regular HTML tags, both types of tags generally work the same. In contrast to BSP extensions, however, various ready-to-use TagLibs are already available in the JSP world and can be easily integrated in the respective JSP context, as shown in the following example:

```
<%@page contentType="text/html"%>
<%@taglib prefix="txt"
          uri="/WEB-INF/MyTxtTagLib.tld" %>
<html>
  <head>
    <title>JSP example</title>
  </head>
  <body>
    <txt:headline size="large">
      My JSP example page
    </txt:headline>
    <txt:paragraph>
      This is an example paragraph
    </txt:paragraph>
  </body>
</html>
```

Listing 6.18 Example for Integrating TagLibs in JSPs

Enterprise JavaBeans

Enterprise JavaBeans model the business logic on the other side of the application. As described in Section 6.3.2, EJBs are divided into three groups:

- **Entity beans**, whose attribute values are saved in a persistent medium (such as a database) and which save typical business objects such as customer data or bills of material (BOM)
- **Session beans**, which encapsulate application-specific access logic for EJBs and are typically addressed externally, for example, from a servlet

▶ **Message-driven beans**, which play more of a subordinate role in a Web application framework, but are very important for distributed applications and integration tasks

Tutorial: JSP Introduction with SAP NetWeaver Developer Studio

Project Structure

After this brief outline of the architecture and how JSPs are used in a complex application, you will then create an example mini-app. Once again, the example involves ResMan, your resource management tool. You want to create a mask to display the reserved resources at an enterprise—whether man or machine—and make it possible to reserve new resources for specific periods or release resources that are already reserved. To do so, there is a Java Server Page named *reservation.jsp*, which is responsible for displaying the corresponding data and which lets you enter data. There is also a servlet named *ReservationServlet*, which accepts the inputs from the JSP and processes them—setting or deleting reservations. Although using a session bean would be a cleaner architectural approach, we have elected to omit it at this point in order to avoid making the example unnecessarily complex.

Project Types

This type of project in J2EE is divided into three to five individual projects:

1. The *Web project*, which contains the actual programming of JSPs and servlets, and therefore covers the presentation logic from the Java side. The development environment supports developers primarily by relieving them of their organizational and infrastructure-related tasks.
2. The *Web application project*, which potentially represents an aggregation of several *Web projects*, and provides developers with distribution information in the form of XML descriptors. The development environment provides suitable masks to help define these XML files, which, in turn, simplifies the process.
3. The *EJB project*, which fully supports the development of Enterprise JavaBeans. It is an analog *Web project*, with one particular difference—it is used to develop the business logic, not the presentation logic.
4. The *EJB assembly project*, which again potentially consists of several *EJB projects*, consolidating them to form a transportable distribution. The distribution information required for this is also located in XML files; again, the corresponding masks simplify their use.
5. The *enterprise application project*, which serves as an umbrella project for *Web application projects* and *EJB assembly projects*, and ties them

together into a distributable package that can be transported to the J2EE server and activated.

Requirements

Some preparation is required before you can start the project:

1. The SAP NetWeaver Developer Studio must be installed and running.
2. The J2EE server must be running.
3. You can connect to an instance of the SAP DB.

Creating the Web Project

Once the preceding prerequisites are met, you can create the project structure. To do so, switch to the **J2EE development perspective** in the SAP NetWeaver Developer Studio by choosing menu path **Window • Open Perspective • J2EE Development** or with the toolbar on the left-hand side. You now have to create a Web project that contains the Java Server Page and the servlet. To do so, choose menu path **File • New • Project...**, click **J2EE** on the left side, and the appropriate project on the right. When you click **Next**, the system prompts you to enter the project name: *ResManWeb*. Leave the default settings and click **Finish** to confirm.

Creating the JSP

You now need a Java Server Page and a servlet. To create the JSP, open the context menu for the new node and choose **New • Jsp....** In the next screen, enter the name of the Java Server Page: *reservation.jsp*. The new page can now be displayed with **ResManWeb • JSP Registry**.

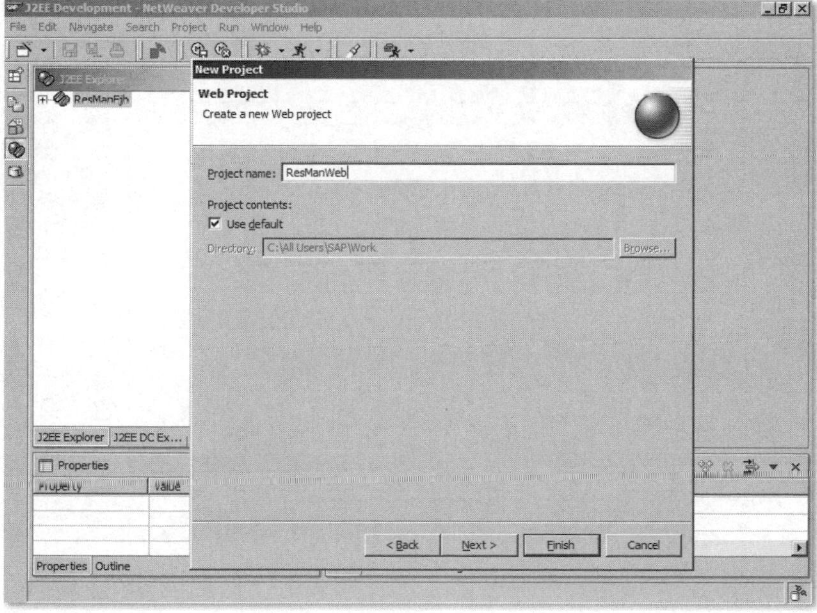

Figure 6.39 Web Project "ResManWeb"

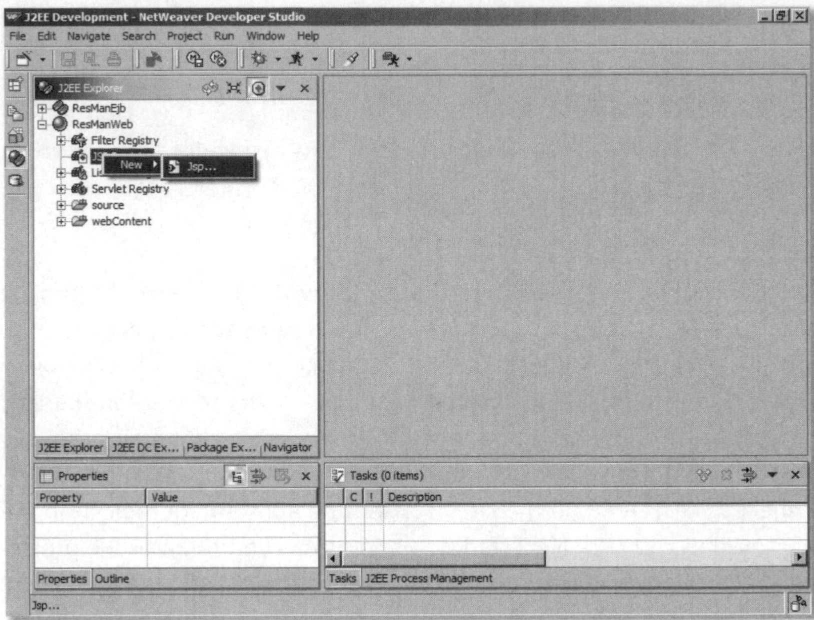

Figure 6.40 New JSP

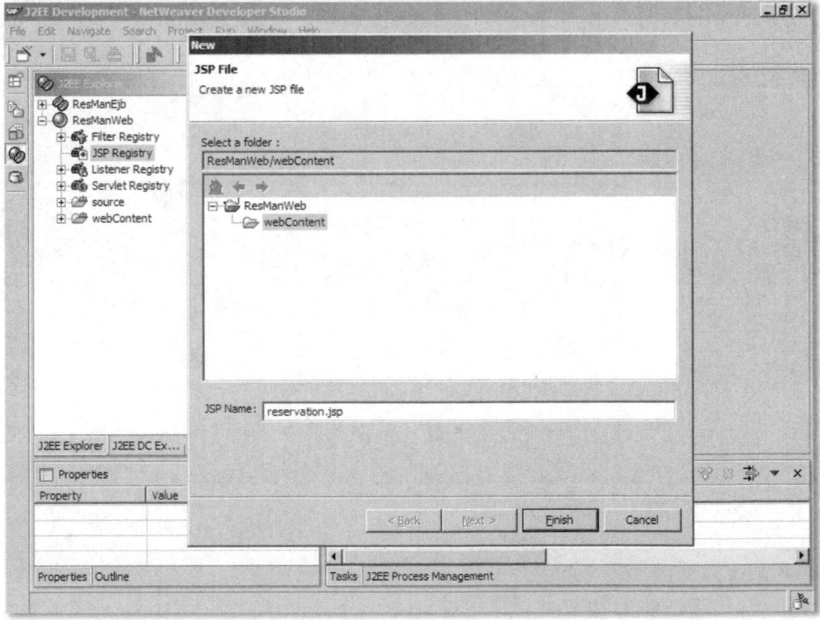

Figure 6.41 Creating reservation.jsp

Aside from a preview function—which incidentally displays only those HTML functions saved in the JSP, but not the server-side functions—you can now implement the JSP. Provided that you have the necessary HTML skills, the basic structure should be easy to understand—except for the output of a system message—and does not require further comment here. The dynamically generated parts of the JSP are flagged by comments in the listing and are described individually below.

Implementing the JSP

```
<%@page import="java.util.ArrayList" language="java" %>
<html>
  <head>
    <title>ResMan</title>
  </head>
  <body>
    System message:
    <%=session.getAttribute("message")%>
    <h1>List of reserved resources</h1>
    <table cellpadding="5">
      <tr>
        <td>Resource</td>
        <td>From</td>
        <td>To</td>
        <td>Comment</td>
        <td> </td>
      </tr>
      <!-- Display reserved resources -->
    </table>
    <hr/>
    <form method="POST" action="/ResMan">
      <table cellpadding="5">
        <tr>
          <td>Resource:</td>
          <td><!-- Selection list of resources --></td>
        </tr>
        <tr>
          <td>From:</td>
          <td>
            <input type="text"
                   name="date_from"
                   size="10"
                   value="0000-00-00"/>
```

```
           
          <input type="text"
                 name="time_from"
                 size="8"
                 value="00:00"/>
        </td>
      </tr>
      <tr>
        <td>To:</td>
        <td>
          <input type="text"
                 name="date_to"
                 size="10"
                 value="0000-00-00"/>
           
          <input type="text"
                 name="time_to"
                 size="8"
                 value="00:00"/>
        </td>
      </tr>
      <tr>
        <td>Remarks:</td>
        <td>
          <textarea name="remark"></textarea>
        </td>
      </tr>
      <tr>
        <td colspan="2" align="right">
          <input type="submit"
                 name="action"
                 value="reserve"/>
        </td>
      </tr>
    </table>
  </form>
</body>
</html>
```

Listing 6.19 Basic HTML Structure for the JSP Version of the ResMan Application

The reserved resources are displayed line by line, with an option to cancel the corresponding entry in each line. Note that this list was provided by the servlet in advance and merely represents the generation of a display, which makes it easy to detect the architectural separation of the individual components. To create the individual table rows, an object with type `ArrayList` is passed in a loop, and the individual entries are merged to create HTML output.

```
<%
  ArrayList list = (ArrayList)
    session.getAttribute("reservations");
  if(list != null) {
    for(int i = 0; i < list.size(); i++) {
      String[] item = (String[]) list.get(i);
%>
  <form name="cancel"
        method="POST"
        action="/ResMan">
   <tr>
     <td><%=item[1]%></td>
     <td><%=item[2]%> <%=item[3]%></td>
     <td><%=item[4]%> <%=item[5]%></td>
     <td><%=item[6]%></td>
     <td>
       <input type="submit"
              name="action"
              value="cancel"/>
     </td>
     <input type="hidden"
            name="resid"
            value="<%=item[0]%>"/>
     <input type="hidden"
            name="date_from"
            value="<%=item[2]%>"/>
     <input type="hidden"
            name="time_from"
            value="<%=item[3]%>"/>
   </tr>
 </form>
<% } %>
```

Listing 6.20 Displaying the List of Reserved Resources

As you can see at the top of the coding above, the program checks whether the servlet has saved the `reservations` attribute in the `session` object. If no reservations exist, you should indicate this condition explicitly with an `else` block:

```
<% } else { %>
  <tr>
    <td colspan="3"
        align="center">
      No entries found
    </td>
  </tr>
<% } %>
```

Listing 6.21 Alternative Display If No Resources Are Reserved

Creating Servlets

The implementation of the Java Server Page is now complete. The next step is to create and implement the corresponding servlet, which ensures that the JSP makes the corresponding attributes available in the session object. To create the servlet, open the context menu for the *ResManWeb* project and select menu path **New · Servlet**. Enter "ResManServlet" as the name and create package `com.sap.resman`. Set the checkboxes next to the `doGet()` and `doPost()` methods, select **HTTP Servlet** as the servlet type, and click **Finish**.

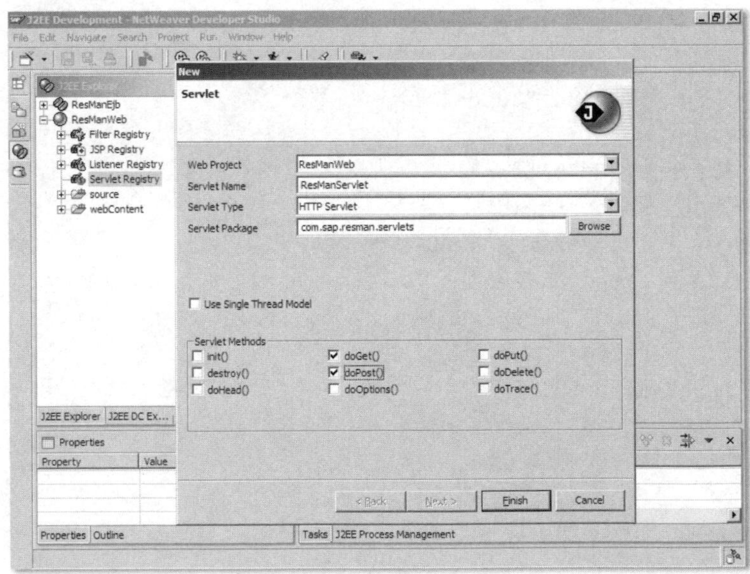

Figure 6.42 The ResMan Servlet

These two methods are then processed in the corresponding URL when an HTTP request occurs in your Web browser. In general, `GET` requests are created when you click on links or enter a URL in your browser, while `POST` requests are used primarily to send form data.

Structure and Tasks of the Servlet

From here on, we will concentrate on only the most relevant aspects for the implementation, and discuss the rest in a conceptual framework. If you like, you can look up the full source coding at *www.sap-press.com*.

The servlet generator in the development environment has already generated a template with the selected methods automatically. Now, your job as developer is to expand this skeleton, or in other words, create the actual implementation. Because the `GET` and `POST` requests essentially have the same function in our example, it makes sense to encapsulate them both in the `doWork()` method instead of dealing with them separately (and thus redundantly). This method establishes the connection to the database via JDBC and fills the necessary variables for the session objects—`reservations` and `resources`—with the corresponding values from the database, using the `populateReservations()` and `populateResources()` methods, which, in turn, are used by the JSP. In addition, the `handleRequest()` method is called at the appropriate juncture to process reservations and cancellations. Additionally, the method forwards the handling of the output to the JSP, by forwarding the request for it to the dispatcher.

Integrating Your Own JAR Libraries

If you plan to use JDBC to create the database connection, you will need a database driver, which is usually saved in a *JAR* (Java archive) file. In many cases, however, especially when these drivers are involved, you cannot assume that they are already contained in the standard distribution of your development environment. Therefore, you need a mechanism that makes it possible to integrate these archives—the driver for the SAP DB (*sapdbc.jar*) in this case—subsequently in the J2EE engine. To do so, open the context menu for the *ResManWeb* project, select **Properties**, and then **Java Build Path** from the menu. Click on the **Libraries** tab. You can now select **Add External JARs...** to add your own library archives. To include them in the distribution process, click on the **Order and Export** tab and set the checkbox next to the corresponding file, to include it in future transports.

In the following example, we will use the two main methods `doWork()` and `handleRequest()`, as well as the `populateResources()` method. Information that is to be used by several methods of a class at the same time has to be available as attributes of an object instance. For this purpose, all the attributes that are related to the database connection are declared as attributes of the object instance:

```
package com.sap.resman;
...
public class ResManServlet extends HttpServlet {
  protected Connection connection;
  protected String database = "database";
  protected String dbuser   = "user";
  protected String dbpass   = "******";
  ...
}
```

Listing 6.22 Saving Connection Data in Object Attributes

Change the values accordingly. These object attributes are now available to all methods of the global class. The `protected` keyword indicates that only instances of the class and its derived class can access the attributes internally. External access to the attributes is not permitted.

We should mention that security-related information—such as the access data for a database connection—should never be hard-coded in a production system. We do so here only to simplify the example.

doWork() The `doWork()` method is called implicitly by the `doGet()` and `doPost()` methods, which process the corresponding HTTP requests. The tasks performed by this part of the application are largely infrastructure-related, for example, opening and closing the database connection and initiating some of the internal methods already mentioned. The error handling is also finalized at this level, to forward any triggered messages to the user.

```
protected void doWork(
  HttpServletRequest request,
  HttpServletResponse response
) throws ServletException {
//Retrieve session object
  HttpSession session = request.getSession(true);
  try {
  //Load SAP DB-JDBC driver for the connection
    Class.forName("com.sap.dbtech.jdbc.DriverSapDB");
  //Establish connection to database
    connection = DriverManager.getConnection(
      "jdbc:sapdb://localhost/"+ database
```

```
        +"?timeout=0", dbuser, dbpass);
    //Call method 'handleRequest()'
      handleRequest(request, response);
    //Call method 'populateReservations()'
      populateReservations(request, session);
    //Call method 'populateResources()'
      populateResources(request, session);
    //Forward query to the JSP
      RequestDispatcher dispatcher =
        request.getRequestDispatcher("/reservation");
    //Try to catch dispatcher errors
      try {
        dispatcher.forward(request, response);
      } catch (IOException e) {
        e.printStackTrace();
      //Escalate error to next instance
        throw new ServletException(e.getMessage());
      }
    //Close database connection
      connection.close();
  //Catch errors from SQL queries
    } catch(SQLException e){
    //Escalate error to next instance
      throw new ServletException("SQLException: " +
        e.getMessage());
  //Catch errors caused by missing driver classes
    } catch(ClassNotFoundException e){
     //Escalate error to next instance
       throw new ServletException(
         "ClassNotFoundException: " + e.getMessage());
    }
  }
```

Listing 6.23 Implementation of the doWork() Method

handleRequest()

The handleRequest() method, which is called implicitly in doWork(), takes care of reserving and canceling the resources. The actual database requests are sent as SQL statements here, and the status messages for the user (for output in the JSP) are filled. The method first checks which action should be performed. This is determined by the action form parameter, which is set depending on whether the **Cancel** or **Reserve** button was pressed. The form parameters required to build the correct SQL statement are read immediately afterwards and the request is then executed on the database. Note that JDBC does not use any transactions in this example. Each statement is inherently atomic. This is not important in this case, however, as only one request is involved, and there are no functional interdependencies between different statements.

Error Handling As in all Java applications, error handling is again performed in the `try ... catch` blocks, and is used to save the error message for the user in plain text, in the `message` attribute of the session object.

```
protected void handleRequest(
  HttpServletRequest request,
  HttpServletResponse response
) throws ServletException {
//Retrieve session object
  HttpSession session = request.getSession(true);
  session.setAttribute("message","");
//Read and evaluate form parameter 'action'
  String action = request.getParameter("action");
  if (action != null) {
  //Check whether 'reserve' is recorded as action
    if(action.equalsIgnoreCase("reserve")) {
      //Retrieve form parameters required to
      //construct SQL statement
        String resid =
          request.getParameter("resource");
        String date_from =
          request.getParameter("date_from");
        String time_from =
          request.getParameter("time_from");
        String date_to =
          request.getParameter("date_to");
        String time_to =
          request.getParameter("time_to");
        String remark =
         (request.getParameter("remark") !=
          null)?request.getParameter("remark"):"";
      //Generate the SQL statement
        String sql = "
          INSERT INTO RES_RES
          VALUES('"+resid+"',
                 '"+date_from+"',
```

```
                '"+time_from+"',
                '"+date_to+"',
                '"+time_to+"',
                '"+remark+"')";
        try {
        //Send query to the database
          Statement statement =
            connection.createStatement();
          statement.executeUpdate(sql);
          statement.close();
        } catch(SQLException e) {
        //Fill status message for user
          session.setAttribute("message",
           "An error occurred during the
            booking.");
        }
    //Check whether 'cancel' is recorded as action
     } else if(action.equalsIgnoreCase("cancel")) {
       //Retrieve form parameters required to
       //construct SQL statement
         String resid =
           request.getParameter("resid");
         String date_from =
           request.getParameter("date_from");
         String time_from =
           request.getParameter("time_from");
       //Generate the SQL statement
         String sql = "
           DELETE FROM RES_RES
           WHERE resid='"+resid+"'
             AND date_from='"+date_from+"'
             AND time_from='"+time_from+"'";
         try {
         //Send query to the database
           Statement statement =
             connection.createStatement();
           statement.executeUpdate(sql);
           statement.close();
         } catch(SQLException e) {
         //Fill status message for user
           session.setAttribute("message",
             "An error occurred during cancellation.");
```

```
            }
        }
    }
}
```

Listing 6.24 Implementation of the handleRequest() Method

populateResources()

To round out your introduction to using servlets and JDBC, we will now briefly examine the `populateResources()` method, which fills the session variable required for the JSP, `resources`, with a list of all resources.

```
protected void populateResources(
  HttpServletRequest request,
  HttpSession session
) throws SQLException {
//Generate the SQL statement
  Statement statement = connection.createStatement();
//Send the statement
  ResultSet records = statement.executeQuery(
     "SELECT resid, description FROM RES_MASTER");
//Create an ArrayList object as container for the
//selected data records
  ArrayList resources    = new ArrayList();
//Loop over query results
  while(records.next()) {
  //Generate a string array to represent the
  //data record
      String[] record = new String[2];
  //Fill the individual parts of the array
    record[0] = records.getString(1);
    record[1] = records.getString(2);
  //Append the array to the ArrayList
    result.add(record);
  }
  records.close();
  statement.close();
//Fill the session variables
  session.setAttribute("resources",resources);
}
```

Listing 6.25 Implementation of the populateResources() Method

Several steps are required before these session variables can be filled, however. You first have to formulate an appropriate SQL statement and send it to the database through an existing connection. The result, with object type `RecordSet`, has to be processed further, and an object with type `ArrayList`—which is similar to an internal table—has to be filled. To do so, the individual string arrays—comparable to a work area—are filled with values successively and then appended to the `ArrayList`. The result can then be used to fill the `resources` session variable, which the JSP can process further for output.

If you're wondering why this method doesn't have any error handling, remember that the signature of the method itself indicates that a `SQLException` can be triggered internally and is then delegated to the outside. Therefore, the calling methods—`doWork()` in this case—are responsible for error handling.

Creating a Web Application Project

Once you're finished implementing the JSP and the servlet, two more steps are required to make the object transportable, as described above. To do so, you first create a new Web application project that contains the distribution data for the relevant components. To do so, choose menu path **File · New · Project...**, select **J2EE** on the left-hand side, and **Web Application Project** on the right, and click **Next**. Enter "ResManWar" as the project name, leave the other default settings as they are, and click **Next**. Now select the projects that belong to this distribution—*ResManWeb* in this case—and click **Finish** to confirm.

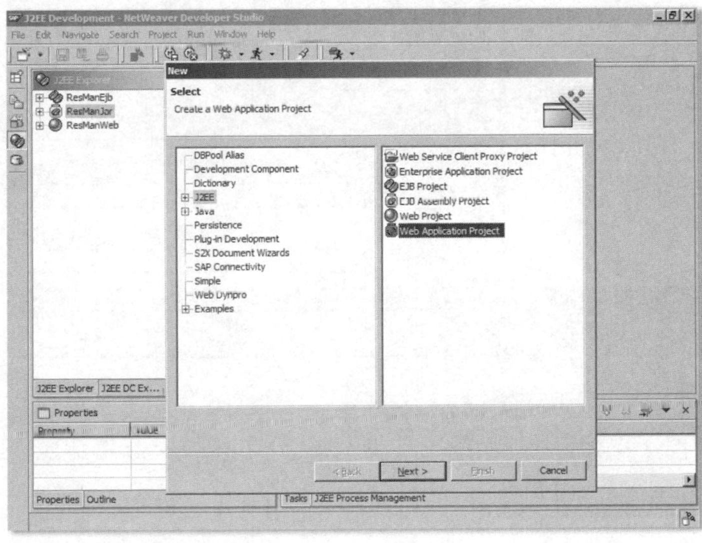

Figure 6.43 The ResManWar Project

Configuring Descriptors When you expand the appropriate node, you'll see two XML descriptors that are valid for this project: *WEB-INF/web.xml* and *WEB-INF/web-j2ee-engine.xml*. They are both XML files that you can also manipulate with a text editor outside of the development environment. They are used for physical and virtual localization of JSPs and servlets during the transport to the J2EE server.

In this example, *WEB-INF/web.xml* is used to create URL mappings and metadata, and configure security/authentication information. Click the file name and switch to the **General** tab. Enter the name of the Web application, "ResMan", as the **Display Name** and enter an appropriate description in the **Description** field. You can leave the other default values alone.

Creating URL Mappings Now click the **Mapping** tab, where you configure the virtual paths to the servlet and the JSP. These mappings create an additional level of abstraction that helps you every time the real URLs of JSPs or servlets change due to their enhancement, separation, or merging. If you studied the listings in the above examples carefully, you will have noticed that some places—such as the dispatcher, which delegates the HTML generation to the JSP—use names that not been defined yet.

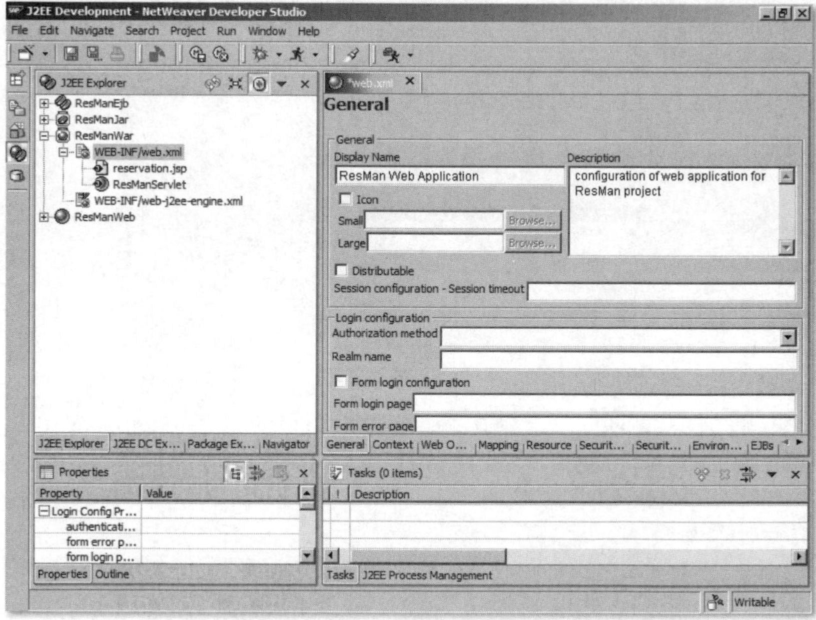

Figure 6.44 The web.xml Descriptor

To do this now, click **Add two new entries to the Servlet Mapping** area, by selecting *reservation.jsp* and *ResManServlet* from the list of servlets that appears. You may recall that the J2EE engine also creates and compiles JSPs as servlets. You can apply that information here and use them as such. Enter the following URL patterns for the respective servlet.

Creating a WAR

To transform the Web project to a transportable state, you must create a new Web archive (*WAR*) file in the last step. To do so, after you have saved all the data, right-click Web project *ResManWar* to display its context menu and select menu item **Build WAR File**.

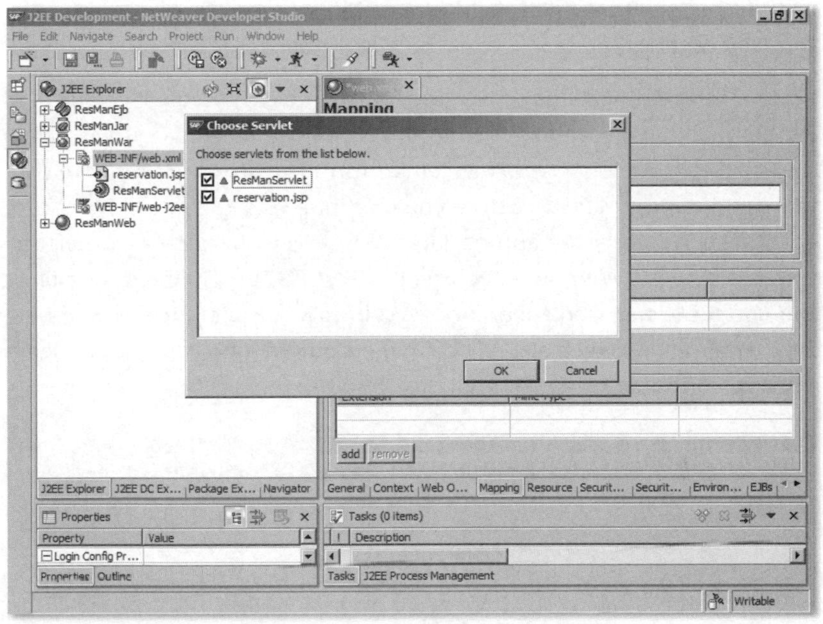

Figure 6.45 URL Mappings

Creating an Enterprise Application Project

To combine the *WAR* and *JAR* files that come from the Enterprise JavaBeans distribution packages and form a finished application distribution, you have to create an *enterprise application project*. The result is an enterprise archive (*EAR*), which is theoretically executable on any J2EE server without requiring any further changes—fully compliant with the Java development paradigm: *Compile once, run anywhere*.

To create a new enterprise application project, choose **File · New · Project...** to start the project wizard. Select the **Enterprise Application Project** under **J2EE** and click **Next**. Enter "ResManEar" as the project name and click **Next**. Select the *ResManWar* Web project as the sole referenced project and click **Finish** to confirm.

A new node now appears in the J2EE Explorer. It contains the application descriptors, *META-INF/application.xml* and *META-INF/application-j2ee-engine.xml*. Select the former and enter "ResManEar" and an appropriate **Description** in the **General** tab.

Defining the Application URL

Now switch to the **Modules** tab. You can now define a URL for your project; the application will be published on the J2EE server under this URL. Choose **ResManWar** from the list on the left and enter "/ResMan" in the **Context Root** field. Your application will then be available under this URL on the J2EE server after the deployment process.

Generating the EAR and Deployment

You are now just two steps away from having an executable JSP version of ResMan. You first have to generate the enterprise archive (*EAR*) and then deploy it to the J2EE server. You can perform the first step using the context menu for *ResManEar*. Before you continue with the deployment process, check whether the appropriate J2EE server is available. To perform this test, choose **Window · Preferences · SAP J2EE Engine** to configure the correct server, and then choose **Window · Preferences · Software Deployment Manager** and click **Check connection**; you should see a positive confirmation as shown in Figure 6.46.

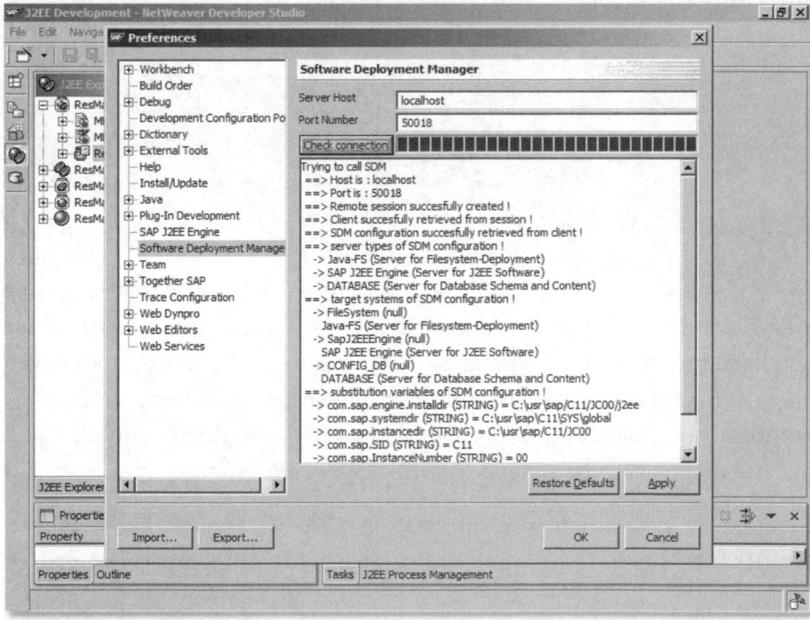

Figure 6.46 SDM Connection Check

You should now see the *ResManEar.ear* file as a subnode of *ResManEar* in the *J2EE Explorer*; select **Deploy** from its context menu to transport it to the J2EE server.

Testing

Assuming that your J2EE server can be reached on a host called *J2EEServer* under port *50000*, you can reach your application under the following URL:

http://J2EEServer:50000/ResMan

In addition, make sure that the corresponding instance of the SAP DB is running properly; if it isn't, use the SAP Management Console to start it.

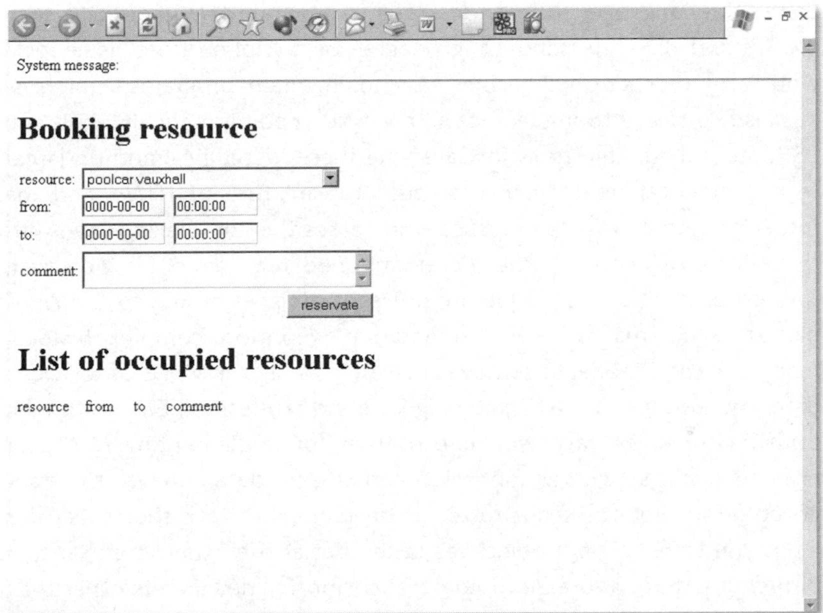

Figure 6.47 Executed ResMan Application

You can now test your ResMan application extensively by reserving resources and canceling existing reservations. At this point, we should point out that the above demonstration application does not perform any syntax check for the date and time information. Therefore, to avoid database errors, be sure to adhere to the specified format.

Web Dynpro

Now that you have already learned about one popular technology for creating Web-based user interfaces under Java, this section will initially examine the concepts of a relatively new SAP user interface technology,

Web Dynpro. The conceptual part of this section is valid for both the Java side and the ABAP side—although the technology has not been released yet for the latter.

You will then lay the cornerstone for implementing the ResMan application with Web Dynpro. After you have examined the SAP NetWeaver Developer Studio and its tools in the context of Web Dynpro programming, you will develop the actual ResMan application in Java.

Overview Web Dynpro is another technology that was developed to implement graphical user interfaces. It was designed to address the specific deficiencies of the existing technologies in the SAP and J2EE environments. Server-side languages that are designed to generate HTML directly, such as JSPs and BSPs, demand a high degree of discipline from developers who want to create extensible, easy to maintain programs—not least because you have to implement all necessary coding manually. JSPs and BSPs are not suitable tools for satisfying these ideological and (in larger teams) practical requirements because the mixture of HTML and the respective script language drastically increases the complexity—and thus the effort—of achieving the aforementioned requirements. Moreover, the responsibilities are frequently not separated according to the MVC pattern, which makes the implementation even more complex. Instead, many JSP and BSP pages retrieve their own data, convert it to localized data, and also handle all dispatching inbound requests to EJBs. Although both technologies have workable options for implementing MVC, for example, using servlets as controllers and EJBs for data retrieval, the associated effort required tends to tempt developers to take shortcuts—this helps you to reach your objectives faster, but at the expense of clarity, a proper structure, and ease of comprehension for developers other than the initial one.

From ITS ... In the early days of SAP Web integration, the Internet Transaction Server (ITS) allowed us to make transactions somewhat Web-capable, but, today, it doesn't even approximate the architecture or the capabilities required of a modern GUI design. Moreover, it generates an unreasonably high load on the network and servers. Once it is linked with a Web server through the CGI interface (Common Gateway Interface), there are three ways for creating Web-capable transactions with the ITS, each of which generates HTML for a browser in accordance with the CGI model.

1. **Emulated transactions**
   You can rebuild transactions in a Screen Painter; in the process, the ITS fills the original dynpros with macros, evaluates the result, and converts it to HTML.
2. **Translated transactions**
   Most of the standard transactions have a template defined in Business HTML, and therefore, templates don't have to be created from scratch. However, the data interchange is still based on filling the actual dynpros with macros.
3. **RFC connections**
   The HTML required for the display can also be retrieved directly from the server, using an RFC call to a remote-enabled function module.

The ITS solution never established itself in actuality, however, because many transactions—especially those involving complex GUI elements—could never be converted properly and the entire process was and is highly susceptible to disturbances anyway.

... to Dynpro ...

Similarly, dynpros are not suitable for Web publication. Although the client/server architecture makes them network-capable, an ITS is required to display them in a Web browser. Moreover, they do not clearly separate the presentation logic, user interaction, and data retrieval, as demanded by the MVC model.

... to Web Dynpro

To eliminate all these deficiencies and expand the development paradigm to meet new requirements such as platform independence, a new, metadata-based language was created to describe graphical user interfaces in the Web—Web Dynpro.

This new technology is a standardized, flexible, extensible solution that is intended to overcome the following factors that are typical of Web-based applications: the instability of the heterogeneous Web environment (which makes it extremely difficult to achieve a uniform presentation for all potential users); poor performance due to iterative load processes; user navigation that can be inefficient at times; and the difficulty of managing session data correctly. The application architecture of Web Dynpro also helps to avoid problems with reusing existing coding (modularization) that can otherwise occur when developing Web-based applications.[1]

1 Other benefits of Web Dynpro include independence of the browser version, 508 accessiblity, internationalization, and support for a wide range of user devices (such as BlackBerry).

The SAP NetWeaver Developer Studio is equipped with various plug-ins, which provide an easy-to-use GUI for creating views and navigating between them. Views can be anchored in *view sets* or exist as single screens. The *inbound* and *outbound plugs* provide an entry to and exit from a view. These navigation points (plugs) can be connected with a navigation link and represent potential navigation between the involved views. Navigations to views can be triggered through the event control. The views that are accessed through the navigation links are then visible.

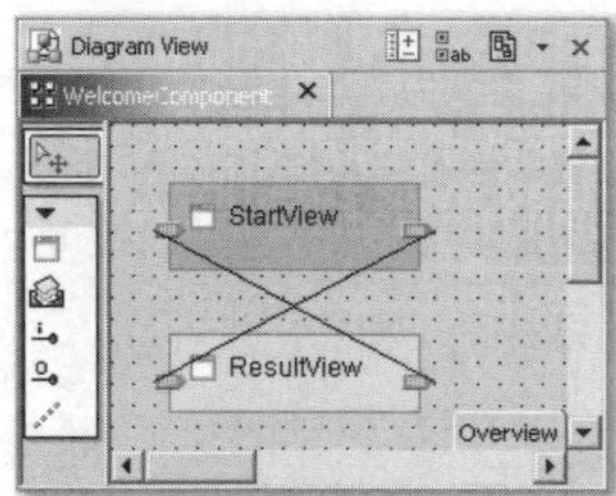

Figure 6.48 Navigation Between Views

Communication Model

Aside from these intentional jumps, the browser does not usually reload a page, but instead uses an internal client (implemented in JavaScript) to address and communicate with the server. This enables you to implement data comparisons or retrieve page contents through delta data packages—which significantly reduces the network load on one hand, but on the other hand, greatly increases the complexity of the communication steps. The metadata approach in Web Dynpro makes this complexity completely transparent for developers, however, avoiding contact with the complexity. If you examine the history and development of Web browsers in general—and the associated compatibility problems in particular—it is soon evident that a modern browser with corresponding JavaScript capabilities is required to successfully conduct comparisons of this type.

The major advantage of the reduced network load, by only transmitting the delta data, can be found in the usability of browser-based interfaces. The typical "jitter" that occurs— because refreshing a Web page requires reloading its entire contents—is lost, resulting in more application-like user guidance. Once again, JavaScript plays a vital role here, by dynamically updating the hierarchical tree structure on which the data model of a Web page is based—the Document Object Model (DOM)—integrating the comparison data from the server selectively.

As was already repeatedly mentioned, Web Dynpro is based on an abstraction layer formulated in XML, which initially gives it a high degree of platform independence. This metadata contains all the information involving the user interface design, connections to data sources, dialog flow control, and the corresponding mapping. It is generated automatically, based on graphically created designs from Web Dynpro projects in the SAP NetWeaver Developer Studio. On this basis, the development environment then generates equivalent coding at compilation time in either Java or ABAP, specifying the platform and making it visible and easy to work with for the end user. **Architecture**

The implementation language—options so far are restricted to Java and ABAP in SAP Web Application Server 6.40[2]—can be selected for the respective target platform at design time. The few components that still have to be implemented manually, such as the connection and access to data sources, can then be entered in the selected language and compiled at deployment time. The resulting coding is then fed into the respective runtime environment and executed there when queries are received.

A Web Dynpro project can be divided into four components, each of which can be subdivided further. Aside from the integrated dictionary, the *Web Dynpro applications* are the central components within a project. Currently, they serve as the definition for using a Web Dynpro Component with specific parameters. Components encapsulate views, along with their corresponding controllers. The last element of a Web Dynpro project—in the MVC concept framework—is the model. **Applications**

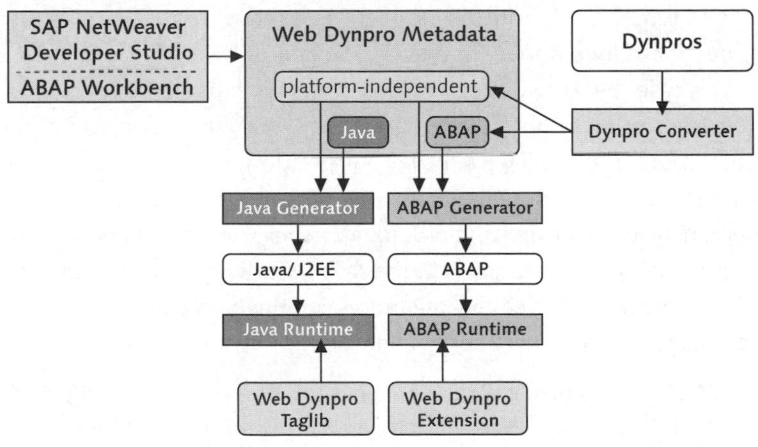

Figure 6.49 The Web Dynpro Architecture

2 Not yet released for customers.

Web Dynpro applications are central components of a Web Dynpro project. They encapsulate components, making them a collection of elementary components from the overall application. When you create a Web Dynpro project, it is the application that is made available to the runtime environment. Web Dynpro Runtime is integrated in the SAP Web Application Server and consists of engines for the supported programming languages. In the current version of SAP Web AS (Release 6.40), the Web Dynpro Runtime includes J2EE and ABAP. The implementation of .NET is planned for in the future. The application metadata is then used to generate an appropriate implementation, based on the integration and the selected platform. Specifically, this involves generated classes that are executed at runtime. The automation of the conventiontied source code generation featured in the SAP NetWeaver Developer Studio enables the consistent implementation of the MVC pattern.

The Web Dynpro application is also the component that the browser calls. As such, it represents the starting point for the program and refers to the initial view. Both the configuration and creation of a Web Dynpro application are performed declaratively, which lets you define settings such as authentication or an expiration time.

In the next section, we will examine Web Dynpro specifically based on Web Dynpro for Java.

Java Dictionary In Web Dynpro projects, the *Java Dictionary* makes it possible for developers to create user-defined data types and structures in an integrated manner—doing so autonomously, without having to maintain a separate project with type "Java Dictionary project." In contrast to the Java Dictionary project described above, however, you can define only simple data types in this case. Because a Web Dynpro project is active only at the presentation layer of an application architecture, you don't need to define database tables because all data retrieval is performed using one or more external modules. Therefore, you can use data types, for example, to force certain validation rules that would not otherwise be possible due to insufficient data type declarations in the Java Dictionary or were not provided. For definitive information regarding creating and configuring data types, see the Java Dictionary section later in this chapter.

Model Because Web Dynpro projects take place at the presentation level exclusively, data manipulation here is categorically prohibited. While Java classes are theoretically capable of retrieving data manually—through JDBC or SQLJ, for example—you should refrain from using this option so as not to compromise consistency and structure. Instead of manual data retrieval, Web Dynpro projects provide *models*: data models that are derived directly from the interface definition of a module in the business logic layer. While this interface definition can have almost any format, WSDL (which you will remember from our discussion of Web services) is the first choice. For that reason, other types of interface descriptions are initially converted to WSDL, which is then used to automatically generate the Java classes that serve as proxies for accessing the respective data model.

Consequently, a Web Dynpro application merely provides the graphical interface for the user, as a front end for any data model. From the perspective of the Web Dynpro application, the data model is interchangeable to an extent; from the perspective of the data model, the downstream Web Dynpro application is also completely interchangeable. This strict adherence to loose coupling between the individual parts of an application once again complies with the MVC model for application development, increasing the reusability of components in the individual layers. Accordingly, you can link data models and application components from many different technological areas with a Web Dynpro. In practice, data models in Web Dynpro appear as flexible tree structures whose individual nodes can be linked with any other nodes of other data models, such as those found in the individual Web Dynpro components. This mapping intertwines the data structures, transferring the inbound and outbound values.

The MVC model within the Web Dynpro concept supports several different types of model linking. The three most important methods are explained below.

UML-XMI

Unified Modeling Language (UML) is a graphical notation used to plan object-oriented software systems. It is widespread in industry and has established itself as a de facto standard. It permits the description of software of any breadth and granularity, and is therefore suitable for communication with both customers and developers. Because UML is a graphical notation that uses diagrams, it requires a representation in a character-based data format to be machine-processed. This is provided by the *XML Metadata Interchange Format* (XMI), which is supported by many vendors of UML software (such as Rational Rose).

Ultimately, the description of a software model and structure by XMI represents an interface description. Although its objectives are much broader than WSDL, transformation technologies such as XSLT can convert it relatively simply. This approach makes it possible to generate an interface for any software model and integrate it in Web Dynpro. Note, however, that such interfaces don't necessarily mask a specific application, as XMI is currently generated more from theoretical models than from actual program coding.

Adaptive RFC

Integration with a BAPI is the preferred method for linking a business model with a Web Dynpro application. On consideration, this is only logical since BAPIs are used exclusively to make the business logic in the SAP world available to external applications, and are also the preferred method for accessing ABAP components and business objects from within Java. The import of an RFC module to a Web Dynpro application is performed interactively in the model-binding concept. Developers can spontaneously log on to a server and select the relevant RFC modules for a specific application from all those available.

Adaptive RFC represents an enhancement to the original RFC model. It features dynamic behavior that enables developers to use the logic encapsulated in BAPIs even after a structural modification. This can be done without creating another model (BAPI) for the modified backend or rebuilding the proxy for the new structure. As a result, the structure defined at development time is no longer used at runtime; instead, the Web Dynpro model synchronizes the structure data with the structure definition on the backend. The context is also defined from these structures. To implement this concept, the context does not create the structure attributes until runtime, which means subsequent changes can be reflected automatically. Accordingly, the Web Dynpro context has a dynamic, adaptive behavior.

From a technical perspective, the generated Java proxies merely represent a higher-level encapsulation of a Java Connector access for an RFC model.

Web Service Definition

Another option for connecting an external model is to integrate a Web service and its interface description. Because Web services are implemented in every programming language and can be provided by a variety of servers, this medium enables Web Dynpro applications to be integrated with almost any data model. This fact is another argument in favor of Web Dynpro technology, because it makes it easy to use advanced GUI technology (such as Web Dynpro) to connect legacy components to the Web, thereby, optimizing the best of existing investments in other systems.

Nonetheless, the primary use of the Web service interface for Web Dynpro is to integrate Enterprise JavaBeans with the Web Dynpro technology, as there is currently no native interface to EJBs, even though both technologies—in the case of J2EE Runtime for Web Dynpro—are based on the same implementation language and can use the same application architecture (J2EE).

Web Dynpro Components

Web Dynpro components encapsulate the actual implementation of a Web Dynpro, its views, and its controllers. Components can generally be assigned to an application, but this is not mandatory. Any integration of the above models also has to take place here in order to map the data structures of the subordinate entities contained in the component—such as controllers and input/output elements of views.

A major aspect in programming Web-based applications is the life cycle of the software components used. Three persistence layers can be defined: *Data structures at application level* are visible to all users of that application, and continue until the application itself is terminated—upon restart of the J2EE server at the earliest. *Data structures based on the user session* are visible only for a single user, but over several requests. They are not deleted until the session is terminated, for example, when the user logs off from the system. Lastly, there are also *data structures at request level*, which are recalculated during each new user request. Each of these layers is represented by the appropriate entities of a Web Dynpro component.

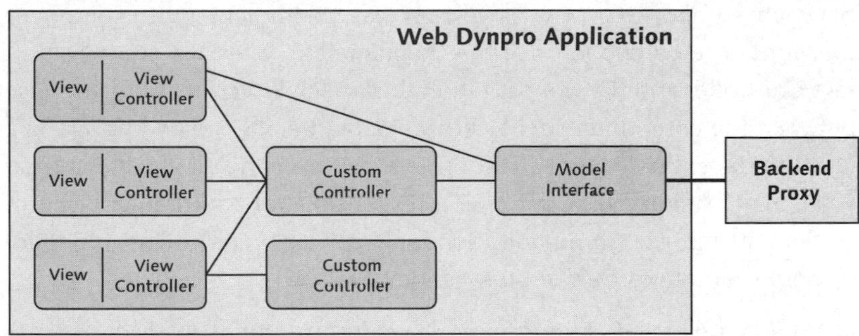

Figure 6.50 Degrees of Persistence of Web Dynpro Entities

Accordingly, Web Dynpro components are persistent for the entire life cycle of an application, which makes sense because they provide structure data that is required—by every user and his or her requests—for external data models. *Custom controllers* are more temporary. These session-dependent entities of a Web Dynpro application oversee connections to external data models and manage the bidirectional data transfer between them. They have to be active for a complete user session—not only to use resources efficiently, but also (and primarily) to make this data available over multiple requests and views. It could be useful, for example, to use the same information in different places in different views, without having to request this data actively from the external data model each time. The delta data comparisons that are used within the Web Dynpro technology, which are intended to reduce network load, would not even be possible if the data model had to be requested completely each time.

Views—which can be grouped together in *view sets* and then into *windows*—represent the shortest-lived independent entity. They save data for the duration of only one request, and usually use it only to retrieve data from the controller or initiate data transport into the underlying system.

Web Dynpro Component Interfaces

Web Dynpro components have *component interfaces*. A component interface is a controller that defines the public access point to the component. None of the other controllers for this component is visible externally. When components are nested, their component interfaces are also responsible for communication among the nested components themselves. Developers must implement the interface functions as method calls.

The obligatory *programmatic interface* is responsible for communication between components. The developer has to implement the interface functions. The components of the Programmatic Interface are the Interface Controller and the Configuration Controller, which serve as interface between the components. They enable data interchange and navigation: The Interface Controller is responsible for exchanging business data, while the Configuration Controller is responsible for controlling the component attributes. Communication between the controllers is implemented via method calls or by triggering events.

Controllers

Controllers are located between model and view, and oversee all communication between the two. They format the model data to enable its presentation in the view. The controller is also responsible for interaction with the user; it processes the user's inputs and forwards them to the model. Lastly, it is accountable for event handling: When the user triggers an event, such as clicking a button, the controller initiates the corresponding action—for instance, executing a method.

Consequently, controllers define the complete control flow within a Web Dynpro application.

As previously mentioned, the Web Dynpro technology uses different controller types than the extended MVC model. The reaction to user interaction occurs in the *view controller*. Every view has a view controller. There are also global controllers for multiple views, which are called *custom controllers*. In addition, every Web Dynpro component automatically has a *component controller*, which is the main controller within the component and belongs in the custom controller category.

Every controller contains data, which is saved in a context. The content of a view controller context (*view context*) usually lasts as long as the view is displayed in the browser. In contrast, the data in the custom controller context (*custom context*) is retained as long as the component is used—for the duration of the active user session.

In addition to the actual user data, contexts also contain metadata that defines the structure of the user data. The contexts are not a passive data store, but instead a highly dynamic, hierarchical data store whose metadata is usually defined at design time. It is also possible to modify the structure of contexts at runtime. In contrast, the contents are unknown until runtime itself. From a technical programming perspective, the context is a central, dynamic class that supplies the corresponding controller with data. The declarations that are defined at design time are used to generate the relevant methods in the context that permit retrieval of the user data at runtime.

The data in the context has a hierarchical structure. This tree structure consists of nodes and attributes, where an attribute is defined as a node without any children (end node). The top element is a root node.

Due to the limited life cycle of the data in the context, the next step is the persistent data retention, which requires transferring the data to the model. To do so, you have to link the contexts, which involves the following steps:

1. The UI element is linked to an element (node or attribute) in the view context. This process is called *data binding*. The user inputs are transferred directly to the view context.
2. The element of the view context is linked with an element of the custom context through a *context mapping*. This makes it possible to temporarily buffer and restore data.

3. The element of the custom context is linked with an element of the model, which is responsible for persistent storage or retrieval of the data.

This approach automates the data transport between view and model in both directions. However, there is an important difference between binding and mapping—*binding* refers to binding a UI element to an element in the view context, while *mapping* describes a connection between contexts.

In addition, every controller contains separate areas for source coding, which developers can use to insert source coding manually. Any coding outside of these special areas is deleted automatically, either by implemented methods or event handling. Examples of events include initialization, calling, or termination of a view, actions initiated by the user, and events called by a controller.

View The view represents the design and is responsible for the graphical display of application data in the browser. It is part of the user interface and is described by a layout. The view is represented by a rectangular area in the browser window. The layout is defined using UI elements, such as labels, text fields, buttons, or tables. Views can be nested within one another and grouped together to form view sets, which are used to display several views in the browser at the same time.

You can use typical Java layout managers, such as FlowLayout or GridLayout, to structure a view. The UI elements are then arranged in accordance with the rules of the layout manager.

Navigation Clicking a link in a Web page usually sends you to the next page. This process is called *navigation*. To implement navigation within a Web Dynpro application, you create links between views, using their outbound and inbound plugs. To set a reference between two views, you merely have to link the outbound plug of the initial view with the inbound plug of the target view.

Accordingly, inbound plugs define the entry points for a view, while outbound plugs enable navigation from the initial view to the next view. These references between views are called *navigation links*. Each outbound plug can have only one navigation link, while inbound plugs can be the target of multiple links. When you create a Web Dynpro application, you set the navigation links with Drag&Drop between the views (or more precisely, their plugs). Although a view doesn't have to have an outbound plug, an inbound plug is essential, or the view could never be accessed. The link information between the plugs is saved separately; the views do not know the links.

Views and view sets cannot be displayed independently. To display them in a browser, we need a new component, the *window*. You assign the views and view sets to the window. Therefore, each application has to have at least one window.

Each window has an interface view, which is the interface to the window. It is linked with a Web Dynpro application and can be called with a URL. Consequently, when you start a Web Dynpro application, the interface view of the start window is the target object.

ABAP: From Dynpro to Web Dynpro

Release 6.40 of the SAP Web Application Server features a new method of developing SAP applications. New development tools are available in the ABAP environment, in particular, a conversion tool that transforms existing dynpros into Web Dynpros.

The new Web Dynpro technology is also based on the MVC design concept. So, when dynpros are converted to Web Dynpros, the screens are converted to Web Dynpro views and the dynpro flow logic is converted to Web Dynpro controllers.

The Web Dynpro Runtime also has to perform various tasks. It has to integrate the functions of dynpro processing and the control framework. The event handling has to be linked to the appropriate ABAP modules. In addition, the dynpro calls from ABAP (such as `LOOP AT SCREEN`) have to be caught and rerouted to the Web Dynpro Runtime. The business logic is not affected by the conversion.

Preview

Because the application is saved as metadata, Web Dynpros are platform-independent. Now that you have learned about the Web Dynpro concepts and architecture, you will now implement an actual Web Dynpro application—again based on ResMan.

Web Dynpro IDE

The SAP NetWeaver Developer Studio is the Web Dynpro development environment. Its Web Dynpro perspective contains tools that help you create Web Dynpro applications, including a WYSIWYG editor, Drag&Drop functions, and wizards for easy-to-use, graphical creation of applications. All programming aspects of the user interface are fully automated during application development within the IDE framework.

Assume, for example, that you want to display data on the screen. This data comes from a context. The developer's task is now to define the layout, contexts, and mappings. The corresponding coding for the user interface and data transport is generated automatically.

By generating the implementation according to specific conventions, the SAP NetWeaver Developer Studio provides for much better consistency within the application than could be achieved manually.

To make all of this possible, the SAP NetWeaver Developer Studio provides the following tools:

Web Dynpro Explorer

The Web Dynpro Explorer gives you an overview of all the components of an application in a hierarchical structure. It displays all the Web Dynpro data, in addition to the necessary Java Dictionary types and source coding.

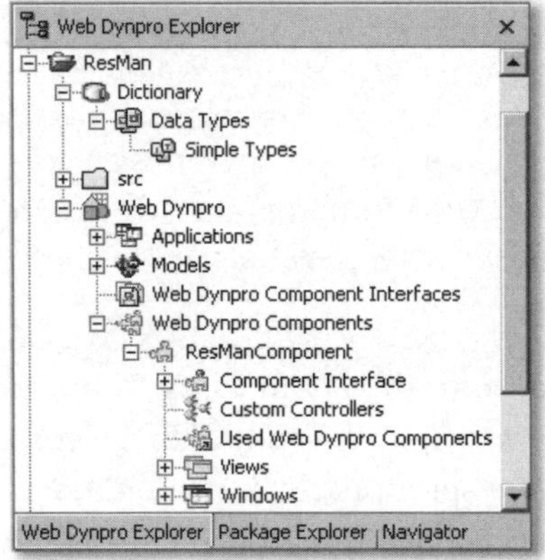

Figure 6.51 Structure of a Project

Application Modeler

You use the Application Modeler to define views and group them in view sets. You assign inbound and outbound plugs to them and set references as navigation links between them.

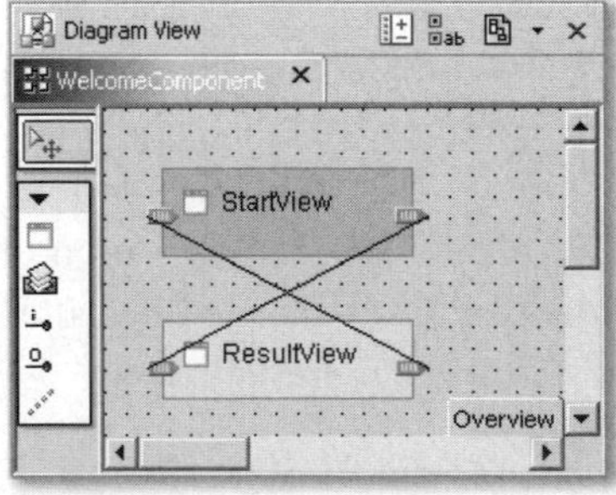

Figure 6.52 Modeled Navigation Between Views

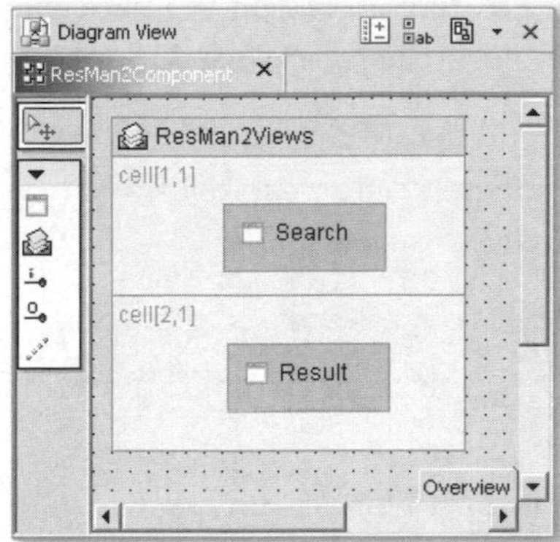

Figure 6.53 Grouping Views Together to Form View Sets

View Designer

You use the View Designer to create the view layout, positioning the UI elements with the Drag&Drop method. Their specific arrangement will depend on your selected layout manager. The editor features WYSIWYG functionality.

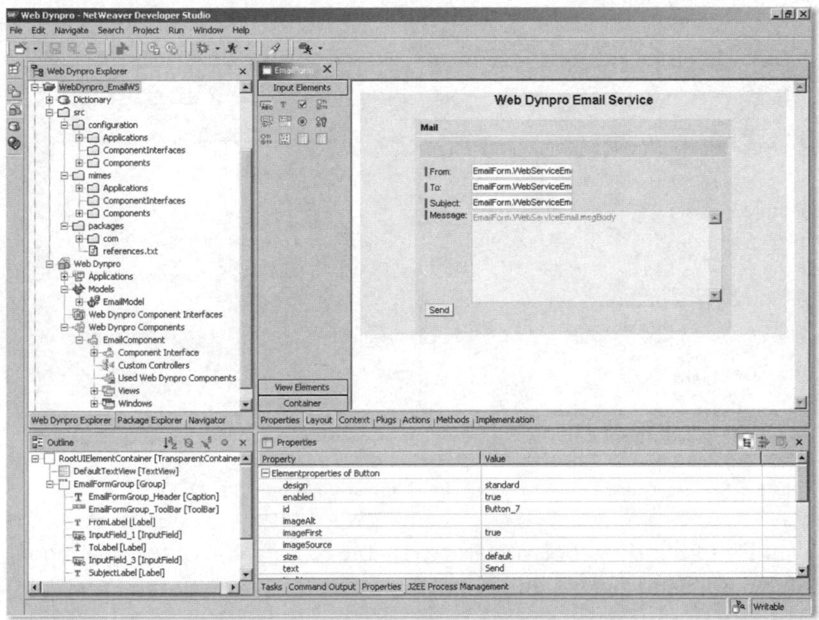

Figure 6.54 View Designer (Upper Right) Within the SAP NetWeaver Developer Studio

Over 30 UI elements are available for display within the views. They are based on controls technology, which permits client-side user interaction (such as scrolling within views) without creating a load on the back-end system. Each UI element has configurable properties, such as visibility and layout information.

The *Outline view* lists all the utilized UI elements. You can edit the properties of each selected element in the *Properties view*.

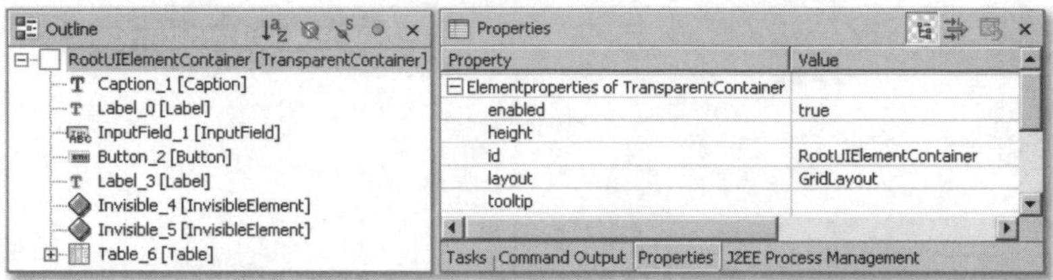

Figure 6.55 Listing and Properties of UI Elements

Controller Editor and Context Editor

The controller and context editor provide graphics-based support for defining the hierarchically organized context structure and the data mapping between the elements, which is a prerequisite for the data flow within the application.

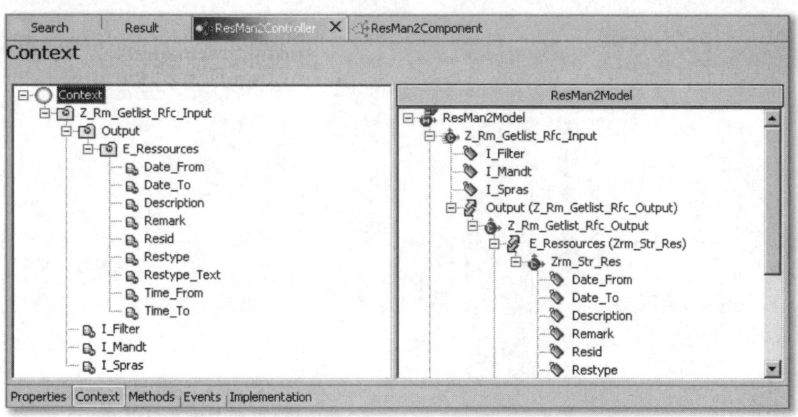

Figure 6.56 Structure of the Context (Left) and the Model (Right)

Web Dynpro model tools are also available to help you define the model, which enables you to supply data from the back-end system. The Message Editor supports the generating and editing of text messages, which you can use easily in a Web Dynpro application. Messages can take the form of errors, warnings, and information messages.

Web Dynpro Development

Web Dynpro application development can be divided into two phases. The first phase is creating the actual application, which is saved entirely as metadata. Essentially, this involves connecting external resources to a model, defining and mapping the contexts, and preparing the layout—including binding the UI elements to the contexts.

The second phase is the implementation, which is independent of these declarative activities and performed exclusively in the controllers. The manual source coding includes any event handling, exception handling, and method implementations.

Events can be used to initiate processing steps. You have to implement their processing logic yourself, using methods that are called when a specific event occurs. Exception handling deals with processing the errors and exceptions that occur at runtime. In addition, you can also program regular methods to encapsulate and deploy specific functions.

The primary focus of Web Dynpro is the visual design of applications, with the objective of minimizing the manual implementation. Web Dynpro reduces the required implementation effort by around 80%; the manual coding is not added until later in the development cycle.

System Requirements

Certain system requirements must be fulfilled to develop and execute Web Dynpro applications. In this case, you need an installation of the SAP NetWeaver Developer Studio to create the applications. The SAP J2EE Engine is used in addition to the IDE. If these components are running on different computers, we recommend allocating 512 MB RAM to each. If both run on the same system, however, 512 MB RAM is the minimum requirement; 1 GB is recommended. An SAP connection is often available in the network. If an SAP connection is not available, or if you want to connect to an SAP System for testing purposes only, we recommend installing a local instance of the Mini Web AS for Java. This slimmed-down standalone version of the SAP Web AS is available from SAP free of charge under the developer license[3] and can be installed on your local workstation. A database is also integrated in the distribution. Various other tools are available, including the Visual Administrator, which lets you configure the Java Engine. JDBC configurations are required here, for example, to permit database access from within applications via JNDI. Yet another tool is the SQL Studio, a frontend that gives developers direct access to the database.

To execute the Web Dynpro, SAP requires Internet Explorer 5.5 and later or Netscape 7 and later. This complete, local software environment can

3 Download from the SAP Developer Network under *http://sdn.sap.com*.

easily consume up to 10 GB of hard disk space; a modern processor with a frequency of at least one GHz is also recommended.

Other Prerequisites

In addition to the hardware and software requirements, knowledge of the technology is also essential. While it is relatively easy to navigate around the SAP NetWeaver Developer Studio, its use consists of more than just Drag&Drop. Creating the structure of a Web Dynpro application alone requires detailed knowledge of the structure of an application. And programming skills are required when you have to create your own implementations (at the latest); if you plan to use Java, you need to know about object-oriented programming and be familiar with several APIs in the J2EE architecture.

Tutorial: Web Dynpro Development

ResMan Example Application

This introduction to Web Dynpro development demonstrates the major aspects of programming. The declarative part is covered first, followed by the implementation. Along the way, you'll get an impression of the development process, based on the characteristic situations of Web Dynpro in the ResMan scenario.

Scenario and Objective

A data model for the ResMan project already exists, as described above. We're not interested in optimizing this structure for practical use here; instead, we'll focus on creating the Web application. The data structures have been defined in the database of an existing SAP System, and the tables have already been filled with test data. An SAP Web Application Server that has access to this database contains remote-enabled function modules that meet our declared functional requirements, which are as follows:

- Creating a list with resources (all, only reserved, only available)
- Book resources (with error handling in case of overlaps)
- Cancel bookings

In the course of the project, you will link the function modules to the Web Dynpro model to integrate the functions and ultimately present the corresponding data in the view. In this example application, you'll create the views responsible for outputting the resource data. The example demonstrates the general procedure quite effectively, and shows you the basics of creating both the declaration and implementation of a Web Dynpro application.

Requirements

To develop the application, the following prerequisites must be met:

1. The SAP NetWeaver Developer Studio is installed and running.
2. The J2EE server (and therefore the SDM—Software Deployment Manager) is running.
3. You have access to an SAP System (ABAP personality). It contains function modules with the functions described above, along with the ResMan user data.

Process

To develop the application, you first define a model that implements the connection to the function module. There is also a custom controller, which is responsible for the data flow. It passes the data for display to the view on one side, while sending the parameters for the function call in the SAP System to the model on the other side. The view has several UI elements. A drop-down box is used, whose contents are extracted a value domain in the Java Dictionary. The user can select a value to determine whether to display all the resources, only reserved resources, or only available resources. As soon as a value in the drop-down box is selected, an event is triggered (dependent on the selected option), which initiates the data retrieval and facilitates the display of the requested data in a table.

Declarative Development

Switch to the *Web Dynpro perspective* within the SAP NWDS. Access to the required tools is available here. You first have to create a *Web Dynpro project*. All the other application components are defined as belonging to this project. To create *Web Dynpro components*, right-click the corresponding elements within the *Web Dynpro Explorer* to call their context menus, and select the **Create** option. A wizard appears to help you create the appropriate component.

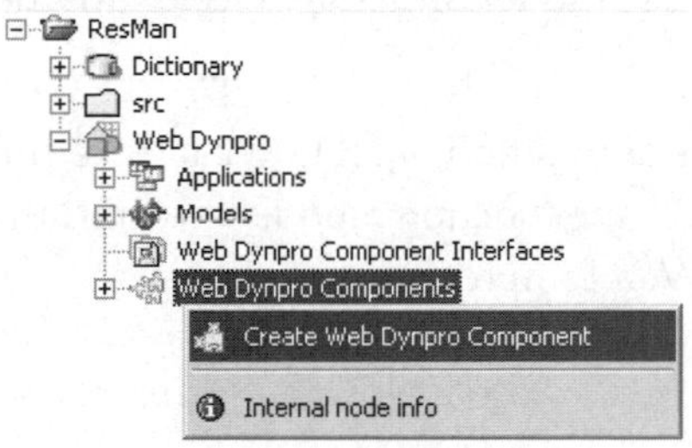

Figure 6.57 The Initial Web Dynpro Structure

Java Dictionary

At first, you define a simple data type called `resourceInput` in the Dictionary and declare it as a `String` (a simple character string). You can define a value domain under **Enumeration**. The values you enter here in the **Description** field will be displayed in a dropdown box at runtime. Therefore, the selected value, and thus the corresponding value field, represents an import parameter of the function module. It indicates which data will be returned to the Web Dynpro application: all, only utilized, or only available resources.

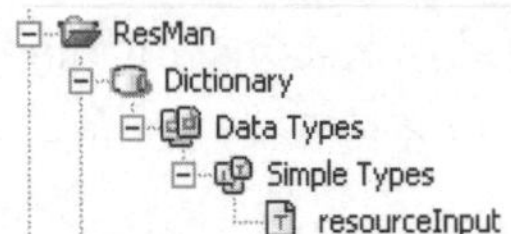

Figure 6.58 The Java Dictionary Structure

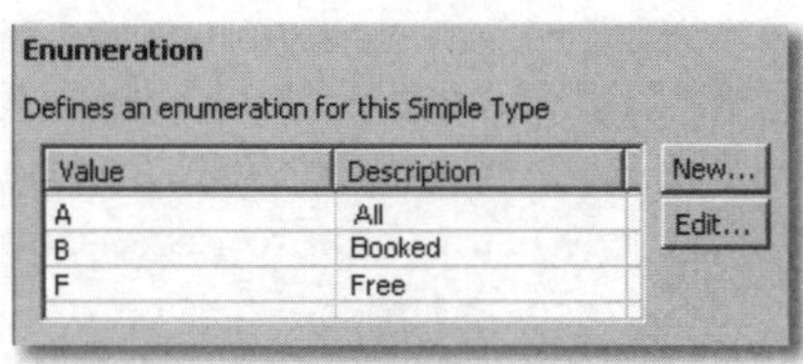

Figure 6.59 Value Domain of Simple Data Type resourceInput

Model

You now define the model, *ResManModel*. Our example involves connecting to functions in an external SAP System. To do so, a remote-enabled function module that encapsulates the business logic must be available on the ABAP side. When you select **Create Model**, a wizard appears. Select **Import RFC Model**, which represents the connection to the SAP System, and specify the connection data. The transmission protocol is RFC. In the next screen, you now select the appropriate function module, `Z_RM_GETLIST_RFC` in our case. As you know, the "Z" designates development objects in the customer namespace in the SAP System. You now define the hierarchical model structure based on the import and export parameters.

The relevant import parameter in this application, I_FILTER, can take the values A (All), B (Booked), and F (Free). The function module then returns the appropriate data records to the Web Dynpro.

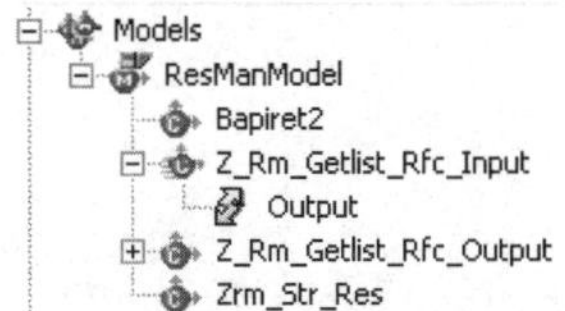

Figure 6.60 The Model Structure

In the next step, you create a component called *ResManComponent* to encapsulate the controllers and views. This component is declared with the *ResManModel* in order to use it later. You now create a custom controller, *ResManController*, under the *ResManComponent* in the project structure. In the next step, you define a new node in the context of this controller, a *model node* called `Z_Rm_Getlist_Rfc_Input`, which is required for the model binding. The node was named similar to the function module here. You now select all the data structures used in the application from the model, mapping them in the global custom context of *ResManController* in the node you just created.

Controllers

Furthermore, the wizard creates the `getResources()` method with return type `void` in the custom controller, as well as a parameter called `value` with type `String` for this method. This parameter will contain the user selection user selection from the drop-down box. The method retrieves the data at runtime. The controller source code is added to the implementation automatically.

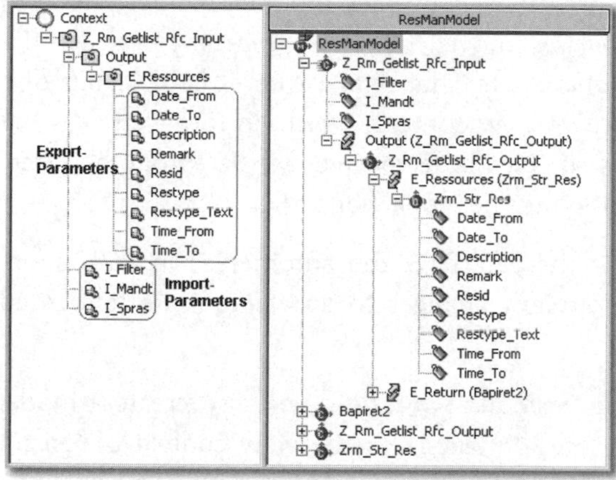

Figure 6.61 Model Binding Between Custom Context (Left) and Model (Right)

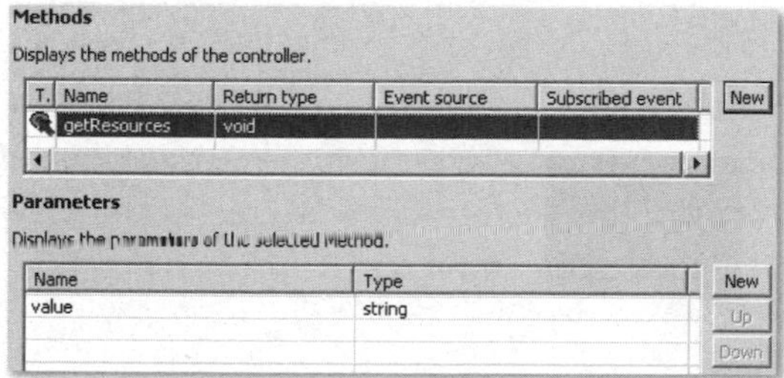

Figure 6.62 Method getResources() and Parameter Value

Views

Now, you can configure the layout of the application. Create a view set in the *ResManComponent* window. Assign a grid consisting of one column and two lines. Embed a view in each field and call these views *Search* and *Result*. The view set allows you to display both views in the browser simultaneously.

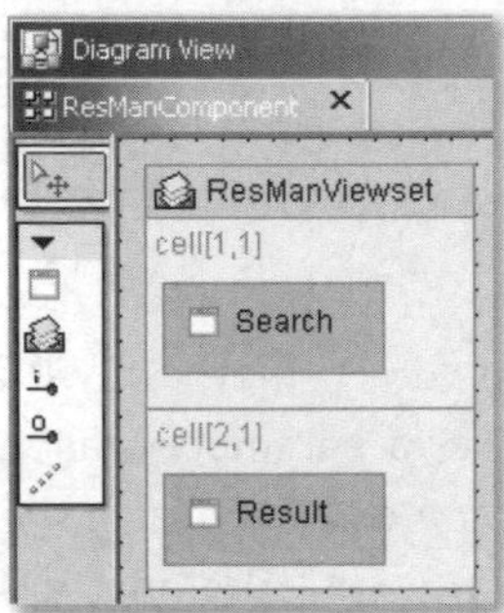

Figure 6.63 The ResMan View Set

You now have to register the global controller, *ResManController*, for both views. As in the *model binding* above, the *context mapping* between the *view context* and the global context takes place here. Each layout of a view can access only its own view context, which, in turn, retrieves the data from the global context. The model receives the data from the external resource and passes it on to the global context.

These connections define the data flow and automate it in both directions at runtime. Therefore, any changes to an element are forwarded automatically.

To implement this in the ResMan application, you also create a model node called `Z_Rm_Getlist_Rfc_Input` in the view context of *Search*. However, it maps only the import parameters of the custom context. You also create a *value attribute* called `resInput`, which points to data type `resourceInput` defined in the Java Dictionary and provides the contents for the drop-down box.

Also, you create a model node called *Resources* in the context of the *Result* view. It maps only the export parameters under the *Output* node of the context of *ResManController*. The custom context creates the view context structures shown in Figures 6.64 and 6.65.

Figure 6.64 Search View Context

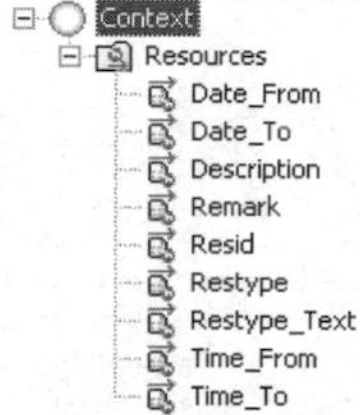

Figure 6.65 Result View Context

View Layout

In the next step, you will create the layout for the view. First configure **GridLayout** as the layout manager. You can now position the UI elements and modify their properties. Now conduct the data binding.

The *Search* view consists of labels and a drop-down box, which is tied to value attribute `resInput` (data binding) in order to transfer and display the options. Adjust the properties of the UI elements to your graphical and functional requirements.

To initiate the data retrieval at runtime, an event is triggered. To enable the view controller to process this event, create an action for it called *Go*. In the process, an event handler called `onActionGo` is created automatically, which is represented by the identically named method of the *Search* view controller. This method contains the event handling.

Lastly, the event is linked with the drop-down box. It has a property called `onSelect`, which you link to event *Go*. The *Go* event is now triggered at runtime as soon as the user makes a selection in the drop-down box.

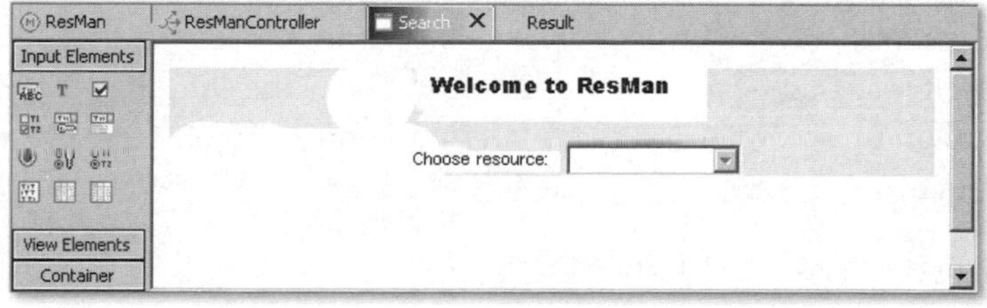

Figure 6.66 Layout of the Search View

In contrast to creating the layout for the Search view, you add only one table to the *Result* view, and assign the `dataSource` property to the *Resources* node of the *Result* view context. The following attributes below the Resources node represent the table columns. Each attribute can now be bound individually, that is, represented as a column. You can also adjust table and column properties, for example, by entering suitable column headers or changing the sequence of the columns.

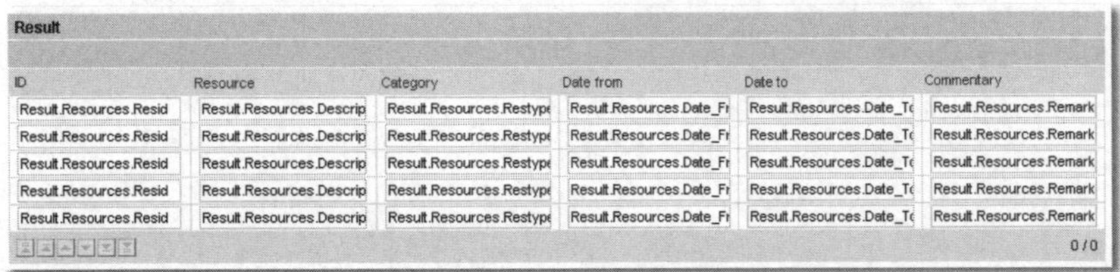

Figure 6.67 Layout of the Result View

Once you have defined the model, the global controllers, and the views (including their view controller), and bound and mapped the elements, you have completed creating the application in line with the requirements. Up to this point, everything is still saved in metadata.

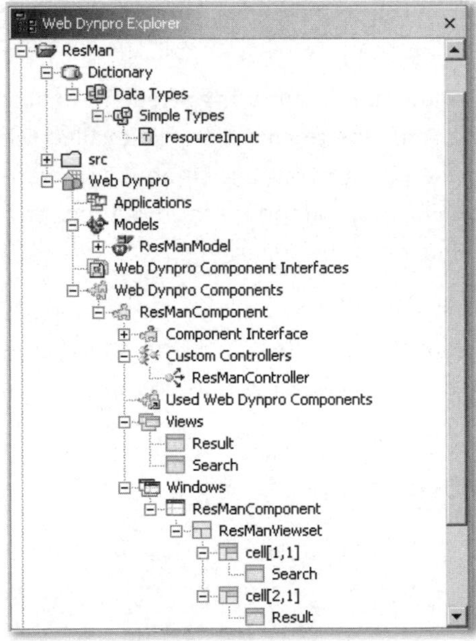

Figure 6.68 The Complete ResMan Project Structure

What we now lack is the manual implementation in the controllers.

You will first learn some general information about Java-side Web Dynpro elements and then begin the actual implementation of the ResMan application.

Implementation

Similar to a Web Dynpro application, the manual implementation is merely inserted in the controllers. A 1:1 relationship exists between a controller and its context. The dynamic controller class is provided to developers as Java object `wdThis()`, and the corresponding context as object `wdContext()`. These two objects are available in all non-static controller methods. The constructor of a controller cannot be modified and resembles the following example:

```
private final IPrivate<controllerName> wdThis;
private final IPrivate<controllerName>.
  IContextNode wdContext;

public <controllerName>(IPrivate<controllerName> wdThis){
  this.wdThis = wdThis;
  this.wdContext = wdThis.wdGetContext();
}
```

Context Node

Every context has a root node, underneath which additional attributes can be defined in a hierarchy. Because the context is completely dynamic, several conventions apply to keep the structure manageable. If you want to receive a node object as a return value, for example, you usually call the corresponding method directly, assuming you know the name of the context object. However, there are also ways of resolving this problem when you are faced with an unknown structure.

Creating a context node triggers the creation of interface `I<contextNode>Node`. In the process, the following specific methods and classes are created:

- **`wdContext().create<contextNode>Element()`**
  Returns an element from this node collection
- **`set<attributeName>()`**
  `get<attributeName>()`
  Set and get methods for an attribute of the node element
- **`.current<contextNode>Element()`**
  Get method for the current node element

- **set<attributeName>()**
  get<attributeName>()
  Set and get methods for an attribute of the current node element
- **.node<contextNode>()**
  Creates a new node object
- **getElementAt(i)**
  Returns element i of the node collection

Controller Class

Controller classes have several predefined places and methods where coding can be inserted. You cannot change the names or parameters of standard methods. For the manual implementation, there are two tags between which programmers can insert coding; this area is enclosed with `//@@begin` and `//@@end`:

```
public void wdDoInit(){
        //@@begin wdDoInit()
           //Own coding...
        //@@end
}
```

Any source coding outside of these tags will be deleted automatically, and without advance warning the next time the class is generated after changes to declarative aspects.

When a controller class is created, certain methods are always created regardless of whether you implement them or not. They are called the *standard methods* of a controller class:

```
// Constructor
public <controllerName>(IPrivate<controllerName>
  wdThis) {
  this.wdThis    = wdThis;
  this.wdContext = wdThis.wdGetContext();
}

public void wdDoInit(){
  //@@begin wdDoInit()
  //@@end
}

public void wdDoExit(){
  //@@begin wdDoExit()
  //@@end
```

```
}

//@@begin others
//@@end
```

Listing 6.26 Standard Methods of a Controller Class

Every controller is a separate, dynamically generated Java class. The controller class surrounds a subordinate dynamic class with type `IPrivate<controller_name>.IContextNode`, which is the context class of the controller. Controllers usually have only one constructor, `<controllerName>`.

Controller classes are instantiated automatically by the Web Dynpro Runtime. In the process, the `wdDoInit()` method is called immediately after the controller is instantiated. The preparatory tasks are defined in this method. In contrast, the `wdDoExit()` method is called immediately before the controller is removed by the garbage collector, and performs cleanup tasks such as logging off from the R/3 System.

Space for custom static methods and attributes is provided at the end of the controller class, between `//@@begin others` and `//@@end`.

Methods

Controller type-specific methods can also be implemented. A view controller, for example, allows you to modify UI elements with the `wdDoModifyView()` method. This is the only place within an implementation that permits changes to UI elements. This method is called immediately before the view is rendered.

You will now implement the application in our view controller, *Search*, and custom controller, *ResManController*. The view controller handles user interaction and data visualization, while the custom controller is responsible for the processing logic and external connections.

You generate a preliminary implementation within the controller tool in order to edit it. However, the true source code generation doesn't take place during this implementation phase: the application consists solely of metadata at design time. The final implementation is generated dynamically during compilation and considers any manually inserted source code.

View Controller

Let us first examine the *Search* view controller. It contains the `onActionGo()` method, which was created automatically and represents the event handler of the connected drop-down box. This method is called automatically by the Web Dynpro Runtime when the user makes a selection in the list. It is supposed to initiate data retrieval; therefore, the following call is implemented in the method:

```
String value = (String)wdContext.getCurrentElement().
  getAttributeValue("resInput");
wdThis.wdGetResManControllerController().
  getResources(value);
```

In the first step, the user input saved in attribute `resInput` is transferred to the local variable `value`. This is followed by the call of the `getResources()` method you created previously for the global controller, *ResManController*. `value` is passed on in the process. The actual data retrieval takes place in `getResources()`. In this example, these two lines represent the complete implementation of the *Search* view controller. The *Result* view controller doesn't require an implementation, as its data retrieval and display are fully implemented through automatic context mapping and data binding.

Custom Controller

The implementation in the custom controller, *ResManController*, is far more complex. You must first declare essential objects in the general area:

```
//@@begin others
JCO.Client client;
ResManModel model;
Z_Rm_Getlist_Rfc_Input input;
//@@end
```

The `client` object is required to implement the connection to the SAP System with JCo. The `model` object represents an instance of the model built in the declarative part, and `input` permits access to the context. The meaning and use of these objects will become clear in the following sections.

The `wdDoInit()` method of the global controller is called immediately after it is instantiated and looks like this:

```
public void wdDoInit(){
    //@@begin wdDoInit()
    //Create a model node object
    input = new Z_Rm_Getlist_Rfc_Input();

    //Bind the object to the model node in the context
    wdContext.nodeZ_Rm_Getlist_Rfc_Input().bind(input);
```

```
    // Instantiate the client by defining
    // the connection to the remote SAP System
    client = JCO.createClient(
       "100",        // Client
       "user",         // User
       "*******",      // Password
       "EN",           // Language: English
       "host.snp.de",  // Host name or IP of system
       "00"            // System number
    );

    // Instantiate the model with the factory
    model = (ResManModel)
    WDModelFactory.getModelInstance(
    ResManModel.class,
    WDModelScopeType.APPLICATION_SCOPE
      );

    // Assign client to the model
    model.setJcoClient(client);

    //@@end
}
```

Listing 6.27 wdDoInit() Method of the Global Controller

Class Z_Rm_Getlist_Rfc_Input represents the type of the model node. The instantiated input object is now bound to the model node in the appropriate context. This object assignment enables the mapping of the data structures. This step is followed by instantiating the connection to the SAP System, which involves specifying the user and system data. The form used here is an extremely simple way of connecting to the system. In a typical scenario, of course, it would be disastrous to specify this data—including the password—hard-coded in the source coding. Procedures are available for enabling a secure login via JNDI, in which the connections are once again maintained centrally as pools on the J2EE server. Finally, you generate the model object in the method and assign the connection to it. This step is necessary to transfer data between the model and the system.

Data Retrieval We are now missing only the implementation of the Web Dynpro-side data retrieval logic: the getResources() method. This is called indirectly (using onActionGo) upon selection in the drop-down box.

```
public void getResources(java.lang.String value){
    //@@begin getResources()
    // Establish connection to SAP System
    client.connect();

    // Set import parameters to value
    input.setI_Filter(value);

  // Set any other optional parameters (statically)
    // input.setI_Mandt("100");   // Client
    // input.setI_Spras("E");     // Language

    try{
// Call remote FM Z_RM_GETLIST_RFC
   wdContext.currentZ_Rm_Getlist_Rfc_InputElement()
                          .modelObject().execute();
    }catch(Exception ex){
       ex.printStackTrace();
    }finally{
       client.disconnect();
    }
    wdContext.nodeOutput().invalidate();

    //@@end
}
```

Listing 6.28 Web Dynpro Data Retrieval Logic

In the first step, the connection to the SAP System is established with connect(). The value variables are then passed on to import parameter I_FILTER, which is sent to the function module and specifies whether all only available, or only booked resources, will be returned. You can also set other parameters, either statically or dynamically. The function module is then called in the subsequent try ... catch block. If an error occurs, the catch branch is processed; in this case, printStackTrace() outputs the error message. The finally block is always executed, and closes the connection to the SAP System. Last but not least, the invalidate() method ensures that the remotely retrieved data is written to the custom context.

When the coding is complete, you select **Source • Organize Imports** from the context menu to ensure that all the necessary libraries are included.

Running the Application

Now that you have completed the application, you perform the last step. You create a new application, *ResManApplication*, in the Web Dynpro Explorer. You then have to save the metadata of the application.

Several prerequisites must be met in order for you to successfully deploy and run the application. The connected SAP System must be active and the corresponding remote-enabled function modules must be available. Also, the J2EE engine and the SDM have to be running; while the J2EE engine primarily provides the runtime environment, the SDM is responsible for deploying the application.

Now choose option **Deploy new archive and run** to run the application you just created. All the necessary program flows are performed during this process, including creating the project structure and generating the implementation, deployment, and running the application in the browser. Alternatively, you can also execute the build, deploy, and run processes separately.

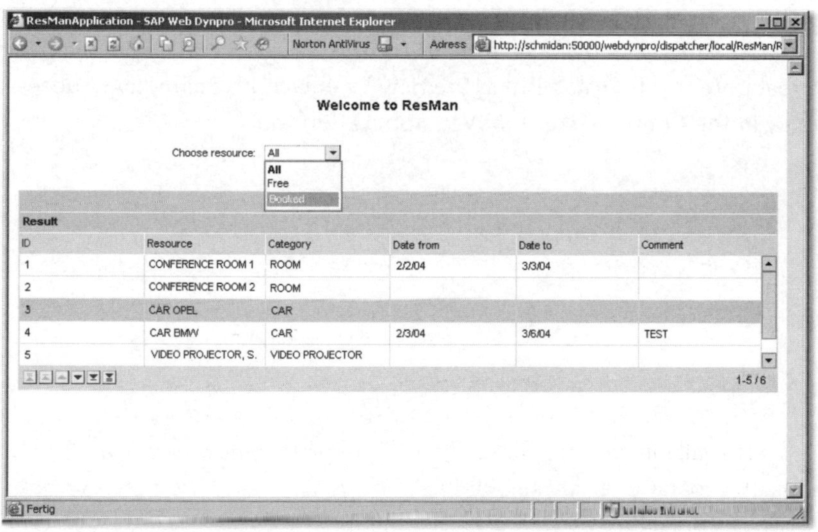

Figure 6.69 ResMan Application Running in the Browser

Result and Summary

You have now created a successful Web Dynpro application. First, within the declarative development, you defined the application's components as belonging to one project and created the user interface. Specifically, this involved the MVC components and the Java Dictionary. You then connected the model with the SAP System and declared the contexts and controller methods. Based on the created data structure, you were able to connect the UI elements—through the controller contexts—down to the model structure. These connections are called *context mapping* and *data binding*.

In the next step, you implemented the controllers. The lion's share of development effort was required by the custom controller, which is responsible for connecting to the remote SAP System, calling the appropriate function module there, and sending it the parameters. The return data transport to the frontend takes place exclusively through the connections in the data structures, and is performed automatically.

After you successfully deployed and ran the Web Dynpro application, the selected data is displayed in the browser.

Conclusion A declarative programming style successfully shifted the focus of the implementation to the design. Thanks to its high degree of automation, Web Dynpro saves developers from having to deal with too much source coding, eliminating many potential sources of errors. Moreover, the development environment adheres strictly to the MVC model, that is, the application is structured and modularized in reusable components that encapsulate the individual functions. This programming approach has great potential for establishing the new Web Dynpro technology successfully in the future market for Web application tools.

7 Application Design

This chapter deals with the problems and issues that developers—even those with many years of experience under their belts—often neglect until it is already too late, namely, strategies for designing software architectures, or design patterns.

7.1 A Typical Problem

If you've been developing applications for more than a week, you've probably had to deal with the following situation:

Your project is done, it's been tested, and it works. You're satisfied with the results. It's 3:30 p.m. on a Friday afternoon and you're looking forward to leaving the office early and driving up to the lake to relax. Your project manager comes into the office and asks you to demonstrate your software one more time. Everything is going smoothly until she drops the bomb:

"By the way, the translator for the application will be here next week. They approved the budget for the Russian translation two weeks ago."

You suddenly become aware of a very large, deep pit in your stomach. No one ever said anything about translation. You're certain that you've studied the specifications in detail. You leaf through them again quickly—nope, nothing about multiple languages. With some trepidation, you ask your project manager about the translation again, and here's your answer:

"So, what's the problem? The marketing brochures for SAP Web Application Server say that all developments support multiple languages."

You jog your memory in a desperate search for a clue. As far as you can remember, the training course you attended last summer on the subject of business server pages (BSPs) didn't mention anything about this support for multiple languages. All you know is that you're facing a tremendous amount of work. You now have to create text tables, find language-tied literals in BSP pages, views, and BSP extensions, and finally learn about how Web applications and Unicode character sets really work—after all, if your application has to be translated into Russian next week, then Japanese can't be far away.

7.2 Design Patterns

Developing software via using a design pattern does not involve examining and implementing every possible event. Instead, it implies gaining a comprehensive understanding of the difficulties of software development, declaring flexibility and ease of maintenance as the supreme objectives, and creating a place and the underlying conditions for the later on-demand implementation. Even if your requirements are solidified in a finalized, approved concept and you're absolutely certain that you will never have to deal with the current project again, as soon as you or your successor have to add a feature or try to reuse your development in a different context, you will have to deal with the aspects that you forgot or ignored the first time around.

You're probably already familiar with many of the patterns that are introduced below. In fact, you probably already use some versions of them today—maybe without even knowing it. Still, you'll find it helpful to know how other people have addressed these problems, as well as learn about the example solutions that are available for many of the aspects you have had to deal with—and will have to deal with in the future—even if you must modify them slightly to meet your needs.

If we tried to list design patterns for every possible situation in software development here, it would far exceed the scope of this book. In general, we recommend that committed developers—especially those with an inclination toward object orientation—read the related literature about design patterns at a more abstract level of software development, in order to learn about the new strategies and procedures for software modeling. The Java developer community is full of enthusiasts for cross-context design patterns. Although some of the approaches are a bit too abstract to be realized directly—a bit of realism and some inductive reasoning would surely help here—we still maintain that design patterns are a better way of learning about new models and designs than delving through source coding for hours or days on end.

7.2.1 MVC

We've already mentioned the Model View Control (MVC) design pattern several times in this book. You already read about the relevant components in Section 5.2 and Section 6.4. Therefore, this section will define the advanced principles of an MVC-based application designed to meet specific requirements.

The objective of the MVC pattern is to decouple the presentation logic from the business logic; this is often combined with the intention to reuse components of both layers independently of the context.

As you know, requests are placed with the *controller*, which is responsible for either instantiating the used *models* or retrieving references to them to initialize dependent *views*. The controller then triggers the business methods for the models, modifying the data in the application or retrieving the data required by the views. Subsequently, it selects a view, depending on the query, or interaction with the events or data involved in the model, and tasks it with creating a display.

Filters

There are many practical requirements that an MVC model can face. A general pattern for realizing these requirements are filters or filter chains, where the latter can be any combination of the former. Filters are generally independent, and don't usually build on one another directly. As you will learn in the following sections, filters are typically used in inbound and outbound filter chains.

Security Aspects

Authentication

Authentication is the process of determining the identity of a user or active entity of a software program. It will usually suffice to authenticate users once each session, if it is passed on transparently to resources and functions for all accesses. In a BSP application, authentication is performed implicitly by a system filter in the BSP application, and does not have to be implemented separately. Although J2EE applications don't imply any pre-implemented authentication mechanisms, the Java Authentication and Authorization Service (JAAS) architecture introduced in Section 5.2.1 provides a generic, extensible mechanism for authorization, even though it has not yet been implemented.

Authorization

Contrary to authentication, authorization can be used at several levels within an application to access a resource or function of that application. Generally, authorization is granted or refused—based on the request data—when a container is accessed, although explicit authorization is also possible for models that require access to application components or system resources.

Validation

You can't always trust the data received in a user request, especially in Web applications based on a stateless protocol like HTTP. First, any input validation logic implemented on the client side, such as in JavaScript, is generally untrustworthy, because many browsers let users deactivate JavaScript. Hiding sensitive values in invisible form fields, to pass them on to the next query, is also frowned upon. Yet, it is not only security aspects that make it absolutely essential to validate queries, especially in a Web application framework—there are also integrity-related issues.

Input Checks

The simplest form of validation involves checking atomic form fields against value ranges or domains. The goal is to ensure that the user has entered valid value ranges—especially when general input fields are involved. Typical uses here include verifying the validity of an email address or ensuring that no negative values are entered.

The next form of validation is based on interaction between several input values, which enables you to model dependencies between form fields, for example. Typical uses include "From/To" field combinations, in which the logical value of the first field cannot exceed the value of the second field, and confirmation fields (used frequently when setting new passwords), which must contain the same values as their twins.

The technical security aspects differ from checks for valid entries and value domains. These aspects should be checked within filters in the application logic, however, instead of shifting the function to filters on the controller—for example, in case the application is used outside of the MVC model.

Hierarchy and Distribution

Navigation

Because a model that aims to achieve modularization and division of areas of responsibility is certainly not conducive to stuffing all of the required functions into a single MVC construct, it must be possible to distribute MVC models and even arrange them in a hierarchy. The first option is navigation between coequal entities, which is similar to the navigation mechanism used in static Web pages. When the user sends a form or clicks on a link, the request is usually routed to another controller, based on the context, which then has to deal with the request itself. Both BSP applications and J2EE applications created with the JavaServer Faces (JSF) or Jakarta Struts technologies feature such navigation mechanisms.

Delegation

In addition to controllers acting in parallel, they can also be nested. In BSP applications, for example, you can have a controller or view collect queries that it previously processed itself and forward them to a sub-controller. If a view addresses a sub-controller directly, the outputs from its view are integrated in the appropriate spot in the calling view. This nesting of MVC constructs is used for the BSP extension HTMLB, for example, to generate generic components—such as table views and tree views—that higher-level controllers or views fill with data, which they, in turn, represent generically. You can even implement your own event and data model in this manner.

Decentralized Event Control

Another important characteristic of MVC is the controller's ability to respond flexibly to other controllers' events. In BSP applications, higher-level controllers can detect events in subordinate or same-level controllers during event processing and respond accordingly. The technical access is implemented using ABAP Objects and is usually quite involved. Unfortunately, models like those in JSF applications, in which callback methods can be defined for specific events for any controller, are not implemented in BSP applications. In contrast, Web Dynpro applications contribute several other improvements.

Data Visualization

Push Versus Pull

Because one of the main objectives of the MVC design pattern is to decouple application logic from presentation logic, you have to decide on the strategy for transporting data from the application to the individual view components. We differentiate between the push and pull principles.

Under the push principle, the controller sets all the variables required by the view. Within the view, the variables are addressed by only the names under which they were transferred. The primary disadvantage of this model is that when the model changes, you not only have to update the view, but also the controller that passes the data.

Under the pull principle, the controller sends references to the involved model to the views, and the views then retrieve the corresponding data autonomously. In addition to eliminating processing requirements at runtime, the main advantage of this approach is that when the model for data transfer changes, you don't have to update the controller, only the view (and even then, only in some cases). Therefore, there are fewer interdependencies among the individual entities.

Multilingual Capability

Now that you've read about the filter types for authentication, authorization, and validation, we will devote the rest of this chapter to the requirements that can be implemented as outbound filters.

One consistently underestimated issue in Web applications is the multilingual capability of an application—primarily because the variety of implementation options on the respective platform cause developers to overlook existing, platform-inherent mechanisms for supporting multiple languages. In general, the implementation of multilingual capability is initially the responsibility of the presentation logic.

One option of preparing the application data model for multiple languages is to provide for language-specific text tables for master data values, from which the texts are read at runtime. This approach inevitably shifts language dependencies into the application and persistence layers, especially when language-dependent conversions—such as currencies, and so on—are involved.

Aspects of messages, notifications, or error reporting—especially in the validation and authentication phase—cannot be modeled by such measures, however. Most platforms follow a different strategy for dealing with the problem: recreating such language-dependent special features in a catalog, where every entry in the catalog must be parameterizable in a simple way, and accessible through a unique key. An outbound filter would then be responsible for identifying such references to catalog entries in the final output and replacing them as necessary.

Multiple Output Formats

Different user devices—browsers, PDAs, smart phones, and so on—usually require different output formats. For that reason, an application intended to be transportable to many different media with minimal additional effort should provide for this possibility from the start. A prerequisite for all of the following strategies is that the type of expected output format can be clearly identified based on the request.

The first step involves providing various views for the individual output formats and including them in the controller, depending on the expected output format. A major shortfall of this approach is that a redundant update of all views is required for all output formats when the model changes. Also, adding a new output device would require changes to all controllers.

A more elegant approach is to equip views with a rendering mechanism for each output format in order to implement a "platform-specific" instance of the "platform-independent" view. In BSP applications, this abstraction option is available through BSP extensions, which can implement platform dependencies as elementary components of a view. In the J2EE world, this option is provided by the TagLibs used in JSPs and rendering services in JSFs.

Delta Handling

The preceding pattern can also fully model delta handling. In order for an application client to be able to create a complete data and rendering model from a delta set of data, it has to manage a separate application status. This is a typical property of rich clients, which ultimately have their own (usually MVC-like) architecture for handling application data and status. BSP, JSP, JSF, and servlet-based applications are typical *thin clients*, which destroy their complete data model and receive it again from the server during each request. Alternatively, ABAP and Web Dynpro applications are rich clients. A primary advantage of rich clients is that they remove an enormous amount of network load caused by the server, due to the extreme reduction of the transmitted dataset. Rich clients, however, model certain parts of an application redundantly—especially when the application on the server has to deal with both client types. In addition, they often require a rollout of the client software.

Compression

In the last step before transmitting the rendered data to the client, the final outbound filter usually applies a compression algorithm, which both client and server have to support. Thin clients, such as browsers, typically use this function to compress the relatively large data quantities involved (compared to rich clients). HTTP version 1.1 and later provides for a negotiation mechanism here, in which the client informs the server of the supported decompression processes in every request, which the server can use to compress the output.

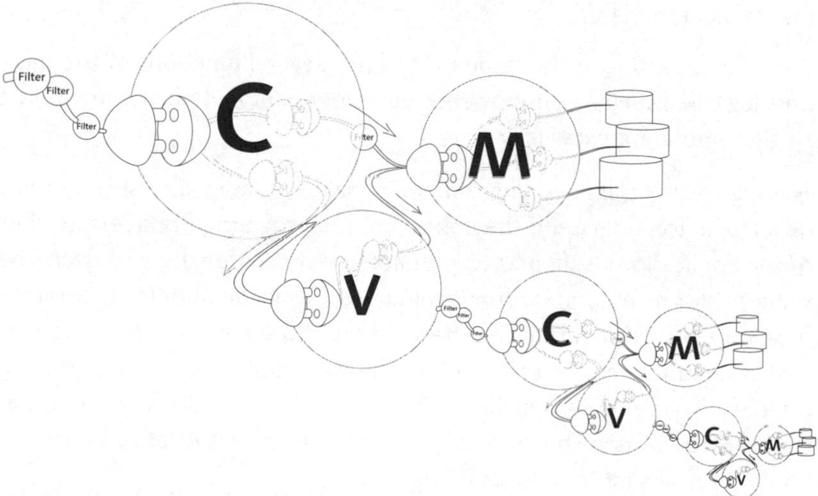

Figure 7.1 The MVC Pattern

This is the only design pattern for the presentation layer that is described in detail in this volume. As we already mentioned, excellent literature for the complex subject area of GUI development is available. In closing, we should mention that the MVC design pattern is very general at its core, and fails to define many aspects that are extremely relevant in reality. Consequently, the different platforms usually have different versions of this design pattern, which originated in the Smalltalk community.

7.2.2 Façade

The model introduced a component of the MVC pattern that—depending on the interpretation—either represents a direct link to the business logic or contains the business logic itself.

The façade pattern provides standardized access to the business logic specifically for these direct connections. The design pattern defines a higher-level business component, which encapsulates and centralizes the interaction between lower-level components. They represent a single interface to the client, concealing the functions of an underlying complex transaction or multiple components. It converts an actual request into multiple requests, which are then routed to the individual, subordinate business components.

Objective The main objective of the façade is to unify several functions of the business logic in a single, context-sensitive component and portray them as a single component externally.

This approach to aggregating functions makes it easier for user interface developers to understand the context of the program interface, and thus of the application itself, and to prepare it as a GUI for the end user. The potential for misinterpretation is minimized, as is the additional communication effort, through a clear declaration of the application's functions that is comprehensible to all sides. The definition of the programming interface is very important here because it institutionalizes this declaration.In other words: The more explicit an interface is, the less you have to know about it's internal functioning.

At this point, especially in the ABAP environment, integration gaps can also be removed, because different modularization options—such as classes, reports, function modules, BAPIs, and so on—can be encapsulated by a single component type.

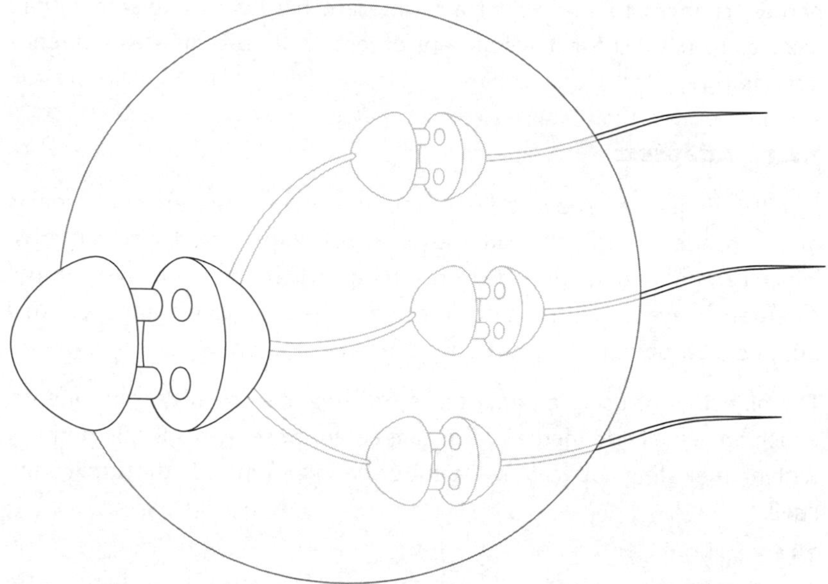

Figure 7.2 The Façade Pattern

In the ResMan example, it would make sense to extend the MVC model by grouping all the function modules for posting, canceling, and requesting resources together in a single class. This would then provide the central repository to deal with the underlying data model for a BSP application, and would save the developers of the visual component from having to find out themselves which options they have for modifying the data—whether via direct use of function modules or direct access with Open SQL.

Context

Another advantage of the façade is that it shifts the context-holding component away from the presentation and toward the application. The controller or BSP page is no longer responsible for holding a context between the presentation and application layers. Instead, this function—which is required for the "lazy initialization" pattern, for example—is at least shifted to the application model.

Using the façade pattern has a positive effect on network load at runtime: Instead of sending many, highly granular method calls between the client and the individual objects, a single method call is now sufficient, which ultimately reduces the latency of the remote calls as well.

The main problem of façades is designing and communicating them well. Because they usually represent an interface between two development parties, changes to the API of a façade are harder to implement than changes to the API for development objects without cross-team dependencies.

7.2.3 Adapters

Just like uniqueness and stability of the utilized interface are core aspects of the façade pattern, the same aspects also apply to adapter patterns, which can be used in any type of resource connection—preferably in the persistence layer. Adapter patterns can also be used to integrate external business components in a system.

Objective The objective of using an adapter is to integrate any two components, which are usually defined and unchangeable, to serve a specific purpose within an existing application—without having to modify the application itself.

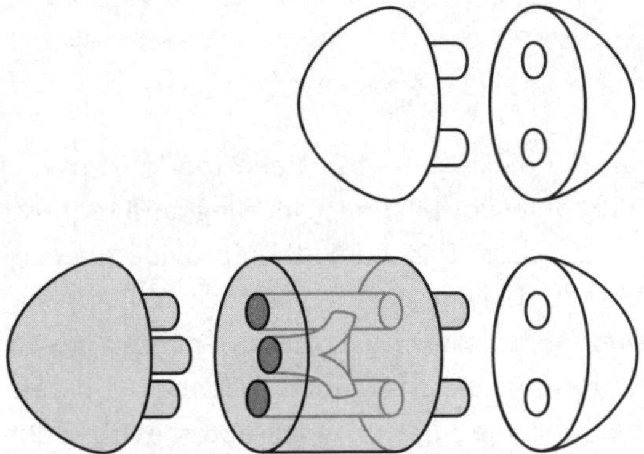

Figure 7.3 The Adapter Pattern

The main problem in integrating third-party components, which were not designed for such use in most cases, is the existing programming interface of the components, which does not immediately fit into the existing model. An adapter reflects a strategy of creating an intermediate component that encapsulates the functions of the component to include once again, making the application available in "bite-sized" portions.

Use Case A typical use case for an adapter is to encapsulate the call of a function module within another function module, whose import and export parameters are better synchronized with the calling program, eliminating the need for typecasting before each call of the component. This approach stabilizes the call of a function module with incorrect typing—which would otherwise result in a spontaneous short dump—and makes the calling program more immune to interface changes in the original component. Moreover, the additional encapsulation level enables you to implement any preprocessing and postprocessing filters for input and output in the adapter.

A problem that you have to consider regarding adapters is that they generate additional load in the overall application, resulting in a certain loss of performance, however small. Moreover, the new encapsulation component requires additional development effort initially, although you'll quickly compensate for it through the multiple preparation of parameters for every call of the surrounding program, which would otherwise be necessary.

7.2.4 Driver Model

The driver model approaches the problem of integrating external components from an entirely different perspective, with different prerequisites. It assumes that no external components exist yet, but will be used for certain types of applications in the future.

Objective

To ensure simple standardization at this point, a primary objective of a driver model is to define the interface in advance, that is, specify the requirements of components, which are of a certain type and used for a specific purpose, explicitly in the form of a programming interface.

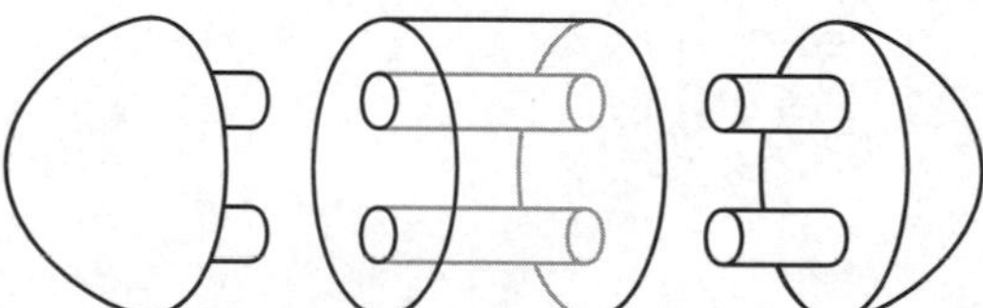

Figure 7.4 Driver Model

This somewhat unusual name stems from the origin of the design pattern. When hardware components are connected to the software, operating systems place certain requirements on components of the same type—such as printers—and formulate these requirements as an interface specification. The objective here is to develop a driver model before you even know which vendors will provide drivers for their hardware components. Of course, a collection of software components that is based on this specification—such as an office suite—has to support all existing and future printer types. You shouldn't have any trouble thinking of analogies for component-based software.

Use Case If it were implemented as a class, the driver model would be a typical use case for an interface or—if some methods can be implemented generically—an abstract class.

Because developers are not omniscient, and also can't foretell the future, they cannot predict how stable the driver model will be. The requirements defined for the interface could prove to be too short-sighted, for example, and demands on the interface can evolve over time. There are generally three options in such cases:

1. If new requirements come from both sides of the application, that is, both from the driver developers and the driver users, there is often no avoiding a new interface specification. The new specification replaces the existing specification and all dependent components—namely the drivers and programs that use them—have to be modified (see Figure 7.5). These incompatibilities usually occur when a new generation of software is distributed.

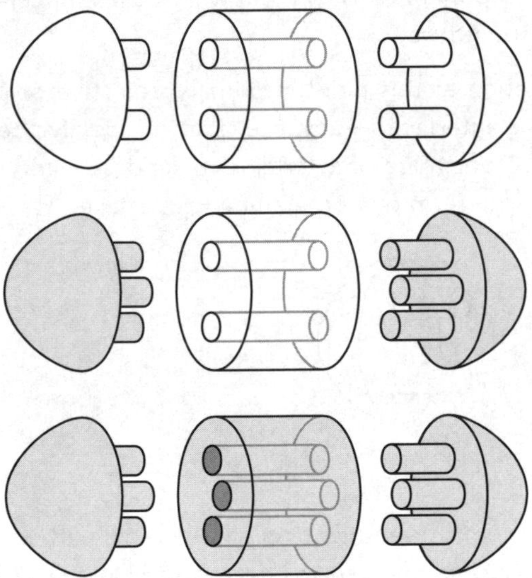

Figure 7.5 New Driver Model

2. The new requirements come mainly from the applications used. In this case, the application could use the adapter pattern that was just described to "squeeze" more out of the interface and implement higher-value functions based on the existing ones (see Figure 7.6). Although this use case occurs fairly frequently, it is often linked with performance problems because the higher-value functions usually consist of multiple sub-accesses to lower-value functions.

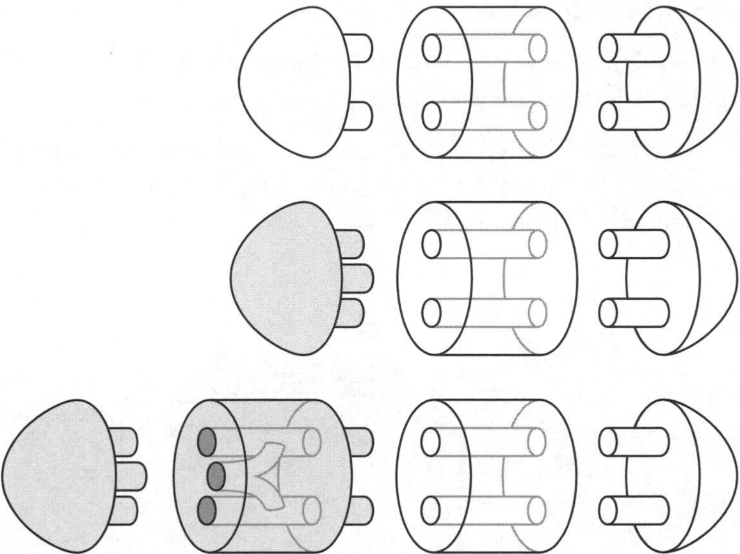

Figure 7.6 Application-Side Adapter

3. The new requirements come mainly from the driver vendor side (see Figure 7.7). This case is more infrequent, and usually results in alternative driver models, in which the driver vendor applies the adapter pattern to the old driver models, which often seem more inefficient as a result.

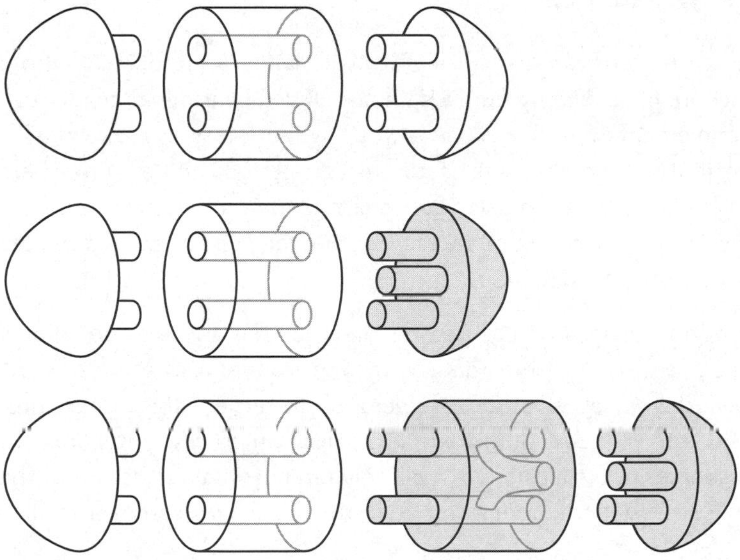

Figure 7.7 Driver Model-Side Adapter

7.2.5 Lazy Initialization

One cross-layer development pattern for increasing performance and reducing the resources tied by an application is *lazy initialization*.

Objective The objective of lazy (or *late*) initialization is to avoid unnecessary access to resources such as files or databases by not supplying the values until they are required for processing (see Figure 7.8).

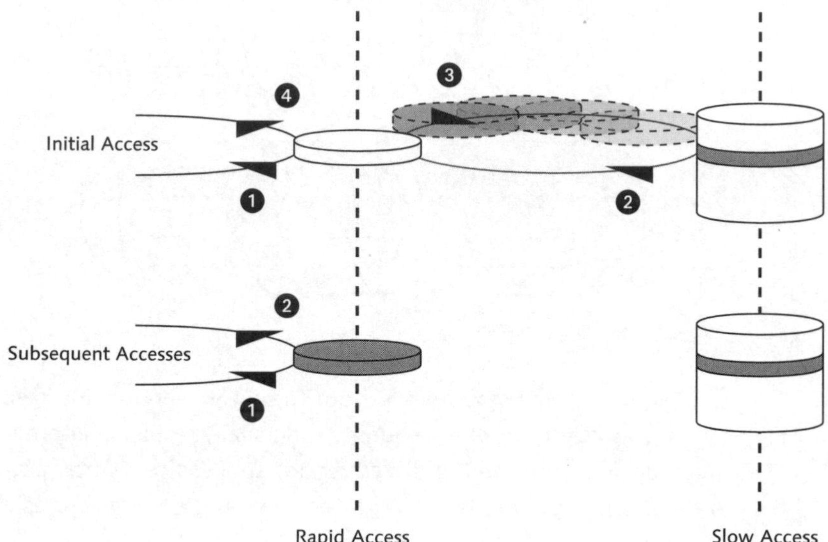

Figure 7.8 Lazy Initialization

Use Case This design pattern can be explained most vividly using objects whose attributes are filled directly from a database. If you consider an object-oriented implementation of ResMan and designed a resource as a class—with attributes such as usage status, usage period, and so on—there would very likely be an initialization phase, either within or outside the constructor of this class, during which all the object's attributes are filled with values from the database.

Now, imagine that an object from class `Resource` also includes binary data, such as images or metadata, retrieved from a Web service. You'll probably ask yourself whether it's necessary to retrieve this rather complex, CPU-intensive data during every initialization process. After all, a list of all resources of a specific type will only rarely contain a picture of the respective component, indicating that this data was retrieved gratuitously.

On the other hand, you can't simply create a number of implementations of the class for different application scenarios. Even though this seems like the most logical step—and, thanks to the inheritance concept, can be implemented relatively simply and non-redundantly for classes—the users of your classes would be faced with the problem of selecting the correct implementation from the wide range that you provide. Therefore, it makes things easier for both sides when there is only one implementation that can cover most of the requirements.

The concept of lazy initialization meets this demand perfectly. You don't have to fill the attributes of a class until the context demands it, that is, requests read access. You might ask how you can determine when an attribute requires read access to an object. Granted, neither ABAP nor Java support context-sensitive callback functions that would implement the method call of a `get()` or `set()` method for accessing the attribute of a class, to pass the name—and in one case, the value of the attribute as well—to the method, and you would only have to implement this method with an access to the resources behind the attribute.

Consequently, you will need a different strategy. Your class must not possess any publicly visible attributes, but instead, it must use methods to encapsulate the access. Therefore, methods such as `getStatus()` and `setStatus()` for an object with class `Resource` would be used, and it would be up to the context to access the attributes of this class exclusively through method calls.

```
public Date getDate() {
  return this.date;
}
```

Listing 7.1 Direct Access to an Initialized Attribute

In addition to filling the most important attributes during the initialization phase of the object, other attributes are filled when the method is first accessed to provide direct availability for subsequent calls. The object's attributes are used as a type of cache, which initially exists as long as the object does.

```
public Image getImage() {
  if(this.image == null) {
      this.image = ... //Retrieval logic
  }
```

```
        return this.image;
}
```

Listing 7.2 Access to an Attribute with Lazy Initialization

Consideration You'll have to carefully consider, and possibly even prove—based on statistical tests—whether you selected the correct attributes for lazy initialization, or whether it might be more efficient to fill them during the initialization phase. The reason for this consideration is that attributes that come from the same source will result in more accesses to that source if lazy initialization is used exclusively. A good example of this consideration is the following question:

Is it better to initialize attributes with a single, complex SQL statement during the initialization phase, or is it better to do so later, with several separate, but more simple statements; for example, without complex `JOIN` statements?

7.3 Developing an ABAP Web Application

You now have to design ResMan, based on the development patterns you just learned about. Although you worked on the same project in previous chapters, you didn't examine the application as a whole. This is exactly what we will do now—with the objective of developing a Web-capable application in ABAP.

Assumptions The data model, as described in Chapter 3, applies. You can assume that the business logic is already available as function modules, as described previously. This situation is fairly typical for developing Web applications and is the starting point for your own developments in many cases. Moreover, you want to implement the entire application as a single-page application, that is, all elements are contained in a single screen and separated from one another through navigation elements such as tab strips, grouping elements, and so on.

At this point, many developers are tempted to look for things to criticize in the existing model, which they inevitably find, and then decide to start the existing application over and "do it right" this time. Unfortunately, this mindset is widespread among developers in small teams. However, the allegedly flawed model was usually created for a reason, and the Where-used list in the ABAP Workbench cannot by itself always ensure that someone else isn't using the application in its existing form. But, perhaps you can eliminate all these factors, the existing components truly fail to meet your needs, and your customer is prepared to pay for a complete redesign. If you're definitely not dealing with an integration or feature enhancement, and there are no financial constraints, it may be advisable to start over with a newer technology and a better model than the one previously used. In all other cases, however, you'll be faced with a system model that you're unfamiliar with and that doesn't meet your current requirements.

So, what is the fastest way to feel at home in a foreign object architecture? In many cases, the adapter pattern introduced above can help you encapsulate the existing components—in this case, the three function modules `Z_KM_GETLIST`, `Z_KM_BOOK`, and `Z_KM_CANCEL`. The type of encapsulation depends primarily on the anticipated front-end technology.

Web Dynpro Application

If you want to implement a Web Dynpro application, remote-capable function modules are the current correct distribution form to use. In addition, Web Dynpro promotes the use of MVC. At the time this book goes to print, SAP has yet to release an implementation of Web Dynpro for ABAP officially.

BSP Application

Conversely, if an MVC-compliant BSP application is your (or your customer's) preferred choice—because Web AS 6.40 is not available or you work on a team that lacks the necessary skills—you can implement and interpret the design pattern yourself.

According to the forward navigation philosophy, you start by creating a stateful BSP application and its corresponding controller. Although stratification in a hierarchy is possible, the simplicity of the application means it is not essential in this case. Create a model that you instantiate in the controller during the initialization phase of the application and connect it to a public attribute of the controller class.

Model

The model must implement only three methods, which act as adapters for the existing function modules. You don't have to consider the lazy initialization pattern for the solitary data retrieval method, since all the data (in the function module) can be retrieved from the database at once with a relatively uncomplicated `SELECT` statement, and no large, secondary datasets—such as images in a detail view—exist.

Views

To build your application, you'll also need a main view, which provides the framework for the application and which integrates header lines with logos, footers as page fragments, and one sub-view each for the search template and output list in the layout. As an alternative to the output list, you should provide for another view for use as an error page, if the search does not deliver any results. You should also consider how the corresponding error messages are passed on to the user, such as those due to incorrect or blank entries in the search template. When in doubt, you can also shift this function to another view, which is then displayed only in case of error or to notify the user.

The easiest way to design views is to use elements of the BSP HTMLB extension; in addition to a drop-down list with the different search categories, they also contain a table view to display the results, and buttons to post and cancel the selected data records. You will also need date and time fields, which must be checked for overlaps and valid entries within the control in order to allow entry of intervals for the bookings.

Controller

In addition to instantiating the model and main view—and delegating the request to the main view—the controller also needs event-handling logic, which requires handlers for searching, booking, and cancellation in this case. The latter two handlers have to read the selected lines in the table view to determine the data records to be modified. The modification itself can be performed by calling the respective methods of the model, possibly iteratively for multiple data records.

Design Pattern Used

In planning your application model, you have already used three of the introduced design patterns, and were able to exclude one due to the existing assumptions and components. You now use the MVC pattern, adapter, and façade—and exclude lazy initialization, because its implementation wouldn't help (and, in fact, would have a negative impact on the application).

7.4 Developing a J2EE Web Application

Assumptions

In this section, you will plan a software model for ResMan. You'll do so by using the options available in the current version of SAP NetWeaver Developer Studio (SAP NWDS). The same assumptions regarding the existence of a dataset and function modules apply as in the ABAP personality. Therefore, your Java-based Web application has to access the ABAP personality in order to access the data and business functions. In this case, the Java Connector (JCo) interface is your preferred tool.

Web Dynpro Application

When you implement a Web Dynpro application, a "clean" MVC model is provided from the start. You can trust that the implementation is correct and proceed according to the instructions in Section 5.2.4 and Section 6.4.2.

To create a more demanding design pattern, however, you'll have to use the technology of a JSP/servlet application, without using a secondary architecture such as Jakarta Struts or JavaServer Faces (JSF). To do so, first create the appropriate project types in SAP NWDS: Web application project, EJB project, and enterprise archive project.

JSP/Servlet Application

The model for this application will involve a stateful session bean. It implements adapters for the respective ABAP-side business logic in its business methods—similar to the BSP application—and functions as a façade for the MVC architecture. In theory, the individual business methods are implemented identically in all cases. First, retrieve an instance of the JCo for the corresponding function module through a Java Native Description Interface (JNDI) lookup. Then, use this connection to implement the remote calls via RFC. Compared to establishing and ending the connection in the corresponding methods of the life cycle, the advantage of the JNDI lookup is that resources are allocated for only the duration of the call, and not during the entire session. Because JNDI lookups are relatively "cheap" in terms of runtime costs and most likely won't become a bottleneck for the application—which can occur if too many connections are open at the same time—this strategy is preferred as long as performance is not compromised.

Model

The view is implemented as a JSP. Unlike the BSP application, you can delegate between multiple views only if you have a JSP TagLib that supports this template procedure; however, this isn't always the case. Therefore, you may be faced with the decision of either omitting the delegation or using scriptlets to implement them explicitly—a relatively costly alternative. You'll also have to choose the GUI controls to use. If you don't have a JSP TagLib for the individual UI elements, which is the norm in the standard delivery, you'll have to reproduce them using HTML markup.

View

The last component to be added to your application is the controller, which you implement as a servlet. Although JSPs that serve as views are also converted to servlets internally, this implementation strategy and the programming paradigm it implies are totally different, because JSP uses a descriptive markup language while servlets use Java as an object-oriented programming language.

Controller

When implementing the servlet, you first have to consider which inbound filters will be needed. Authentication and authorization aren't relevant in this specific case, but input validation might be.

We recommend first merging the two callback methods—`doPost()` and `doGet()`—in a shared method in the servlet that processes the requests. This method should then implement the life cycle of an MVC application in a pragmatic manner.

The event handlers then decide which business methods to call and how the data is to be saved or modified in the session. The session data here is only the data in the output list, which should be retained after a server roundtrip (for making a reservation) in order to avoid the relatively "expensive" remote access to the function module for data retrieval.

After the event handling and data retrieval, the controller servlet forwards the request to the JSP that we described above.

Deployment Now that you've developed the application, you must oversee the central configuration of the JCo connections on the J2EE server during the subsequent deployment. The typical deployment steps are also required to establish suitable connections between the individual project types—Web application project, EJB project, and enterprise archive project. In particular, this involves providing a session bean, which implements the business logic and is supplied to the Web application as a JNDI object through the local or remote interface, depending on the physical distribution of the application to one or more hardware components.

Conclusion As you can see, the current implementation of Web applications based on JSPs and servlets raises many issues that the model doesn't resolve. Actual projects that rely on servlet technology for deployment reasons will most assuredly try to use servlet extensions—like JavaServer Faces or Jakarta Struts together with JSP TagLibs—that automate most of the manual implementation and decisions regarding the proper extensions to use for the servlet model.

8 Performance Aspects

A good application must be more than just powerful and user-friendly. Ultimately, whether users accept an application depends on keeping the response times for users as low as possible, while balancing the resources an application uses and the benefits it provides.

8.1 Performance under ABAP

ABAP and Open SQL

A major strength of the ABAP programming language is its seamless integration of database access through its own database query language (Open SQL). This close integration between the ABAP runtime environment and the database was borne of necessity, however, because nearly all the resources of an SAP System are saved as data in the database. Consequently, the performance of ABAP program coding is highly dependent on the efficiency of the database accesses.

We differentiate between two categories of program coding:

- Program coding for dialog programs, for example, to display a business partner's open items
- Program coding for analyzing large quantities of data, for example, programs that analyze the current set of open items and generate dunning notices from this data

Development Projects

In our experience, it is the latter category of program coding that requires you to consider performance aspects during the design phase, because any errors in the flow structure or data retention of the programs will demand a major effort to be corrected. Therefore, to ensure good performance, developers must weigh both analytical and design aspects, and pay equal attention to both when planning ABAP development projects. Subsequent changes to low-performance coding are often difficult, and also run the risk of ruining a program that is functioning, however slowly, by adding new errors.

Growing Datasets

In development projects, performance critical aspects of the overall development have to be identified early on. Over the course of the implementation, you should repeatedly check whether the performance of these critical areas is sufficient—especially in the context of the expected data volumes—keeping in mind the tendency of data volumes to grow over time, which manifests itself in so many applications.

"Acceptable" performance of an analysis program is often dictated by the time window available on the production computer in daily job planning; the dataset analysis has to be completed before this window closes. If the application is not fast enough to analyze the dataset within the available time window, the application itself is useless (or at least unusable), and the entire development effort may have been for naught.

Where dialog programs are involved, "acceptable" performance is harder to classify. If the program coding in question is called by a frequently used transaction, its performance can be a key factor in appraising the usability of the entire application. The primary measure for "good" performance of a dialog application is the response time—the time it takes for the application to respond to a user request.

8.1.1 Rules for Boosting Performance

There are several general rules for optimizing the performance of ABAP program coding. These rules are only rough guides, however, and should not be applied blindly without an in-depth analysis of the given situation. It is also true that good program coding strikes a balance between performance and coding elegance and simplicity.

Database Queries

The transfer of data between the database and the SAP application server accounts for most of the program runtime in typical applications. Therefore, minimizing the amount of transmitted data can give you a big boost in performance.

One common example of superfluous data transfer between the database and the application server is using the asterisk, instead of an explicit field list, `(*)` in `SELECT` statements. If you need only a few of the fields contained in a database table, you should specify them explicitly in a `SELECT` statement. The same applies to `UPDATE` and `MODIFY` statements.

To further reduce the amount of data transferred, avoid using `IF ... ENDIF` and `CHECK` statements to define logical constraints for the selected field. Instead, add these conditions to the `WHERE` clause of the `SELECT` statement.

In many cases, you must access another table to determine whether a data record is required. If you use nested `SELECT` statements for this, the transmitted data quantity will generally be larger than if you had linked the involved transparent tables with a `JOIN` or a view. The use of subqueries is another alternative.

SAP R/3 applications often entail data models that consist of header tables and subordinate item tables. To process these item records efficiently, you can use SELECT ... UP TO ... ROWS to read the header data in packages and then use SELECT ... FOR ALL ENTRIES to read the item data.

8.1.2 Performance Analysis Tools

SAP provides several powerful analysis tools for ABAP developers, which can also help you optimize performance. These tools are:

- Runtime Analysis (Transaction SE30)
- SQL Trace (Transaction ST05)
- Coverage Analyzer (Transaction SCOV)
- Code Inspector (Transaction SCI)

Runtime Analysis

You can use Transaction SE30 to analyze the runtime of transactions, reports, and function modules. This measures the time required to call the individual ABAP modularization units, as well as the time required for Open SQL statements. Because modularization units are generally nested, both gross and net values are reported for the runtime of a modularization unit.

The runtimes are output in an ABAP List Viewer (ALV) list, which you can easily export to a spreadsheet program or sort by any column. Sorting by net percentage in descending order is especially useful, because the modularization unit or Open SQL statement that required the longest runtime appears at the top of the list. In addition, a pushbutton is available to jump directly to the corresponding code segment, letting you quickly analyze the critical parts.

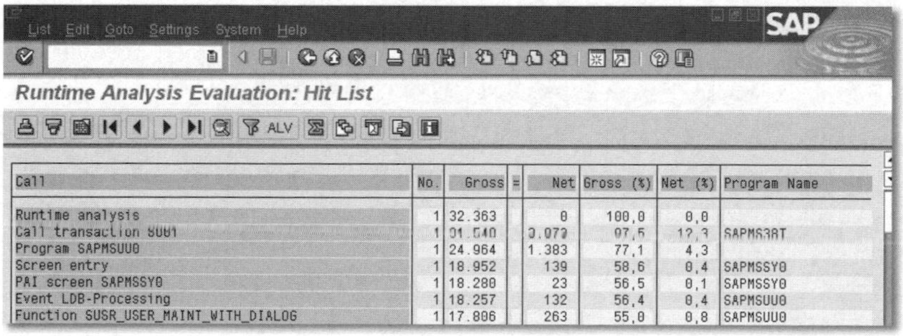

Runtime Analysis Evaluation: Hit List

Call	No.	Gross	=	Net	Gross (%)	Net (%)	Program Name
Runtime analysis	1	32.363		0	100,0	0,0	
Call transaction SU01	1	31.540		3.977	97,5	12,3	SAPMS38T
Program SAPMSUU0	1	24.964		1.383	77,1	4,3	
Screen entry	1	18.952		139	58,6	0,4	SAPMSSY0
PAI screen SAPMSSY0	1	18.280		23	56,5	0,1	SAPMSSY0
Event LDB-Processing	1	18.257		132	56,4	0,4	SAPMSUU0
Function SUSR_USER_MAINT_WITH_DIALOG	1	17.806		263	55,0	0,8	SAPMSUU0

Figure 8.1 Runtime Analysis

In addition to runtime information, Transaction SE30 also provides other helpful data, such as the call structure and memory usage of the analyzed coding.

SQL Trace

The SQL Trace is extremely useful for analyzing SQL statements. You can activate and deactivate the SQL Trace with Transaction ST05, as well as prepare and analyze the trace results. Because the SQL Trace requires processing resources and hard disk space itself, you should activate it only briefly, as required, and then deactivate it soon afterwards. We also recommend using the filter options that are available in Transaction ST05.

The general procedure is to activate the trace first, then execute the transaction, report, or function module that you want to analyze. Once execution is complete, you deactivate the trace and analyze the results.

The trace results are output as a list that includes the runtime of the SQL statement, the table involved, and the executed operation, among other details. Statements with long runtimes are highlighted. As in Transaction SE30, you can jump directly to the coding segment where the analyzed SQL statement was executed. You can also display metadata for the affected table in the ABAP Dictionary, along with the technical parameters of the table. By far the most important feature for performance analysis, however, is the **Explain** button: It displays the database strategy of the analyzed SQL statement, where you can check whether the database optimizer was able to locate a suitable index, and determine how many index fields were used, both of which give you valuable insight into boosting performance.

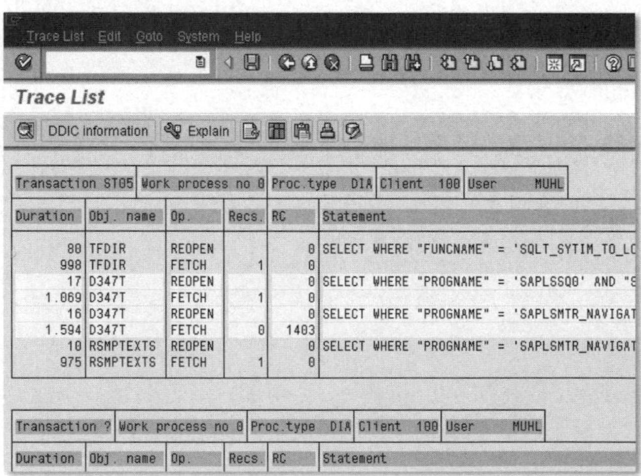

Figure 8.2 SQL Trace

Coverage Analyzer

The Coverage Analyzer counts the number of calls of a given modularization unit system-wide. With this tool, you can easily tell how often a given transaction or function module was called during the recording period. For that reason, you can determine which coding segments are executed most frequently and focus your optimization efforts on these objects.

Code Inspector

The Code Inspector enables you to analyze individual objects—function groups, reports, classes, interfaces, and so on—or lists of objects, and search them for common programming errors. The user configures the test scope. Tests are available for syntax, security, and performance, and can be activated individually. The performance tests check several of the rules described above and can help you localize the cause of deep-rooted performance problems.

8.2 Performance under Java

Is Java Slow?

Java is commonly believed to suffer from performance problems. Its critics claim that Java is too slow, that the garbage collector (automatic memory cleanup) occupies the entire CPU time, and that the interpretation of the Java Virtual Machine (JVM) makes the hourglass icon a symbol of productivity. Granted, Java did not initially win over people because of its blinding speed, but due to its security features, network capability, and portability to other operating systems. However, the current version of Java has changed drastically. In particular, the JVM has been optimized and equipped with new functions. But, among many software developers who have switched to Java from other programming languages, Java still has a reputation of being far too slow, while programming languages such as C, C++, Delphi, ABAP, or Assembler have far greater performance. Studies show, however, that this criticism is unjustified in the majority of cases, and that Java can now keep pace with the other programming languages.

In addition, Java also provides a maximum of scalability and availability. Many of the memory management problems that occur in C and C++, for example, have been solved in Java. Because the language was designed under the umbrella of security, potentially insecure language constructs such as explicit *memory management* and *pointer arithmetic* have been avoided. Consequently, Java applications don't crash due to incorrect memory pointers and are immune to buffer overruns and other security attacks that can occur because of direct memory access.

But, before we deal with the subject of performance under Java, we should first clarify exactly what "performance" means.

Fundamentals of Performance Optimization

Performance is more than just a measure of processing speed; it also involves input/output operations and memory use. Therefore, the performance of a computer that has only a small amount of RAM will be far worse when running a fast program with large memory requirements than when running a slow program with low memory requirements. Conversely, if a program's memory requirements are low, it often requires much more computing power. If this computing power is not available, a fast input/output speed is required. As you can see, computing power, working memory, and input/output devices are all directly interrelated and are all tremendously important for program performance.

In general, for a program to be considered high-performance, it must use existing resources efficiently. If a large amount of main memory is available to a program, it makes much more sense to cache the data and keep it in the main memory than to access the comparatively slow database or hard disk after each operation. In many cases, however, main memory is limited, so only data that is used constantly is cached in main memory. As application developer, you need to find a balance between optimized resource utilization and waste; separating the two is the foundation for performance optimization.

Engage Users During Wait Times

Despite efforts to develop high-performance programs according to the defined optimization rules, end users still complain that programs are too slow. This is especially true in cases where users have to interact directly with a program. For example, consider a Web browser. If the browser doesn't display the complete Web page until all the page contents have loaded, you would think the program is slow. Conversely, if the browser displays the contents that have already been loaded at runtime, regardless of whether other objects still have to be downloaded, you'd perceive the program as being faster, although a performance measurement of both applications would produce identical results. Therefore, it's vital that you have some kind of visual to indicate to users that the program is currently working, instead of leaving them hanging—staring at a static screen. Web browsers, for example, indicate the data transmission progress with the hourglass mouse pointer, or a percentage display in the status bar, so users always know how long they have to wait.

Knowledge Is Performance

In addition, a program should provide a way for users to cancel the current operation at any time—to empower end users by giving them control over the program at all times. Remember: no one wants to feel subordinate to a program. Therefore, you should always follow one basic rule: If wait times are unavoidable despite performance optimization, you must inform the user of the ongoing progress of the current program.

8.2.1 Rules for Boosting Performance

You now know the fundamentals of high-performance programming. A software solution has to use existing resources efficiently and consider the users' sensibilities. But these two factors alone are not sufficient to create an efficient program. You need two other things: knowledge and curiosity. Many performance problems are ultimately due to sloppy programming or, put another way, a lack of knowledge of the high-performance solution options. As a Java developer, in addition to having a good development environment like SAP NetWeaver Developer Studio (SAP NWDS), you should also have local access to the Java API documentation and Java source code. You can configure paths to the documentation and the source coding in the settings for SAP NWDS, giving you direct access to all necessary information at the click of the mouse during development.

When you subject your software to performance tests, you have to do so at different levels, using both micro and macro (benchmark) tests. Micro tests are an excellent way to optimize small, isolated program modules. Macro tests, in contrast, give you a general overview of your software. The two test types are complementary. In addition, you should always perform multiple test runs to get reliable results. In general, you should assume that the cost of making changes increases exponentially as the project progresses. To avoid this, you should design your test pattern by keeping in mind all possible eventualities.

Profilers

In any case, we strongly recommend that you run these performance tests as frequently as the situation demands. Several options are available for Java developments. On Windows systems, for example, you can monitor the Windows Task Manager during program execution. A major deficit of the Windows Task Manager, however, is that it cannot examine your Java program. *Profilers* solve this dilemma. Besides the many commercial profilers available on the market, Sun's JVM already integrates a simple profiler called *Hprof*. It uses the *Java Virtual Machine Profiler Interface* (JVMPI), a still-experimental interface for profilers. Hprof is a tool that allows you to monitor and measure performance parameters in an active program, such as CPU time used, the number of allocated objects, or, the number of calls made for specific methods. By manually inspecting the generated log files (or using an analysis program), you can determine which parts of the program generate the greatest load, and therefore warrant further scrutiny for optimization potential.

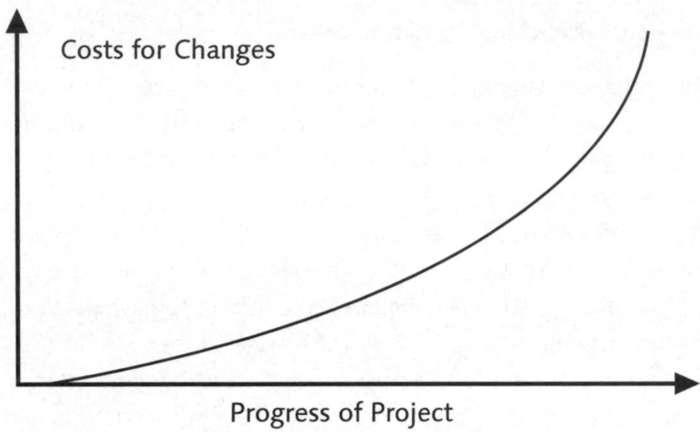

Figure 8.3 Cost Analysis

Hprof is started by a JVM parameter as indicated below:

```
Java -Xrunprof[:help][:<parameter>=<wert>,...] MainClass
```

The options listed in Table 8.1 are available:

Option	Description	Default Value
`heap=dump|site|all`	Returns the content of the heap (dump), generates stack traces that show which memory was allocated where (site), or both (all)	all
`cpu=samples|time|old`	Samples the calculation time of methods (samples), runtime and execution frequency (times) or the format used in earlier JVMs (old)	off
`monitor=y|n`	Output information for thread synchronization	n
`format=a|b`	Binary or ASCII output	a
`file=<file>`	Saves the output in a file	Java.hprof (.txt)
`net=<host>:<port>`	Transmits the data via a TCP connection	off
`depth=<value>`	Depth of stack traces	4

Table 8.1 Options for Starting Hprof

<table>
<tr><th>Option</th><th>Description</th><th>Default Value</th></tr>
<tr><td>cutoff=<value></td><td>Percentage for ranking list</td><td>0.0001</td></tr>
<tr><td>lineno=y|n</td><td>Displays line numbers</td><td>y</td></tr>
<tr><td>thread=y|n</td><td>Specifies the threads in the stack trace</td><td>n</td></tr>
<tr><td>doe=y|n</td><td>Display termination of the JVM</td><td>y</td></tr>
</table>

Table 8.1 Options for Starting Hprof (cont.)

The following brief example demonstrates how to use Hprof:

```
/**
  * PerformTest.Java
  **/
package de.snp.perf.demo;

public class PerformTest {
  public void slowMethod(){
    for(int i=0; i<500000; i++);
  }
  public void mediumMethod(){
    for(int i=0; i<5000; i++);
  }
  public void fastMethod(){
    for(int i=0; i<500; i++);
  }
  public static void main(String[] args){
    PerformTest pf = new PerformTest ();
    pf.slowMethod();
    pf.mediumMethod();
    pf.fastMethod();
  }
}

/** Execute the class **/
Java  -Xrunhprof:cpu=samples de.snp.perf.demo.PerformTest
```

Listing 8.1 Example for Using Hprof

Once Hprof is complete, the current directory contains file *Java.hprof.txt*, which has all the relevant performance information for the application that you just tested.

8.2.2 Performance Analysis Tools

SAP has also implemented several features for improving performance, as new technologies like SAP NetWeaver require continuous high performance. Several different tools are available.

Monitoring Functions

Extended monitoring functions help you administer and support Java applications. A new logging and tracing function reduces the time required to solve problems, while the availability of your system is increased through support of *distributed statistics records* and integration in the existing *Computing Center Management System* (CCMS). Distributed Statistics Records (DSRs) are analyses of statistics records that provide information about a system's performance. The response times of the J2EE Engine and all its installed applications and databases are collected and compared with one another.

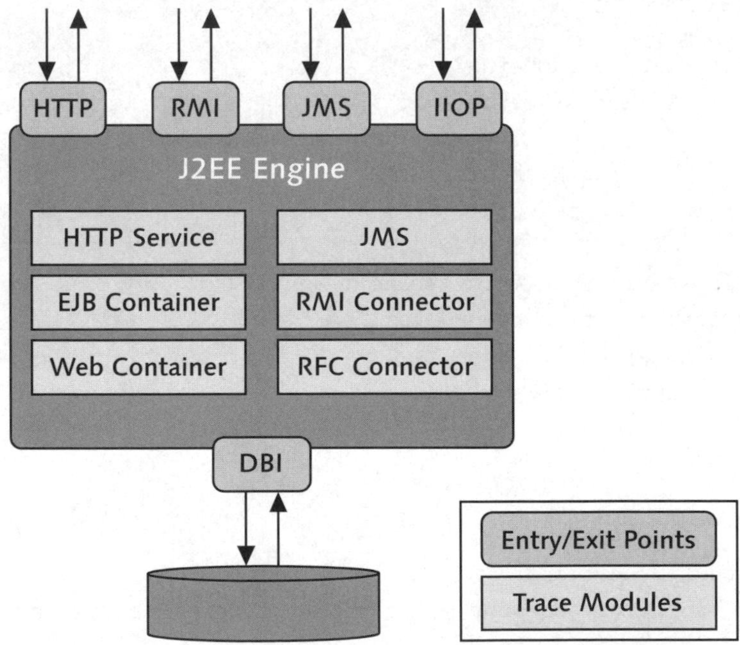

Figure 8.4 Distributed Statistics Record

Logging

The CCMS enables you to monitor, control, and configure your SAP System. As already mentioned, this system has been enhanced with monitors in SAP Web AS 6.40, which are generated by the Monitoring Service on the J2EE Engine and monitor the most important server parameters.

The monitoring architecture in the J2EE Engine is based on JMX, the Java Management standard, which means external tools can also access the monitoring data. The JMX standard provides a uniform method of making it possible to administer Java applications and services. In contrast to many other approaches, it does not involve specifications developed through the Java Community Process. It describes a model, design patterns, an API, management services for applications and networks, and monitoring services for Java. In theory, the standardized JMX interface enables you to address any compliant application from any JMX-capable management console. You can display all this data in summary form in the Visual Administrator, which helps you retrieve status information for the most important resources. This provides you with an easy way to check whether your systems are working properly, and locate the source of the problem if they're malfunctioning. The individual monitors can send alert messages as soon as defined thresholds are exceeded. The events that occur are written to the log file, which you can analyze with the Log Viewer. The Log Viewer enables you to search for log files containing specific error and event information on multiple servers, quickly and efficiently.

Application Tracing

Another useful tool is the Application Tracing Service, which helps you quickly eliminate system errors in J2EE applications. It provides traces that contain all the information about the current process of an application, without having to restart the JVM in debugging mode. You can see, for example, which classes are loaded and how much memory they use, and determine whether your application is using the available system resources optimally or wasting them.

Performance Traces

The SAP J2EE Engine also features powerful performance trace functions (see Figure 8.5), which you can use to monitor system performance and the load on system resources centrally. The performance is also monitored using statistics that you can view in the Visual Administrator.

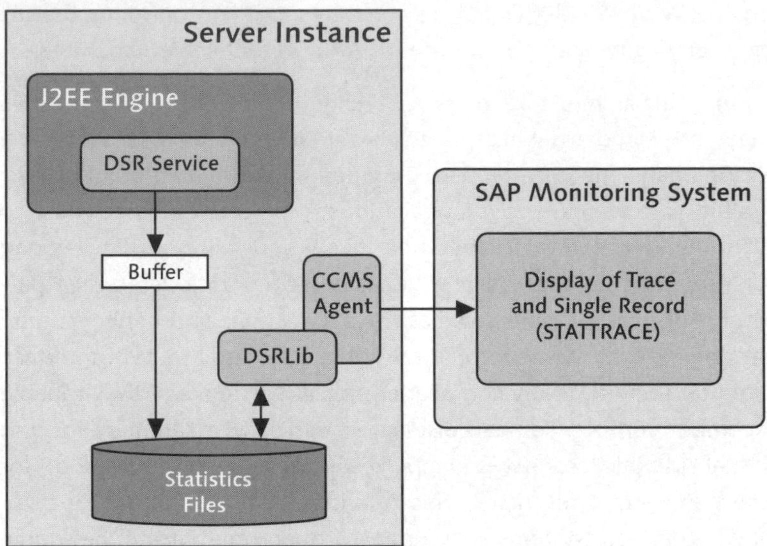

Figure 8.5 Performance Trace

Alert Monitor

The system resources, managers, and services send data to the central system, where it is handled by the Alert Monitor. All monitoring functions are based on alerts, which are warning messages that display disturbances quickly and reliably. You can configure freely definable thresholds to trigger alerts when a threshold value is exceeded or undershot. The Alert Monitor is the central tool for monitoring and managing distributed systems efficiently. It quickly and consistently displays any problems that occur. Alerts draw your attention directly to critical situations, informing you of occurring problems through automated methods instead of making you search for them yourself.

The Alert Browser helps you analyze alerts. Once you have solved a problem, or are sure you can ignore it without detrimental effects, you set the alert status to *Completed*. The corresponding alert then disappears from the display and is saved in the alert database.

The Alert Monitor sends alerts upwards through the monitor tree—the color assigned to a node always indicates the highest alert in all the elements of its branch. If a host system is displayed in red, for example, then one or more components in that host system's monitor tree have a red alert.

The essential values of the individual managers and services of the J2EE Engine—such as memory usage, pool utilization, or queue sizes—are displayed akin to a traffic light system in the Visual Administrator monitor service, clearly signifying whether and how your applications are working at all times.

To achieve optimal performance, the underlying system must meet the corresponding requirements.

Best Practices

To achieve the maximum availability, the Web container, the EJB container of the Web AS, and the underlying database system should each be located on different, physically separate systems. This will result in good performance for even large requests. Figure 8.6 illustrates this design model.

If you still think that Java is too slow, then clean programming, combined with a newly installed architecture, should convince you of the contrary.

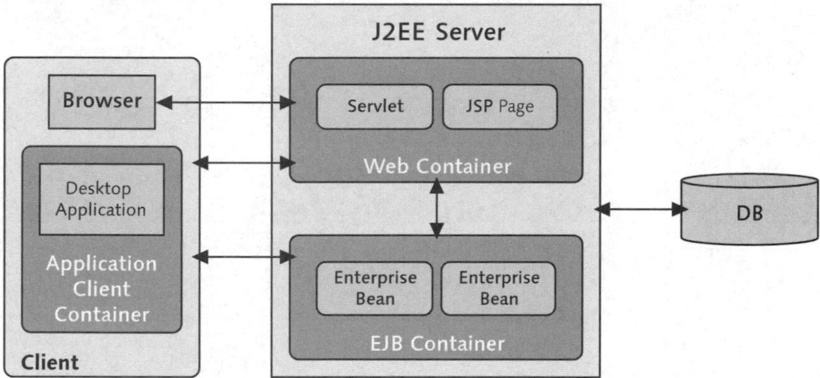

Figure 8.6 Three-Tier Architecture

9 Outlook

The development and integration of the "new" world of SAP are already well advanced—but have they progressed far enough? The best choice at the present is clearly this: Take the best of both worlds.

TCO as Motivator for Technological Focus

Implementing the best solution from the user's perspective often requires a large degree of technical heterogeneity. At the same time, heterogeneous solutions—which have to integrate widely differing technologies to create sensible scenarios—harbor their own technical and economic pitfalls that can drive the expenses for implementing and operating such solutions to unplanned or even unmanageable levels. In large IT landscapes, the effort required to merely maintain existing interfaces consumes huge sums—and these costs are rarely transparent. Eliminating this problem in current software solutions is one of the motivations for SAP's decision in recent years—to become a software vendor that, in its own words, is "technology driven and business oriented."

Technology Is Becoming More Important

Beginning with the concepts of the mySAP Technology, and even more with its announcement and implementation of the Enterprise Services Architecture (ESA) strategy with SAP NetWeaver, SAP has transformed itself from a vendor of business software solutions to a true technology provider. Consequently, technology will play an even greater role in future SAP projects. Of course, the solution's general capabilities for solving business problems remain the prime consideration, but the underlying basic technology is becoming more of a factor in determining the feasibility—and especially the cost-effectiveness—of a software solution.

Far, but Not Far Enough

Implementing SAP's visions in actual tangible products that stand up to practical demands is an arduous, stony path—and SAP still has a long way to go. The current version of the SAP Web Application Server (SAP Web AS) has taken several important steps in this direction, however. At the same time, the system is still far from fully integrating the ABAP and Java/J2EE worlds, or even putting them on an equal footing.

An Important Maturity Process

We hope you have reached the same conclusion after reading this book. Several more SAP release cycles will be required before the Java environment attains an ease of use of both development and administration that even approximates the standards of the "old" SAP world—which, of course, are quite high. You should remember, however, that even the now robust SAP R/3 technology had its teething problems and was not perfect from the start. Every new technology has to mature and prove itself; this applies especially to the Java/J2EE technology in the SAP environment.

The Right Direction

You should not discount the progress that has been made. SAP's decision to pursue this objective is still the right one, as the company had to move towards open technologies to remain competitive in the long term. SAP still seems committed to doing so, and we hope it will succeed.

Maximum Benefit Through Selective Use

For users and developers in the SAP environment, how you use the new technologies will ultimately determine how much you benefit from this new strategic orientation. The only logical approach here is this: *Take the best of both worlds*. For each new application, you should examine in detail how you can best use the strengths of both environments to implement the current project.

After reading this book, you should now have an overview of the available options. In general, the number and quality of available techniques, and their possible combinations, will increase in every new SAP release.

Rate Technologies Properly

In future, the fundamental challenge for SAP development—aside from implementing business contexts efficiently, practically, and cost-effectively—will be the ability to judge which technology or combination of technological options is best suited to ensure project success in the short- to mid-term.

You have to repeat this appraisal process for every new release of the SAP Basis technology, and don't hesitate to include existing applications in your examination. You should investigate in detail whether revising existing applications with new technologies (such as Web Dynpro) is sensible and economical.

Application Design as a Factor for Success

An attractive design of new or revised applications can already support and simplify this process today, independently of future technologies. One noteworthy example is the consistent separation of persistence, business logic, and presentation logic, which can be implemented completely independently of a given programming language or technology. Consistent implementation of this principle today is a critical prerequisite for implementing successful projects with SAP technology in the future.

Service Architecture

One technical objective of SAP's NetWeaver strategy is to divide the existing, rather monolithic business software into smaller, easier-to-use units, namely, the services. This makes it possible to connect functions between different modules in a way never before possible. The new xApps, which are based on the service architecture, prove that this approach is a promising one. They link existing business processes, functions, and data models to give customers new, custom-tailored applications at little additional effort.

Web services—a means for supplying and using cross-application functions that is already available today—are surely an important building block for creating flexible, robust, future-proof applications.

The increasing separation of application layers and Web services is certainly a big part of SAP's strategy, one which will provide a refined way of breaking down and combining applications and application components—especially those from other software vendors.

Application Toolkit

Another component of the strategy is to give users of a software solution increasingly more options for designing the functions of an application simply by combining application modules, but without requiring them to develop software in the conventional sense. While this approach is not entirely new, it is facilitated by the more modular structure of the applications and is becoming much easier to implement from a technical perspective. Examples here include the GUI Machine and options for defining new, custom workflows in SAP CRM.

Consequences for Developers and Decision-Makers

In light of current announcements and SAP products already on the market, one thing is certain: The job description for SAP developers is going to change drastically in the coming years. If you plan to develop applications that indisputably harness the vast potential of new technologies, you'll definitely require state-of-the-art skills to do so.

This requirement has the following implications for developers:

- They will have to understand and use more technologies than before. In particular, the importance of Web technologies is increasing at a breakneck pace.
- The technological share of a developer's expertise will increase, compared to application expertise.

For decision-makers, this means:

- Technological aspects of an application will have to be considered early on, possibly even in the design phase itself.

Important: Critical Appraisal and Feedback

"State-of-the-art" development does not mean implementing every new technology and uncritically chasing the latest trends. On the contrary, all new possibilities have to be examined critically in terms of their benefit for the enterprise, feasibility of implementation, and stability—and compared with all other existing possibilities—before their deployment is seriously considered. It's important to give SAP as much information as possible to clarify why certain technologies were accepted or rejected, because only constructive feedback from the customer will truly improve the products.

In the coming years, the increasing variety of technologies available for satisfying project requirements will make project work in the SAP environment more challenging.

To execute and manage SAP development projects successfully in the long term, you will have to rely on the right technologies to solve the task at hand.

We hope this book will help you to choose them.

A Glossary

This glossary contains explanations for most of the technical terms used in this book.

.JAD Java Application Descriptor. A descriptive file, for example, for MIDlet.

.NET Microsoft's platform for XML-based Web services. Contains tools to develop and use Web-based applications. A new technology for programming in the Internet and implementing globally distributed applications. .NET competes with SunONE.

ABAP Advanced Business Application Programming. A programming language and environment for developing, using, and executing mySAP application components.

ABAP Dictionary A central, redundancy-free repository for all application and system data in the SAP System. The ABAP Dictionary is part of the R/3 Repository. Transaction SE11.

ABAP Editor A tool in the ABAP Workbench to develop and maintain ABAP programs. The ABAP Editor provides many specialized functions for developers. Transaction SE38.

ABAP Interpreter Interprets ABAP programs.

ABAP Objects Object-oriented enhancement of the ABAP Workbench. It features a Virtual Machine (VM) that can execute applications with and without ABAP objects.

ABAP program A program written in the ABAP programming language. There are two kinds of ABAP programs: report programs (ABAP reports) and dialog programs.

ABAP VM (Virtual Machine) Executes ABAP intermediate coding at runtime. Forms the core of the ABAP runtime environment (also: ABAP Personality).

ABAP Workbench SAP's graphical development environment. The integrated tools of the ABAP Workbench provide a wide range of functions.

Abstract class → class

Abstract method → method

ActiveX ActiveX can be used to program software modules based on Microsoft's COM and DCOM standards. These OCX/OLE controls (→ OLE) are largely plug-ins and usable primarily under Microsoft Windows.

Aggregation A special type of relationship between objects defined in the UML specification. It represents a whole/part relationship in which the life cycle of the part is not dependent on that of the whole. Example: Object "tire" (part) has a relationship to object "car" (whole). The tire can continue to exist even if the car is destroyed.

Activate, activation Activating SAP development elements makes them available to the runtime system.

ALE Application Link Enabling. ALE supports the integration of distributed applications. This platform-independent solution enables SAP and non-SAP systems to communicate with one another, making it possible to implement cross-application, cross-component business processes and information flows.

Application hierarchy An organization tool for displaying all business applications in the SAP R/3 System. Transaction SE81.

Application hierarchy An organization tool for displaying all business applications in the SAP R/3 System. Transaction SE81.

API Application programming interface. APIs are interfaces to application programs. They provide developers with standardized libraries, allowing the use of existing services.

Applet → Java applet

Applet container Runtime environment for applets. Consists of a Web browser and a Java plug-in (on the client).

Application client container Runtime environment for client applications. Runs on the client and can establish status-specific connections with the J2EE server.

Application server Server for application programs. Can refer to a server in the LAN that runs applications used by many clients (such as groupware; in contrast to pure file server services), or can be used as a transaction server or middleware in a three-tier architecture (→ Three-tier architecture). The Web Application Server (→ Web AS) is used for Web applications.

ASCII American Standard Code for Information Interchange. The standard encoding of letters, numbers, and other symbols. ASCII consists of 128 symbols (7-bit) and does not contain any international characters. A non-standard extension to 8-bit contains another 128 country-specific characters. → Unicode

Association A relationship between classes or objects. Stronger forms of association are aggregation and composition.

Attribute Property of an object. A variable that is assigned to a class. Class attributes, in contrast, apply to multiple objects, independently of the object instantiation.

Authorization Permission to carry out a specific activity in the R/3 System. Authorizations are saved in the user's profile.

Authorization concept The structure and functions associated with authorization assignment and checking in the R/3 System. You use authorizations to protect the system from unauthorized or unwanted access.

AWT A class library provided in Java. It consists of elements for designing user interfaces. It is part of the JFC. The Swing library is the successor technology.

Backend Refers to the data storage layer within the layer model. In contrast, a backend system means connecting an independent IT system (SAP or non-SAP system) with its own database. In addition to ERP systems, Web services can also be integrated in the Web Dynpro framework.

BAPI Business Application Programming Interface. BAPIs represent a standard for communicating between business systems. They implement object integration at both a technical and user department level; form standardized, business-based, and object-oriented programming interfaces to the business objects; and enable communication with SAP components. BAPIs are based on professional terminology and represent a highly semantic interface. They do not use any screen dialogs. BAPIs are defined as methods of SAP business objects or SAP interface types in the Business Object Repository and are implemented as function modules.

BAPI Explorer An environment for developing BAPIs. Its hierarchy area can be used to display application components, other Workbench tools can be called from the navigation area. Transaction BAPI.

Batch input An interface that enables the transfer of large volumes of data to an SAP System. A sequence of transactions can be saved as a stack in a batch input session. The session can be processed at any time; the database is not changed or updated until then. This method can be used to save large amounts of data in the SAP System in a short amount of time.

Background processing Processing that runs autonomously and does not require user interaction.

Beans → JavaBeans

Binding Assignment of a UI element to an element of a view controller context structure.

Bottom-up modularization A principle of system development from specialized to general, therefore sometimes also called "generalization." → Top-down

BPM Business Process Management. A component in the SAP NetWeaver architecture to enable cross-system business processes. The technological basis is the SAP Exchange Infrastructure (XI).

Breakpoint A selected point in the source coding where execution (in debugging mode) is interrupted, in order to analyze the program flow. → Debugger

BSP (Business Server Page) Business Server Pages are Web pages that contain business logic in addition to a layout description. They are implemented by embedding ABAP coding in HTML pages.

Build The build process takes place within J2EE and Web Dynpro development. When a build is executed, all development objects are grouped together in packages. In Web Dynpros, this step largely involves generating the actual implementation from the metadata.

Business Connector XML-based connection of business partners across the supply chain. The Business Connector therefore enables the integration of heterogeneous systems over the Internet.

Business Framework An open, component-based product architecture that includes both R/3 and non-R/3 systems. SAP Business Framework makes it easier to maintain and upgrade systems, as well as interact between different systems.

Business logic Represents the actual processing logic and is a separate layer—between the presentation and data collection layers—in the layer model.

Business object An actual instance of a specific object type (ABAP) or a specific class (Java) at runtime.

Business Object Builder A tool for creating and modifying business object types. You can use it to access business object type definitions directly, test and generate business object types, and generate a Where-used list. You can also create subtypes for existing business object types. Transaction SW01.

Business Workflow SAP's concept for optimizing business processes through integrated, cross-function business processes.

Byte code Intermediate coding that is generated from Java programs is called "byte code." This coding is platform-independent and is executed by the JVM.

Caching A storage procedure for accelerating information processing that is used in various ways; for example, to buffer Web pages in a browser, or to accelerate access to hard disks and databases.

Call-by-reference When used to call methods, these methods are given the references in the parameters.

Call-by-value When used to call methods, these methods are given the values in the parameters.

Casting Explicit type conversion of variables, attributes, or objects.

CATT Computer Aided Test Tool for generating test data and testing business processes.

CBS Component Build Service. A component of the Java Development Infrastructure (JDI), it stores Java archives and supports the build processes from the DTR contents.

CGI Common Gateway Interface. Programming interface on Web servers. Parameters from the client—from HTML forms, for instance—can be passed on to a program or a script that is then executed on the server, using environment variables or the stdin interface.

Change request → Transport request

Changing parameter A parameter that is passed on to a function module, manipulated within it, and then returned in change form. It functions as both an import and an export parameter and is transferred by reference.

Class A class is one of the main characteristics of object orientation. It consists of attributes and methods, and employs data encapsulation. The concept is based on analyzing data simultaneously instead of sequentially. Inheritance between the classes sets up a hierarchical structure. Objects are instantiated from concrete classes.

Class, abstract A class that cannot be used to form an instance. It is merely used to add a structure to the inheritance hierarchy and give uniform properties to the subclasses.

Class attribute This type of attribute is assigned to a class and is completely independent of any given instance.

Class Browser Browser component of the Class Builder. The Class Browser supports navigation in the R/3 class library, which contains ABAP classes and interfaces.

Class Builder A component of the SAP development environment for modifying classes and interfaces. Transaction SE24.

Class, concrete A class from which objects may be created.

Class inheritance Structure of a class hierarchy in which the subclasses inherit all the properties of the higher-level class.

Class, inner When classes are nested, the class that is within another class. It is intended to control visibility.

Class library A collection of routines that provide development functions. The class library is completely independent of the application's architecture.

Class method This type of method is assigned to a class and is completely independent of any given instance.

Client In commercial and organizational terms, a self-contained unit in an R/3 System. Data and Customizing settings can be client-specific or cross-client.

CMS Change Management Service. → SL

COM Component Object Model. An object-oriented component model developed by Microsoft. Its objective was to increase software reusability. To enable access to object components over networks as well, COM was enhanced to create DCOM (Distributed COM) in a later stage.

Compiler A compiler completely converts the source coding of a program into machine language, creating an executable (but platform-dependent) file.

Component controller Every Web Dynpro component automatically has a component controller, which represents the main controller in the component and belongs to the family of custom controllers.

Component interface Public controller and thus interface to a Web Dynpro component.

Component (Web Dynpro) Web Dynpro components encapsulate views and controllers. They structure the application and make it possible to reuse entire application components. Component interfaces are also used.

Composite Application Framework The Composite Application Framework enables xApps to be created quickly and easily, using tools, methods, rules, and modules.

Composition The definition of a composition as it is used in design patterns should not be confused with the official UML specification. As defined in this book, a composition describes a simple relationship between objects that is implemented through references. According to UML specifications, composition is a special form of relationship between objects that represents a whole/part relationship in which the life cycle of the part depends on that of the whole. Example: Object "file" (part) has a relationship to object "folder" (whole). If the folder is deleted, the file is also deleted.

Consolidation route The regular transport path of a Repository object from the integration system to the consolidation system. The consolidation route is defined by the development class and the transport layer for each Repository object. The routes are required for each involved transport layer in order to transport changes.

Consolidation system A system into which tested, stable developments can be transported. Consolidation systems can be quality assurance systems, where final testing is performed; when minor developments are involved, the production system can also be used as the consolidation system. → Development system, Production system

Constructor A method that is carried out automatically when an object is created and sets the initial attribute values. The constructor can also call other methods and (super)constructors.

Container Server-side component of the runtime environment. → EJB, JSP, Servlet

Container-managed persistence The EJB container controls the storage of Entity Beans in the database, which means direct database access is no longer necessary.

Context Contexts are objects from the development environment comprised of key fields that must be entered; relationships between these fields; and other fields that can be derived from them.

Context (Web Dynpro) Hierarchically structured, dynamic data store of a controller. In addition to the actual user data, contexts also contain metadata that defines the structure of the user data. The metadata is defined at design time, while the contents remain unknown until runtime.

Context Builder To create, maintain, and test contexts. Transaction SE33.

Control Framework The basic technology for Enjoy controls, based on ABAP Objects.

CORBA Common Object Request Broker Architecture. A software architecture that makes it possible for objects to communicate with other remote objects. Not dependent on a specific programming language or system platform.

CSF Client-side framework. Enables client-side rendering of Web Dynpro pages. This approach reduces the load on the server and accelerates page reproduction. The CSF consists of a JavaScript library approximately 80 KB in size (compressed).

CSS Cascading style sheets. Defines style properties that control the appearance of elements in Web pages.

CSV Comma-separated values. A data interchange format. Field contents are separated by commas or semicolons, while line breaks separate table rows.

Custom tags User-defined JSP elements that encapsulate repetitive tasks. Custom tags are managed in tag libraries.

Data Modeler A tool for creating data models. The Data Modeler supports the creation of data models and their mapping to the ABAP Dictionary. Transaction SD11.

Database A database generally refers to a relational database. It saves data in tabular form. SQL statements are used to access the data.

Database, logical A special ABAP program that combines the contents of specific database tables. A logical database can be appended as an attribute of an ABAP program. It supplies that program with hierarchically structured table lines that can originate from different database tables. This saves developers from having to program the data retrieval themselves. The term "logical database" encompasses both the actual program and the corresponding dataset.

Database commit A database operation that finally executes all database changes within an LUW to the database.

Database rollback If an error is detected within an LUW, a database rollback resets all the database changes made since the start of that LUW (that is, since the last database commit).

Database transaction → LUW

Data element A development object that is assigned to a data type and which has content, such as data from a field or a table.

Data encapsulation The properties of an object are encapsulated within that object and not visible from the outside. This is achieved through strict application of the security concept.

Data type Data types describe the technical properties of the data objects. The data type is determined during declaration, for example, integer or string. Important data types are Char (fixed-length string), Float (floating point number), integer, and string (variable-length string).

DCOM Distributed Component Object Model. Enhances the COM model with an option to access object components across networks.

DDIC → ABAP Dictionary

Debugger A tool for identifying and eliminating errors in programs. It runs a program step by step and can be interrupted at runtime (Breakpoints), and also shows the contents of variables and their changes at processing time clearly. The debugger is integrated in the ABAP Workbench.

Declarative programming Characterizes the programming paradigm. In contrast to imperative programming, in which a sequence of commands is programmed, declarative programming describes a problem or a program at a high level of abstraction. It is implemented in Web Dynpro in that the application is saved in metadata, which is ultimately used to generate the actual implementation automatically. This makes for platform-independent programs.

Declaration The definition of variables, attributes, or objects. Often used in combination with initialization.

Deployment descriptor Describes a module (→ JAR or → EAR) and configures it for the specific use. Consists of one or more XML files.

Deployment Deployment is a component of developing server-side components. It means making the server components available on a server.

Design pattern A design pattern systematically names, motivates, and explains a general pattern that solves a repetitive design problem in object-oriented systems. It describes the pattern, the solution, where the solution can be applied, and the consequences of its application. It also provides implementation tips and examples. The solution is a general pattern of objects and classes that solve the problem. The solution is tailored and implemented to solve the problem in a specific context. (As defined by Erich Gamma)

Development class Related data is assigned to a development class to ensure simple, trouble-free transport. Development classes have been renamed as packages since Basis Release 5.0A.

Development system This system is used for software implementation, and usually for Customizing as well. → Consolidation system, Production system

Development environment → IDE

Development cycle (Web Dynpro) After a Web Dynpro application is created (Edit), the source code is generated at first (Build). After subsequent publishing on the Web AS (Deploy), the Web application is executed (Run) in the browser. The software development cycle of Web Dynpros involves the following steps: Edit – Build – Deploy – Run.

Dialog program A program consisting of screens, which can be started with a transaction code.

DOM Document Object Model. W3C standard for object orientation and programming interface for XML documents. DOM competes with Simple API for XML (SAX). In contrast to SAX, DOM uses an object tree for XML access, which is easier to handle but not suitable for large documents.

Domain A domain defines technical attributes of fields, such as the number of places. Similar fields can be assigned to the same domain, grouping them together. When the domain is modified, the fields are updated automatically, which guarantees consistency. → Value domain

DTD Document type definition. Definition of the document type and meanings of tags of HTML and XML documents. → XML Schema

DTR Design Time Repository. DTR is a component of the Java Development Infrastructure (JDI). It manages central development objects, such as tables, Java classes, and Web Dynpro project files, enabling versioning of all project components and synchronization among the developers.

Dynpro DYNamic PROgram. This technology is used to build graphical screens. A dynpro consists of a screen image and the underlying structure logic.

EAR Enterprise Archive. An EAR file is a standard .jar file that contains J2EE modules to build different J2EE applications that use the same components.

ebXML Electronic Business XML. Framework for an open, XML-based architecture that enables the use of business information globally in an interoperable, secure manner.

Eclipse A freely extensible IDE for developing and testing applications. Was written completely in Java.

EIS Enterprise Information System. System components that manage information, such as databases and ERP systems.

EJB Enterprise JavaBeans. EJBs are server-side components that enable the implementation of object-oriented, distributed application services. Its runtime environment is called "EJB Container."

EJB Container Runtime environment for EJBs. Controls the life cycle of a Bean and provides the Beans with various services (name/directory service) and APIs (such as JDBC). The EJB Container is also responsible for tasks such as transaction/resource management, scalability, persistence, security, and database access.

Enjoy controls Enjoy controls are reusable, object-oriented ABAP components that are intended to improve the appearance of the SAP System as part of the enjoySAP initiative.

enjoySAP An approach to developing custom user interfaces that are tailored to users' specific needs in order to make work more efficient.

Entity Bean Represents persistent business objects that are saved in a database via object-relational mapping.

Event When a certain system state is achieved, an event is triggered, which initiates a processing block.

Event block A group of ABAP program statements called by the runtime system. They are executed when a certain event is triggered, such as program initialization or a certain user interaction.

ERP Enterprise resource planning. ERP systems employ targeted workflow management to provide for enterprise-wide resource planning. ERP can consist of systems for manufacturing, financials, human resources, sales, and material resources. R/3 is an ERP system.

Error handling → Exception handling

ESA Enterprise Services Architecture. ESA is an architecture for service-based business applications implemented using SAP NetWeaver technology. It provides cross-enterprise business processes that integrate all involved SAP and non-SAP systems.

Exception (handling) An exception is an occurrence of an error at runtime. Errors can be trapped specifically. Exception handling refers to the catching and processing of errors.

Export parameter Value that a function module passes on to the calling program. → Import parameter

Framework A class library that gives the user a certain type of application. Developers adapt the framework to their needs by forming subclasses and using their objects.

Function Builder Tool for developing and managing function modules and function groups. You use the Function Builder to create, change, test, and document function modules. The Function Builder contains a function library, which serves as a central storage facility for all function modules. Transaction SE37.

Function A process triggered either within a program or through user interaction.

Function module External subroutines, written in ABAP, that can be developed in the Function Builder. They're managed in a central function library and can therefore be called from any ABAP program. They have a unique, defined interface.

Function library Central storage facility for function modules.

Function code The unique key for a function to control the screen flow. The function code is interpreted by the ABAP program. It is either entered by the user or assigned to a function key.

Function group A set of logically related function modules. Typically, functions that use the same data are assigned to the same function group.

Garbage collector The garbage collector cleans up at runtime of a Java program, releasing memory by deleting objects that are no longer referenced.

GUI status The GUI status contains a menu bar with menus, an application toolbar, and a function key menu. → Menu Painter.

GUI title This GUI element allows you to define the title for a screen. → Menu Painter

GuiXT GuiXT is a tool for customizing the SAP R/3 user interface. Many different configuration options are available to create a custom design.

Hash A hash function, such as SHA-1 (Secure Hash Algorithm) and MD5 (Message Digest), is an algorithm for generating unique, brief byte sequences (similar to checksums). These one-way functions are used like a digital fingerprint as a digital signature (→ Signature). While the signature does not reveal anything about the file content, it is nearly impossible to create another file with the same hash result.

HTMLB HTML Business for ABAP. A complete set of easy-to-use Web controls. Lets you implement complex HTML elements as summary tags.

IAC Internet Application Component. An R/3 Internet application that enterprises can use to run transactions, functions, and program reports in a Web browser. Requires an ITS.

ICM Internet Communication Manager. Web AS component. It is responsible for maintaining communication between an SAP System and the outside world (Internet) using HTTP, HTTPS, and SMTP protocols. It can act as both server and client.

IDE Integrated Development Environment. A development environment that provides easy-to-use tools to simplify program implementation. SAP NetWeaver Developer Studio is the IDE in Web Dynpro.

IDoc Intermediate document. Standard SAP format for electronic document interchange between systems.

Import parameter Value that a calling program passes on to a function module. → Export parameter

Inbound plug (Web Dynpro) Entry point to a view. Is connected with an outbound plug of the start view.

Include 1.) A non-independent ABAP program. Include programs contain program components. They are called by a main program and are only executable together with a main program. A function that is placed in an include program can be called by any number of different report programs.
2.) Insertion of other parameterizable JSPs in the context of a higher-level JSP. Not related to the include concept in the SAP terminology.

Initialization Initial assignment of a variable, attribute, or object. Often used in combination with declaration.

Instance In the object-oriented terminology, an instance is an actual object of a class.

Instantiation Generation of a new instance, for example, to create an object.

Interface 1. An interface consists exclusively of abstract methods, but does not define their functions. Instead, the corresponding class has to implement the interface (or interfaces). Therefore, interfaces are a way to compensate for the non-existent multilevel inheritance.
2. An interface defines the interaction between objects. It consists primarily of abstract methods. The corresponding classes have to implement these methods.

Interface inheritance Inheritance of interfaces.

Intermediate code → Byte code

Internal table → Table, internal

Interpreter The source program is interpreted during its execution, and not compiled as machine coding beforehand. Java classes (*.java) are precompiled in byte code (*.class), which is interpreted (parsed and executed line by line) at runtime. The runtime environment is implemented by a platform-specific Virtual Machine (VM), which makes the actual program coding platform-independent.

ITS Internet Transaction Server. Interface between the R/3 System and the Internet. The ITS enables Internet and intranet users to communicate with the R/3 System directly by running business transactions, function modules, and program reports as IACs.

J2EE Java 2 Enterprise Edition. A platform developed by Sun Microsystems for developing and operating multilayer, Java-based enterprise applications. J2EE represents an enhancement of J2SE and provides additional packages. → Java

J2EE component J2EE applications consist of J2EE components. A J2EE component is a functional software unit that is embedded in the J2EE application with its corresponding classes and files. Java servlets and EJBs are two examples of possible J2EE application components.

J2EE module A J2EE module consists of one or more J2EE components that have an identical container type and a component deployment descriptor.

J2EE server Runtime environment for a J2EE product. A J2EE server provides EJBs and Web containers.

J2ME Java 2 Micro Edition. For Java-enabled devices such as cell phones and PDAs.

J2SE Java 2 Standard Edition. → JDK

JAR Java archive. JARs group Java classes and other resources together in a compressed file, enabling more complex functions.

Java An object-oriented, platform-independent programming language suitable for use in the Internet. Java is an interpreter language whose runtime environment is implemented by a Virtual Machine (→ VM).

JavaBeans Java Beans are reusable Java components that can be integrated as elements in applications. JavaBeans compete with OLE.

Java byte code → Byte code

Java Dictionary A central, redundancy-free repository for metadata and therefore, a directory of all data-relevant information. The Java Dictionary is part of the Repository.

Java servlet technology A technology that can be used to define HTTP-specific servlet classes. A servlet class extends the capabilities of the request/response programming model to an application server.

Java Web Start → JWS

Java applet A Java program integrated in a Web site that is loaded from the Web server over the Internet or intranet to the client and run in a Web browser there. It is subject to stringent security requirements and has no direct access to the computer's resources.

Java application An independent, executable program that was programmed in Java and has full access to all the computer's resources.

Java IDL Java API to enable use of CORBA.

JavaMail Java API for email.

JavaOS Java Operating System. Operating system that can run Java programs directly.

JavaScript A macro language that can be integrated in HTML. It is interpreted in the client-side browser. Technically speaking, JavaScript is completely independent from Java; the only similarities are its name and syntax. It is especially well suited for direct local processing, such as input validation. The CSF (client-side framework) in Web Dynpro is based on JavaScript, which makes it possible to process user interactions on the client and minimize server requests.

Java Server Pages technology This technology makes it possible to insert small pieces of servlet coding directly in a text-based document. A JSP consists of two parts: a static part (HTML, WML, XML, etc.) and a dynamic part (JSP elements).

JAXM Java API for XML Messaging. Supports the transfer of XML data via HTTP, FTP, and SMTP.

JAXP Java API for XML Parsing. A standardized API for accessing XML content under Java. Consists of SAX and DOM. → JDOM

JBC Java byte code. → Byte code

JCA J2EE Connector Architecture. Defines standardized Java interfaces to simplify the integration of enterprise applications within J2EE-based Java applications. Java developers can use these interfaces to access databases, e-business applications, and legacy systems. → JCo

JCo Java Connector. Java connector from SAP R/3 to BAPI via SAP RFC. SAP Java Connector is an independent middleware component and enables two-way communication between the Java and ABAP personalities on Web AS. An API and additional middleware interface convert Java calls to RFC calls and vice versa.

JCP Java Community Process. An open, community-based process for developing specifications, reference implementations, and compatibility kits for Java technology. The objective of the JCP program is to promote the further enhancement of Java, while maintaining its platform independence. JCP has two separate executive committees for the consumer/embedded and enterprise markets.

JDBC Java Database Connectivity. An object-oriented interface for Java programs to access databases. Enables SQL statements to be sent to databases easily, provided the database has a JDBC driver.

JDI Java Development Infrastructure. Enables team-based development of Java and Web Dynpro. The JDI is integrated directly in SAP NetWeaver Developer Studio. It consists mainly of the components DTR, CBS, and SL.

JDK Java Development Kit (also called J2SE). A collection of tools (libraries, compiler, interpreter, applet viewer, debugger, and so on) for programming in Java.

JDO Java Data Objects. An API for transparent database access. Enables developers to store Java objects transparently, without having to consider the peculiarities of the database. Prerequisite: A JDO-compatible DBMS is used.

JDOM Java Document Object Model. DOM for Java, JAXP

JES Java Embedded Server. Intended for use on home gateways, to connect networked households to the outside world and enable remote control of household appliances. Contains Personal Java for Embedded Devices. → J2ME

JFC Java Foundation Class. The JFC contains classes of the GUI, such as Swing and the look and feel.

Jini Java Intelligent Network Infrastructure. Java/RMI-based middleware technology for the simple integration of various devices in networks. In the home networking area, Jini competes with UPnP (Microsoft's Universal Plug&Play home networking standard).

JMS Java Message Service. Features a complete set of APIs that enable developers to use the widespread features of various messaging systems.

JMX Java Management Extensions. A universal, open technology for managing adapted legacy systems and implementing new management solutions. JMX features tools for creating distributed, modular, dynamic Web-based solutions for managing Java-based devices, applications, and service-driven networks.

JNDI Java Naming and Directory Interface. Features a standardized interface to directory services such as ADS, NDS, LDAP, and DNS. An object can be linked to a name and located through that name. JNDI enables the retrieval, storage, and deletion of objects in a directory service.

JNI Java Native Interface. Controls calls of platform-specific functions under Java.

JNLP Java Network Launching Protocol. Protocol for copying JWS applications. Java applications can be installed through a Web browser and are then executable outside of the browser.

JRA SAP Java Resource Adapter. Resource adapters (also called "connectors") connect the server with external data sources (EIS). They are represented by a Java archive. A resource adapter is installed on the server and enables communication between it and the EIS.

JRE Java Runtime Environment.

JRun Web server extension by Macromedia, including servlet and JSP support.

JSP Java Server Page. JSPs enable developers to embed Java in HTML pages. An HTML page is generated on the server side at runtime, forming a Web page. The JSP runtime environment is called a "Web container."

JSTL Java Standard Tag Library. A popular tag library used for JSP development.

JVM Java Virtual Machine. → VM

JWS Java Web Start applications are transferred via JNLP and run independently of the Web browser in a separate JVM; in contrast to Java applications, however, they are subject to similar restrictions as Java applets.

Layout manager The configured layout manager defines how UI elements are displayed in a view. Two frequently used elements are the FlowLayout and the GridLayout. The FlowLayout arranges all the elements in its sequence and sets a simple line break at the bottom of the window. In contrast, the GridLayout divides the screen into a grid in which each cell can be assigned a UI element.

LDAP Lightweight Directory Access Protocol. Standard protocol for accessing directory services. LDAP is generally used to supply organizational and user data, as well as other sources such as files and devices in the Internet or in enterprise networks.

List An output list is a standard function in R/3. A list is the formatted output of data from a database query.

Local object A development object used for private purposes. Local objects belong to development class $TMP and are not transported to other systems. It is possible to display other user's local objects, however.

Lock object A lock object is a virtual connection of several SAP tables that synchronizes concurrent access to the same dataset by two different users.

LUW Logical unit of work. An inseparable sequence of database operations hat must be executed in its entirety or not at all. The logical unit of work, or database transaction, plays an important role in ensuring data integrity in the DBMS. Ensures full processing of multistep processes. The transaction is not made final (commit) until all the single processes are performed correctly; otherwise all changes are undone (rollback).

Mapping In Web Dynpro, involves mapping one context element to another, which enables automatic data transport from the frontend to the backend.

Menu Painter A tool for designing the GUI. The Menu Painter can be used to define the menu bar, application toolbar, and function key menu. The graphical user interface consists of a GUI title and a GUI status. Transaction SE41.

Message-driven bean Combines features of session beans and JMS so that a business component to receive JMS messages asynchronously.

Metadata Data that describes other data. Metadata is data definitions that are usually stored in a data dictionary (ABAP or Java Dictionary). In contrast, metadata created for a Web Dynpro project is saved based on XML, which is used to generate the actual application later.

Method An operation that can be executed on an object. Methods are called with the method ID and the interface parameters.

Method, abstract An abstract method does not contain an implementation. If a class has an abstract method, that class has to be declared as abstract as well. The purpose of using abstract methods is that all classes that inherit a class have to implement the respective method, making them uniform.

Middleware Link between system and application. Builds on the transport layer and provides extended functions to applications. Middleware is often used in remote method calls.

MIDlet J2ME application for MIDP devices. Multiple MIDlets and other resources can be grouped together in a .jar archive to form a MIDlet suite. → Java applet

MIDP Mobile Information Device Profile. Extends J2ME libraries for the device class of small, mobile, wireless devices, such as cell phones and PDAs. Can execute MIDlets.

MIME Multipurpose Interchange Mail Extensions. Standard for designating the format of multimedia files, for example, for multimedia email and for encoding any binary files as e-mail attachments.

Modification Browser A special editor with modification wizards for changing/enhancing standard SAP programs.

Module Modules are special ABAP processing blocks for screen processing. They are integrated in the flow logic and not executable on their own.

Module pool An ABAP module pool is a program type. It collects modules. Therefore, a module pool represents a pool for dialog modules and cannot be executed independently.

Multithreading A processing method in which programs are split into multiple subroutine threads that are processed in parallel. → Thread

MVC Model View Controller. This concept organizes the components of a system independently of one another, making them much more flexible. This design paradigm is applied consistently under the Web Dynpro technology. The model contains the data (or is responsible for collecting it), while the view displays it. The controller is responsible for communication between view and model, guaranteeing their independence.

Native SQL Native SQL enables the use of database-specific SQL statements in an ABAP program. An ABAP program with database-specific SQL statements does not usually run on different databases. → Open SQL

Next screen Attribute of a screen. The next screen is the screen displayed after the current screen in a transaction flow.

Object Instance of a class. Objects contain data (attributes) and provide services as methods.

Object catalog Directory of all Repository objects that comprise the SAP System. The object catalog contains at least the following information for each object: Object type, object name, original system, owner, and development class.

Object list A list of change requests. Whenever objects are changed, they are added to the object list of a task. When a task is released, its object list is placed in the object list of the request to which it is assigned. Transport

Object Navigator Navigation tool for managing development objects. The user interface of the Object Navigator works like a file manager, by grouping development objects together in object lists within a hierarchical structure. Transaction SE80.

Object-relational mapping The process of mapping object-oriented data to a relational database system.

ODBC An API that applications use to access databases. The API decouples databases and applications. All database systems are now ODBC-compatible. To achieve this, database vendors have to provide an ODBC driver. ODBC-compatible applications can therefore access different databases.

OLE Object Linking and Embedding. A Microsoft standard for composed documents that is based on the COM specifications. Documents can be embedded in and linked with one another to create a link to the source document. OLE competes with CORBA. → ActiveX

OO, OOP Object-oriented programming. Data (properties) and the corresponding operations (methods) are bundled in classes or objects. Examples of OO languages include Java, ABAP, and C++.

Open SQL A set of SQL statements defined by SAP and a subset of the SQL standard. Open SQL enables database queries from the R/3 System, regardless of which database system is used.

Outbound plug (Web Dynpro) Exit from a view. Enables navigation and is linked with an inbound plug of the target view.

Overloading (methods) When two identically-named methods of a class have different signatures, this is called overloading.

Packages Classes and interfaces in Java can be grouped together to form packages. Packages have a hierarchical structure and are used to group together different classes that belong to a common work area.

PAI Process After Input. A processing block in the screen flow logic that is processed after the screen is displayed. → Dynpro, Module, PBO

Parameter Data required to execute an object method (→ Import parameter) or returned by the method after it is called (→ Export parameter). The parameters belonging to a method are determined within the object type definition. The interface of the method call is determined when the parameters are defined.

Parent class → Superclass

Patterns Patterns describe programming language-independent concepts for solving problems in system development. They can occur at different levels of abstraction, for example, to describe an architecture. Design patterns (→ Design patterns) are much more popular. They solve recurring problems with patterns in an abstract manner.

PBO Process Before Output. Processing block that is processed after a screen is called but before it is actually displayed. → Dynpro, Module, PAI

Personality The Web AS features ABAP and Java personalities, each of which comprises the development and runtime environment. The Java Connector (JCo) is used for two-way communication.

Polymorphy A method used in OOP. It dictates that inherited methods in the derived class can be implemented differently than in the basic class. It is implemented by overwriting the basic class in the hierarchy view. Accordingly, object polymorphy can exist in only inheritance hierarchies. A derived object can appear in place of a specific object anywhere in a program, because an object of a derived class is polymorphic. It can respond as either an object of a derived class or an object of a basic class.

Pretty Printer ABAP source coding highlighting. It goes through the source coding and makes it easier to read by indenting lines and writing keywords in all caps.

Private This keyword makes attributes and methods visible only within their own class.

Processing block A group of program statements executed as a unit. When an event occurs, the assigned processing block is called and processed. → Event, Event block, Module, Subroutine

Production system The system that is intended for actual operations; it contains the enterprise data and must only contain released system components. → Development system, Consolidation system

Program status A program status can be defined for each program in the SAP System. They include: Test program, system program, customer production program, and the SAP standard production program.

Program type Each program in the SAP System can be assigned a program type. They include: Executable program, module pool, INCLUDE program, function group, subroutine pool, interface pool, class pool. A pool is a collection of similar programs. Only the "Executable programs" can be run independently.

Protected This keyword releases the element within the inheritance hierarchy, but not to the outside.

Public This keyword makes the corresponding element visible to everyone.

RAR Resource adapter archive. This archive contains all the interfaces, classes, and system-dependent libraries.

Reference A reference is a link from one place in the main memory to another. This link makes it possible to not only pass elements on by value, but with their reference as well.

Report program An ABAP program that reads and analyzes data from database tables without changing the database. Every ABAP report program has program type "1" and is linked with a specific logical database. These values are passed on in the program attributes. When an ABAP report program is executed, the output list is either displayed on screen or sent to a printer.

Repository Central storage facility for all ABAP Workbench development objects, such as program objects, function group objects, and Dictionary objects.

Reuse components Reusable components, such as function groups and classes.

Reuse Library Library of reuse components.

RFC Remote Function Call. RFC is an SAP interface protocol that simplifies the programming of communication processes between systems. RFCs enable predefined functions to be called and executed in the same system or on a remote system.

Rich client A client that contains client-side processing logic in addition to displaying data. In contrast, a thin client is responsible for only the display logic.

RMI Remote Method Invocation. A Java standard for distributed programming. RMI enable objects on remote systems to communicate with one another. The objects respond like local objects.

Runtime analysis A test environment for transactions, programs, and function modules.

Runtime environment A runtime environment enables programs to be executed and provides the libraries required to do so. In Web AS, the ABAP Engine and J2EE Engine are the runtime environments. The Web Dynpro runtime environment encapsulates the engines of the supported programming languages (platforms). Currently, only the Java personality is available for Web Dynpro in Web AS 6.30.

SAML Security Assertion Markup Language. An XML security standard for exchanging authentication and authorization information.

SAP GUI/SAP client Graphical user interface for the R/3 System. It enables access to applications, data input, and data output. Different SAP GUIs are available, primarily:

- SAP GUI for HTML: Runs in a browser
- SAP GUI for Java: Platform-independent Java application
- SAP GUI for Windows: Standard GUI for Windows; no restrictions compared to other SAP GUIs

SAP NetWeaver SAP NetWeaver is the next generation of mySAP technology. It integrates information and business processes across different technology platforms, using Internet standards and Web services. This openness guarantees compatibility with J2EE and other platforms. NetWeaver is also the foundation for xApps and ESA. Its flexibility allows you to develop comprehensive, service-focused business solutions.

SAP NetWeaver Developer Studio An Eclipse-based IDE for developing Web applications; encompasses the complete Web Dynpro development cycle.

SAP Web AS SAP Web Application Server. The SAP Web AS is an open, scalable, high-availability infrastructure for developing dynamic, cross-enterprise Internet applications. It is based on application server technology and has been enhanced with Web functions. It is the new technological basis of all mySAP solutions and the core of the SAP R/3 Enterprise System.

SAP XI eXchange Infrastructure. SAP XI is based technically on the Web AS and guarantees application integration for inter-enterprise and cross-enterprise business processes between software solutions from different vendors. It is based on an open, standardized interface based on XML and Java. The technological integration is achieved through support for multiple standards, protocols, and connectors such as JTTP, XML, SOAP, and the JCo. SAP XI also meets the challenge of recording and adequately assigning the different meanings of the exchange data in the business concepts of the respective enterprise and system. This shared collaboration knowledge principle is the foundation for saving the information and is implemented by SAP XI to exchange information with other systems.

SAX Simple API for XML. A programming interface for XML processing. SAX competes with DOM. In contrast to DOM, SAX passes the XML document sequentially and only saves certain XML elements, which enables very large documents to be processed as well. → JAXP, JDOM

Screen Painter Tool for creating the screens of a dialog transaction. Drag&Drop can be used to compose the layout. The elements can refer directly to the Dictionary and the corresponding properties. Transaction SE51.

Scriptlet Refers to a block of script block within an HTML page that starts with <% and ends with %>. Only procedural Java coding is permitted between the markers.

Security concept Attributes of an object should not be visible or modifiable from the outside. Methods must be used to access these attributes.

SDM Software Deployment Manager. → SL

Selection screen Screen of an ABAP report program. Selection criteria can be entered in a selection screen; and control the program to analyze the database and generate a results list.

Selection table Internal table in which selection criteria are stored. Selection tables standardize the storage of complex selections.

Service A service provided in the system. Service orientation describes components that are independent of one another but can provide services and information, implemented using method calls and return values. The principle of Web services.

Servlet Servlets make it possible to integrate HTML in Java source coding. An HTML page is generated on the server side, forming dynamic Web pages. The servlet runtime environment is called a "Web container."

Session A user session begins with a security check. The session-dependent data can be saved. If the session were not used, each connection would have to be authenticated separately. Sessions are used in the Internet to implement portals with protected or personalized pages.

Session (SAP) A window in which an application function can be processed. When a user logs on to the R/3 System, the window opens the first session. Each user can open up to six sessions concurrently.

Session bean A type of Bean that is responsible for client requests. There are two types of session beans: → Stateful and stateless.

Signature (of a method) The externally visible method name and information regarding the sequence and types of the formal parameters. The signatures of two identically named methods can be distinguished whenever at least one parameter is different.

SL Software Logistics. SL is a component of the Java Development Infrastructure (JDI) and consists of the Change Management Service (CMS), which manages versioning of the individual software components, and the Software Delivery Manager (SDM), which is responsible for deploying Web Dynpros and J2EE applications.

SOAP Simple Object Access Protocol. A protocol for exchanging information in a decentralized, distributed environment. It is based on XML and typically used with HTTP. SOAP contains conventions that implement the method calls for objects, their responses, and standardized data types.

SQL A largely standardized language for accessing data stored in relational databases.

SQL trace A test tool used for database tuning.

Status → GUI status

Structure A structure is a complex type and consists of components that can have any type themselves. Structures are used in ABAP programs, for example, and to type interface parameters of function modules.

Stub Establishes the connection between two remote objects and is responsible for their communication.

Search help A search help is an ABAP Dictionary object used to define input help functions.

Subclass Class that is derived from a superclass through inheritance in a hierarchy structure.

Subroutines The processing of subroutines is initiated by an ABAP statement. Subroutines can be given parameters through an interface.

SunONE Sun Open Net Environment is a framework and development environment (IDE) for Web applications; its Open Smart Web services standardize interfaces for Web-based software and services. ONE uses XML and SOAP, and sometimes competes with Microsoft's .NET.

Superclass The class from which another class (a subclass) inherits in a hierarchy structure.

Swing API for creating graphical user interfaces (GUI). Part of the standard scope of the JDK.

Syntax check A check phase within a compiler or interpreter that checks the correctness of the commands and their sequence.

System field System fields are variables that are specified and managed by the SAP System and that save certain information, such as error codes.

Table A tabular collection of data. A table consists of columns (attributes) and rows (data records). Each table row can be identified uniquely through its primary key.

Table, internal A data structure that only exists at program runtime. It consists of any number of identically structured table rows and contains data filtered and/or combined from database tables.

Tag A tag is a command used to format texts. In most cases, opening and closing tags are used to enclose the respective content. Tags can be nested to form a structure.

Tag library Tag libraries define a set of custom tags and contain objects that implement those tags.

Template Templates define a structure that can be filled with content. They are often used to generate static and dynamic Web pages.

Text elements Developers can freely define the text elements of a program. They include: → List headers, selection texts, and text symbols.

Text symbols Text constants specified and maintained outside a program. Text symbols are used instead of text literals in programs because they help keep programs language independent and make them easier to maintain. Each text symbol must have a three-character identifier.

Thin client A thin client represents an application at the software level that is solely responsible for displaying data. If processing logic is integrated, the client is called a rich, thick, or fat client. A Web browser is an excellent example: If it only displays static HTML pages, it is a thin client. If client-side processing logic is integrated (as is the case in the Web Dynpro technology), such as JavaScript-based input checks, it is a rich client.

Thread A thread is an executing component in a process that can potentially be run in parallel. Threads are used to realize parallel processing within a program. A thread can have various states, which the scheduler uses to allocate CPU time to all the threads in the system. → Multithreading

Three-tier architecture In this architecture, an application consists of three layers. Each layer is implemented separately and is independent of the others. The tiers are divided into the presentation layer (GUI, Frontend), the processing layer (business logic) and the data retention layer (usually databases and back-ends).

Title, title bar → GUI title

Top-down modularization A principle of system development from general to specialized, therefore sometimes also called "specialization." → Bottom-up

Transaction A logically self-contained process in the R/3 System. From the user's point of view, it involves performing an action, such as creating a list. From the developer's point of view, a transaction is a complex object that consists of a module pool and screens, and is called by specifying a transaction code.

Transaction code A sequence of characters that identifies an SAP transaction. Entering a transaction code in the command field calls that transaction in the R/3 System.

Transaction data Data that is dependent on ongoing operations (transaction-based) and therefore changed frequently. Example: Current warehouse stocks. → Master data

Transport group All systems that access a common transport directory.

Transporting Copying R/3 system components from one system to another. The components to be transported are contained in the object list of a transport request.

Transport layer Groups together all development objects that use the same transport routes to reach the target system(s).

Transport Organizer A tool for managing centralized and decentralized ABAP Workbench development projects and Customizing projects.

Transport request A document for copying corrections between different system types. A transport request records released corrections. When the request is released, the transport is performed. Transaction SE10.

UDDI Universal Description, Discovery and Integration. A type of registry in which services are registered and found. It represents the start of the client activity and has the potential to respond to its requests automatically. This directory service was created to find business partners and publish products and services. → Web services

UI element A screen element that can be placed in a view. Examples include labels, text fields, and tables.

UML Unified Modeling Language. Unifies software programming languages, specifications of distributed applications, object-oriented analysis and design, and system modeling.

Unicode Unicode is an internationally standardized 16-bit character set. It contains some 40,000 different characters. → ASCII

Using parameter Parameter passed on to a subroutine.

UTF-8 Unicode Transformation Format-8. A Unicode character set that covers nearly all languages.

Value domain A set of values that are assigned to a simple data type in the ABAP Dictionary.

View An application-specific logical view of one or more tables in the ABAP Dictionary.

Visibility The external visibility of certain data and interfaces (attributes, methods) of a class can be defined with the keywords `public`, `private`, and `protected`.

VM Virtual Machine. A runtime environment that interprets and executes program coding and intermediate coding. The VM is installed on the respective system, which makes the actual program coding platform-independent.

Web container Runtime environment for servlets and JSPs; also manages their life cycles.

WebDAV Web Distributed Authoring and Versioning. WebDAV is a standard for cross-enterprise interaction over the Internet. It specifies protocols for locking documents, metadata standards, deletion and retrieval functions, a characteristic-based search for Web resources, and naming operations; also supports copy and move functions.

Web Dynpro A new UI technology from SAP for designing graphical user interfaces that makes it easy to develop browser-based applications. In the long term, all SAP applications will be based on Web Dynpro, which is characterized by declarative programming. Metadata is used to generate the actual implementation, which complies with the MVC pattern and results in a structured, consistent application that is constructed from reusable components. Web Dynpros are platform-independent and easy to enhance. Graphical tools are provided to create and run them. → Dynpro

Web Dynpro application Component of a Web Dynpro project that represents the application. It is made available to the runtime environment (deployment) and represents the starting point for the Web application (through a browser call).

Web Dynpro controller Controllers are the link between view and model, and are responsible for the control flow. They contain the context as data store. In general, there are view controllers and view-independent custom controllers.

Web Dynpro model Part of the MVC architecture within the Web Dynpro application. It is responsible for data retrieval, and therefore for connecting to external databases or other data retrieval logic. Examples include connections to an SAP System or to Web services.

Web Dynpro project A Web Dynpro project encompasses all project-relevant data. It consists of the Java Dictionary and the actual Web Dynpro application, which in turn consists of applications, components (views and controllers), and models.

Web Dynpro view Views are part of the MVC concept. They are the Web Dynpro components that are displayed in the browser. They consist of a layout formed from UI elements. Views can be grouped together to form view sets. Each view possesses a view controller, which is responsible for user interaction and has a local data store.

Web Dynpro view set Used to group views together, in order to display multiple views at the same time.

Web Dynpro window A window encapsulates views and view sets, and is the unit that is assigned directly to a component.

Web service XML-based applications and services that are provided to enterprises and users over the Internet. → UDDI, WSDL, SOAP

Where-used list Indicates where a selected object is used in the system.

Work area A one-row table structure that can be assigned values at runtime.

Workbench → ABAP Workbench

Workflow A sequence of steps processed either by people or by the system. It is monitored by the Workflow Manager and can be controlled with event-related response mechanisms.

WSDL Web Service Description Level. A standardized description of Web services. Enables the creation of automated calls to use services.

X.509 An ITU-T standard for certificates and authentication services used to determine the issuer's name and digital signature. Certificates under the X.509 standard can also be email certificates used for the secure transmission of email and files, and can also be used for identification on Web sites.

xApps SAP xApps are a new generation of application programs. Based on SAP NetWeaver, xApps connect heterogeneous systems to enable cross-enterprise business processes independently of the underlying infrastructure.

XMI XML Metadata Interchange. Format for exchanging software source coding over the Internet. Intended to unify XML, UML, and MOF.

XML eXtensible Markup Language. A file format for exchanging structured data over the Internet. XML itself is not a descriptive language like HTML, but instead a kind of meta-language that can be used to generate other specialized languages. XML documents are increasingly used to enable cross-enterprise collaboration, such as the exchange of business documents over the Internet. → Web services, XSL, XSLT.

XML schema Defines the type and structure of XML documents. Intended to replace DTD.

XSL eXtensible Stylesheet Language. Used to format XML documents. → XSLT

XSLT eXtensible Stylesheet Language Transformation. Language that can be used to transform XML documents. Used frequently in Internet applications to transform XML to (X)HTML. → XSL

B Sources and Further Reading

Books

Alur, Deepak; Crupi, John; Malks, Dan: *Core J2EE Patterns.* Prentice Hall 2003.

Bergsten, Hans: *JavaServer Pages*. O'Reilly & Associates 2004.

Färber, Günther; Kirchner, Julia: *mySAP Technology.* Galileo Press 2002.

Flanagan, David: *Java in a Nutshell.* O'Reilly & Associates 2002.

Gamma, Erich; Helm, Richard; Johnson, Ralph E.: *Design Patterns.* Addison-Wesley Professional 1997.

Heinemann, Frédéric; Rau, Christian: *Web Programming with the SAP Web Application Server. The complete guide for ABAP and Web developers*. SAP PRESS 2003.

Hohpe, Gregor; Woolf, Bobby: *Enterprise Integration Patterns. Designing, Building, and Deploying Messaging Solutions*. Addison-Wesley Professional 2003.

Hunter, Jason; Crawford, William: *Java Servlet Programming.* O'Reilly & Associates 1999.

Keller, Horst; Jacobitz, Joachim: *ABAP Objects – The Official Reference.* SAP PRESS 2003.

Keller, Horst; Krüger, Sascha: *ABAP Objects.* Addison-Wesley Professional 2002.

Matzke, Bernd: *ABAP/4: Programming the SAP R/3 System.* Addison-Wesley Professional 2000.

Monson-Haefel, Richard: *Enterprise JavaBeans*. O'Reilly & Associates 2002.

Roman, Ed; Ambler, Scott W.; Jewell, Tyler: *Mastering Enterprise JavaBeans. 2nd Edition.* John Wiley & Sons 2001.

Roßbach, Peter; Schreiber, Hendrik. *Java Server and Servlets.* Addison-Wesley Professional 2000.

Online Resources

SUN Microsystems: *Java Web Service Tutorial. http://java.sun.com/webservices/*

SUN Microsystems: *J2EE 1.4 Tutorial. http://java.sun.com/j2ee/1.4/*

C About the Authors

Bernd Noll works at SNP AG as Delivery Manager for the development area, and is also responsible for development of the SNP Realtime Business Monitor (RBM), SNP's proprietary, SAP-based solution for automated monitoring and control of business key process indicators (KPIs)—"business monitoring."

Since completing his degree in business administration, Mr. Noll has honed years of experience programming in both SAP and non-SAP environments, and has been both project manager and IT manager. He joined the SNP Group in 2001. His particular expertise lies in the management of RBM projects, Web-oriented SAP development, and the SAP Business Workflow/Webflow area.

Dr. Andreas Schlindwein started developing with SAP soon after finishing his master's degree in physics. An ABAP developer with years of project experience in various SAP Systems and modules, his expertise is in performance-optimized ABAP development and SAP Business Workflow/Webflow.

Dr. Andreas Schneider-Neureither is CEO and Chairman of SNP Schneider-Neureither & Partner AG, Heidelberg. He is responsible for the areas of consulting, development, sales, and training.

After receiving his PhD in theoretical physics, he initially worked as an IT consultant and developer in numerous major projects at leading companies. He founded Schneider-Neureither & Partner GmbH in 1994, together with his wife, Petra Neureither. After the company became incorporated in 1998, he assumed the responsibilities of CEO and Chairman of SNP Schneider-Neureither & Partner AG.

Dr. André Schüngel also holds a PhD in physics. While earning his degree, he cultivated a profound knowledge of theoretical and practical programming. In addition to his years of experience in professional software development with various programming languages, he is a recognized expert of Java/J2EE applications and ABAP Objects. His areas of expertise include application architecture and middleware.

Dominik Wittenbeck holds a master's degree in business data processing and has years of experience in Web development and integration projects involving both SAP and J2EE. He is a member of the RBM Core Development Team and is a recognized specialist for Web services in the SAP environment.

In addition to these authors, many others were instrumental in creating this book. The following individuals made major contributions:

- **Nico Gärtner**
  Nico Gärtner holds a master's degree in business data processing. He is an ABAP developer and a specialist for Web technologies and DHTML. He is also a member of the RBM development team.
- **Alexander Knapstein**
  Alexander Knappstein also holds a master's degree in business data processing. He works as a J2EE and ABAP developer. His specialties are application integration and Web technologies, especially Web services and service-oriented models.
- **Andreas Schmidsberger**
  Andreas Schmidsberger holds a master's degree in business data processing and works as a developer for ABAP and Java/J2EE. His area of expertise is front-end technologies.

- **Andreas Schöttler**
  Andreas Schöttler is a computer scientist. His specialties are Java and J2EE development. He is a member of the RBM development team and is responsible for developing the Java components.
- **Martin Uhl**
  Martin Uhl holds a master's degree in business data processing. He works as an ABAP developer—particularly in the framework of RBM projects.

SNP Schneider-Neureither & Partner AG is an SAP consulting firm that supports its customers in the implementation and optimization of their SAP solutions. The company was founded in 1994 by Dr. Andreas Schneider-Neureither and his wife, Petra Neureither, as a limited liability partnership, Schneider-Neureither & Partner GmbH. After it became incorporated in 1998, the company went public in 2000. SNP Schneider-Neureither & Partner AG currently employs a staff of 80. Its head office is located in Heidelberg, Germany, with other offices in Germany (Stuttgart, Dusseldorf, Leuna), Austria (Vienna, Linz), and Switzerland (Zurich).

SNP Schneider-Neureither & Partner AG focuses on providing technology, process, and application consulting for the SAP market. It is constantly expanding its expertise in the areas of SAP technology consulting, enterprise application integration optimization, service & support, system landscape optimization, SAP workflow, monitoring, and process and application consulting.

SNP Schneider-Neureither & Partner AG developed the SNP Realtime Business Monitor to optimize company performance. This solution, which is based entirely on SAP technology, helps to automate business performance monitoring by examining critical KPIs and business processes in realtime, enhanced with automatic initiation and tracking of solutions for any known problems. SNP AG also provides services for optimizing service and support organizations and solution management, based on the SAP Solution Manager and Support Desk.

Index

3-tier architecture 22

A

ABAP 71
  business logic 345
  presentation logic 362
ABAP application 436
ABAP development environment 138
ABAP Dictionary 139, 141, 459
ABAP Editor 139, 459
ABAP Interpreter 459
ABAP Objects 83, 137, 147, 459
ABAP Personality 26, 459
  authorizations 46
ABAP program 459
ABAP VM (Virtual Machine) 26, 459
ABAP Web service 315
  SOAP request 327
  SOAP response 328
ABAP Workbench 138, 207, 459
ABAP/Java integration 60
Abstract class 459
Abstract method 459
abstract, keyword, Java 129
ActiveX 459
Adapters 430
Adaptive RFC 396
Aggregation 459
Alert monitor 452
ALV 138
American Standard Code for Information Interchange (ASCII) 460
Applet 460
Applet container 172, 460
Applets 49, 168
Application class 150
Application client archive 173
Application client container 460
Application hierarchy 459
Application integration 20
Application layer 24
Application Link Enabling (ALE) 29, 315, 459
Application Modeler 402
Application platform 20
Application programming interface (API) 460
Application server 460
Application Tracing Service 451
Application tracing, Java 451
Arrays, Java 100, 121
  multidimensional 100
Assembler 445
Assembly project 58
Association 460
Attributes, Java 118, 460
  hiding 126
Authentication
  J2EE 52
  Java 203
Authorization 46, 460
  EJBs 53
  J2EE 53
  Java 204
Authorization concept 460
Authorization field 46
Authorization object 46
Authorization profile 47
Authorization system 46
AWT 460

B

Back-end 460
BAPI 345, 460
BAPI Explorer 139, 346, 460
Basic authentication 53
Batch input 460
Batch input session 460
Bean-managed persistence (BMP) 179, 286
Beans 461
Binding, JNDI 190, 461
Bottom-up modularization 461
BPM 461
Branching, CVS 245
Break, statement, Java 110
Breakpoint 145, 461
BSP application 149, 437
  stateful 152
  stateless 153

BSP extensions 155, 364, 367, 438
Buffer control, JSP 187
Build 461
Business Application Programming
  Interfaces (BAPI) 137, 345
Business Connector 28, 461
Business Framework 461
Business intelligence 20
Business logic 344, 461
  Java 170, 214
Business object 346, 461
Business Object Builder 139, 461
Business Object Repository 346
Business Server Pages 23, 42, 138, 151,
  364, 461
Business Workflow 461
Byte code 461
Byte code enhancer 287

C

C++ 445
Caching 31, 461
CALL METHOD, statement 86
Call-by-reference 461
Call-by-value 461
CASE, statement 79
Cast, Java 99
Casting 461
CATT 461
CBS 461
Certificate interfaces 202
CGI 462
Change Management Service (CMS)
  58, 239
Change request 462
Changing parameter 462
Class 459, 462
  ABAP 147
  ABAP Objects
    abstract 89
    final 89
  abstract 462
  concrete 462
  inner 462
  Java 115
    abstract 129
    defining 116
    extending 125
CLASS ... ENDCLASS, statement 84
Class attribute 462
Class Browser 462
Class Builder 139, 147, 462
Class inheritance 462
Class library 462
Class members 119
Class method 462
Class pools 73
Client 462
Client tier 52
Clients, Java 167
CMS 462
Code Inspector 144, 443, 445
Collision control, CVS 245
COM 462
COM/DCOM Connector 29
Comments, Java 94
Common Client Interface (CCI) 195
Compiler 462
Component Build Service (CBS) 58,
  215, 238, 461
Component controller 399, 462
Component interface 398, 462
Component model technologies, Java
  174
Component, Web Dynpro 462
Composite Application Framework 21,
  462
Composite profile 47
Composite role 47
Composition 463
Compression 427
Computing Center Management
  System (CCMS) 59, 450
Concurrent Version System (CVS) 244
Connection context 273
Connection management, Java 195
Connection pool 264, 300, 304
Connectors 28
Consolidation routes 159, 463
Consolidation system 463
Constants
  ABAP 74
  Java 99
Constructors 117, 463
Container 463
Container services 171

Container-managed persistence (CMP) 179, 280, 463
Containers, Java 170
Context (Web Dynpro) 463
Context Builder 463
Context Editor 404
Continue, statement, Java 111
Contracts 195
Control Framework 362, 463
Control structures
ABAP 78
Java 107
Control technology 137
Controller Editor 404
Controllers 150, 398, 409, 423
ABAP 438
Java 439
CORBA 33, 178, 190, 463
Coverage Analyzer 443, 445
Credentials 203
Cryptographic services 202
CSF 463
CSS 463
CSV 463
Custom controller 397, 399, 416
Custom controls 362
Custom Tags 463
Customizing requests 161
CVS 240

D

Data Control Language (DCL) 255
Data Definition Language (DDL) 255
Data Dictionary project, Java
creating 226
Data element 464
Data encapsulation 464
Data Manipulation Language (DML) 255
Data Modeler 139, 141, 463
Data objects, ABAP 74
Data structures, Java
deployment 233
Data types 141, 464
ABAP 75
Java creating 228
JCo 302
Database 463
Database commit 464
Database independence 30
Database integration 30
Database layer 24
Database queries
performance 442
Database rollback 464
Database tables 142
defining 230
Database transaction 464
Database, logical 464
DB access layer 265
DCOM 33, 464
DCOM Connector 315
Debugger 464
Debugging 144
Declarative programming 464
Decrement operators 101
DELETE, statement 83
Delivery routes 160
Delphi 445
Delta handling 426
deltav 243
Deploy process 233
Deployment 440, 464
Deployment descriptor 182, 464
Design patterns 464
Design Time Repository (DTR) 58, 215, 238
Development class 464
Development cycle, Web Dynpro 465
Development environment 465
Development objects
ABAP 143
Java 216
Development paradigm, Java 212
Development projects
ABAP 441
Development system 465
Dialog program 465
Diff algorithm 245
Distributed statistics record (DSR) 59, 450
DNS 190
DO, statement 80, 109
Doc comment 132
Document management systems 240
Document Object Model (DOM) 196

Document Type Definitions (DTD) 196
Documentation conventions 132
DOM 465
Domain 143, 465
Driver model 431
DTD 465
DTR 465
Dynpro 145, 362, 391, 465

E

EAR 465
ebXML 465
ebXML Registry 197
eCATT 165
Eclipse 465
EIS 465
EJB 465
  assembly project 221, 372
  class diagram 332
  container 171, 175, 350, 453, 465
  project 220, 372
  proxy class 61, 312
Electronic Data Interchange (EDI) 29
Encapsulation, Java 128
Endless loops, Java 110
Enjoy controls 465
enjoySAP 137, 465
Enterprise application project 222, 372, 387
Enterprise archives 173
Enterprise information system (EIS) 167, 170
Enterprise JavaBeans 174, 176
  deployment 182
Enterprise JavaBeans archives 173
Enterprise Services Architecture (ESA) 18, 36
Entity bean 170, 220, 279, 466
  life cycles 177
equals(), method, Java 122
ERP 466
Error handling 466
  JSP 186
ESA 466
Escape sequences, Java 97
Event 466
Event block 466
Event handler 152
Event, ABAP Objects 89
Exception 466
Exception handling 466
  Java 112
Exchange connections 276
Executable programs, ABAP 72
Export parameter 466
Extended program check 144
extends, keyword, Java 125
Extreme Programming (XP) 249

F

Façade pattern 428
Field symbols 77
Filters 423
  servlets 219
final, keyword, Java 127
for, statement, Java 109
Form-based authentication 53
Framework 466
Function 466
Function Builder 139, 466
Function code 466
Function group 73, 466
Function library 466
Function module 146, 466

G

Garbage collection, Java 122
Garbage collector 466
Generation limit 145
Get method, Java 118
Group, J2EE 52
GUI status 146, 466
GUI title 146, 466
GuiXT 466

H

Hash 466
Host expressions 272
Host variables, Java 271
Hprof 447
HTMLB 367, 438, 467
HTTP 240, 241
HTTP error pages 186

I

IAC 467
IBM WebSphere 19
ICM 467
IDE 467
Identifiers, Java 95
IDoc 29, 315, 467
IF, statement, ABAP 78
If, statement, Java 107
implements, keyword, Java 130
Import parameter 467
Import queue 162
import, statement, Java 124
Inbound call 300
Inbound plug (Web Dynpro) 392, 467
Include programs 73
Includes 467
  JSP 189
Increment operators 101
Information integration 20
Inheritance
  ABAP Objects 88
  Java 124, 127
  preventing 127
Initialization 467
INSERT, statement 81
Instance 467
Instance members 119
Instantiation 467
Integration Engine 24, 30
Interface 467
Interface inheritance 467
Interface pools 73
Interface, ABAP 147
Interfaces, ABAP Objects 87
Interfaces, Java 129
Intermediate code 467
Intermediate Language (IL) 26
Internal table 77, 467
Internet Application Component (IAC) 40, 137
Internet Communication Framework 152
Internet Communication Manager (ICM) 23, 24
Internet Inter-Object Request Broker Protocol (IIOP) 178
Internet service, ABAP 148
Internet Transaction Server (ITS) 18, 137, 390, 467
Interpreter 467

J

J2EE 91, 467
  security 51
J2EE applications, architecture 167
J2EE component 468
J2EE module 468
J2EE server 171, 468
J2ME 91, 468
J2SE 91, 468
Jakarta Struts 424, 439, 440
JAR 173, 222, 468
JarClientAPI 222
Java 468
  business logic 347
  presentation logic 369
  security 48
  versioning and transport 58
Java API for XML Registration Services (JAXR) 197
Java applet 468
Java application 438, 468
Java Application Descriptor 459
Java archive 222
Java Authentication and Authorization Service (JAAS) 202
Java byte code 468
Java Community Process 451
Java Connector (JCo) 28, 298
Java Cryptography Architecture (JCA) 202
Java Cryptography Extensions (JCE) 202
Java Data Dictionary 269
Java Data Objects (JDO) 198, 287
Java Database Connectivity 198
Java Database Objects (JDO) 217
Java Development Infrastructure (JDI) 50, 237
Java Dictionary 214, 217, 223, 407, 468
Java IDL 468
Java Message Service (JMS) 191, 354, 355
Java Naming and Directory Interface (JNDI) 173, 175, 190, 350

Java Native Interface (JNI) 298
Java platform 91
Java Remote Method Protocol (JRMP) 178
Java security model 51
Java Server Pages (JSP) 23, 42, 169, 184, 219, 370
  error handling 186
  life cycle 186
  technology 468
Java Standard TagLib (JSTL) 185
Java Transaction API (JTA) 192, 200
Java Virtual Machine (JVM) 90
Java Virtual Machine Profiler Interface (JVMPI) 447
Java Web services 331
Java Web Start 468
Java XML API (JAXP) 196
Java XML RPC API 197
Java, concepts 90
JavaBeans 174, 176, 468
  components 188
  deployment 182
JavaMail 468
JavaOS 468
JavaScript 468
JavaServer Faces 424, 439, 440
JAXM 468
JAXP 468
JAXR API 197
JBC 469
JCA 469
JCo 60, 61, 469
JCP 469
JDBC 170, 261, 264, 265, 469
  API 197
  drivers 199
  result set 278
  with SQLJ 276
JDI 469
JDK 469
JDO 469
  development 288
JDOM 469
JES 469
JFC 469
Jini 469
JMS 469
  client 354
  provider 354
JMX 451, 469
JNDI 469
  lookup 439
  lookup service 171
JNI 469
JNLP 469
JRA 470
JRE 470
JRun 470
JSP 470
JSP/servlet application 439
JSTL 470
JUnit 248
JVM 470
JWS 470

K

Key management interfaces 203
Keywords, Java 95
Knowledge Management (KM) 20

L

Layout manager 470
Lazy initialization 434
LDAP 190, 470
Life cycle management 21
List 470
Listeners, servlets 219
Lists 363
Literals, ABAP 74
Local object 470
Lock object 143, 470
Logging, Java 450
Logical databases 256
Loops, ABAP 79
LUW 470

M

main, method, Java 120
Mapping 470
Mass transport 162
Master Data Management (MDM) 20
ME, self reference, ABAP 117
Media types 187
Members 116
Memory management 445

Memory pipes 25
Menu Painter 145, 470
Message broker 355
Message management, Java 196
Message-driven bean 354, 470
  deployment descriptor 359
  life cycle 357
Metadata 470
Method 471
  ABAP
    redefining 126
  ABAP Objects 85
  abstract 471
  Java 114, 118
    abstract 129
    overwriting 126
METHOD ... ENDMETHOD, statement 85
Method signature 114
Microsoft .NET 19
Middleware 297, 471
MIDlet 471
MIDP 471
MIME 471
MIME objects 151
MIME Repository 156
Model 394, 408, 423
  ABAP 437
  Java 439
Modification Browser 139, 471
Modifiers 128, 131
MODIFY, statement 82
Module 471
Module pool 72, 471
Monitoring functions
  Java 450
Multilingual capability 425
Multiple output formats 426
Multithreading 471
MVC 42, 138, 370, 422, 471
  authentication 423
  authorization 423
  data visualization 425
  hierarchy and distribution 424
  multilingual capability 425
  validation 423

N

Naming conventions
  ABAP 132
  Java 131
Native JDBC 262
Native SQL 32, 265, 471
.NET 459
.NET Connector 29
Next screen 471
null, keyword 101

O

O/R mapping 281
Object 471
Object catalog 471
Object class 46
Object list 471
Object Navigator 140, 471
Object services 257
Object/relational persistence 279
Object-oriented programming 91
  ABAP 83
  attributes 92
  class definition 92
  classes 92
  encapsulation 93
  inheritance 93
  methods 92
  objects 92
Object-relational mapping 32, 472
Objects, Java 116, 121
  creating 118
  finalization 122
ODBC 472
OLE 472
Open Database Connectivity (ODBC) 198
Open SQL 30, 80, 255, 472
  Performance 441
Open SQL Engine 217, 263, 265, 268
Open SQL for Java 261
Operators, Java
  + 105
  assignment 104
  bit 102
  Boolean 104
  instanceof 105
  new 105

point operator (.) 105
priorities 106
relational 103
type conversion 105
Outbound call 306
Outbound plug (Web Dynpro) 392, 472
Outline view 404
Overloading 115, 472
Overwriting 126
preventing 127

P

Packages 143, 472
Java 123
Packaging, Java 172
PAI 362, 472
Parameters 472
ABAP 75
Java 115
Parent class 472
Patterns 472
PBO 362, 472
People integration 20
Performance
ABAP 441
analysis tools 443
Java 445
Performance trace 145
Java 451
Persistence Service 257
Persistent objects 257
Personality 472
Pluggable Authentication Module (PAM) 203
POH 362
Pointer arithmetic 445
Point-to-point model, JMS 193
Polymorphy 472
POV 362
PreparedStatement object 266
Presentation layer 23
Presentation logic 361
Pretty Printer 472
Private 472
Process integration 20
Processing block 473
Production system 473
Profilers 59, 447
Program status 473
Program structure, ABAP 72
Program type 473
Programmatic interface 398
Programs 144
Project life cycle, Java 207
Properties view 404
protected 473
public 473
Publish/subscribe model, JMS 194

Q

Queue 356, 357

R

R/3 17
RAR 173, 473
Realm 52
Reference 473
Reference equivalence 122
Remote Function Call 29
Report 144
Report program 473
Repository 473
Resource adapter archives 173
Return, statement, Java 111
Reuse components 138, 473
Reuse Library 139, 473
Revisions, CVS 245
RFC 29, 60, 61, 298, 473
Rich client 473
RMI 190, 473
Role, J2EE 47, 52
Runtime analysis 140, 145, 443, 473
Runtime environment 473

S

SAAJ API 197
SAML 473
Sandbox model 49
SAP Business Warehouse (BW) 20
SAP Enterprise Portal 20
SAP Exchange Infrastructure (XI) 20, 197, 315
SAP GUI 473
SAP GUI for HTML 40, 213
SAP GUI for Java 38

SAP GUI for Windows 36
SAP J2EE Engine 26
  standards 27
SAP List Viewer 138
SAP Mobile Infrastructure 20
SAP NetWeaver 19, 474
SAP NetWeaver Developer Studio 44, 58, 182, 207, 438, 447, 474
  Java Dictionary 214
  perspectives 218
  testing 248
  user interface 209
SAP Query 71
SAP technology 17
SAP Web Application Server 18, 20
  architecture 21
  as Web service client 35
  as Web service provider 35
  components 24
  frontends 36
  transport system 56
  versioning 54
SAP xEM 21
SAP xMA 21
SAP xPD 21
SAP xRPM 21
SAPconnect 314
SAPPhone 314
SAX 474
Screen 138
Screen Painter 145, 474
Scriptlets, Java 186, 474
SDM 474
Search help 143, 475
Security
  J2EE 51
Security concept 474
Security management, Java 196
Security policy, Java 204
SELECT, statement 80
Selection screen 363, 474
Selection table 474
Server cache 25
Service 474
Service gateway 318
Service interface 316
Service Provider Interface (SPI) 202
Service-oriented architecture (SOA) 17
Servlet 219, 370, 474
Servlet specification 183
Session (SAP) 475
Session beans 170, 180, 221, 347, 475
  as Web services 350
Sessions, Java servlets 25, 183
Set method, Java 118
Short-circuit evaluation 104
Signature 475
Simple API for XML (SAX) 196
Simple Object Access Protocol (SOAP) 197
Single transport 162
SL 475
SOAP 29, 33, 475
SOAP Runtime 62, 316
SOAP transport binding 330
SOAP with Attachments 330
SOAP with Attachments API for Java (SAAJ) 197
Software Delivery Manager (SDM) 58, 239
Software Logistics (SL) 58, 239
SQL 255, 475
SQL for Java (SQLJ) 198
SQL processor 268
SQL processor layer 265, 268
SQL Studio, creating data 235
SQL trace 140, 265, 443, 444, 475
SQLJ 269
  debugging 275
  development 271, 274
  Syntax 270
SQLJ Checker 275
SQLJ result set iterator 278
Stateful session beans 348
Stateless session beans 348
Statement cache 267
Statement pooling 266
static, keyword, Java 119
Status 475
Structure 475
Stub 318, 475
Stub/skeleton 178
Subclass 475
Subroutine pools 72
Subroutines 475
SunONE 475

super, keyword, Java 125
Superclass 475
Swing 475
Switch, statement, Java 108
Synchronized, statement, Java 111
Syntax check 144, 475
Syntax elements, ABAP 72
System data container 165
System field 475

T

Table, internal 476
Tag 476
Tag Browser 367
Tag library 367, 476
Tagging, CVS 246
TagLibs 371
TagLibs, JSP 185
Team collaboration, Java 237
Template 476
Test configuration 166
Test data container 166
Test scripts 165
Testing
  ABAP 165
  Java 248
Text elements 476
Text symbols 476
Thin client 476
this, keyword, Java 117
Threads, Java 111, 476
Three-tier architecture 476
Throw, statement, Java 112
throws, statement, Java 113
Title bar 476
Top-down modularization 476
Topic 355, 356
Total cost of ownership (TCO) 19
Tracing 31
Transaction 476
  SCI 443, 445
  SCOF 445
  SCOV 443
  SE11 459
  SE24 462
  SE30 443
  SE37 466
  SE81 459
  ST05 443, 444
Transaction capability 31
Transaction code 476
Transaction data 476
Transaction management, Java 195, 196
Transaction Service 257
Transport group 476
Transport layer 159, 160, 476
Transport Management System (TMS) 159, 164
Transport Organizer 56, 139, 163, 477
  extended view 164
  tools 164
Transport process 57
Transport protocols, EJB 177
Transport request 477
Transport system 56, 157
Transporting 476
Try-catch-finally, statements, Java 113
Type conversions, Java 99

U

UDDI 33, 34, 197, 477
UI element 477
UML 477
UML-XMI 395
Unicode 477
UPDATE, statement 82
URL mappings 386
User master record 47
User, J2EE 52
Using parameter 477
UTF-8 477

V

Value domain 477
Variables
  ABAP 74
  Java 98
Variants 166
Vendor SQL 264
Version catalog, ABAP 157
Version control, CVS 245
Versioning 54
  ABAP 157
  Java 237
View 152, 400, 410, 423, 477

ABAP 437
Java 439
View controller 399, 415
View Designer 403
View set 392, 398
Views 142, 398
Visibility areas, ABAP Objects 84
Visibility, Java 128, 477
Visual Administrator 268, 451
VM 477

W

WAR 173, 220
Web Application Builder 148, 343, 364
Web application project 372
Web archive 173, 220
Web components, Java 169
Web container 453, 477
Java 172
Web Dynpro 23, 44, 138, 216, 369, 389, 477
for ABAP 437
Web Dynpro application 393, 437, 438, 477
Web Dynpro components 397
Web Dynpro controller 477
Web Dynpro Explorer 402
Web Dynpro IDE 401
Web Dynpro model 477
Web Dynpro project 478
Web Dynpro view 478
Web Dynpro view set 478
Web Dynpro window 478
Web project 218, 372
Web service client project 222
Web service technologies, Java 174
Web services 18, 29, 33, 60, 61, 315
ABAP 315
Java 331
process flow 33
Web tier 52
WebDAV 215, 240, 477
locking 242
metadata 243
namespace management 241
Where-used list 478
WHILE, statement 79
while, statement, Java 108
Windows 398
Work area 478
Workbench requests 161
Worker threads 25
Workflow 478
WSDL 33, 34, 478

X

X.509 53, 478
X/Open XA 202
xApp 21, 478
XI 474
XMI 478
XML 478
XML descriptors 220, 221
XML Metadata Interchange Format (XMI) 395
XML schema 196, 478
XML Stylesheet Language Transformation (XSLT) 196, 478
XSL 478

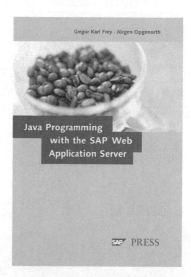

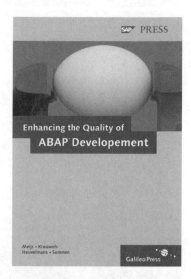

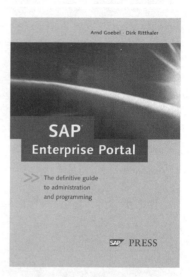

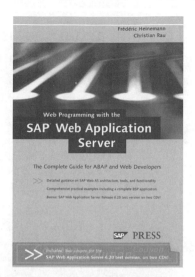

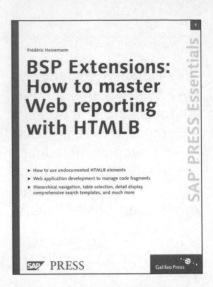